Research in Physical
Education and Sport:
Exploring Alternative Visions

8

14

Research in Physical Education and Sport:
Exploring Alternative Visions

Edited by

Andrew C. Sparkes

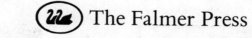 The Falmer Press

(A member of the Taylor & Francis Group)
London • Washington, D.C.

UK The Falmer Press, 4 John St., London, WC1N 2ET
USA The Falmer Press, Taylor & Francis Inc., 1900 Frost Road, 101, Bristol, PA 19007

First published 1992

Library of Congress Cataloging-in-Publication data are available on request

A catalogue record for this book is available from the British Library

ISBN 0 75070 074 2 cased
ISBN 0 75070 075 0 paperback

Cover design by Caroline Archer

Set in 10.5/11.5 pt Bembo
Graphicraft Typesetters Ltd., Hong Kong

Printed in Great Britain by Burgess Science Press, Basingstoke on paper which has a specified pH value on final paper manufacture of not less than 7.5 and is therefore 'acid free'.

Contents

Contents

Introduction

Andrew C. Sparkes

When I first contacted the contributors to this volume I did so on the basis that they were involved in forms of research that differed from much of the traditional fare that has characterized physical education (PE) and sport in recent years. Each was invited to outline their particular vision of research and provide an example of how this vision shaped the ways in which they went about attempting to understand the social world. Consequently, this is not a 'how to do it' book, a book about techniques that attempts, for instance, to give detailed prescriptions about how to conduct an interview. Rather, it is about how the authors locate themselves as researchers in terms of the personal meanings, understandings and interpretations they bring with them to the process of enquiry and how these influence their conceptualization and use of interviews or any other data generating procedure. Their responses to my invitation provide powerful insights into a variety of research traditions that are influenced by theoretical perspectives ranging from phenomenology and symbolic interactionism to critical theory, feminism and post-structuralism. In this sense their work is a collective invitation to consider how we might begin to explain and understand the complexities of PE and sport in our society by slipping on alternative sets of lenses so that we are able to see the world around us, our relationship to it and each other, in different ways.

To locate the range of visions that are presented I provide in chapter 1 an extended review of the paradigms debate of which this present volume is, in part, both a reaction to, and a product of. It is a lengthy chapter because I have assumed that many readers are coming to the debate for the first time and therefore require an extensive coverage of some of its key issues to illustrate just what it is about alternative paradigms research that actually makes it alternative. Indeed, what are alternative paradigms an alternative to? Furthermore, what does it mean to call oneself an interpretive or critical researcher and what implications does this have for the research process? With such questions in mind I begin by considering the nature of paradigms and suggest that *all* research

1

is informed by deep philosophical assumptions and commitments that shape the manner in which individuals and groups conceptualize both the nature and the purpose of the research enterprise. To highlight this point the notion of validity is focussed upon since this term has very different meanings in the positivist, interpretive and critical paradigms. The assumptions undergirding each of these paradigms is considered in detail although greater attention is given to the interpretive and critical paradigms since all the contributions in this volume draw upon them for their inspiration. The differences between the three paradigms are highlighted and it is suggested that interpretive and critical research forms provide viable alternatives to positivistic research. I conclude that the research emanating from any given paradigm should be judged according to criteria that are consistent with its starting premises so that as a research community we are able, not only to understand their differences, but to celebrate them as a source of theoretical vitality and creativity.

In chapter 2 Stephen Smith draws upon strands from European phenomenology to consider how we might go about studying the lifeworld of physical education. His phenomenological orientation contrasts directly with much of the current work in pedagogical research that bases understanding on systematic, formalized and generally quantifiable, observation procedures. Stephen invites us to observe in a different way, a pedagogic way, that implicates us in a situation of responsibility for the child's movement towards maturity whereby we must not only look *at* the child, and *for* the child, but also to take note of how the child is placed so that we can look *after* her or him. To illustrate his points Stephen provides examples from his own research involving phenomenological descriptions of children's physical activities in a variety of contexts, and the recollections of undergraduate students of physical education regarding their experiences of physical activity during childhood. These examples, along with the other issues raised by Stephen throughout his chapter as to how this kind of research might encourage a different form of pedagogical consciousness regarding the children in our care, suggests that phenomenological enquiry has the potential to make a major impact on how we conceptualize physical education in the future.

The process of phenomenological interviewing in which participants reconstruct their experience and reflect upon its meaning is used by Sherry Woods in chapter 3 to describe and understand the contextual realities of being a lesbian physical educator. Historically, these teachers have represented a silent minority in education and little is known about their experiences. Consequently, a major goal of Sherry's research was to break this silence and provide these women with a voice so that a process of dialogue and change might be initiated. A thematic analysis of her interviews reveals the shared experiences of these teachers in terms of the underlying assumptions they make about being a lesbian physical educator, the personal and professional split they have to maintain between their identity as a lesbian and a PE teacher, and the ways in which they utilize a range of lesbian identity management techniques to survive in the school as a place of work. These experiences are located within the framework of oppression theory and highlight the prevalence of homophobia, sexism and heterosexism within schools and the ways in which these operate to structure the daily lives of lesbian PE teachers so that they remain locked into a cycle of isolation, silence, fear and powerlessness. However, in line with the intention that her research should promote change, Sherry suggests that this cycle can be broken by lesbian PE teachers openly acknowledging their presence to each other so that they can begin the process of developing the positive collective identity that is so essential for interrupting and challenging the effects of homophobia and heterosexism in PE and sport.

In chapter 4 the voices of teachers are again given due attention by Tom Templin and myself as we utilize a life history approach to explore the meanings of marginality for those that teach physical education in schools. Our starting position is that if we are to understand why PE teachers teach as they do then we need to know something about them as people who have a past, a present and aspirations for the future, that is, we need to understand more about their lives. We suggest that one good way to do this is to explore with them their life histories and, in particular, the life stories they can tell. The resurgence of interest in this approach is outlined and the contemporary concern to locate the subjective reality of individuals in a wider social, economic, political and historical context that structures their lives is discussed in detail. To illustrate the potential of life histories to assist our understanding of teachers we draw upon data from an ongoing study of the lives and careers of PE teachers to focus on the dialectical relationship between subjective and objective careers and how these operate to shape the views and prospects of those who teach a low status subject like PE in schools. As part of this process the personal views of PE teachers from different generations regarding their marginality and the positioning of their subject relative to others are located in a historical landscape to reveal how their personal troubles are linked to broader social issues. This point is reinforced by a detailed consideration of the double marginality experienced by many women PE teachers in an educational system that is dominated by men. In relation to these, and other issues raised within the chapter, we conclude by considering the potential of life history studies to empower teachers and initiate change by providing a forum for their voices in the research process.

A different focus on the voices of PE teachers is provided by Gill Clarke in chapter 5. Drawing upon symbolic interactionism and ethnomethodology Gill's attention is directed to the process of teaching and learning in physical education lessons and how these are accomplished through the central medium of language. Her case study examines in detail the patterns and nature of talk between PE teachers and students in a series of gymnastics lessons and provides us with insights into how meanings and definitions are framed by the language used as these lessons unfold. The analysis provided suggests that classroom discourse subtly shapes what happens between teachers and students in the achievement of 'common' knowledge. Lessons are seen to serve many functions and to be the result of joint actions that do not just happen but are actively accomplished. Attention is given to how order is maintained and issues of interactional power are explored by utilizing the concept of frame to illustrate how teachers are able to establish particular behavioural frames and impose certain definitions of the situation upon students. In relation to these issues Gill considers what it means to become defined as a socially, procedurally, and linguistically competent student and how this process influences the quality of interactions that many students experience with their PE teachers during lessons.

One of the most powerful critiques to emerge within the social sciences in recent years has been that of feminism and in chapter 6 Sheila Scraton and Anne Flintoff focus on feminist research. The first half of the chapter provides an introduction to the key debates associated with this form of enquiry in terms of method, methodology, epistemology and the complex relationship between theory and practice. It is suggested that these debates could, and should, inform and challenge much of the current research in PE. Sheila and Anne indicate that while there are many different perspectives on feminist research the common strand that unites them is their fundamental link to feminist politics which has as its primary aim the creation of change and improvement in women's lives. They emphasize that feminist research is research *for* women, rather than simply research *on* women. To illustrate this point a range of feminist perspectives and their applications to PE are considered. The second half of the chapter provides an example of feminist research in action by focussing upon a recent study of the relationship between gender and girl's PE in a city-based local education authority. Here, the possibilities and problems of applying this approach to research in PE unfold as the dynamics of this form of engagement are documented in detail. In closing, Sheila and Anne suggest ways in which feminist research should influence the research agenda in PE during the coming years.

Action research has a limited history in PE research yet a considerable history in the broader fields of education and social psychology. Although there has been a rigorous debate about the nature of action research within educational discourse for over a decade, the debate seems to have eluded the world of physical education. When action research has been used in PE it has often been misunderstood and misdirected. With these as his starting points Richard Tinning, in chapter 7, provides an explanation of action research and locates this approach in a historical context. The epistemological assumptions underpinning various interpretations of this form of enquiry, such as technical, practical and emancipatory action research, are discussed, together with the different kinds of knowledge and human interests that such interpretations favour or reflect. It is argued that action research is a particular form of critical social science which is ultimately related to issues of power, epistemology and emancipation. Following this, several examples of action research in PE are outlined with particular reference to the knowledge and interests they represent to illustrate how they have often reinforced a technical and individualistic orientation to teaching while ignoring issues of power and dominance. Richard provides a contrast to these examples by discussing his own involvement with emancipatory action research over the last ten years with pre-service and in-service PE teachers and highlights the possibilities and problems associated with this approach in the context of an award bearing course. The chapter concludes with a call to refocus attention on the fundamental values of action research so that its potential to improve the lives of teachers is realized.

The potential of curriculum history to inform the field of physical education is the focus of attention for David Kirk in chapter 8 where he explains what is distinctive about *curriculum* history compared to other historical work in education and physical education. By providing examples from his own work on the social construction of PE in post-war Britain and its influence on the contemporary debates surrounding this subject, David offers a particular view of curriculum history and illustrates the kind of material this approach produces, along with the sources of struggle it illuminates regarding attempts to define what is 'useful' knowledge in PE. His analysis suggests that in the broader context of curriculum research and critical pedagogy that curriculum history is indispensable for the following reasons. First, it supplies an antidote to the tendency of contemporary culture to become imprisoned in the lurid present. Second, it specifically exposes the contested nature of the processes of selecting, organizing and distributing knowledge, and the ways in which these processes are part of, and contribute to, the production of circuits of power in our society. Third, by revealing the contested nature of curriculum, historical research highlights the ways in which schooling intersects with power relations in society and their substantiations through relations of class, race, sex and age. Finally, curriculum histories, by unveiling the political nature of knowledge production and the ways in which human agency is circumscribed and structured over time, feeds into and informs contemporary struggles over definitions of knowledge in PE by assisting those involved in these struggles to identify the broad terrain of ideological contestation and the specific sites of struggle. In conclusion, David argues that curriculum history has a very practical, strategic and political source that can act as a force for change in society and he suggests that physical educators need to actively draw on this source in their attempts to control the process of defining their subject.

In the emerging literature on alternative paradigms research in recent years much has been written about the process of enquiry but little has been said about the end product. As a consequence, chapter 9 by John Evans, along with those that follow by Keith Lyons and myself, begin to redress the balance by problematizing the ways in which we write about our research and represent the people we work with in our papers and reports. By reflecting critically on his own engagement in an ethnographic study of a group of innovative physical educators John raises issues about how researchers conceptualize and characterize the thinking and actions of those they interact with in the field, and how they go about the business of conducting and reporting ethnographic educational research. He suggests that the researcher's interests are always present and yet at the same time remain deviously silent in the production of ethnographic texts that claim to capture and analyze the reality of a given social situation. In relation to this, John explores how he became increasingly dissatisfied with the research role he adopted in his study, with the way in which he conceptualized and represented the thinking and actions of the teachers and with his inability to convey the diachrony and complexity of either the social and intellectual changes, or the educational reform processes which these people experienced. The insights provided by John highlight how the processes of writing, representation and theorizing are inseparable and bound together in a dynamic relationship. Furthermore, these insights into the limitations of much ethnographic writing suggest that we need to both rethink how we write about, represent and describe the actions of teachers, and better conceptualize the nature of teachers' thinking and their subjectivity. This would certainly involve some experimental writing in an attempt to finds ways of describing the complexity, the multi-dimensionality, the organization and disorder, and the uncertainty and incongruities of the social worlds that we and others inhabit.

People rarely just *do* research. At some point their 'results' are shared with other people and Keith Lyons in chapter 10 argues that the forms this sharing takes in physical education ought to be questioned and not taken for granted. He suggests that it is useful to regard ethnographic research as a way of receiving and telling stories that offers parts for many voices that are rich in meaning. Drawing upon a three-year ethnographic study of five teachers of boys' PE in two secondary schools Keith presents several stories to illustrate how this form of research is in fact a celebration of the finding, making and sharing of stories as a means of relating lived experiences to others. The ways in which Keith tells his stories provides both a marked contrast to, and a critique of, the standard forms of representation to be found in the majority of ethnographic writing and begins to indicate to us how alternative tales from the field might be told so that the voices of teachers are privileged as their authority and authorial voice are placed centre stage. Like John Evans in the previous chapter, Keith reflects upon his own involvement with the teachers and pupils that he worked with and makes explicit what he feels were shortcomings in his fieldwork. He also calls upon insights from literary theory, anthropology and personal construct psychology to highlight the difficulties inherent in representing field experiences in a textual form. Finally, Keith considers the emerging influence of post-modernism and how it might influence how ethnographers write their stories in the future.

The final chapter in the book, chapter 11, also draws upon recent debates within anthropology and sociology to explore and problematize the ways in which researchers represent not only the people in their studies but themselves in their written texts. It is argued that our 'findings' are inscribed in the way we write about things and they are not detached from the presentation of observations, reflections and inter-pretations that are associated with particular forms of engagement in the research process. As a consequence, I suggest that there can be no such thing as a neutral report since the conventions of text and the language forms used by researchers of all paradigmatic stances are actively involved in the *construction* of realities. In relation to this, insights from post-structuralism are provided to indicate that language is not a mirror of reality since it is language that constitutes reality and, therefore, various languages will construct specific aspects of reality in their own ways. The point is emphasized that *all* researchers use writing and rhetorical devices as part of their method and practices of persuasion and I highlight some of these to illustrate how researchers working in different paradigms call upon specific rhetorical conventions to persuade the reader of the auth-ority of their findings. Following this, I focus specifically on how the voices of both subjects and researchers are located in the realist, con-fessional, and impressionist tales told by ethnographers in order to indicate different forms of writing that those committed to alternative paradigms research in PE might like to consider in the future. Having outlined some of the problems and possibilities associated with telling tales in different ways, I conclude by suggesting that we should all be encouraged to develop a reflexive self-awareness of the rhetorical and stylistic conven-tions we use so that they can be brought within our explicit and metho-dological understanding. In the light of this more informed understanding of our textual practices we might then begin the principled exploration of alternative modes of representation that are more suited to our hopes and aspirations as researchers dealing with complex and multiple social realities.

Having briefly summarized the contributions to this volume it is clear that a range of visions have been made available for consideration. None of the authors make any claim that theirs is the only vision or that their views should be privileged above all others. Rather, they suggest that their own particular form of engagement with the research process has something valuable to contribute in terms of how we conceptualize, understand and attempt to explain many of the key issues and problems that confront us in the world of physical education and sport. Nobody would deny that in the coming years there is much work to be done in refining and developing the visions that are emerging within alternative paradigms research. In this context it is hoped that the insights the authors have provided will stimulate your interest and encourage you to develop this interest in the future as part of your own research endeavours.

Chapter 1

The Paradigms Debate:
An Extended Review and
a Celebration of Difference

Andrew C. Sparkes

During recent years in a range of academic disciplines within the natural and social sciences there has been an intense debate going on regarding the nature of research. This debate has led to major upheavals in how we conceptualize the research process, ourselves as researchers, and how we come to understand the world around us. As a consequence, Phillips (1987) suggests that during the last three decades the epistemological status of science has been called into question.[1] Indeed, several influential books on the philosophy of science have included the word *revolution* in their titles,[2] and Lincoln (1985, 1989a and 1990) believes that a paradigm revolution is taking place in the academic disciplines ranging from business administration and organizational theory to occupational therapy. Using a more aggressive metaphor Gage (1989) talks of the paradigm wars that raged in the world of educational research during the 1980s and reached their sanguinary climax in 1989. There appears to be much unrest within the world of research in general and the social sciences in particular. According to Bernstein (1976):

> the initial impression that one has in reading through the literature in and about the social disciplines during the last decade or so is that of sheer chaos. Everything appears to be 'up for grabs'. There is little or no consensus — except by members of the same school or sub-school — about what are the well-established results, the proper research procedures, the important results, the important problems, or even the most promising theoretical approaches to the study of society and politics. There are claims and counterclaims. (pp. xii)

Within this turbulent intellectual landscape the world of physical education (PE) has not gone untouched.[3] Towards the latter part of the 1980s

signs of this debate began to manifest themselves with increasing fre-
quency in a range of scholarly journals.[4] We have been able to witness
vociferous exchanges between advocates of particular ways of researching
into the world of PE who have argued eloquently for the beauty and
appropriateness of their views in relation to other contrasting visions. The
net effect of these exchanges has led Hellison (1988) to suggest that
'Winds of change are ruffling the study of teaching in physical education.
New research paradigms are being advocated both in education and
physical education . . . the employment of alternative approaches to research — are no longer confined to isolated pockets of "fringe" scholars'
(pp. 84–6). Likewise, Bain and Jewett (1987) note how the historical
dominance of the empirical paradigm in PE is being challenged by the
interpretive and critical paradigms in such a way that the focus and methodology of research is changing.

For many of us who study PE these are exciting times in which
alternative visions of research challenge each other as they contribute their
own particular insights to the terrain of knowledge in this area. I, for one,
welcome a multiplicity of visions and, rather than perceive intellectual
conjunctures such as the present one as conjuncture of crisis, I take the
current debate to be a sign of growing maturity, confidence and efferves-
cence within the PE community. Indeed, I would be more likely to talk
of crisis if the debate was *not* taking place. As Metzler (1981) comments in
relation to PE pedagogy:

> What was once a fairly small cadre of relatively like-minded
> scholars is growing larger and more diverse. Both are healthy
> trends. It is quite likely that the impending debates will result in
> methodological and epistemological splits in our ranks. That too
> is healthy, as long as we can look past those differences while
> working together for a shared agenda in research on teaching and
> teacher education, (p. 110)

Having indicated that a debate is taking place in PE and many other
disciplines my next task is to attempt to provide some kind of framework
for making sense of the debate and the contributions contained in this
volume. This task is extremely difficult as there are many complex strands
running through the debate and in choosing to focus upon some aspects
others are necessarily ignored. As Smith (1989) comments 'The terms used
to acknowledge this discussion have become common currency: quantitative versus qualitative, scientific versus naturalistic, empiricist versus
interpretive, and so on. No matter which labels are selected, however,
there is still a lack of clarity as to what is involved in this discussion' (p. 1).
In such a context, I need to signal that while, as a neophyte researcher,
I am excited by the current debate I am also confused by it. Therefore,
this introductory chapter needs to be seen as an expression of my own confusions in which I present a personalized view of the ways in which I have
attempted to, and am still attempting to, make sense of what is going on.

Consequently, my introduction can only be partial and is replete with a range of distortions. For instance, while I discuss three particular views of research in this chapter I find two of them (the interpretive and the critical) more interesting and satisfying than the other (positivist) in terms of my own personal engagement in the research process. Also, since all the chapters in this book are located within the interpretive and critical paradigms I devote more time to discussing these in detail. Having said this, my intention is not to advocate one view over another but to highlight key issues within the current debate so that each viewpoint can be positioned relative to the others in such a way that the contribution of each to our understanding can be properly acknowledged. Furthermore, I want to emphasize that this is the way I see things and it should not be taken to be a widely agreed upon position. Others will tell the story in different ways.

In order to provide a provisional framework for understanding what I take the debate to be about I begin by considering the nature of paradigms and the manner in which they operate to shape the research process as a totality. Next, I outline the basic assumptions of three of the major paradigms that have impacted upon the world of PE in recent years. These are the positivist, interpretive, and the critical paradigms. In order to illustrate how the basic assumptions of each of these shape the work of researchers I provide brief details of the different ways that each conceptualizes the issue of validity within its boundaries. Having outlined some of the major differences I conclude that attempts to accommodate different paradigms are problematic and that they need to be seen as viable and valuable alternatives in their own right that should be judged accordingly using appropriate criteria.

The Nature of Paradigms

The individual research act does not take place in a vacuum but in the social context of 'invisible colleges', that is, a community of scholars who share similar conceptions of proper questions, methods, techniques, and forms of explanation. Schulman (1986) has suggested that the term most frequently employed to describe such research communities, and the conceptions of problem and method they share, is *paradigm*. This term is most often associated with the work of Kuhn and his book *The Structure of Scientific Revolutions* which takes a historical view of scientific development and was first published in 1962. It is impossible to do justice to the issues raised by Kuhn and detailed discussions of his work are available elsewhere.[5] For our purposes it needs to be recognized that there are various ways of defining what a paradigm is and Kuhn himself used the term in more than twenty different ways in his book (see Masterman, 1970). Bearing this in mind, Patton (1978) provides a useful working definition:

A paradigm is a world view, a general perspective, a way of breaking down the complexity of the real world. As such, paradigms are deeply embedded in the socialization of adherents and practitioners: paradigms tell us what is important, legitimate, and reasonable. Paradigms are also normative, telling the practitioner what to do without the necessity of long existential or epistemological consideration. But it is this aspect of paradigms that constitutes both their strength and weakness — *their strength in that it makes action possible, their weakness in that the very reason for action is hidden in the unquestioned assumptions of the paradigm.* (p. 203, my emphasis)

More recently Guba and Lincoln (1989) have argued that paradigms are basic *belief* systems that represent the most fundamental positions we are willing to take and which cannot be proven or disproven, 'If we could cite reasons why some particular paradigm should be preferred, then, those reasons would form an even more basic set of beliefs. At some level we must stop giving reasons and simply accept whatever we are as our basic belief set — our paradigm' (p. 80). The adoption of a paradigm for Lincoln (1990) 'literally permeates every act even tangentially associated with inquiry, such that any consideration even remotely attached to inquiry processes demands rethinking to bring decisions into line with the world view embodied in the paradigm itself' (p. 81). At a most fundamental level different paradigms provide particular sets of lenses for seeing the world and making sense of it in different ways. They act to shape how we think an act because for the most part we are not even aware that we are wearing any particular set of lenses.

As with any form of belief system, the values and assumptions individuals adopt regarding the nature of the research enterprise are a product of their life history during which a personal stock of recipe knowledge and system of relevancies is developed via the process of socialization. Therefore, to become a competent and accepted member of a given research community, the individual must not only learn the content of the field but also a particular way of seeing the world that eventually becomes not only unquestioned but unquestionable. For Popkewitz (1984) 'Learning the exemplars of a field of inquiry is also to learn how to see, think about and act towards the world. An individual is taught the appropriate expectations, demands and consistent attitudes and emotions that are involved in doing science' (p. 3). At the heart of this socialization process is the taking on of certain assumptions regarding questions of *ontology* and *epistemology*.

Ontological assumptions revolve around questions regarding the nature of existence, that is, the very nature of the subject matter of the research — in our case, the social world. As Burrell and Morgan (1979) point out, social scientists are faced with the basic ontological question:

whether the 'reality' to be investigated is external to the individual — imposing itself on individual consciousness from without — or the product of individual consciousness; whether 'reality' is of an 'objective' nature, or the product of individual cognition; whether 'reality' is a given 'out there' in the world, or the product of one's mind. (p. 1)

The former may be classed as an external-realist view while the latter is an internal-idealist position. Linked to issues of ontology are a second set of assumptions of an epistemological kind that refer to questions of knowing and the nature of knowledge.

These are assumptions about the grounds of knowledge — about how one might begin to understand the world and communicate this as knowledge to fellow human beings. These assumptions entail beliefs, for example, about the forms of knowledge that can be obtained, and how one can sort out what is regarded as 'true' from what is to be regarded as 'false'. Indeed, this dichotomy of 'true' and 'false' itself presupposes an epistemological stance. It is predicated upon a view of the nature of knowledge itself: whether, for example, it is possible to identify and communicate the nature of knowledge as being hard, real and capable of being transmitted in tangible form, or whether 'knowledge' is of a softer, more subjective, spiritual or even transcendental kind, based on experience and insight of a unique and essentially personal nature. The epistemological assumptions in these instances determine extreme positions on the issue of whether knowledge is something which can be acquired on the one hand, or something which has to be personally experienced on the other. (*ibid*, p. 2)

The former may be classed as an objectivist view while the latter is a subjectivist epistemology. A third set of assumptions identified by Burrell and Morgan that are linked to ontological and epistemological issues, but conceptually separate from them, concerns *human nature*. Any form of research that involves people in a social context involves making assumptions of this kind and in particular about the relationship between people and their environment. Some might adopt an extreme view in which people are seen as responding in a mechanistic and deterministic way to the situations that confront them in their external world. Such a stance would take people and their experiences to be *products* of the environment in which they are conditioned by their external circumstances. This is a deterministic view. An opposing view would posit that people are much more in control of their lives and are actively involved in creating their environment. In this voluntaristic view people are the controllers and not the controlled and there is a sense of agency, autonomy and 'free will'. Clearly, these are extreme views of human nature and most researchers would probably locate their assumptions somewhere on a continuum between the two poles that would allow for the influence of both situational and voluntary factors to be considered in relation to how people think and act. Nonetheless, assumptions regarding this relationship are constantly made.

The position taken with regard to the three sets of assumptions outlined will have a bearing on how researchers set about gathering data in order to understand the social world. Some might adopt a *nomothetic* approach that emphasizes the importance of basing research upon systematic protocol and technique:

> It is epitomised in the approach and methods employed in the natural sciences, which focus upon the process of testing hypotheses in accordance with the canons of scientific rigour. It is preoccupied with the construction of scientific tests and the use of quantitative techniques for the analysis of data. Surveys, questionnaires, personality tests and standardized research instruments of all kinds are prominent among the tools which compromise nomothetic methodology. (*ibid*, pp. 6–7)

In contrast, others may adopt an *ideographic* approach which is based on the view that to understand the social world we need to gain first-hand knowledge of the subject under investigation. Such an approach emphasizes the importance of getting close to one's subject and exploring its detailed background and life history:

> The ideographic approach emphasizes the analysis of the subjective accounts which one generates by 'getting inside' situations and involving oneself in the everyday flow of life — the detailed analysis of the insights generated by such encounters with one's subject and the insights revealed in impressionistic accounts found in diaries, biographies and journalistic records. The ideographic method stresses the importance of letting one's subject unfold its nature and characteristics during the process of investigation. (*ibid*, p. 6)

In drawing attention to the kinds of assumptions that researchers make I have made no attempt to argue a case for any of them. My point is that *all* researchers make assumptions of some kind or other in relation to issues of ontology, epistemology, human nature and methodology and that these assumptions tend to cluster together and are given coherence within the frameworks of particular paradigms. What this means is that we cannot, and do not, enter the research process as empty vessels or as blank slates that data imprints itself upon. Essentially, ontological assumptions give rise to epistemological assumptions which have methodological implications for the choices made regarding particular techniques of data collection, the interpretation of these findings and the eventual ways they are written about in texts and presented orally at conferences (see Evans, chapter 9 in this volume; Lyons, chapter 10 in this volume; Sparkes, 1989, 1991 and chapter 11 in this volume). At the most fundamental level this will mean that those operating with different sets of paradigmatic assumptions will see the world in a different way, go about investigating it in different ways and report their findings in different ways.

Essentially, as Morgan (1983) points out, any form of science is a process of *engagement* whereby scientists engage a subject of study by interacting with it through a *particular frame of reference*. Therefore, what is observed and discovered in the object, that is, its objectivity is as much a product of this interaction and the protocol and technique through which it is operationalized as it is of the object itself. Such a stance 'emphasizes the importance of understanding the possible modes of engagement' (p. 13). This form of understanding is crucial in terms of the paradigms debate since, according to Earls (1986), the researcher's basic assumptions concerning the nature of reality, truth, the physical and the social world infuses all aspects of the investigative process. Therefore, the often quoted advice that the 'problem' will determine both the approach and the methods of investigation is grossly misleading and is an example of a prevailing confusion between *philosophical* and *technical* issues (see Bryman, 1984; Sparkes, 1989). The former concerns the appropriate foundations for the study of society and its manifestations whereas the latter is concerned with the appropriateness or superiority of the methods of research in relation to one another, for example, direct observation of events versus the survey.

This confusion has been exacerbated by the indiscriminate use of such terms as method, research methods, and methodology in the literature. In an attempt to clarify matters, Bulmer (1984) offers the following classifications: (a) general methodology (philosophical issues in my sense), which donates 'the systematic and logical study of the general principles guiding sociological investigation . . . (and) . . . has clear and direct lines to the philosophy of social science'; (b) research strategy or research procedure, which refers to the way in which particular empirical studies are designed and carried out and, 'what notions about the task of sociological research are embodied in the approach used'; and (c) research techniques (technical issues in my terms), which refer to the 'specific manipulative and fact finding operations which are used to yield data about the social world', for example, questionnaire construction, observation schedules, interviews, participant observation techniques, and various forms of statistical analysis (pp. 4–5).

Bulmer suggests that the choice of research strategy and techniques is rarely independent of philosophical issues. However, in terms of the view that I have articulated so far I would argue that they can *never* be independent but are inseparable in making sense of the research process within any given paradigm. According to Popkewitz (1984), methods are not simply technical skills that exist independently of the purpose and commitment of those who do the research; rather, techniques emerge from a theoretical position that reflects certain values, beliefs and dispositions towards the social world. Hence, in terms of the meanings attached to any method and the interpretation of the data produced by them, it is not the problem that determines the method but rather a prior intellectual, emotional, and political commitment to a given philosophical position that orients the researcher to conceive of, and formulate, the problem within the context of these commitments.

In identifying what is crucial and what is not crucial to the paradigms debate Smith (1990a) points out that there is little to be gained by devoting our attention to alternative research techniques and their specific applications and that such a focus is unproductive. That is, the paradigms debate is *not* simply about the *techniques* of research although it does have implications for how techniques are chosen and used. For example, those who adhere to a realist ontology and an objectivist epistemology are likely to prefer techniques that differ from those who hold to an idealist ontology and a subjectivist epistemology. Therefore, the real issues of the paradigms debate do not revolve around technical issues because, as both Locke (1986) and Schempp (1988) have pointed out, the techniques of research are flexible and no method of data collection is inherently linked to any one world view. As a consequence, techniques of data gathering do not constitute the uniqueness of a paradigm. In relation to this Erickson (1986) provides a good example in his discussion of a data collection technique known as 'continuous narrative description' that has been used in social and behavioural research since the latter part of the nineteenth century and involves a play-by-play account of what an observer sees observed people doing. He emphasizes that the use of this technique will vary according to the paradigmatic assumptions held by the researcher:

> The technique of continuous narrative description can be used by researchers with a positivist and behaviourist orientation that deliberately excludes from research interest the immediate meanings of actions from the actor's point of view. Continuous narrative description can also be used by researchers with a non-positivistic, interpretive orientation, in which the immediate (often intuitive) meanings of action to the actors involved are of central interest. The presuppositions and conclusions of these two types of research are very different, and the content of the narra-tive description that is written differs as well. If two observers with these different orientations were placed in the same spot to observe what was ostensibly the 'same' behaviour performed by the 'same' individuals, the observers would write substantively differing accounts of what had happened, choosing very different kinds of verbs, nouns, adverbs and adjectives to characterize the actions that were described. (p. 120)

Clearly, the uniqueness of a paradigm comes in the particular perspectives of those who use the techniques. Therefore, the crucial features of the paradigms debate according to Smith (1990a) revolve around the complex webs of background knowledge and the philosophical commitments that researchers bring with them, either explicitly or implicitly to their researches. In relation to this Hawkins (1987) notes how such assumptions 'are rarely consciously and deliberately adopted. They tend to be taken for granted, intuitively acquired, almost inherited — like some intellectual gene from whatever popular culture happens to have fathered us' (p. 372). This is why an awareness of paradigmatic assumptions is crucial to the debate since they shape the ways that the world is seen. With this in mind I want to now provide portraits of the three of the paradigms that have influenced research within PE. However, before beginning this task I want to make the reader aware of some of the dangers associated with my approach.

First, there is a need to acknowledge the timely warning provided by Locke (1989) and Siedentop (1987 and 1989) regarding the dangers of trying to simplify paradigmatic differences via the use of caricatures and cartoons. Often, such an approach leads to fruitless disputes and professional animosities in which a few leading scholars are singled out as villains or heroes (there are rarely heroines in a male-dominated research world as Griffin (1989) reminds us) and the complexity of their views and the variety of the contributions they have made to the field of study is ignored.[6] Furthermore, as Hawkins (1987) comments:

The temptation is that by labelling something, we think everyone will know what we are talking about. It would be nice if that were true. Unfortunately, many of the labels we use are associated, even in a scientific culture like ours, with various connotations that often misrepresent the position the labels are intended to designate. In these cases the labels become polemical ghosts, intellectual punchbags erected to serve as sparring partners for the opponent. (p. 370)

In what is to follow I have no desire or interest in cartooning the beliefs and works of individual scholars. However, I do admit that in order to highlight key issues within the paradigms debate, I present ideal-type characterizations of paradigms that have all the faults inherent in such forms of representation. For example, as with all stereotypes and generalizations they may not be true in all cases. Furthermore, as with any ideal-type or caricature, only the central tendencies and dimensions of each paradigm are revealed, and this strategy invariably glosses over certain distinctions within a paradigm and does not give full weight to their internal disagreements about procedures and perspectives. Paradigms are not homogeneous or monolithic and there are many contrasting traditions contained within any one particular paradigm, that is, there is internal diversity within paradigms. For example, if we take just the interpretive paradigm we find Jacob (1987 and 1988) drawing upon work in North America talking of six traditions that range from human ethology to cognitive anthropology while Atkinson *et al* (1988) review seven approaches that have been used in British educational research that range from symbolic interactionism to neo-Marxist ethnography, and feminism.[7] To complicate matters even more there are also considerable internal disagreements regarding whose work is representative and about what constitutes the main features of a given tradition within a particular paradigm.[8]

In such a confused situation caricatures can provide a service in that they draw on central and recognizable features. Indeed, if the caricature did not bear some resemblance to the subject it claims to represent then it would not be able to perform its function and be recognizable. In this context we need to be aware that while it would be wrong to suggest that each paradigm contains homogenous schools of thought, it would also be an error not to recognize that certain intraparadigmatic similarities exist. For example, Giddens (1976) claims that the schools of thought contained within the interpretive paradigm are closely associated with philosophical idealism while the positivistic position is closely associated with philosophical realism. Therefore, in the light of the dangers and limitations that I have signalled the manner in which I proceed to draw on the concept of paradigms as a disciplinary matrix of assumptions needs to be seen as a heuristic device that polarizes world views for the sake of discussion, without, I hope, denying the complexities of the research approaches involved in any of them. Like Eisner (1990a) I am fully aware that the complexities of the research process cannot be neatly separated and captured in a few categories or dimensions but as he argues 'you also know, as I do, that analysis requires separation, even if the parts are part fiction ... I address each aspect separately because language itself is a diachronic, not a synchronic, medium. I bracket in order to illuminate and write in parts because I write rather than paint' (p. 88).

The Positivist Paradigm

According to Jacob (1988) 'Until recently, educational research has drawn primarily from psychological traditions that operate within a positivistic approach' (p. 16). Some of the terms associated with this approach include empiricist, empirical-analytical, behaviourist, radical behaviourist and quantitative. Not surprisingly, Giddens (1974) notes that, while positivism as a philosophy has a long and illustrious history, this term has acquired a variety of meanings.[9] He suggests:

> Positivism in philosophy, in some sense revolves around the contention, or implicit assumption, that the notions and statements of science constitute a framework by reference to which the nature of any form of knowledge may be determined. Positivism in sociology may be broadly represented as depending upon the assertion that the concepts and methods employed by the natural

sciences can be applied to form a 'science of man', or a 'natural science of society'. (p. 3)

This view was forcefully articulated by Auguste Comte in France during the early part of the nineteenth century and his advocacy of this view forms part of a tradition that has had a substantial impact on how we conceptualize and seek to conduct research on social phenomena today. According to Smith (1989):

> By the middle to late nineteenth century, an approach to the study of social life modelled on the natural sciences was in the process of being firmly established. The desire to master social life expressed itself in a concern for the discovery of social laws; in the development of a methodology that stressed the observation of experiences, experiments, and comparisons; in the separation of facts from values; and in the separation of the cognizing subject from the object of cognition. (p. 45)

In view of the historical importance of positivism and the tremendous gains in knowledge it fostered within the natural sciences during the last century it is understandable that it became the dominant paradigm for research within PE as this discipline gradually emerged. This dominance is evident more in some countries than others and Crum (1986) has argued that with regard to sport pedagogy research the majority of work in North America has been carried out in what he calls a descriptive-explanatory framework. In relation to this, Harris (1983a, p. 83) notes how the study of PE has historically been rooted in the biological sciences, for instance with exercise physiology, biomechanics/kinaesiology there are obvious linkages while motor learning, motor development and sport/exercise psychology also have strong biological components. Due to this close link with the life sciences it is hardly surprising that physical educators, for the most part, have utilized a research paradigm that was developed in the natural sciences. For her, 'This choice of a model for seeking truth has perhaps been facilitated by the almost unquestioned respectability this research paradigm is granted within academia in general'.

Others have also noted this tendency and McKay *et al* (1990) have argued that one major strategy that has been used to enhance the credibility and security of PE has been the emulation of empirical-analytical science at the expense of other world views. Kirk (1989) suggests that this approach forms an orthodoxy within research on teaching in PE that, 'is guided in particular by a belief in the need for objective measurement of teaching and learning in real-life situations, which can be achieved through empirical observations of life in classrooms and in the gym, the construction of standardized instruments to collect data from these observations, and the often sophisticated deployment of statistical techniques in the analysis of the data' (p. 124). In essence, those operating within this framework believe that the social world can be investigated in much the same way as the physical or natural world and that the methods, techniques and modes of operation of the natural sciences are the best way to explore the social world. Such a belief is based on a host of interrelated assumptions and commitments that Popkewitz (1984) believes act to shape this paradigm. These are as follows:

1 Theory is to be universal, not bound to a specific context or to actual circumstances in which generalizations are formulated.
2 There is a commitment to a disinterested science in which statements of science are believed to be independent of the goals and values which people may express in a situation. That is, facts are free of the values and interests of those who produce them.
3 The social world exists as a system of variables that are distinct and analytically separable parts of one interacting system. Variables are to be studied independently of one another. It is believed that by identifying and interrelating variables, the specific cause of behaviour within the system can be known. A cause is a relationship among empirical variables that can be explained or manipulated to produce conditionally predictable outcomes.
4 There is a belief in formalized knowledge which involves making clear and precise the variables of inquiry prior to research. Concepts should be operationalized, defined in such a way that there is an invariant definition which can be used to test and compare data. By making units of analysis invariant, the researcher can create 'independent' and 'dependent' variables to identify how one unit influences others, and how manipulation of one variable can produce 'effects' upon other variables.
5 The search for formal and disinterested knowledge creates a reliance upon mathematics in theory construction. Quantification of variables enables researchers to reduce or eliminate ambiguities and contradictions. (pp. 36–8)

These, and other assumptions that undergird positivism are outlined in Figure 1.1. While space does not allow a thorough interrogation of all these assumptions it is important to note that positivism adopts a realist-external ontology, an objectivist epistemology and prefers a nomothetic methodology.

With regard to ontology, positivism postulates that the social world external to individual cognition is a real world made up of hard, tangible and relatively immutable facts that can be observed, measured and known for what they really are.

Whether or not we label and perceive these structures, the realists maintain, they still exist as empirical entities. We may not even be

Figure 1.1: *Assumptions underlying the positivist, interpretive and critical paradigms*

ASSUMPTIONS	PARADIGM		
	POSITIVIST	INTERPRETIVE	CRITICAL
ONTOLOGY	EXTERNAL-REALIST	INTERNAL-IDEALIST, RELATIVIST	EXTERNAL-REALIST *OR* INTERNAL-IDEALIST
EPISTEMOLOGY	OBJECTIVIST, DUALIST	SUBJECTIVIST, INTERACTIVE	SUBJECTIVIST, INTERACTIVE
METHODOLOGY	NOMOTHETIC, EXPERIMENTAL, MANIPULATIVE	IDEOGRAPHIC, HERMENEUTICAL, DIALECTICAL	IDEOGRAPHIC, PARTICIPATIVE, TRANSFORMATIVE
INTERESTS	PREDICTION AND CONTROL (TECHNICAL)	UNDERSTANDING AND INTERPRETATION (PRACTICAL)	EMANCIPATION (CRITICISM AND LIBERATION)

aware of the existence of certain crucial structures and therefore have no 'names' or concepts to articulate them. For the realist, the social world exists independently of an individual's appreciation of it. The individual is seen as being born into and living within a social world which has a reality of its own. It is not something which the individual creates — it exists 'out there'; ontologically it is prior to the existence and consciousness of any single human being. For the realist, the social world has an existence which is as hard and concrete as the natural world. (Burrell and Morgan, 1979, p. 4)

Consequently, 'things' such as intelligence, social class, self-esteem, motivation, and so on are conceived of as independent and separately existing entities — they exist whether we conceive of them or not. Since they are taken to be mind-independent and exist outside of the individual then they can be described and known for what they really are by researchers who aspire to a detached objective 'God's eye' point of view to see the world from nowhere in particular (cf. Putnam, 1981). That is, for positivists the ideal would be for the researcher to somehow gain a view the world from a detached vantage point outside of it rather than from a place within it. This separation of mind and the world, or dualism, is a key issue because it leads to the view that truth has it source in this independently existing reality. Consequently, Guba (1990) argues, 'If there is a real world operating according to natural laws, then the inquirer must behave in ways that put questions directly to nature and allow nature to answer back directly. The inquirer, so to speak, must stand behind a thick wall of one-way glass, observing nature as "she does her thing"' (p. 19). Such behaviour is based on the premise that the researcher can explicate nature's secrets without altering them in any way.

Since reality can be known for what it actually is by the researcher adopting an unbiased and detached stance, it is important to control any possible sources of bias. Therefore, within the positivist framework a manipulative methodology is adopted which attempts to control both researcher bias and other external variables in the environment so that nature's secrets can be revealed for what they are. In this context a certain set of techniques are taken to be epistemologically privileged. Smith and Heshusius (1986) emphasize, 'for quantitative inquiry, techniques stand separate from and prior to the conduct of any particular piece of research' (p. 9). Indeed, the correct application of these techniques is deemed not only necessary but essential to match the criteria of internal and external validity plus reliability within this framework. Talking of research on teaching in PE, Siedentop (1983) suggests:

We have learned a great deal about data collection. We have many different tools for collecting data . . . There is healthy attention to and discussion of what constitutes good data, precisely the kind of interest that is characteristic of one of the most important self-correcting mechanisms of science, the continual asking, in one way or another, of the fundamental scientific question 'How do you know? which translates most often into 'What methods did you use to collect your data?' (p. 5)

Given their basic assumptions concerning the nature of reality then for positivists to 'know' this reality is to be able to describe or reflect it accurately. Consequently, Goetz and LeCompte (1984) argue:

Validity is concerned with the accuracy of scientific findings. Establishing validity requires (i) determining the extent to which conclusions effectively represent empirical reality; and (ii) assessing whether constructs devised by researchers represent or measure the categories of human experience that occur. (p. 210)

Therefore, any given judgment is 'true' when it corresponds to this external reality and false when it does not. Thus, a *correspondence* theory of truth is adhered to whereby, according to Smith (1984) 'True statements are judged to have accurately reflected the qualities and characteristics of what is out there whereas false ones are those judged to have in some way distorted the nature of that independently existing reality . . . The significant point is that truth has its source in an independently existing reality — a reality that can be known for what it really is' (p. 385). He goes on to comment that the process of observation, or empirical verification, is essential to our ability to judge whether or not a statement is true and how, for the positivist the dangers of subjectivity are a great worry in this area. Therefore, the quest is for objectivity, or as was said earlier to see the place from no particular place in it so that the values, desires and emotions of the researcher do not influence the object of study. To achieve this objectivity positivists adhere to certain prescribed methods (techniques) within a formalized process of investigation often called the 'scientific method'. These are taken to act as a constraint upon the researcher in terms of protecting her or him from distorting the qualities and characteristics of the object of study.

At the level of practice, adherence to these procedures will ensure that the study has been properly conducted. And if this is the case, we must accept the results, regardless of how we might feel about them. In other words, these are results to which all 'rational' people must accede, and disagreements can be reconciled by a properly done appeal to an independent reality. These procedures are neutral and non-arbitrary in that they stand over and beyond any one individual's interests, dispositions, or place in the world. (*ibid*)

More recently, Smith (1988, p. 20) has argued that for positivists the proper application of formalized methods (technical procedures) are taken to allow the researcher to penetrate through the level of how things *seem* to any given person, at any given time and place to the level of how things *are*. This methodological penetration allows us to see nature in its own terms (cf. Rorty, 1982) which itself acts as the ultimate constraint on our knowledge. This reality is seen as, 'that permanent neutral matrix to which we may appeal to settle competing knowledge claims'. Not surprisingly, methods that accurately measure what they are designed to measure, that is, those that 'see' the world from no particular place within it are highly prized since it is believed that they protect against the intrusion of our subjective selves and allow valid claims to be established. Methods within positivism are taken to be the guarantors of truth, and knowledge is believed to rest on firm foundations.[10]

The Interpretive Paradigm

Alternative ways of making sense of social reality have always existed and in direct contrast to positivism stands the interpretive paradigm. I have chosen to use the term 'interpretive' because according to Erickson (1986), it refers to a whole family of approaches and is useful for three reasons:

> (a) It is more inclusive than many others (for example, ethnography, case study); (b) it avoids the connotation of defining these approaches as essentially non-quantitative (a connotation that is carried by the term *qualitative*), since quantification of particular sorts can often be employed in this work; and (c) it points to the key feature of family resemblance among the various approaches — central research interest in human meaning in social life and its elucidation and exposition by the researcher. (p. 119)

As indicated, a range of research traditions can be located within the interpretive paradigm that go under various names including; ethnography, hermeneutics, naturalism, phenomenology, symbolic interactionism, constructivism, ethnomethodology, case study and qualitative research. Not surprisingly, Smith (1987) argues 'The body of work labelled qualitative is richly variegated and its theories and methods diverse to the point of disorderliness' (p. 173). Locke (1989) suggests 'At the best, qualitative research is a field characterized by zesty disarray' (p. 2). While Jacob (1988) claims 'What has been called "qualitative research" conveys different meanings to different people. Needless to say, this has caused considerable confusion among educational researchers' (p. 16). In her view it is inappropriate to view qualitative research as *one* approach. However, while there are differences between these traditions there are also many similarities in their approaches and for the purposes of simplicity I shall use them interchangeably throughout this section while using 'interpretive' as an umbrella term for discussing general issues.

Talking in an optimistic vein to a North American audience Locke (1987) comments, 'Few members of the Academy will be surprised by the prediction that we are in for a prolonged love affair with qualitative research methods in general and, to a lesser degree, the qualitative research paradigm in particular. That is where the cutting edge of research on pedagogy is located now, and where it is likely to remain for some time to come' (p. 86). However, Harris (1983b) suggests that the interpretive paradigm has received relatively little attention within PE. In relation to this Lincoln (1989) points out that the bulk of qualitative studies have only just begun to see the light of day in the United States and it needs to be recognized that 'it is only recently — within the last fifteen years or less — that scholarly journals have seriously considered publishing the products of qualitative inquiry (p. 237).[11]

Like positivism, the interpretive paradigm has deep historical roots and it emerged forcefully in the nineteenth century as a critical reaction to the former. An influential figure in this reaction was Wilhelm Dilthey who argued strongly that, whereas the natural sciences dealt with a series of inanimate objects that can be seen existing outside of us, this could not be so for the social sciences. The focus of the latter concerns the products of the human mind and these products are intimately connected to human minds, including all their subjectivity, interests, emotions and values. Dilthey concluded that:

> society is the result of conscious human intention and that the interrelationships among what is being investigated and the investigator are impossible to separate. For all people, lay people and social scientists alike, what actually exists in the social world is what people think exists. There is no objective reality as such, which is divorced from the people who participate in and interpret that reality . . . From this perspective, human beings are both the subject and the object of inquiry in the social sciences, and the study of the social world is, in essence, nothing more than the study of ourselves. (Smith, 1983, p. 35)

This legacy remains with us and interpretive researchers believe that while the natural science approach with its positivistic assumptions may be appropriate for the study of the physical world they are not appropriate for the study of the social world which they see as having very different characteristics. Popkewitz (1984) argues, the unique quality of being human is found in the symbols people invent to communicate meaning or an interpretation for the events of daily life, 'To an atom, the language of culture means nothing. To people immersed in Azanda or American life, the ideas, concepts and languages of interactions create ways of expressing and defining the possibilities and limitations of human existence' (p. 41). Since human beings are thinking, conscious, feeling, language-, and symbol-using animals, interpretive researchers do not feel drawn towards the natural science approaches for understanding the social world. Rather, they take the humanities to be a more appropriate starting point, especially social history since it emphasizes the interpretation of the past through what people have left behind them. In relation to this Burrell and Morgan 1979 argue:

> The interpretive paradigm is informed by a concern to understand the world as it is, to understand the fundamental nature of the social world at the level of subjective experience. It seeks explanation within the realm of individual consciousness and subjectivity, within the frame of reference of the participant as opposed to the observer of action . . . It sees the social world as an emergent social process which is created by the individuals concerned. Social reality, insofar as it is recognized to have any existence outside of the consciousness of any single individual, is regarded as being little more than a network of assumptions and inter-subjectively shared meanings . . . Everyday life is accorded the status of a miraculous achievement. Interpretive philosophers and sociologists seek to understand the very basis and source of social reality. They often delve into the depths of human consciousness and subjectivity in their quest for the fundamental meanings which underly social life. (pp. 28–31)

The interpretive paradigm is undergirded by a network of ontological and epistemological assumptions that are very different to those of positivism (see Figure 1.1). They adopt an internalist-idealist ontology, a subjectivist epistemology and prefer an ideographic methodology. For example, Guba (1990) in explaining *constructivism*, argues that facts do not exist in some external reality since facts can only become facts *within* some theoretical framework. As a consequence, reality can only exist in the context of a mental framework (construct) for thinking about it, that is, 'reality' can only be seen through a window of theory, whether implicit or explicit. If this is the case, then it also means that reality can only be seen through a value window which means that all facts are value laden and many constructions are possible. Finally, knowledge is seen as the outcome or consequence of human activity, that is, knowledge is a human construction, which means that it can never be certifiable as ultimately true but rather it is problematic and ever changing.

> *Ontologically*, if there are always many interpretations that can be made of any inquiry, and if there is no foundational process by which the ultimate truth or falsity of these several constructions can be determined, there is no alternative but to take a position of *relativism*. Relativism is the key to openness and the continuing search for ever more informed and sophisticated constructions. Realities are multiple, and they exist in people's minds . . . *Epistemologically*, the constructivist chooses a *subjectivist* position . . . If realities only exist in respondents' minds, subjective interaction seems to be the only way to access them. (*ibid*, p. 26)

Therefore, with regard to ontology, interpretivists take reality to be mind-dependent and adopt an internalist-idealist position on this issue. They argue that there are multiple realities and that the mind plays a central role, via its determining categories, in shaping or constructing these. Consequently, there can be no separation of mind and object since the two are inextricably linked together — the knower and the process of knowing cannot be separated from what is known, and facts cannot be separated from values. However, as Smith (1989) reminds us, 'Mind-dependence here does not mean that the mind "creates" what people say and do, but rather that how we interpret their movements and utterances — the meanings we assign to the intentions, motivations, and so on of ourselves and others — becomes social reality as it is for us. In other words, social reality is the interpretation' (p. 74).

Such an approach clearly rejects the positivistic notion of an independently existing reality that can be known through a neutral set of procedures. Since social reality is mind-dependent there can be no data that is free from interpretation, there can be no 'brute data' out there on which to found knowledge or verify our positions. As Smith (1988) argues, 'Methods themselves, including statistical procedures, are not and cannot be interpretation-free. And if this is so, then the knowledge claims supported by methods cannot be interpretation-free' (p. 20). The same author comments:

> Whereas an externalist perspective holds to the independence of the instrument from the attribute or object measured, the internalist position finds this separation impossible to accept. For this latter position, an instrument does not simply reflect or mirror reality *but contributes to constructing or defining social reality*. Social scientists, then, through the use of their measuring instruments, *are actually participants in the process of making social reality* rather than discoverers of the qualities and characteristics of an independently existing reality. (Smith, 1989, p. 84, my emphasis)

Therefore, according to interpretivists a 'God's eye view' of the world is impossible, we cannot hope to see the world outside of our place in it — all that we can ever have are various points of view that reflect the interests, values and purposes of various groups of people. In view of this interpretivists focus on the interests and purposes of people (including the researcher), on their intentional and meaningful behaviour, then by attempting to construe the world from the participant's point of view they try to explain and understand how they construct and continue to reconstruct social reality, given their interests and purposes. As Wolcott (1990a) talking about his own work comments 'I do not go about trying to discover a ready-made world; rather I seek to understand a social world we are continuously in the process of constructing' (p. 147). Brown (1990) also notes, 'The characteristic which sets naturalistic research apart from other approaches to research is the focus on the participants' perspectives of the phenomena under study or the culture within which the study is being conducted. This approach from within the culture in terms of participant categories has been termed in anthropology as the emic approach' (p. 1).

According to Wolcott (1990b) the term ethnography is derived from anthropology, and means literally 'a picture of the "way of life" of some identifiable group of people' (p. 188). In relation to ethnography Fetterman (1989) suggests that an emic perspective — the insider's or native's perspective of reality — is at the heart of this form of research, and that this perspective 'is instrumental to understanding and accurately describing situations and behaviours . . . An emic perspective compels the recognition and acceptance of multiple realities. Documenting multiple perspectives of reality in a given study is crucial to an understanding of why people think and act in the different ways they do' (p. 30). As a consequence, Woods (1986) feels that ethnography:

> is concerned with what people are, how they behave, how they interact together. It aims to uncover their beliefs, values, perspectives, motivations, and how all these things develop or change over time or from situation to situation. It tries to do all this from *within* the group, and from within the perspectives of the group's members. It is *their* meanings and interpretations that count. This means learning *their* language and customs with all their nuances, whether it be the crew of a fishing trawler, a group of fans on a football terrace, a gang a grave-diggers, the inmates of a prison or a religious seminary . . . These have each constructed their own highly distinctive cultural realities, and if we are to understand them, we need to penetrate their boundaries, and look out from the inside, the difficulty of which varies according to our own cultural distance from the group under study. In any event, it will mean a fairly lengthy stay among the group, first to break down the boundaries and be accepted, and second to learn the culture, much of which will be far from systematically articulated by the group . . . It is, thus, no ordinary picture. A snapshot gives merely surface detail. The ethnographer is interested in what lies beneath — the subjects' views, which may contain alternative views, and their view of each other . . . The ethnographer thus aims to represent the reality studied in all its various layers of social meaning in its full richness. (pp. 4–5)

To gain such insights means spending an extended period of time with the group and often the researcher attempts to becomes a full and active member of the group in order to learn about their way of life from the inside, to feel what it is like for the people in the situation. According to Brown (1990) the primary goal of the use of participant-observation as a data collection strategy 'is for the researcher as instrument of data collection to live the "slice of life" with the participants and to generate her own constructions of the events and the interactions which are observed and which are lived. These constructions, along with the constructions of the participants, form the data from which interpretations are made' (p. 1). While this role of participant-observer[12] is a central method in ethnography the researcher can also draw upon a wide range of methods to help understand the views of the participants. These include, various forms of interviewing (unstructured, structured, life history/ autobiographical, key informant), projective techniques, archive analysis along with the analysis of other written documents, the analysis and collection of non-written sources (for example, maps, photographs and film, artefacts, video and audio tapes) and standardized tests plus other measurement techniques to provide quantitative data where required (see Fetterman, 1989; Hammersley and Atkinson, 1983). However, as Wolcott (1990b) is quick to point out:

> The most noteworthy thing about ethnographic research techniques is their lack of noteworthiness . . . There is no way one could ever hope to produce an ethnography simply by employing many, or even all, of the research techniques that ethnographers use. Ethnography . . . is *not* a reporting process guided by a specific set of techniques. It is an inquiry process carried out by human beings . . . it is not the techniques employed that make a study ethnographic, but neither is it necessarily what one looks at; the critical element is interpreting what one has seen. (pp. 191–202)

Interpretive Research and the 'Researcher as Instrument'

The views expressed so far place the human being as interpreter at the centre of the ethnographic research process. Indeed, Hammersley and Atkinson (1983) in recognizing the role of the researcher as an active participant in the research process note "He or she is the research instrument *par excellence*' (p. 18). In relation to participant-observation in ethnography Ball (1990) notes how very often, 'Not only do researchers go into unknown territory, they must go unarmed, with no questionnaires, interview schedules, or observation protocols to stand between them and the cold winds of the raw real. They stand alone with their individual *selves*. They themselves are the primary research tool with which they must find, identify, and collect the data . . . My point is that ethnographic fieldwork relies primarily on the engagement of the self, and that engagement can only be learned enactively' (pp. 157–8).

For Ball, this means that in conducting an ethnographic study the social skills and creative intelligence of the researcher, rather than a set of technical competencies, are of crucial importance as she or he is involved in any fieldwork interaction on at least three levels: (i) in terms of 'normal interaction, fieldworkers must strain to keep their everyday 'good' researcher *persona* in place, (ii) as data gatherers, fieldworkers must sift and select 'data' from what is going on. This includes what should be said and done next, if appropriate, in order to elicit more data, and (iii) as reflexive analyst, the fieldworker must weigh the impact and effects of their presence, their *personae* and the respondent's perception of them, for the status, usefulness, and limitations of the data recorded. He concludes:

> Data are a product of the skills and imagination of the researcher and of the interface between the researcher and the researched. The choices, omissions, problems and successes of the fieldwork will shape the process of the research in particular ways . . . Indeed, what counts as data, what is seen and unnoticed, what is and is not recorded, will depend on the interests, questions, and relationships that are brought to bear in a particular scene. The research process will generate meaning as part of the social life it aims to describe and to analyze. (*ibid*, pp. 169–70)

Since, in interpretive research, the researcher is the instrument Brown (1988) reminds us, 'There are no reliability and validity coefficients for the researcher who is observing and interviewing participants in the natural setting' (p. 95). In view of this it should come as no surprise to find that, for interpretivists, methods (techniques) are not seen as guarantors of truth as they are in positivism. Smith (1989) notes 'An interpretive researcher cannot come to a study with a pre-established set of neutral procedures but can only choose to do some things as opposed to others based on what seems reasonable, given his or her interests and purposes, the context of the situation, and so on. In other words, there are no privileged methods for interpretive inquiry' (p. 157). Rather, we find, as Reason and Rowan (1981) have argued, 'validity in new paradigm research lies in the skills and sensitivities of the researcher, in how he or she uses herself as knower, and as inquirer. Validity is more personal and interpersonal, rather than methodological' (p. 244).

Furthermore, since within an interpretivist framework the anti- or non-foundational assumption is made that there is no independent reality or data that is free from interpretation on which to found knowledge, which means that knowledge cannot be built upon a certain or indubitable base, then truth or validity cannot be a matter of correspondence as it is in positivism. For interpretivists, it becomes a matter of *coherence*. Smith (1984) notes, 'For interpretive inquiry, the basis of truth or trustworthiness is social agreement; what is judged true or trustworthy is what we can agree, conditioned by time and place, is true or trustworthy' (p. 386). Therefore, within a coherence theory of truth a proposition is judged to be true if it coheres (is connected and consistent) with other propositions in a scheme or network that is in operation at a particular time, thus making coherence a matter of internal relations as opposed to the degree of correspondence with some external reality. For Popkewitz (1984) 'What is "real" and valid is so because of mutual agreement by those who participate. Objectivity, then, is not a law that guides individuals but the result of an intersubjective consensus that occurs through social interaction' (p. 42). He emphasizes that while this is so for individuals interacting, it also applies to the scientific community itself, 'The knowledge of science is considered valid and "truthful" only insofar as it reflects the consensus of the scholarly community. The scientific community presupposes conventions and agreement about appropriate knowledge' (p. 42).

Inherent in such a position is the notion that at certain times and in certain situations, agreement will be greater in degree and extent than others. Truth then is what we make it to be based upon shared visions and common understandings that are socially constructed. For example, in considering the meaning of validity in cooperative inquiry Heron (1988) adopts the stance that the 'real world' is, 'already construed by us. We can never get at it outside our constructs to find out whether our statement corresponds to it' (p. 41). He goes on to suggest that validity relates to when, 'propositional knowledge asserted by the research conclusions is coherent with the experiential knowledge of the researchers as co-subjects, and their experiential knowledge is coherent with their practical knowledge in knowing how to act together in their researched world' (*ibid*, pp. 42–3). In considering aspects of this form of validity in more detail he comments:

> Firstly, the research conclusions need to be coherent with each other: they are consistent with each other, interdependent and mutually illuminating. Secondly, the inquirers are in agreement about these conclusions . . . the agreement sought between inquirers is not total unanimity, but the illumination of a common area of inquiry by differing individual perspectives. Validity is enhanced by a diversity of views that overlap. It is not found simply in the common properties of the different views, but rather in the unity-in-variety of these views . . . Agreement of this sort cannot be absolute, at any rate so far as coherence with experience is concerned, and in the early stages of developing a researched world. It admits of degrees. It is a matter of judgment when the degree of agreement is so low that it constitutes a criterion of inadmissible disagreement. (*ibid*, pp. 43–4)

The key point here is the manner in which Heron emphasizes notions of coherence in terms of what validity means to cooperative inquiry and the procedures that he suggests for enhancing the validity of conclusions in this form of research. In relation to this Fetterman (1989) argues that the success or failure of an ethnographic report depends on the degree to which it 'rings true to natives and colleagues in the field' (p. 21). However, such agreement does not guarantee the validity of the findings in any foundational sense. Here, an example from my own research will help illustrate the point. During 1983–86 I conducted a case study of a teacher-initiated innovation within a PE department at a large urban coeducational comprehensive school in England.[13] During the academic year 1983–84 I adopted the role of researcher-participant and also used interviews and documentary analysis. From 1984–86 I had to rely on interviews only. During the first year of the study I interpreted the newly-appointed department head's management style as autocratic, in terms of how he used the various forms of power at his disposal to ensure the adoption of certain innovations in the department. On discussing this issue with him in 1984, it became evident that he strongly believed that he was using a democratic management style. Note, this teacher was not disagreeing with my reporting of events, conversations or interviews which he saw as accurate and reliable. However, in effect he was disagreeing with my interpretation as researcher; there was a definite mismatch in this sense.

However, in 1984–86 this same teacher attended a diploma course in educational management and the understanding he gained from it led him to reassess his previous actions and to conclude that he had been autocratic in his approach. Therefore, in 1984 the subject disagreed with my interpretation but in 1985 he agreed with it retrospectively; so where does this leave my interpretation? Does his agreement enhance the credibility of my interpretation and, conversely, does his initial disagreement reduce the credibility of my interpretation? What if the study had ended in 1984 and I had not been able to gain access to his reappraisal in 1985? Where would this have left my original interpretation?

My interpretation as researcher stands as simply that; an *interpretation* of a set of events. Agreement or disagreement by the subjects of this interpretation need not necessarily reduce or enhance its credibility. To believe otherwise is to adopt a stance that is somewhat simplistic in that it ignores those aspects of power that develop in social relationships, plus it infers that 'lay' assessments (by subjects) are validators of 'professional' (researcher) judgments and interpretations. Thus an insider's view is assumed to be more credible than an outsider's view, even when very often the researcher is able to, and aspires to, gain insights into behaviours and processes that are beyond those available to the people involved in the action. Furthermore, Schutz (1967) reminds us that lay people produce their own distinctive sociological accounts of their various social worlds (first-order constructs), and these will very often differ from those produced by the sociological researcher (second-order constructs) since each is formulated in relation to different interests.[14] As Miles and Huberman (1984) point out, 'Even if people do not themselves apprehend the same analytical constructs as those derived by researchers, this does not make such constructs invalid or contrived' (p. 19).

This is not to deny the importance of the researcher discussing her or his findings to check for their accuracy and to confirm that certain words were used in a conversation or that certain events took place. It is also appropriate for the researcher to discuss his or her interpretations of events with those involved in the study, given that agreements and disagreements are illuminating in themselves and provide a rich source of data that is itself pertinent to the researcher's analysis and ongoing interpretation. Therefore, these interactional episodes are themselves subjected to analysis that allows the researcher's interpretation to be extended and enriched. Consequently, taking findings back to the field should not be seen as a test of the 'truth' but an opportunity for reflexive elaboration (see Sparkes, 1989). As Fetterman (1989) suggests:

> These readers may disagree with the researcher's interpretations and conclusions, but they should recognize the details of the description as accurate. The ethnographer's task is not only to collect information from the emic or insider's perspective, but also to make sense of all the data from an etic or external social science perspective. An ethnographer's explanation of the whole system may differ from that of the people in the field and at professional meetings. However, basic descriptions of events and places should sound familiar to native and colleague alike. (pp. 21–2)

Differences regarding interpretation can take place within a community of scholars even when the same group have been the subject of the study. Ball (1990, p. 167) explores this issue and notes that it would not be uncommon for ethnographies to turn out differently when different researchers conduct the fieldwork. However, he believes that the differences would be a matter of emphasis and orientation rather than in the story being told. For him the 'complexity and the "becomingness" of social life belies the possibility of a single, exhaustive or definitive account. And both as an analytical decision-making process and as a social process, we should expect different researchers to pick their way through fieldwork differently'. Quite simply, decisions about who to talk to, where to be, and when to be in certain places will have an impact upon what data is and is not collected. Also, decisions made in the field regarding sampling, the role adopted and the kind of relationships established, and the events and encounters participated in 'will contribute to the construction of a particular fieldwork trajectory and a limited set of possibilities for interpretation . . . The presence, the effect, and the biases and selections of the researcher cannot be removed from qualitative research. Qualitative research cannot be made "researcher proof"'.

What we are left with in interpretive research is a situation in which multiple interpretations are possible regarding the same group under study each of which can be coherent in themselves. That is, there can be many 'truths' available. The problem then becomes that of choosing between a multitude of interpretations of a given event or process, that is, on what basis does choice take place within a process that is essentially locked into a hermeneutic circle?[15] According to Harris (1983a):

> . . . a major problem associated with interpretive cultural research is the likelihood of multiple interpretations concerning the same

> culture or subculture. The problem of multiple interpretations may arise at the time a researcher studies a culture, or it may arise when the interpretations of two or more researchers who have studied the same culture are compared ... Confronted with multiple interpretations, is there any way to determine which is best or most nearly correct? This is a major problem for those who conduct interpretative cultural research because there is no ultimate, agreed-upon authority to which investigators can turn to adjudicate or arbitrate among alternative interpretations. (p. 90)

What this means is that in relation to a coherence theory of truth it is possible for there to be any number of internally coherent systems of belief, and because there are no criteria for choosing among them, it cannot be known which is the 'right' one (cf. Greyling, 1982). Within such a framework there is always the possibility of one interpretation of reality coexisting with another interpretation of reality because with its anti-foundational assumptions there can be no independent, absolute or external criteria on which to decide between two plausible cases. However, this does not mean that 'anything goes' or that we accept all interpretations since to do so would be to do away with the concept of a 'mistake'. As Soltis (1984) reminds us, to be open to other people's views and interpretations is not to be empty minded; at the end of the day 'it does not release us from exercising judgment' (p. 9). This is so, even though interpretivism adopts a relativistic stance. Relativism is a complex concept and has been discussed in detail elsewhere.[16] Rorty (1985) claims that there are three main views associated with this term:

> The first is the view that every belief is as good as any other. The second is that 'true' is an equivocal term, having as many meanings as there are procedures of justification. The third is the view that there is nothing to be said about either truth or rationality apart from descriptions of the familiar procedures or justifications which a given society — ours — uses in one or another area of inquiry. (pp. 5–6)

Most interpretivists adhere to the third view. This means that they do *not* hold to the view that propositions do not have the property of being true. They simply insist that judgments of truth are always relative to a particular framework, paradigm, or point of view. Therefore, relativism holds that proposition X can be true for an individual in framework Y1 but false for individuals in framework Y2. It all comes back to the point that was made earlier concerning the coherence theory of truth and the issue of internal relations. Consequently, *not everything goes*, since judgments are made by researchers operating within the interpretive paradigm who differentiate between a 'good' piece of research and a 'bad' one by utilizing the criteria appropriate to their own particular framework.

Regarding the issue of criteria for passing judgment, Smith (1984), suggests that this term can have several meanings. In its strong form it can mean a 'standard against which to make judgment' (p. 383), and in this sense it has definite foundational connotations in that the criterion becomes a point of reference that can be applied directly to differentiate the 'good' from the 'bad', the correct from the incorrect; this is how research *must* be done. In its softer form it can refer to a 'characterizing trait' which has at best 'mild prescription for inquirer behaviour and does not necessarily refer to something that is held to be foundational'. In this sense there is little hint of prescription or orthodoxy, since all that is being articulated are the characterizing traits of a particular research approach that simply indicates that this is the way that researchers seem to be doing things in this area or tradition at the present; this is how research *can* or *may* be done.

Recently, Smith (1990b) has outlined how over the last few years interpretive researchers have discussed the process and products of this form of inquiry in the form of lists. Initially, these lists were thought of as the first step on the road to a more definitive criteria but now they are accepted for what they actually are, 'an open-ended, always evolving, enumeration of possibilities that can be constantly modified through practice' (p. 178). In relation to this, Guba and Lincoln (1989) use lists to indicate how the quality of constructivist research might be judged. These criteria include those of trustworthiness, credibility, transferability, dependability and authenticity. Listings are provided for each of these, for example, with regard to authenticity the following are mentioned; fairness, ontological authenticity, catalyatic authenticity and tactical authenticity. All these are presented as ways to help in passing judgment on the goodness of constructivist research. Similarly, Harris (1983a) considers that at least three levels of interpretation appear necessary for the careful pursuit of 'good' interpretive research:

> The research must be grounded in the shared understandings about the culture developed between the researcher and the members of the group being examined; it must include the researcher's insights about details of the culture that are not well articulated by members of the group; and it must include theoretical generalizations that go beyond the particular details of the culture to link the study to relevant portions of other research. (p. 92)

Athens (1984) in considering how to evaluate qualitative studies also suggests three criteria. First there is 'theoretical import', 'the contribution they make toward the development of new concepts or theories or the refinement and further development of existing ones' (pp. 261–5). A second criterion that can be used is whether or not the scientific concepts developed in the study are empirically grounded. The final criterion is 'scientific credibility'. Since no study is intrinsically credible or incredible the researcher must make it so, 'The way in which a researcher makes a study credible is by supplying an adequate account of his or her research along with a description of its results. An account is merely a story told by the researcher about how he or she performed the research in question'.

But remember, these criteria are not absolute and do not prevent researchers from different frameworks and theoretical orientations conducting studies of the same group or culture and coming up with different interpretations after having carried out good pieces of interpretive research. In such situations Harris (1983a, p. 92) suggests that adjudication takes place in ways that are similar to legal situations. That is, the means by which one interpretation in a courtroom is judged to be better than another, 'is by the presentation of sufficient evidence to convince the judge or jury of its relative soundness. In a similar fashion, when confronted with two different interpretations of a culture, all that a third person may be able to do is to examine the two sets of evidence presented and decide which seems to be the stronger'. Of course, the notion of 'stronger' returns us to the hermeneutic circle in which *all* researchers, regardless of their paradigmatic stances, utilize a range of rhetorical devices to persuade and convince the reader of the worthiness of their particular interpretation of the world, that is, truth is rhetorically constructed (see Sparkes, 1991 and chapter 11 in this volume). Ultimately, as Taylor (1971) reminds us, 'a good explanation is one which makes sense of the behaviour; but then to appreciate a good explanation, one has to agree on what makes good sense; what makes good sense is a function of one's readings; and these in turn are based on the kind of sense one understands' (p. 14). We end up coming back to the point that truth is what we agree to be true at any particular time.

Therefore, for interpretivists there are no absolute minimums to work out differences in interpretations since the hermeneutic process has no definite beginning or end and contains no specific procedures or established criteria to determine who has got it absolutely 'right' or 'true'. Fortunately, as Harris (1983a) rightly argues, while choices between conflicting interpretations sometimes have to be made, it is not usually a matter of choosing one interpretation and eliminating another, 'Two or more interpretations often lend a richer or broader view of a culture than any interpretation could provide alone' (p. 92). In a world of multiple realities, multiple truths can exist, and this means that for interpretive researchers the meanings associated with the term validity are very different from those of positivistic researchers. Indeed, notions of validity as used by positivists may be meaningless to interpretive researchers, implying, as they do, some impersonal, automatic truth.

The Critical Paradigm

There has been a limited amount of critical research in PE but there are signs that this kind of research is increasing.[17] As with the positivistic and interpretive paradigms there are many diverse strands within the critical framework. For Guba (1990) the label *critical theory* is in many ways inadequate to encompass all the alternatives that can be swept into this paradigm. He suggests that a more appropriate label might be 'ideologically orientated inquiry' which would include neo-Marxism, materialism, feminism, Freireism, participatory inquiry, and other similar traditions as well as critical theory itself. Likewise, Gibson (1986) comments 'It is vital to grasp at the outset that there is no such thing as a unified critical theory. Rather, there are critical *theories*. Critical theory is a label which conceals a host of disagreements among different writers . . . In spite of this heterogeneity, there are commonly-shared assumptions' (p. 3). He suggests that the central intention of critical theory is *emancipation*, that is, enabling people to gain the knowledge and power to be in control of their own lives.

Furthermore, this approach wholeheartedly rejects positivism along with any notions of value freedom in terms of the research process. For example, Carr and Kemmis (1986, p. 103) are quite scathing regarding the ontological assumptions of positivism (realism) since, for them, it takes the 'objective' character of reality for granted and then interprets that reality as something governed by inescapable laws. In doing so they feel it tends to confirm a spurious respectability on prevailing 'commonsense' and offers no way of effecting practical change, other than through technical control. They conclude, 'Positivist theories, by failing to recognize the importance of the interpretations and meanings that individuals employ to make their reality intelligible, fail to identify the phenomena to be explained. In consequence, the kind of theories that they produce are often trivial and useless, even though they may appear to be sophisticated and elaborate'.

In terms of its historical roots, various writers operating within the critical paradigm have acknowledged the contribution that the work of the Frankfurt School has made to the emergence of a critical social science.[18] According to Popkewitz (1984) this group of scholars refashioned and rethought Marxism by 'focussing upon the formation of consciousness, culture and everyday life, and how these formations maintain the legitimacy of existing political and social interests. The language and intent of such theory is political — to consider moments of domination, ideology, hegemony, and emancipation in social life and social change' (pp. 16–17; see also Popkewitz, 1990). In relation to this Harvey (1990) argues:

> Critical social research is underpinned by a critical-dialectical perspective which attempts to dig beneath the surface of historically specific, oppressive, social structures . . . At the heart of critical social research is the idea that knowledge is structured by existing sets of social relations. The aim of critical methodology is to provide knowledge which engages the prevailing social structures. These social structures are seen by critical researchers,

in one way or another, as oppressive structures . . . A totalistic approach denies the relevance of looking at one element of a complex social process in isolation and argues that elements have to be looked at in terms of their interrelations and how they relate to the social structure as a whole. So critical social research is concerned with the broad social and historical context in which phenomena are interrelated. It is concerned with revealing underlying social relations and showing how structural and ideological forms bear on them. Critical social research, then, is interested in substantive issues, and wants to show what is really going on at a societal level. Not only does it want to show what is happening, it is also concerned with doing something about it. Critical social research includes an overt political struggle against oppressive social structures. (pp. 1–20)

In terms of ontological and epistemological assumptions there appears to be two major strands running within the critical paradigm. One is closely associated with positivism while the other relates to interpretivism. Burrell and Morgan (1979) use the term *radical structuralist* to identify one strand. They suggest this strand adopts an external-realist ontology, an objectivist epistemology, and holds a somewhat deterministic view of people that leads them to concentrate upon structural relationships within a realist social world via the analysis of deep-seated internal contradictions and the analysis of power relationships. A second strand identified is associated with *radical humanism* which has much in common with the interpretive paradigm in that it adopts an internal-idealist ontology, a subjectivist epistemology, and a more voluntaristic view of people. Consequently, in what Anderson (1989a) has called a critical-interpretive approach, reality is taken to be socially constructed, knowledge is seen as being context-specific and value laden (also see Bain, 1989).

However, such similarities does not mean that there are no tensions between those working in the interpretive and critical paradigms. The concern of critical researchers to locate the thoughts and actions of individuals and groups in the context of wider sociohistorical, political and economic movements has meant that while they have been sympathetic towards the interpretive approach in terms of its subjectivist epistemology (in which reality is constructed and sustained through the meanings and actions of individuals), they take research undertaken within this paradigm as having major weaknesses. As Carr and Kemmis (1986) argue:

But achieving a correct understanding of individuals' meanings is only a necessary preliminary to social enquiries, and it is misguided to regard this as the whole substance of the theoretical enterprise. For the emphasis of the interpretive model on the subjective meanings of action tends to imply that social reality is nothing over and above the way people perceive themselves and their situation. But social reality is not simply structured by concepts and ideas. It is also structured and shaped by such things as historical forces and economic and material conditions. Moreover, these things also structure and affect the perceptions and ideas of individuals so that 'reality' may be misperceived as a consequence of the operation of various ideological processes. Uncovering these processes and explaining how they can condition and constrain interpretations of reality are vital requirements that are largely neglected by the 'interpretive' approach. (p. 104)

One of the major concerns for critical researchers has been the alleged macro-blindness of interpretive research that, with its concern to understand how people construct and reconstruct their realities in the gymnasium and on the sports field, has tended to ignore the power relationships within which people operate when these realities are constructed, and so tells us little about how individual and group behaviour is influenced by the way in which society is organized. Evans (1987) and Hargreaves (1980) have argued that such studies have resulted in distorted and incomplete accounts of life in schools because they have adopted a position of 'splendid isolation' whereby classrooms are taken to exist in a social and cultural vacuum that is not touched by the economic demands, political pressures and social influences of the wider society. As such the contexts in which teachers work have been ignored. In summarizing these concerns, Sharp (1982) has argued that not enough attention has been given to the underlying nature of the, 'structural patterns of social relationships (that) pre-exist the individual and generate specific forms of social consciousness' (p. 48).

Therefore, while critical researchers can agree with interpretivists that organizations and institutions are the product of shared meanings that are actively created by people via intersubjective negotiation, they emphasize that the results of any negotiations over meanings by individuals or groups takes place, and are determined within, a social and organizational context that is permeated by *unequal* power relations that are related to such issues as social class, gender, sexual orientation, race/ethnicity, disability, etc. That is, social reality is not constructed in a free and voluntary process since negotiations are shaped by particular organizational relations, structures and conditions. In view of this, while critical researchers seek to understand the world from the point of view of the participants and ask questions regarding how meanings are constructed and maintained, they also pose questions in terms of 'what counts?'. For example, Anderson (1989a), in drawing on the work of Bates (1980), suggests the following as a set of critical research questions regarding the nature of knowledge in organizations.

(i)   What counts as knowledge?
(ii) How is what counts as knowledge organized?
(iii) How is what counts as knowledge transmitted?

(iv) How is access to what counts as knowledge determined?
(v) What are the processes of control?
(vi) What ideological appeals justify the system? (p. 6)

As indicated, for the critical researcher, the interest is in how specific forms of knowledge, ways of knowing, and certain values are privileged and legitimized, that is, given meaning and authority relative to others. The central emphasis is upon human consciousness and the ways in which it is shaped and limited by existing social arrangements in such a way as to serve the interests of some groups in our society at the expense of others. To explore these issues a *relational* analysis is often utilized. According to Dewar (1990) this form of analysis attempts to understand *how* our practices in PE have been constructed, *why* they have been constructed in certain ways, and *who* and *what categories* of individuals benefit from these decisions (p. 74). Therefore, a relational analysis 'questions how practices are structured in physical education in ways that may help to legitimate, reproduce or challenge the social relations of power and privilege that exist in Western capitalist patriarchal societies' (p. 74).

Dewar (1991, p. 20) in discussing a relational analysis of gender in sport argues that such work begins with the assumption that sporting practices are historically produced, socially constructed and culturally defined to serve the needs and interests of powerful groups in society. In this sense, sport is seen as a cultural representation of social relations and is not assumed to be neutral, objective and ahistorical. She adds, 'Rather, it is seen as a set of selected and selective social practices that embody dominant meanings, values and practices which are implicated in the creation and maintenance of hegemonic social relationships' (see also Apple, 1979 and 1982). In summarizing the beliefs inherent in such a critical perspective Griffin (1990) notes:

(i) Society is made up of groups with power and privilege and groups without power and privilege.
(ii) Social institutions in a society perpetuate the status quo of power imbalance among groups.
(iii) The powerful and the privileged have a vested interest in maintaining their power and privilege (maintaining the status quo).
(iv) The powerless and disadvantaged have a vested interest in social change.
(v) These competing interests result in conflict and tension which is often below the surface of apparent harmony and consensus.
(vi) The role of the critical perspective is to bring the contradictions between apparent harmony/consensus and conflict/tension to light, to 'problematize' the status quo.
(vii) A critical perspective is concerned with 'why/why not' questions and is critical of 'how' questions that do not

consider 'why' (who's interests are served?). The intention is to change the world, not describe it.

(viii) A critical perspective believes in the the importance of changing individual and group consciousness in creating social change. (p. 2)

These interests shape the ways in which critical researchers conduct their studies. For example, they might draw upon the data collection techniques associated with ethnography as discussed in relation to the interpretive paradigm. However, as Harvey (1990) points out a critical approach to ethnography is different in that it 'attempts to link the detailed analysis of ethnography to wider social structures and systems of power relationships in order to get beneath the surface of oppressive structural relationships' (pp. 11–12). He suggests three ways in which this can be done. The first is to consider the subject group in a wider social context. This is taken to be the weakest form of critical ethnography. Indeed, it may not be critical at all if it just takes the form of 'analyzing functional relationships between subject group and the wider social milieu'. The second is to focus on the 'wider structural relations and examine the ways in which the social processes that are evident in the subject group are mediated by structural relations'.

The final and strongest form is to incorporate ethnography directly into a dialectical analysis in which the understandings from the former are analyzed in relation to the social structures that shape the lives of people. Therefore, while the first two approaches tend to explore the group and then situate it, the latter approach begins with structural relationships and then undertakes an ethnographic study in order to facilitate a structural analysis. As Harvey (1990) emphasizes, the important thing about critical ethnography is that the probing of the subjects' meanings is not the end of the story, 'The group operates in a sociohistorically specific milieu and is not independent of structural factors. Their meanings may appear to be group centred but are mediated by structural concerns' (p. 12). Therefore, as Anderson (1989b) comments:

... like other ethnographers — particularly those who define themselves as interpretivists — critical ethnographers aim to generate insights, to explain events, and to seek understanding. They also share with interpretivist ethnographers the view that the cultural informant's perceptions of social reality are themselves theoretical constructs ... Where critical ethnographers differ is in their claim that informant reconstructions are often permeated with meanings that sustain powerlessness and that people's conscious models exist to perpetuate, as much as to explain, social phenomenon. Critical ethnographers, therefore, attempt to ensure that participants in research 'are not naively enthroned, but systematically and critically unveiled' (Anderson, 1989b, p. 253)

As part of this unveiling, researchers investigate the process by which certain meaning structures become accepted as natural, taken-for-granted, and legitimate and then consider whose interests they represent. Next they actively engage with members of the group under study in order to assist them develop alternative meaning structures in order to facilitate social transformation and emancipation. As Bain (1989, 1990a and 1990b) has emphasized, for critical researchers the purpose is not simply to describe the world but to *change* it by empowering those people involved in the research. Part of this empowerment process involves providing them with the insights necessary to demystify and critique their own social circumstances and to choose actions to improve their lives.

Consequently, while critical researchers argue that *any form* of social research is always a political act which constitutes an assertion of interests which cannot, therefore, be value free (see Brigley, 1990), they acknowledge that their own form of research, which is undergirded by emancipatory interests, is openly ideological. This means that explicit interests and values are substituted for implicit ones and the researcher disclaims any notions of 'value neutrality' since the aim is to challenge the status quo and contribute to a more egalitarian social order. For example, with regard to feminist research, Ramazangolu (1989) comments:

> The notion of a feminist standpoint from which to produce knowledge is a response to the need to connect feminist understanding of social life with feminist political practices. Feminism constitutes attempts to transform the bases of current social, economic and political relationships between men and women . . . Sociological knowledge from a feminist standpoint . . . would also be knowledge *for* women. It would mean taking gender seriously in what we look for, together with the political implications of revealing gendered relationships. The political commitment to social transformation distinguishes research *on* women, which can be taken from any methodological position, from research *for* women, which is politically and methodologically feminist. (p. 428)

Likewise, Lather (1986) notes, 'the overt ideological goal of feminist research is to correct both the invisibility and the distortion of female experience in ways relevant to ending women's unequal social position' (p. 68).[19] With regard to two of the other traditions that she feels have provided a major thrust to critical research in recent years she suggests, 'The overt ideological goal of neo-Marxist critical ethnography is to expose the contradictions and delusions of liberal democratic education in order to create less exploitative social and economic relations' (p. 70). While for Freirian 'empowering' research, 'The openly ideological goal is to blur the distinction between research, learning, and action by providing conditions under which participant's self-determination is enhanced in the struggle toward social justice' (p. 73).

Such emancipatory interests call for a different form of engagement than that associated with positivistic and interpretive research forms. As Guba (1990) notes:

> If the aim of inquiry is to transform the (real) world by raising the consciousness of participants so that they are energized and facilitated toward transformation, then something other than a manipulative, interventionist methodology is required. Critical theorists (ideologists) take a dialogic approach that seeks to eliminate false consciousness and rally participants around a common (true?) point of view. In this process, features of the world are apprehended and judgments are made about which of them can be altered. The result of effective, concerted action is transformation. (p. 24)

Consequently, participatory forms of engagement are required. That is, research is undertaken with the *full participation of the people who are involved in the situation under study so that they are empowered to transform this very situation themselves.* As Bain (1989) outlines, there is a reciprocity between researcher and researched that serves not only to corroborate the interpretation of data but also to provide participants with insights that might serve as the basis for action and change. This latter issue is important since in critical research people are defined as participants in the research process rather than subjects to be studied. As such, they help to frame questions, to interpret data, and to examine and explore how the insights gained from their engagement in this process might assist in the promotion of change. Indeed, for Griffin (1990) this sharing of decision-making and sense-making between the researcher and the participant is essential if both are to enrich their own understanding of their lives in relation to dominant ideologies and then engage in planning and collective action to change their situation as part of the research plan.

Not surprisingly, notions of validity within critical research differ from those of the positivistic and interpretive paradigms. As Brigley (1990) suggests in relation to collaborative research in education, this form of research implies 'radical changes in the relationship between researcher and research subject, and in accepted notions of truth and validity in social research' (p. 29). He goes on to argue that while collaborative enquiry begins with the understandings and realities of the subject it also has a transformative function that enables participants to recognize factors which frustrate their aims and aspirations and to develop strategies to eliminate them:

> An endogenous research model . . . offers the optimum collaboration by permitting participants to define the enquiry, choose the methodology and employ their own theory of knowledge to validate research findings. In the generation of constructs, hypotheses and typologies in endogenous research, it is

the participant who determines their relevance to social practice
... Within such research paradigms, relationships of empathy
and negotiation between researcher and research subject replace
positivist detachment and objectification.... They have to be
nurtured and sustained by consensus-seeking techniques such as
group therapy, if the knowledge yielded by the research is to be
experiential and practical, as well as propositional in character
.... In this way, researchers and participants may establish a
form of research collaboration which takes full account of participants' views of their research needs. For the final test of a
research's validity is its being understood by practitioners as
relevant to, and therefore potentially transformative of, their
situation. (*ibid*, p. 30)

Likewise, Anderson (1989b) argues that critical ethnography with its aim
of social critique, its concern to locate respondent meaning in larger
impersonal systems of political economy, and its 'front-endedness', 'raises
validity issues beyond those of mainstream naturalistic research' (p. 253).
In view of this Lather (1986) has begun the difficult task of recon-
ceptualizing validity within the context of openly ideological research and
suggests the following guidelines to guard against the researchers' biases
distorting the logic of evidence in this form of research. First, with regard
to construct validity there is a need for systematized reflexivity in order
to indicate how *a priori* theory has been changed by the logic of the
data. Second, face validity needs to be seen as much more integral to
the process of establishing data credibility whereby member checks are
involved that recycle the data analysis and tentative results back to at least
a sub-sample of the respondents and the findings are refined in the light
of the subjects's reactions. Finally, there is *catalytic validity* which, 'refers
to the degree to which the research process reorientates, focusses, and
energizes participants in what Freire (1973) terms "conscientization",
knowing reality in order to better transform it' (p. 67). Therefore,
validity in critical research relates not only to the trustworthiness and
credibility of the interpretation but also how effective the research process
has been in actually empowering the participants and enabling them to
create change.

Notions of catalytic validity would seem to be specific to the critical
paradigm given its aims of empowerment and emancipation. Lather
(1986) acknowledges that this conceptualization of validity is by far the
most unorthodox since it 'flies directly in the face of the essential positivist tenet of researcher neutrality' (p. 67). Indeed, this form of validity
has no reference point within positivistic research and consequently it
makes little sense to those operating with positivist assumptions. Similarly, since the main purpose of research for many interpretivists is to
understand the world from the participant's point of view without necessarily changing it, then notions of catalytic validity are also problematic
within this paradigm. Therefore, as Anderson (1989b) argues, 'The critical

ethnographer's concern with unmasking dominant social constructions and the interests they represent, studying society with the goal of transforming it, and freeing individuals from sources of domination and repression continues to make any discussion of validity, as defined by both positivist and interpretive researchers, difficult' (p. 254). This communication is difficult because the meanings attached to the term validity are context bound and specific to the conceptual framework in which they are used. Quite simply, a critical researcher gives the term validity a different meaning than a positivistic or an interpretive researcher.

Comment

It would appear that the paradigms discussed offer differing visions of the research process. As Eisner (1988) argues, different paradigms provide their own particular portrait of the world and 'the terms they employ slice the pie in different ways and harbor their own assumptions' (p. 15). Therefore, just as the word 'space' when used in Newtonian and Ensteinian physics has quite different meanings in each, so the term 'valid' has different meanings when used by advocates of the positivist, interpretive and critical paradigms since in all three the term is embedded in a contrasting set of assumptions, theories and purposes. This is in accordance with the principle of semantic holism that suggests the meaning of any term is determined by its location in a total network of associated meanings and relationships in such a way that changes in one part of the system can bring about changes in the meaning of interrelated terms within the network. Consequently, the term valid derives its meaning from its location within a wider conceptual web of meanings and associations that is the paradigm, and in effect becomes a different term in each paradigm. As Cherryholmes (1988) emphasizes with regard to but one form of validity:

> Construct-validity and research discourses are shaped, as are other discourses, by beliefs and commitments, explicit ideologies, tacit worldviews, linguistic and cultural systems, politics and economics, and power arrangements.... *Different discourses produce different 'truths'*. (p. 107, my emphasis)

If this is the case then, quite simply, people will conceptualize validity in different ways depending on their paradigmatic orientation. They will see the social world differently and go about studying it in different ways depending on their purposes and interests. This is not to infer that one vision is better than another. Only, that they are different and should be understood in their own terms when judgments are to be made about their particular research forms. Therefore, none of the paradigms that have been discussed is the paradigm of choice, that is, the *right* one.

Rather, as Guba (1990) comments, 'Each is an alternative that deserves, on its merits (and I have no doubt that all are meritorious), to be considered' (p. 27). He goes on to argue that the dialogue is not to determine which paradigm is, finally, to win out. Instead it is about taking us to another dimension in which all these paradigms will be replaced by other paradigms whose outlines we are, as yet, dimly aware of. Importantly, this new paradigm or paradigms will not provide a closer approximation to the 'truth' but will simply be more informed and sophisticated than the visions we presently entertain. In saying this we need to be cautious and careful with regard to how alternative paradigms research is cultivated and nurtured in the future within the domain of PE. As Schempp (1990) reminds us:

> Research paradigms, like most educational movements, are often susceptible to becoming fads. What is popular today is often taken to be the new panacea born of some magnificent intellectual nova. While it is often enjoyable to bask in the warmth and light of such nova, it is usually short lived and soon passed over in favor of the next latest and greatest idea . . . In ushering a new paradigm, we must also be cautious. Preservation and celebration of present research traditions are important conditions for continuing the expansion of our body of knowledge. Too often, new research agendas are suggested at the expense of current traditions. The cost for such proclamations is ignoring hard fought battles that have given us insight into the teaching of sport and physical education. (p. 82)

Therefore, the contribution that a variety of paradigms can make to our understanding needs to be recognized. However, in terms of the current paradigms debate, it needs to be acknowledged that it is inappropriate for positivistic criteria to be utilized when passing judgment on a piece of interpretive research or critical research and vice versa. To do so just doesn't make sense given the starting position of each and only leads to confusion and a closing down of any possible dialogue. For example, if positivist criteria (based on foundational assumptions) are used to judge the worth of interpretive work (based on anti-foundational assumptions), then the outcome is a forgone conclusion since, given the assumptions of the former, the latter can only be defined as inadequate no matter how good the interpretive study is in its own terms. Of course, the reverse also holds true. It needs to be recognized that they are separate, distinct and alternative paradigms and so studies in each need to be judged by criteria that are consistent with their own internal meaning structures in relation to the basic epistemological and ontological assumptions, interests and purposes of each world view.[20]

In relation to this Chalmers (1982 and 1990) emphasizes the inappropriateness of transferring the methods and standards of the natural or physical sciences to other areas of study like sociology and history. He suggests that there is no timeless and universal conception of science and scientific method that can serve the purpose of appraising *all* claims to knowledge. For him the going is much tougher than that because we cannot legitimately defend or reject items of knowledge simply because they do not conform to some ready-made criterion of scientificity.

> If some area of knowledge, such as Freudian psychology or Marx's historical materialism, to take two favourite targets of philosophers of science, were to be criticized on the grounds that they did not conform to my characterization of physical science, then it would be implied that all genuine knowledge must conform to the methods and standards of physical science. *This is not an assumption I am prepared to make, and is one that I think would be very difficult to defend.* (Chalmers, 1990, p. 9, my emphasis)

Essentially, there are many ways of knowing, understanding and explaining the world. Therefore, as Lincoln (1989b) argues, 'Until we, as a research community, are more familiar with the traditions our colleagues have adopted, we cannot fully comprehend the meanings they would make of their inquiries, nor can we judge their work in a way that is consonant with their starting premises and intents' (p. 238). This sentiment is echoed by Siedentop (1983) who feels that an examination of initial assumptions is so important that there should be a brief section in research studies that make explicit 'the view of man (sic) from which these methodologies arise' (p. 11). He suggests that such a section would not only alert the reader to the basic point of view of the researcher but, more importantly, it would also require the researcher to consider seriously the implications of the questions asked and the assumptions underlying the methodologies used to answer those questions.

> Therefore, let me suggest that part of our efforts in the next few years be directed toward a lively debate concerning the basic assumptions and research strategies compatible with each set of assumptions. It seems to me that such a debate would be the best way we could avoid becoming efficient technocrats who cannot see beyond their data nor integrate those data so that they might eventually have an impact on some of the larger questions facing our profession. Without that kind of debate, we might risk becoming a group that knows more and more about less and less. (*ibid*, p. 14)

This is not to imply that positivistic researchers should engage in interpretive or critical research or vice versa, unless of course they choose to do so. The point to be emphasized is that unless each becomes conversant with the basic assumptions of the other then it is likely that deafness by dissonance will occur as adherents offer blind allegiance to their particular paradigm and refuse to acknowledge the contribution that other ways of knowing can offer to our understanding of the world of PE. In such situations the possibilities for dialogue and debate are reduced and the critical capacities of the research community are substantially diminished as we become like ships that pass in the night. Clearly this kind of scenario is not in our best interests and Hellison (1988) while recognizing that differences exist between various paradigms, suggests that 'two ships passing in the day and radioing to each other their most defensible cases with their assumptions made as clear as possible might be preferable to seeing which ship can sink the other' (p. 87). In relation to this Lincoln (1989a) reminds us:

> If higher education scholars are not aware of the paradigm revolution in the academic disciplines, they risk engaging in research which does not compete with that of other disciplines in its breadth, its vision, or its innovativeness . . . the paradigm revolution in all the disciplines studied carries with it new languages, new terminology, and new forms of discourse. To fail to be familiar with these new languages and new forms of discourse is to be out of the conversation with many of today's cutting edge researchers. Higher education scholars and decision makers cannot afford to be unable to converse substantively with scholars from other disciplines, or indeed, with vanguard scholars from their own disciplines. They must have a working vocabulary and set of concepts in order to share, to utilize, and shape their own inquiries. (p. 9)

Elsewhere, I have argued (Sparkes, 1991) that we need to develop a polyvocal research community that encourages many voices and visions to be articulated as this would enhance theoretical vitality and understanding in PE. Here, different paradigms (old, newly emerging, and yet to be conceived), and the traditions contained within them, are given the chance to provide whatever they can offer. If one voice, or paradigm, dominates then there is a real danger that we end up just speaking to ourselves. This can lead to a form of tunnel vision whereby some problems are explored exhaustively while others are not even perceived. Hearing only one voice leads to other problems as well. For example, it can lead to individuals with excellent research skills but with a trained incapacity to think in theoretically innovative ways. On this issue Coser (1984) comments, 'Much of our present way of training as well as our system of rewards for scientific contributions encourages our students to eschew the risks of theoretical work and to search instead for the security that comes with proceeding along a well-travelled course, chartered though it may be by ever more refined instruments of navigation' (p. 298). He goes on to warn us that in such conditions there is a danger that the methodological tail ends up wagging the substantive dog!

Of course, making the effort to listen to the voices of others and to understand assumptions that are not familiar to our own is difficult. It is not easy to think a thought with the mind of another, especially when the person has an approach that seems antithetical to one's own. Indeed, the truly open-minded scholarship required to engage in this kind of thinking may be the exception rather than the rule at present. However, as we approach the twenty-first century we need to cultivate such open-minded scholarship and encourage a pluralistic stance that recognizes that there is no single, legitimate way to make sense of the world. As Eisner (1990b) argues:

> Different ways of seeing give us different worlds. Helping people participate in a plurality of worlds made, I believe, is what education ought to try to achieve. The ability to participate in a variety of worlds need not lead to a Tower of Babel: And the specter of everyone marching to the same drummer or forced to speak an official social-science Esperanto thrills me not. *We need multiple voices and we need people who can understand them.* (p. 12, my emphasis)

Likewise, Bain (1990a, p. 9) comments, 'If we want to create a new world we must have new ways of seeing the world. We must have new visions and new voices'. As a consequence, the ability to hear and understand different voices in a spirit of intellectual curiosity and respect is essential if theoretical vitality is to be nurtured within the PE community. In developing these abilities and becoming more aware of research paradigms that offer alternatives to our own, even if we disagree with them, we become far less parochial. Furthermore, recognizing and learning to celebrate ambiguity and diversity introduces a certain humility as we are continually made aware of the precarious quality of our particular ways of knowing and our own research agendas. This instability will be ongoing as the landscape of PE continues to shift as consciousness is raised and what was once considered settled and sacrosanct is reexamined and challenged. In the coming years the conversation within the research community will get deeper, more complex and more problematic as new forms of thinking about knowing and knowledge emerge. Exciting times are ahead and we should approach the future with a sense of optimism.

Acknowledgments

I would like to thank John Evans (University of Southampton), Gareth Nutt (Cheltenham and Gloucester College of Higher Education) and Philip Hodkinson (Crewe and Alsager College of Higher Education) for their helpful comments on an earlier draft of this chapter.

Notes

1 For insights into some of the many discussions taking place within the natural sciences see Bohm and Peat (1987), Chalmers (1982 and 1990), Laura (1988) and Levidow (1986).

2   Two influential books with 'revolution' in their titles are those of Hesse (1980) and Hacking (1981).

3   Throughout this chapter I use PE as an umbrella term that incorporates a wide range of physical activities that include sports. My own perspective is clearly shaped by my interest in sociology and educational issues and my reading of the literature needs to be seen in relation to these interests. In view of this I have attempted to indicate links with other areas by providing references that the reader might like to explore.

4   Indicators of the debate are to be found in the following journals: *Journal of Teaching in Physical Education* (see Schempp, 1987 and 1988; Siedentop, 1987; Sparkes, 1989 and 1991); *Research Quarterly for Exercise and Sport* (see Bain, 1989; Locke, 1989; Schutz, 1989; Siedentop, 1989); *Quest* (see Bain, 1990a; Beamish, 1981; Glassford, 1987; Harris, 1981 and 1983a; McKay *et al*, 1990); *Physical Education Review* (see Evans, 1987; Sparkes, 1986 and 1992); *International Review for the Sociology of Sport* (see Ingham, 1991; Luschen, 1990; Zibgniew, 1990); *Sociology of Sport Journal* (see Chalip, 1990; McKay, 1986; Messner, 1990); *The Sport Psychologist* (see Martens, 1987).

5   Insights into the work of Kuhn are provided by Barnes (1986) and Chalmers (1982). It needs to be recognized that Kuhn himself in an expanded edition of *The Structure of Scientific Revolutions* in 1970 did not see the concept of paradigms as strictly applicable to the social sciences since he saw this domain as being made up of numerous competing views in which none were dominant. This is in contrast to his conceptualization of a mature paradigmatic discipline in the natural sciences which is characterized by a single dominant paradigm whose principles define what 'normal' science is in that domain during any particular historical period.

6   Examples of the negative impact that the targeting of individuals as villains of the piece can have on the research agenda are outlined by Blalock (1984, chapter 6).

7   Just as questions have been raised in relation to the appropriateness of the term paradigm for framing the ways in which researchers carry out their work, so questions have been asked about the appropriateness of using the notion of 'traditions'. For insights into this debate on traditions see Atkinson *et al* (1988), Buchmann and Floden (1989), Jacob (1987, 1988 and 1989), Lincoln (1989b).

8   For disputes over the nature of testing and theory development within the tradition of ethnography see Hammersley (1985) and Woods (1985). For more recent differences of opinion within this tradition see the exchange between Hammersley (1990) and Stanley (1990).

9   For a more detailed history of positivism see Giddens (1974 and 1979).

10 At this stage I was going to discuss the post-positivist paradigm that has emerged as a reaction to the numerous critiques of positivism in recent years. I decided against this because in many ways, as Guba (1990) suggests, post-positivism may be seen as a modified version of positivism. For example, there is a shift from 'naive' realism to 'critical' realism with regard to ontology. The latter holds that the real world is indeed driven by real and natural causes but that humans, because of their imperfect sensory, perceptual and cognitive capabilities are unable to truly grasp it as it is. Although it is accepted that reality can never be known for what it really is there is little doubt that the ultimate truth (reality) is 'out there' beyond the individual. Therefore, realism remains the central concept and prediction and control the major concern.

In terms of epistemology a modified objectivism is adopted. It is accepted that it is impossible for researchers to view the world from nowhere in particular. Since objectivity cannot be achieved in an absolute sense it is now a regulatory ideal whereby researchers attempt to remain as neutral as possible and hold up their own biases for critical scrutiny by the research community. Furthermore, whereas early positivists liked to operate in the tightly controlled environment of the laboratory which dislocated people from the context in which they normally acted, many post-positivists are in favour of conducting their enquiries in the natural setting in which people work and live. That is, much greater attention is now given to context. In relation to this, while techniques that provide high levels of precision are favoured, post-positivists are prepared to utilize interpretive techniques at the data gathering stage of their work. However, the use of such techniques is often seen as a preliminary to conducting more 'rigorous' forms of enquiry (in their terms) at a later date. Most importantly, these techniques are used within a framework that contains the assumptions associated with positivism/post-positivism. Consequently, when they are used they are used in a modified form so that the methodological safeguards derived from the natural sciences can be applied. While the song does not remain exactly the same it appears to be very familiar. For a powerful counter view to that of Guba (1990) see Phillips (1990).

11   For example, if we take specific editions of journals devoted to a particular issue as an indicator of their readiness and willingness to accept research of a different genre then the following moments are significant since they are when issues devoted to interpretive research appeared. In 1986 the *Journal of Teaching in Physical Education* Vol 6, No 1, published a special monograph dedicated to naturalistic research. Following this in 1987 an editorial comment by Templin and Griffey (1987) specified that both quantitative and qualitative research perspectives were appropriate for this journal. In 1987 the *American Educational Research Journal* devoted a special section with a view from the Publications Committee to broaden the methodological and disciplinary ranges of the published articles in this journal. The invited paper by Smith (1987) is of particular interest since its task was to outline the criteria appropriate for judging the work of several traditions within the interpretive paradigm. In 1989 the *Research Quarterly for Exercise and Sport* (Vol 60, No 1) focussed upon qualitative research in detail. These public declarations can be read as a recognition of *differences* between research paradigms.

Once again, we need to be aware that cultural differences exist and Crum (1986) indicates that there has been a very strong German tradition in sport pedagogy based on what he classifies as hermeneutic research at the expense of positivistic research forms. In Great Britain the approach has been more eclectic and the dominance of positivism has not been so overpowering as it has in North America. For example, the first edition of the *Physical Education Review* in 1978 contained a paper by Ward and Marsh that drew on phenomenological theory. However, it was not until 1986 that an edited book by Evans made a collection of qualitative studies available to a more general readership.

12   For a more detailed consideration of the role of participant observer, associated roles, and the nature of relations in the field see Burgess (1984 and 1985) and Hammersley and Atkinson (1983).

13   For a more detailed discussion of this issue see Sparkes (1989). Further details of this study of teacher-initiated innovation that was conducted from an interpretive stance are available in Sparkes (1986b, 1987, 1988a, 1988b, 1990a, 1990b and 1990c).

14   First-order constructs may be taken to be the 'facts' of an ethnographic study while the second-order constructs are the 'theories' that an analyst uses to organize and explain these facts. Therefore, the researcher spending time in a PE department will witness events taking place, for example, a system of streaming

by ability may be evident in games lessons. This is a descriptive property of the social setting being studied. However, such 'facts' do not speak for themselves and the researcher must also deal with another form of first-order construct which involves the situationally, historically, and biographically mediated interpretations used by the members of the PE department to account for the given descriptive property. That is, why does streaming take place *from the view-point of the teachers?* Therefore, both the descriptive properties of the social setting studied (streaming by ability) and the teachers' interpretations of what stands behind these properties are first-order constructs.

In contrast, second-order constructs are those used by the researcher to explain and make sense of the patterning of the first-order constructs through the lens of a particular theoretical framework. At times first-order constructs and second-order constructs can converge. It is not unusual, however, for them to diverge. Often, when there is a lack of convergence the researcher has something novel to say about the social situation that is not perceived by the participants. The more theoretically engaging second-order constructs in essence represent 'interpretations of interpretations'. For a more detailed consideration of these issues see Van Maanan (1983).

15 The notion of hermeneutics originally referred to the interpretation of texts and was developed in relation to the social sciences by Wilhelm Dilthey (1833–1911). Central to hermeneutics was that a knowledge of context or background was essential for any interpretation to take place. The process is circular in that any part of a text or social-historical event requires the rest of the text or event to make it intelligible. Similarly, the whole can only be understood if it is under-taken in terms of the various parts or events. Therefore, the act of interpretation involves a constant movement back and forth between the parts and the whole. Giddens (1976) notes that researchers in many traditions within the social sciences engage in what he calls the 'double hermeneutic' in order to make sense of the social world, that is, they are involved in second-order interpretations of people's first-order interpretations. A more detailed focus on hermeneutics can be found in Outhwaite (1986) and Smith (1989). For a discussion of hermeneutics in relation to sport see Harris (1981).

16 Relativism is discussed in detail by Bernstein (1983) and Gellner (1985).

17 For useful introductions to a critical position that attempts to locate PE, sport, the body and leisure in a wider sociohistorical, economic and political context see the edited volumes by Cantelon and Gruneau (1982), Evans (1988), Jennifer Hargreaves (1982), Horne *et al* (1987), Kirk and Tinning (1990), Mangan and Park (1987), Messner and Sabo (1990), Wimbush and Talbot (1988). Also see Deem (1986), Gruneau (1983), Hoberman (1984), John Hargreaves (1986), Kirk (1988).

18 For more detailed considerations of the Frankfurt School see Gibson (1986), Giroux (1983a and 1983b) and Roderick (1986).

19 As Scraton (1990) and Scraton and Flintoff (chapter 6 in this volume) remind us there are various strands of thought within feminism and it is not an homo-geneous domain. Feminist scholars have provided a major impetus to the devel-opment of a critical perspective. For some examples see Birrell (1989), Birrell and Cole (1990), Dewar (1987, 1989 and 1991), Duncan (1990), Jennifer Hargreaves (1990), Griffin (1989), Lenskyj (1990), Palzkill (1990), Talbot (1988), and Thompson (1988).

20 Adopting a purist position I have argued elsewhere (Sparkes, 1989) that the positivistic and the interpretive paradigms are fundamentally different and incom-patible in that they are philosophically, ideologically, ontologically and epistemo-logically distinct. Therefore, a synthesis is not possible because in their pure

forms they are contradictory since they are based on at least one set of opposing metatheoretical assumptions that are in endemic opposition. These paradigms are alternatives in the sense that one can operate in different paradigms sequentially over time, but mutually exclusive, in the sense that it is not possible to operate in each of these paradigms at any given point in time, because in accepting the assumptions of one, the assumptions of the other are denied. The same would hold for the relationship between the interpretive paradigm and the radical structuralist position within the critical paradigm which adheres to an external-realist ontology and an objectivist epistemology. Clearly, the radical humanist or interpretive-critical strand within the critical paradigm is based on the same epistemological and ontological assumptions as the interpretive paradigm. However, this should not be taken to signify total compatibility since the interests and purposes of each are very different. Also see Smith (1990a) and Smith and Heshusius (1986) for a commentary on incompatibility.

References

ANDERSON, G. (1989a) 'Invisibility, legitimation, and school administration: The study of non-events', paper presented at the annual meeting of the American Educational Research Association, San Francisco, March.

ANDERSON, G. (1989b) 'Critical ethnography in education: Origins, current status, and new directions', *Review of Educational Research*, 59, 3, pp. 249–70.

APPLE, M. (1979) *Ideology and Curriculum*, London, Routledge & Kegan Paul.

APPLE, M. (1982) *Education and Power*, London, ARK Paperbacks.

ATHENS, L. (1984) 'Scientific criteria for evaluating qualitative studies' in DENZIN, N. (Ed) *Studies in Symbolic Interaction — Volume 5*, London, JAI Press Inc, pp. 259–68.

ATKINSON, P., DELAMONT, S. and HAMMERSLEY, M. (1988) 'Qualitative research traditions: A British response to Jacob', *Review of Educational Research*, 58, 2, pp. 231–50.

BAIN, L. (1989) 'Interpretive and critical research in sport and physical education', *Research Quarterly for Exercise and Sport*, 60, 1, pp. 21–4.

BAIN, L. (1990a) 'Visions and voices', *Quest*, 42, 2, pp. 2–12.

BAIN, L. (1990b) '*Research in sport pedagogy: past, present and future*', keynote address, AIESEP World Convention, Loughborough, August.

BAIN, L. and JEWETT, A. (1987) 'Future research and theory-building', *Journal of Teaching in Physical Education*, 6, 3, pp. 346–62.

BALL, S. (1990) 'Self-doubt and soft data: Social and technical trajectories in ethnographic fieldwork', *International Journal of Qualitative Studies in Education*, 3, 2, pp. 157–71.

BARNES, B. (1986) 'Thomas Kuhn' in SKINNER, Q. (Ed) *The Return of Grand Theory in the Human Sciences*, Cambridge, Cambridge University Press, pp. 85–100.

BATES, R. (1980) 'Educational administration, the sociology of science, and the management of knowledge', *Educational Administration Quarterly*, 16, 2, pp. 1–20.

BEAMISH, R. (1981) 'The materialist approach to sport study: An alternative prescription to the disciplines methodological malaise', *Quest*, 33, 1, pp. 55–71.

BERNSTEIN, R. (1976) *The Restructuring of Social and Political Theory*, Philadelphia, PA, University of Pennsylvania Press.

BERNSTEIN, R. (1983) *Beyond Objectivism and Relativism*, Oxford, Basil Blackwell.

BIRREL, S. (1989) 'Racial relations theories and sport: Suggestions for a more critical analysis', *Sociology of Sport Journal*, 6, 3, pp. 212–27.

BIRREL, S. and COLE, C. (1990) 'Double fault: Renee Richards and the construction and naturalization of difference', *Sociology of Sport Journal*, 7, 1, pp. 1–21.

BLALOCK, H. (1984) *Basic Dilemmas in the Social Sciences*, London, Sage.

BOHM, D. and PEAT, F. (1987) *Science, Order and Creativity*, London, Routledge.

BRIGLEY, S. (1990) 'Critical paradigms: Some problems of implementation', *British Educational Research Journal*, 16, 1, pp. 29–40.

BROWN, M. (1988) 'Reconstruction of which reality? Qualitative data analysis' in GOETZ, J. and ALLEN, J. (Eds) *Qualitative Research in Education: Substance, Methods, Experience*, Proceedings of the First Annual Conference of the Qualitative Interest Group, Georgia Center For Continuing Education, Athens, GA, January, pp. 91–103.

BROWN, M. (1990) 'The emic approach: An introduction' in BROWN, M. (Ed) *Processes, Applications and Ethics in Qualitative Research*, Proceedings of the Third Annual Conference of the Qualitative Interest Group, Georgia Center For Continuing Education, Athens, GA, January, pp. 1–6.

BRYMAN, A. (1984) 'The debate about quantitative and qualitative research: A question of method or epistemology?', *British Journal of Sociology*, 35, pp. 75–92.

BUCHMANN, M. and FLODEN, E. (1989) 'Research traditions, diversity and progress', *Review of Educational Research*, 59, 2, pp. 241–48.

BULMER, M. (1984) 'Introduction: Problems, theories and methods in sociology — (how) do they interrelate?' in BULMER, M. (Ed) *Sociological Research Methods: An Introduction*, London, Macmillan, pp. 1–33.

BURGESS, R. (1984) *In the Field: An Introduction to Field Research*, London, George Allen & Unwin.

BURGESS, R. (Ed) (1985) *Strategies of Educational Research: Qualitative Methods*, Lewes, Falmer Press.

BURRELL, G. and MORGAN, G. (1979) *Sociological Paradigms and Organizational Analysis*, London, Heinemann.

CANTELON, H. and GRUNEAU, R. (Eds) (1982) *Sport, Culture and the Modern State*, Toronto, University of Toronto Press.

CARR, W. and KEMMIS, S. (1986) *Becoming Critical: Education, Knowledge and Action Research*, Lewes, Falmer Press.

CHALIP, L. (1990) 'Rethinking the applied social sciences in sport: Observations on the emerging debate', *Sociology of Sport Journal*, 7, 2, pp. 172–8.

CHALMERS, A. (1982) *What Is This Thing Called Science?* Milton Keynes, Open University Press.

CHALMERS, A. (1990) *Science and its Fabrication*, Milton Keynes, Open University Press.

CHERRYHOLMES, C. (1988) *Power and Criticism: Post-structural Investigations into Education*, New York, Teachers College Press.

COSER, L. (1984) 'Two methods in search of substance' in BULMER, M. (Ed) *Sociological Research Methods: An Introduction*, London, Macmillan, pp. 294–307.

CRUM, B. (1986) 'Concerning the quality of the development of knowledge in sport pedagogy', *Journal of Teaching in Physical Education*, 5, 4, pp. 211–20.

DEEM, R. (1986) *All Work and No Play: The Sociology of Women's Leisure*, Milton Keynes, Open University Press.

DEWAR, A. (1987) 'The social construction of gender in physical education', *Woman's Studies International Forum*, 10, 4, pp. 453–65.

DEWAR, A. (1989) 'Recruitment in physical education: Toward a critical approach' in TEMPLIN, T. and SCHEMPP, P. (Eds) *Socialization into Teaching: Learning to Teach*, Indianapolis, IN, Benchmark Press, pp. 39–58.

DEWAR, A. (1990) 'Oppression and privilege in physical education: Struggles in the negotiation of gender in a university programme' in KIRK, D. and TINNING, R. (Eds) *Physical Education, Curriculum and Culture: Critical Issues in the Contemporary Crisis*, Lewes, Falmer Press, pp. 67–99.

DEWAR, A. (1991) 'Incorporation or resistance?: Towards an analysis of women's responses to sexual oppression in sport', *International Review for the Sociology of Sport*, 26, 1, pp. 15–23.

DUNCAN, M. (1990) 'Sports photographs and sexual difference: Images of women and men in the 1984 and 1988 Olympic Games', *Sociology of Sport Journal*, 7, 1, pp. 22–43.

EARLS, N. (1986) 'Conflicting research assumptions and complementary distinctions', *Journal of Teaching in Physical Education*, 6, 1, pp. 30–40.

EISNER, E. (1988) 'The primacy of experience and the politics of method', *Educational Researcher*, 17, 5, pp. 15–20.

EISNER, E. (1990a) 'The meaning of alternative paradigms for practice' in GUBA, E. (Ed) *The Paradigm Dialog*, London, Sage, pp. 88–102.

EISNER, E. (1990b) 'Objectivity in educational research', paper presented at the annual meeting of the American Educational Research Association, Boston, April.

ERICKSON, F. (1986) 'Qualitative methods in research on teaching' in WITTROCK, M. (Ed) *Handbook of Research on Teaching* (3rd edn), New York, Macmillan, pp. 119–61.

EVANS, J. (Ed) (1986) *Physical Education, Sport and Schooling: Studies in the Sociology of Physical Education*, Lewes, Falmer Press.

EVANS, J. (1987) 'Teaching and learning in physical education: Towards a qualitative understanding', *Physical Education Review*, 10, 1, pp. 30–9.

EVANS, J. (Ed) (1988) *Teachers, Teaching and Control in Physical Education*, Lewes, Falmer Press.

FETTERMAN, D. (1989) *Ethnography: Step by Step*, London, Sage.

FREIRE, P. (1973) *Education for Critical Consciousness*, New York, Continuum.

GAGE, N. (1989) 'The paradigm wars and their aftermath: A "historical" sketch of research on teaching since 1989', *Educational Researcher*, 18, 7, pp. 4–10.

GELLNER, E. (1985) *Relativism and the Social Sciences*, Cambridge, Cambridge University Press.

GIBSON, R. (1986) *Critical Theory and Education*, London, Hodder and Stoughton.

GIDDENS, A. (Ed) (1974) *Positivism and Sociology*, London, Heinemann.

GIDDENS, A. (1976) *New Rules of the Sociological Method*, New York, Basic Books.

GIDDENS, A. (1979) 'Positivism and its critics' in BOTTOMORE, T. and NISBET, R. (Eds) *A History of Sociological Analysis*, London, Heinemann, pp. 237–86.

GIROUX, H. (1983a) *Theory and Resistance in Education: A Pedagogy for the Opposition*, London, Heinemann.

GIROUX, H. (1983b) *Critical Theory and Educational Practice*, Deakin, Deakin University Press.

GLASSFORD, R. (1987) 'Methodological reconsiderations: The shifting paradigms', *Quest*, 39, pp. 295–312.

GOETZ, J. and LECOMPTE, M. (1984) *Ethnography and Qualitative Design in Educational Research*, Orlando, FL, Academic Press.

GREYLING, A. (1982) *An Introduction to Philosophical Logic*, Totowa, NJ, Barnes & Noble.

GRIFFIN, P. (1989) 'Gender as a socializing agent in physical education' in TEMPLIN, T. and SCHEMPP, P. (Eds) *Socialization into Physical Education: Learning to Teach*, Indianapolis, IN, Benchmark Press, pp. 219–34.

GRIFFIN, P. (1990) '*What is a critical perspective in research*', paper presented at the annual meeting of the American Educational Research Association, Boston, April.

GRUNEAU, R. (1983) *Class, Sport and Social Development*, Amherst, MA, University Press.

GUBA, E. (1990) 'The alternative paradigm dialog' in GUBA, E. (Ed) *The Paradigm Dialog*, London, Sage, pp. 17–27.

GUBA, E. and LINCOLN, Y. (1989) *Fourth Generation Evaluation*, London, Sage.

HACKING, I. (Ed) (1981) *Scientific Revolutions*, Oxford, Oxford University Press.

HAMMERSLEY, M. (1985) 'From ethnography to theory: A programme and paradigm in the sociology of education', *Sociology*, 19, 2, pp. 244–59.

HAMMERSLEY, M. (1990) 'What's wrong with ethnography? The myth of theoretical description', *Sociology*, 24, 4, pp. 597–615.

HAMMERSLEY, M. and ATKINSON, P. (1983) *Ethnography — Principles in Practice*, London, Tavistock.

HARGREAVES, A. (1980) 'Synthesis and the study of strategies: A project for the sociological imagination' in WOODS, P. (Ed) *Pupil Strategies*, London, Croom Helm, pp. 162–98.

HARGREAVES, J. (Ed) (1982) *Sport, Culture and Ideology*, London, Routledge & Kegan Paul.

HARGREAVES, J. (1990) 'Gender on the sports agenda', *International Review for the Sociology of Sport*, 25, 4, pp. 287–305.

HARGREAVES, J. (1986) *Sport, Power and Culture*, London, Polity Press.

HARRIS, J. (1981) 'Hermeneutics, interpretive cultural research, and the study of sports', *Quest*, 33, 1, pp. 72–86.

HARRIS, J. (1983a) 'Broadening horizons: Interpretive cultural research, hermeneutics, and scholarly inquiry in physical education', *Quest*, 35, pp. 82–96.

HARRIS, J. (1983b) 'Interpretive cultural research: A direction for expansion of scholarly inquiry in physical education', *Proceedings of the National Association of Physical Education in Higher Education Annual Conference*, IV, Indiana, January, pp. 94–113.

HARVEY, L. (1990) *Critical Social Research*, London, Unwin Hyman.

HAWKINS, A. (1987) 'On the role of hermeneutics in sport pedagogy', *Journal of Teaching in Physical Education*, 6, 4, pp. 367–72.

HELLISON, D. (1988) 'Our constructed reality: Some contributions of an alternative perspective to physical education pedagogy', *Quest*, 40, pp. 84–90.

HERON, J. (1988) 'Validity in co-operative research' in REASON, P. (Ed) *Human Inquiry in Action: Developments in New Paradigm Research*, London, Sage, pp. 40–59.

HESSE, M. (1980) *Revolutions and Reconstructions in the Philosophy of Science*, Brighton, Harvester Press.

HOBERMAN, J. (1984) *Sport and Political Ideology*, London, Heinemann.

HORNE, J., JARY, D. and TOMLINSON, A. (Eds) (1987) *Sport, Leisure and Social Relations*, London, Routledge & Kegan Paul.

INGHAM, A. (1991) 'Some not so new arguments in support of heterodoxy: Agendas in the study of sport', *International Review for the Sociology of Sport*, 26, 1, pp. 53–62.

JACOB, E. (1987) 'Qualitative research traditions: A review', *Review of Educational Research*, 57, 1, pp. 1–50.

JACOB, E. (1988) 'Clarifying qualitative research: A focus on traditions', *Educational Researcher*, 17, 1, pp. 16–24.

JACOB, E. (1989) 'Qualitative research: A defence of traditions', *Review of Educational Research*, 59, 2, pp. 229–35.

KIRK, D. (1988) *Physical Education and Curriculum Study: A Critical Introduction*, London, Croom Helm.

KIRK, D. (1989) 'The orthodoxy in RT-PE and the research/practice gap: A critique and an alternative view', *Journal of Teaching in Physical Education*, 8, 2, pp. 123–30.

KIRK, D. and TINNING, R. (Eds) (1990) *Physical Education, Curriculum and Culture: Critical Issues in the Contemporary Crisis*, Lewes, Falmer Press.

KUHN, T. (1962) *The Structure of Scientific Revolutions*, Chicago, IL, University of Chicago Press.

KUHN, T. (1970) *The Structure of Scientific Revolutions* (2nd edn-enlarged), Chicago, IL, University of Chicago Press.

LATHER, P. (1986) 'Issues of validity in openly ideological research: Between a rock and a soft place', *Interchange*, 17, 4, pp. 63–84.

LAURA, R. (1988) 'New frontiers in the philosophy of science and new age education', *Educational Philosophy and Theory*, 20, 1, pp. 63–9.

LENSKYJ, H. (1990) 'Power and play: Gender and sexuality issues in sport and physical activity', *International Review for the Sociology of Sport*, 25, 3, pp. 235–45.

LEVIDOW, L. (Ed) (1986) *Radical Science*, London, Free Association Books.

LINCOLN, Y. (1985) 'Introduction' in LINCOLN, Y. (Ed) *Organizational Theory and Inquiry: The Paradigm Revolution*, London, Sage, pp. 29–40.

LINCOLN, Y. (1989a) 'Trouble in the land: The paradigm revolution in the academic disciplines' in SMART, J. (Ed) *Higher Education: Handbook of Theory and Research — Vol 5*, New York, Agathon Press, pp. 57–133.

LINCOLN, Y. (1989b) 'Qualitative research: A response to Atkinson, Delamont and Hammersley', *Review of Educational Research*, 59, 2, pp. 237–9.

LINCOLN, Y. (1990) 'The making of a constructivist: A remembrance of transformations past' in GUBA, E. (Ed) *The Paradigm Dialog*, London, Sage, pp. 64–87.

LINCOLN, Y. and GUBA, E. (1985) *Naturalistic Inquiry*, London, Sage.

LOCKE, L. (1986) 'Qualitative research in the gymnasium: New responses to old problems' in PARE, C., LIRETTE, M. and PIERON, M. (Eds) *Research Methodology in Teaching Physical Education and Sports*, Quebec, Department of Physical Education, University of Quebec at Trois-Rivieres, pp. 35–56.

LOCKE, L. (1987) 'The future of research on pedagogy: Balancing on the cutting edge', *The Academy Papers No 20, The Cutting Edge in Physical Education and Exercise Science Research*, Champaign, IL, Human Kinetics, pp. 83–95.

LOCKE, L. (1989) 'Qualitative research as a form of scientific inquiry in sport and physical education', *Research Quarterly for Exercise and Sport*, 60, 1, pp. 1–20.

LUSCHEN, G. (1990) 'On theory of science for the sociology of sport: New structuralism, action, intention and practical meaning', *International Review for the Sociology of Sport*, 25, 1, pp. 49–63.

McKAY, J. (1986) 'Marxism as a way of seeing: Beyond the limits of current "critical" approaches to sport', *Sociology of Sport Journal*, 3, 3, pp. 261–72.

McKAY, J., GORE, J. and KIRK, D. (1990) 'Beyond the limits of technocratic physical education', *Quest*, 42, 1, pp. 52–76.

MANGAN, J. and PARK, R. (Eds) (1987) *From 'Fair Sex' to Feminism*, London, Frank Cass & Company Ltd.

MARTENS, R. (1987) 'Science, knowledge and sport psychology', *Sport Psychologist*, 1, pp. 29–55.

MASTERMAN, M. (1970) 'The nature of a paradigm' in LAKATOS, I. and MUSGRAVE, A. (Eds) *Criticism and the Growth of Knowledge*, Cambridge, Cambridge University Press, pp. 59–89.

MESSNER, M. (1990) 'Men studying masculinity: Some epistemological issues in sport sociology', *Sociology of Sport Journal*, 7, 2, pp. 136–53.

MESSNER, M. and SABO, D. (Eds) (1990) *Sport, Men, and the Gender Order: Critical Feminist Perspectives*, Champaign, IL, Human Kinetics.

METZLER, M. (1987) 'Editorial', *Journal of Teaching in Physical Education*, 6, 6, pp. 109–10.

MILES, M. and HUBERMAN, A. (1984) *Qualitative Data Analysis*, Beverly Hills, CA, Sage.

MORGAN, G. (1983) 'Research as engagement: A personal view' in MORGAN, G. (Ed) *Beyond Method: Strategies for Social Research*, Beverly Hills, CA, Sage, pp. 11–18.

OUTHWAITE, W. (1986) *Understanding Social Life: A Method Called Verstehen*, Lewes, Jean Stroud Publisher.

PALZKILL, B. (1990) 'Between gymshoes and high-heels — the development of lesbian identity and existence in top class sport', *International Review for the Sociology of Sport*, 25, 2, pp. 221–34.

PATTON, M. (1978) *Qualitative Evaluation Methods*, Beverly Hills, CA, Sage.

PHILLIPS, D. (1987) *Philosophy, Science, and Social Inquiry*, Oxford, Pergamon Press.

PHILLIPS, D. (1990) 'Post-positivistic science: Myths and realities' in GUBA, E. (Ed) *The Paradigm Dialog*, London, Sage, pp. 31–45.

POPKEWITZ, T. (1984) *Paradigm and Ideology in Educational Research: The Social Functions of the Intellectual*, Lewes, Falmer Press.

POPKEWITZ, T. (1990) 'Whose future? Whose past? Notes on critical theory and methodology' in GUBA, E. (Ed) *The Paradigm Dialog*, London, Sage, pp. 47–66.

PUTNAM, H. (1981) *Reason, Truth, and History*, Cambridge, Cambridge University Press.

RAMAZANOGLU, C. (1989) 'Improving on sociology: The problems of taking a feminist standpoint', *Sociology*, 23, 3, pp. 427–42.

REASON, P. and ROWAN, J. (1981) 'Issues of validity in new paradigm research' in REASON, P. and ROWAN, J. (Eds) *Human Inquiry: A Sourcebook of New Paradigm Research*, Chichester, England, Wiley & Sons, pp. 239–50.

RODERICK, R. (1986) *Habermas and the Foundations of Critical Theory*, New York, St Martin's Press.

RORTY, R. (1979) *Philosophy and the Mirror of Nature*, Princeton, NJ, Princeton University Press.

RORTY, R. (1982) *Consequences of Pragmatism*, Minneapolis, University of Minnesota Press.

RORTY, R. (1985) 'Solidarity or objectivity?' in RAJCHMAN, J. and WEST, C. (Eds) *Post-Analytic Philosophy*, New York, Columbia University Press, pp. 3–19.

SCHEMPP, P. (1987) 'Research on teaching in physical education: Beyond the limits of natural science', *Journal of Teaching in Physical Education*, 6, 2, pp. 111–21.

SCHEMPP, P. (1988) 'Exorcist II: A reply to Siedentop', *Journal of Teaching in Physical Education*, 7, 2, pp. 79–81.

SCHEMPP, P. (1990) 'Culture, change and teaching in physical education' in TELEMA, R., LAAKSO, L., PIERON, M., RUOPPILA, I. and VIHKO, V. (Eds) *Physical Education and Life-Long Physical Activity*, Proceedings of the AIESEP World Convention, University of Jyvaskyla, Finland, June, pp. 73–84.

SCHULMAN, L. (1986) 'Paradigms and research programs in the study of teaching: A contemporary perspective' in WITTROCK, M. (Ed) *Handbook of Research on Teaching* (3rd edn), New York, Macmillan, pp. 3–36.

SCHUTZ, A. (1967) *The Phenomenology of the Social World*, Evanston, IL, Northwestern University Press.

SCHUTZ, R. (1989) 'Qualitative research: Comments and controversies', *Research Quarterly for Exercise and Sport*, 60, 1, pp. 30–5.

SCRATON, S. (1990) *Gender and Physical Education*, Deakin, Deakin University Press.

SHARP, R. (1982) 'Self-contained ethnography or a science of phenomenal forms and inner relations', *Journal of Education*, 164, 1, pp. 48–63.

SIEDENTOP, D. (1983) 'Research on teaching in physical education' in TEMPLIN, T. and OLSEN, J. (Eds) *Teaching in Physical Education*, Champaign, IL, Human Kinetics, pp. 3–15.

SIEDENTOP, D. (1987) 'Dialogue or exorcism? A rejoinder to Schempp', *Journal of Teaching in Physical Education*, 6, 4, pp. 373–6.

SIEDENTOP, D. (1989) 'Do the lockers really smell?', *Research Quarterly for Exercise and Sport*, 60, 1, pp. 36–41.

SMITH, J. (1983) 'Quantitative versus interpretive: The problem of conducting social inquiry' in HOUSE, E. (Ed) *Philosophy of Evaluation*, London, Jossey-Bass Inc, pp. 27–51.

SMITH, J. (1984) 'The problem of criteria for judging interpretive inquiry', *Educational Evaluation and Policy Analysis*, 6, 4, pp. 379–91.

SMITH, J. (1988) 'The evaluator/researcher as person vs. the person as evaluator/researcher', *Educational Researcher*, 17, 2, pp. 18–23.

SMITH, J. (1989) *The Nature of Social and Educational Inquiry: Empiricism Versus Interpretation*, Norwood, NJ, Albex Publishing Corporation.

SMITH, J. (1990a) 'Are there differences that still make a difference', paper presented at the annual meeting of the American Educational Research Association, Boston, April.

SMITH, J. (1990b) 'Alternative research paradigms and the problem of criteria' in GUBA, E. (Ed) *The Paradigm Dialog*, London, Sage, pp. 167–87.

SMITH, J. and HESHUSIUS, L. (1986) 'Closing down the conversation: The end of the quantitative-qualitative debate among educational researchers', *Educational Researcher*, 15, 1, pp. 4–12.

SMITH, M. (1987) 'Publishing qualitative data', *American Educational Research Journal*, 24, 2, pp. 173–83.

SOLTIS, J. (1984) 'On the nature of educational research', *Educational Researcher*, 13, pp. 5–10.

SPARKES, A. (1986a) 'Beyond description: The need for theory generation in physical education', *Physical Education Review*, 9, 1, pp. 41–8.

SPARKES, A. (1986b) 'Strangers and structures in the process of innovation' in EVANS, J. (Ed) *Physical Education, Sport and Schooling: Studies in the Sociology of Physical Education*, Lewes, Falmer Press, pp. 183–93.

SPARKES, A. (1987) 'Strategic rhetoric: A constraint in changing the practice of teachers', *British Journal of Sociology of Education*, 8, 1, pp. 37–54.

SPARKES, A. (1988a) 'Strands of commitment within the process of innovation', *Educational Review*, 40, 3, pp. 301–17.

SPARKES, A. (1988b) 'The micropolitics of innovation in the physical education curriculum' in EVANS, J. (Ed) *Teachers, Teaching and Control in Physical Education*, London, Falmer Press, pp. 157–77.

SPARKES, A. (1989) 'Paradigmatic confusions and the evasion of critical issues in naturalistic research', *Journal of Teaching in Physical Education*, 8, 2, pp. 131–51.

SPARKES, A. (1990a) *Curriculum Change and Physical Education: Towards a Micropolitical Understanding*, Deakin, Deakin University Press.

SPARKES, A. (1990b) 'Power, domination and resistance in the process of teacher-initiated innovation', *Research Papers in Education*, 5, 2, pp. 59–84.

SPARKES, A. (1990c) 'Winners, losers and the myth of rational change in physical education: Towards an understanding of interests and power in innovation' in KIRK, D. and TINNING, R. (Eds) *Physical Education, Curriculum and Culture: Critical Issues in the Contemporary Crisis*, Lewes, Falmer Press, pp. 193–224.

SPARKES, A. (1991) 'Towards understanding, dialogue, and polyvocality in the research community: Extending the boundaries of the paradigms debate', *Journal of Teaching in Physical Education*, 10, 2, pp. 103–33.

SPARKES, A. (1992) 'Validity and the research process: An exploration of meanings', *Physical Education Review*, 15, 1, pp. 29–45.

STANLEY, L. (1990) 'Doing ethnography, writing ethnography: A comment on Hammersley', *Sociology*, 24, 4, pp. 617–27.

TALBOT, M. (1988) 'Understanding relationships between women and sport: The contributions of British feminist approaches in leisure and cultural studies', *International Review for the Sociology of Sport*, 23, 1, pp. 31–41.

TAYLOR, C. (1971) 'Interpretation and the sciences of man', *Review of Metaphysics*, 25, pp. 3–25.

TEMPLIN, T. and GRIFFEY, D. (1987) 'Editorial', *Journal of Teaching in Physical Education*, 7, 1, pp. 1–4.

THOMPSON, S. (1988) 'Challenging the hegemony: New Zealand women's opposition to rugby and the reproduction of capitalist patriarchy', *International Review for the Sociology of Sport*, 23, 3, pp. 205–12.

VAN MAANEN, J. (1983) 'The fact of fiction in organizational ethnography' in VAN MANAAN, J. (Ed) *Qualitative Methodology*, London, Sage, pp. 37–55.

WARD, E. and HARDMAN, K. (1978) 'The influence of values on the role perception of men physical education teachers', *Physical Education Review*, 1, 1, pp. 59–69.

WIMBUSH, E. and TALBOT, M. (Eds) (1988) *Relative Freedoms: Women and Leisure*, Milton Keynes, Open University Press.

WOLCOTT, H. (1990a) 'On seeking — and rejecting — validity in qualitative research' in EISNER, E. and PESHKIN, A. (Eds) *Qualitative Inquiry in Education: The Continuing Debate*, London, Teachers College Press, pp. 121–52.

WOLCOTT, H. (1990b) 'Ethnographic research in education' in JAEGER, R. (Ed) *Complementary Methods for Research in Education*, Washington DC, American Educational Research Association, pp. 187–206.

WOODS, P. (1985) 'Ethnography and theory construction in educational research' in BURGESS, R. (Ed) *Field Methods in the Study of Education*, London, Falmer, pp. 51–78.

WOODS, P. (1986) *Inside Schools: Ethnography in Educational Research*, London, Routledge & Kegan Paul.

ZIBGNIEW, K. (1990) 'Theoretical dilemmas in the sociology of sport', *International Review for the Sociology of Sport*, 25, 1, pp. 41–8.

Chapter 2

Studying the Lifeworld of Physical Education: A Phenomenological Orientation

Stephen J. Smith

Over fifty years ago Edmund Husserl spoke of a crisis in our understanding of the world brought on by a gross neglect of the natural, pre-
theoretical attitude to life from which all theoretical understanding
derives. Such neglect was due, he said, to the fact that we have turned our
attention away from the lifeworld (*lebenswelt*), the world that is experienced
in the 'natural, primordial attitude', the world that is 'taken for granted',
'pregiven' and 'already there' — the 'unspoken ground' and 'grounding
soil' of our most theoretical accomplishments (Husserl, 1970, pp. 103–
186). Husserl was especially critical of the ways in which our natural, pre-
theoretical attitude to the lifeworld falls victim to scientific interpretation.
What was required in his estimation was no less than a suspension of
belief in 'all objective theoretical interests, all aims and activities belonging to us as objective scientists or even simply as (ordinary) people desir-
ous of (this kind of) knowledge' (p. 135), coupled with a kind of intuitive
inquiry which treats the lifeworld as both point of departure and continuing point of return.

This claim of a crisis in understanding carries particular meaning for
those of us pursuing a human science of physical activity. It makes us
suspicious of the kind of connections that are assumed to exist between
our experiences of physical activity and the kinesiological and sociocultural sciences of that activity. We begin to question the relation of our
scientific discourses to the meanings we derive for ourselves from our
games, sports, dances and physical recreations. The claim also gives pause
for thought regarding the connectedness of pedagogical science to those
experiences of physical activity which comprise the lifeworld of physical
education. For, as we continue to fashion a pedagogical science that
emulates other sciences of behaviour, we risk overlooking the lifeworld of
physical education in all its experiential complexity.

Studying the lifeworld of physical education requires, in the first
instance, an attentiveness to experiences that comprise our collective sense

of educating children in desirable physical activity. We need to suspend belief in how children's physical education can be explained and be prepared to describe how it is possible for an adult to stand in an educative relation to a child within particular, somewhat unique, situations that carry significant connotations of physical maturation. We turn our attention, in other words, to the possibility of a relation grounded in a certain domain of valued human activity. We ask what this situated relation might be like: what it might be like to be with children as they engage in physical activity and as we attempt to influence the direction that their physical development might take. And in attempting to describe these situations as vividly as possible, there emerge possibilities that could be regarded as the framework for a pedagogical interest in physical education.

My intention in this chapter is to outline the features of this orientation to the lifeworld of physical education. Taking up the lead of second generation phenomenologists, like Schutz and Luckmann (1973), who sought to define the structures of the lifeworld and to describe them, as Heidegger (1962) and Merleau-Ponty (1962) did, in terms of concretely lived meaning, I look to the 'Utrecht School' of phenomenology which stands out as having produced some of the most concrete, descriptive and evocative accounts of lifeworld experience. Here I think of the phenomenological orientation which Langeveld instigated with the 1944 publication of *Beknopte Theoretische Pedagogiek* (Introduction to Theoretical Pedagogy) and subsequently developed in concert with the phenomenological pursuits of his colleagues Beets, Buytendijk, Linschoten and Van den Berg. I also think of more recent Dutch writers like Beekman, Bleeker, Levering and Mulderij who continue the work of the 'Utrecht School' (see van Maanan, 1978–79 for a detailed discussion of the 'Utrecht School'). Outside The Netherlands I have in mind the translations and interpretations of this phenomenological work by such philosophers of education as Denton, Greene, Troutner and Vandenberg, as well as the inspired phenomenological analyses of van Maanan, Barritt and their respective students. I shall draw upon aspects of this work in sketching out the features of a phenomenological orientation to the lifeworld of physical education.

In the first section, called *orienting to the lifeworld*, I talk about how we can recognize the lifeworld of physical education by taking closer note of what children actually do while being physically active. Stepping back a little from our research-driven ways of looking at children engaged in physical activity, I describe an alternative view, a different observational stance, and one which puts us back in touch with the nature of children's physical experiences. The second section, *grounds for being interested*, is intended to examine those adult dispositions that allow us to recognize a lifeworld of physical education worth studying. Here I describe the intentionality that is at work in our quest for a theory of the lifeworld of physical education. In the third section I bring the preceding considerations to bear upon our understanding of *the domain of physical education* as it is ordinarily defined. Certain lifeworld concepts are addressed, concepts which, as Heidegger (1962) said, 'remain our proximal clues for disclosing this area concretely for the first time' (p. 29). Finally, I outline a *research agenda* for studying the lifeworld of physical education. Here my purpose is not to lay out a prescriptive method, but rather to illustrate the features of a research approach which orients us to the lifeworld of physical education.

Orienting to the Lifeworld

How might we become more aware of the lifeworld of physical education? How might we recognize our involvement with children in physical activity contexts? How might we come to see more clearly where the child is and what the child is, what our relation to the child is, and how we might stand with the child in a given yet questionable world of meanings?

Such questions must take account of the dominant research tradition of systematic observations of teaching-learning episodes. Account must be taken of what Locke (1977) said pedagogical research in physical education should be.

> Research on teaching physical education includes only studies which employ data gathered through direct or indirect observation of instructional activity . . .
> The observation would have to be systematic in the sense that it was conducted so as to extract quantifiable units of data which could meet reasonable standards of reliability and validity. (p. 10)

Here Locke was only echoing the thoughts of educational researchers at large who claimed that what qualifies as research demands a more refined form of observation than that of everyday life. But whereas Locke has since broadened his sense of what is acceptable in pedagogical research (Locke, 1989) his earlier definition of systematic observation still holds for the dominant research tradition within physical education which focusses upon quantifying 'academic learning time'. Even in the *Handbook of Research on Teaching* we are told that there are different forms of observation and these may be placed on a continuum indicating degrees of formality. On one side are the highly 'tacit' observations of everyday life; a little more formal are those everyday observations which are 'situation-specific'; while most formal, which is to say most overt and consciously manipulable, are the 'systematic question-specific observations' of trained viewers (Evertson and Green, 1986, p. 164). According to this delineation, what qualifies as observation for the purpose of research is that which is formalized in a deliberate and systematic manner as a response to pre-determined empirical questions.

Attempts to systematize observation have, of course, produced gains in the research field of physical education pedagogy, taking the field from a 'dismal science' (Locke, 1977) to 'new knowledge and cautious optimism' (Placek and Locke, 1986). But, although we can now see the conditions of 'effective teaching' with greater clarity than ever before (cf. Harrison, 1987), still the question remains: has this refinement of observation, this move away from the observations of daily life, helped us to see the children we encounter in physical education contexts any more clearly? Perhaps in our efforts to become more systematic we have forgotten what it means to be truly observant of children. Speaking from a phenomenological tradition of educational inquiry, Beekman (1983) says: 'Seeing, but not being seen; hearing, but not being heard, that would be objective, quantifiable, reliable, and replicable. But would I understand?' (p. 38). 'How would I know what children are doing? How would I know what the activity means to them or what they are learning if I am not "really out there interacting with the children" (p. 39)? And how would I know what pedagogy could be if divorced from this everyday, interactional context?

The pedagogical research task requires a committed mode of everyday observation. It requires us to not only look at the child, but also to take note of how the child is placed. Observing means looking with care. 'The word "observing" has etymological connections to "preserving, saving, regarding, protecting". The teacher serves the child by observing from very close proximity while still maintaining distance' (van Manen, 1986, p. 19). This is the significance of pedagogic observation — that it is a way of observing children whereby we are constantly challenged to look out for particular children and to see what they do as potentially contributing to their maturity.

Beets (1952) outlines the ways this significance might be appreciated. He describes various situations of watching young children playing soccer and highlights the different ways in which we might observe what is going on. In the first case, Beets writes about the adult who just happens to be passing by a soccer field. This person can become interested for a while in what is happening there, yet he or she can just as easily leave the situation behind without having had any real effect upon the children's play. In the second case, Beets refers to the adult observer who is known to the children in more than a passing sort of way. As mother or father of one of the children, the adult is in a position to observe the children in a far more engaged and responsible manner. Even so, this kind of observation still leaves room for a deeper pedagogical stance. So Beets goes on to talk of a third case where the adult who watches the soccer game has special responsibility for the education of the children. He says:

> They know me and I know them. When I stand still and watch while they are playing, I am an outsider in a certain sense, since now I observe them from a scientific or an educational vantage point of 'pedagogue' or 'diagnosticus'. But I am also involved,

since I am and feel that I am responsible for their education. I stand beside the parent — on the side of the educators. Now I observe in a special manner, however. I have learned to adopt a scientific vantage point and my observing is observation from that 'vision'. (p. 16)

Each of these cases not only reflect different stances taken up by the passer-by, the parent, or the pedagogue, they also express different forms of interaction between children and their observers. They are different ways of responding to the children's activity. So, if from an empirical point of view we would want to argue for observations that are increasingly 'systematic' and 'question-specific', then certainly from a pedagogical point of view we would want to argue for observations that are guided by particular sorts of questions that have to do with what our commitment is to the child. The significance of pedagogic observation is that not only does it mean that the child is seen, but it also carries an admonition that we should stand in the midst of the child's activity and call upon our own ability to respond to what we see happening there. Borrowing from a more technicist North American language, it allows for 'skillful' handling of the child, where 'A skillful observer develops sensitivity to the uniqueness of personality and becomes increasingly able to interpret the language of behavior' (Dowley, 1969, p. 517). To observe the child pedagogically means, in effect, being implicated in a situation of responsibility for the child's movement towards maturity. It means 'being a child-watcher who keeps in view the total existence of the developing child' (van Maanan, 1986, p. 18).

Let me give a more concrete illustration of this form of observation. Consider watching some young children at play. From a park bench I see two small girls on a circular slippery slide. One stands at the top while the other straddles the raised edge of the slide, and starting at the bottom, she begins to pull herself up the slide by gripping under the edge and allowing her outside leg to dangle freely. 'This is fun,' she says to her friend at the top. 'Why don't you try it?' Now half-way up, she decides to try something new. 'Hey, watch what I can do!' Standing on the edge and then bracing herself with her arms against the pillar around which the slide curves, she edges up further. Her friend at the top, however, becomes perturbed by what she sees. Her concern shows even more as the adventurous one reaches the casing that covers the top of the slide — the curved plastic casing that offers no purchase for this girl and that has no guard rail to stop her from slipping over the edge and falling down onto the packed sand below — the casing that this girl is trying to climb over.

I have been watching what these girls are doing and now I, too, am concerned for the child who is at this moment precariously situated on the top of the slide. In fact I am concerned for them both, because both of them find the situation risky, albeit in decidedly different ways. The little girl standing at the top is scared by the antics of her friend, while the

latter child finds herself in a danger that she had not been able to anticipate nor one over which she can now exert some control. Her bravado,
her attempt to impress her friend and I suspect, myself, has prevented her
from appreciating the inevitable consequence of what she does.

As I watch these two little girls I feel responsible for what has now
transpired. I have not shown either of them 'what is the nature of mature
adulthood toward which she is striving' (van Manen, 1979, p. 14). I have
not helped them see a risk that is not necessarily a likely danger. An
action component is missing from this situation, quite apart from the
action of stopping the child from climbing up the slide. Unfortunately it
is too late to act in any way. The child falls off the slide. My heart stops
as I see her sprawled on the ground. A slight relief — she starts crying as I
rush over to where she lays. I am relieved — although she has fallen
heavily, fortunately the little girl has suffered only some minor bruising. I
help her up, allowing her to hobble around for a little while, before she
and her friend head off to the swings. But as I return to the park bench,
having done my job of consoling her after the fall, I feel more than a little
responsible for what has happened and for what may well have been a
more serious injury. I should have stepped in before the child put herself
in danger, before a fall became imminent, although I am not at all sure,
even now, that preventing the child from going further up the slide
would have been the best action to take. What would my concern for
danger do for the child who watches from the top in a state of concern?
How would she be helped by my pointing out the danger that lurks in the
playground? On the other hand, the vitality has gone from the little girls'
movements. I watch them now on the swings and I cannot help think that
something has been lost for these girls as a result of the fall and the lack of
observance of that which led up to it. The children have gained an awareness of safety at the expense of an awareness of movement. A potential
opportunity to teach them and for myself to learn about the nature of
their movement has been lost.

This situation shows that, while 'looking on' provides a measure
of security for the child, at times it obscures the difference between
watching and truly observing the child's activity. Are we there simply to
watch the child, to ensure that activity is safely and correctly performed,
or does the fact that we are in attendance mean the situation is potentially
a pedagogical one? Can we 'convert by way of a pedagogic intention
some incidental subject or problem situation into a situation where a
certain question or problem becomes a critical one for the young person'?
(van Maanan, 1987, p. 22). Can we act in such a way that both children
can see in the risks of the activity an opportunity for safe movement
exploration? To be sure, there will remain a risk in the situation involving
the girl climbing up the slippery slide, yet it is the observer's awareness of
this risk that can create an upswing in their being together on the playground. These children on the slide look to the adult who sits on the park
bench. And now that this vantage point is sighted it creates a site for their
explorations. The adult is caught in a situation where he or she can either

stay seated and leave the children to their own devices, or where the child's glance can be acknowledged and the movement possibilities of the situation drawn out. Either way, a decision has been made.

Of course not every instance of physical activity requires that something decisive happen on our part. One must be sensitive to the difference between critical instances and those which are not, since pedagogy fails as much at the extreme of investing absolutely everything with momentous significance as it does at the other extreme of seeing nothing at all as decisive. The truth of the matter may be that the most important decision is the one to be there for the sake of the child's explorations. This decision potentially circumscribes not only a position, a posture towards physical activity, but also a situation that gives meaning to the particular decisions one might make regarding what to do with the children one faces. The decision to observe children's activity creates a situation in which one is implicated no matter what one decides to do in specific instances (cf. Bollnow, 1972, p. 376). It creates a situation of responsibility for children.

This kind of watchfulness enables us to question more detached and supposedly more scientific kinds of observation. Consider, in this regard, a fairly extreme case described by Beekman (1983). He writes: 'I would be like the observers of a playground in Holland, counting their own made up categories but not understanding. This is described very clearly in *Kinderen Buiten Spel* (The Play for Children Out-of-Doors) where so-called objective observers went inside an unobtrusive workman's shack, made a peeping hole, and made coded observations. In their protocols we find scores of "activities" numerically coded'. But would I understand what is going on? asks Beekman. 'The meaning of the experience is missing. For instance, if you were really "in" the park, you would see girls hanging around on bikes. Doing nothing? Or being social? How do you know, until you are really out there interacting with children?' (p. 39). It would seem that such procedures which deny the adult's place on the playground also deny the point of observing children in the first place. They deny the point of being with children and seeing how our presence influences the nature of their activity. Unlike these detached, impersonal observations of children, which we find advocated by 'academic learning time' researchers (see Metzler, 1989), the kind of watchfulness we want to capture in the methodology of our pedagogical research entails not merely looking at children, nor even just looking out for them, but rather looking *after* them.

Grounds for Being Interested

This way of observing physical activity requires an admission of our involvement in the activity of children. Although we need to take sufficient distance to question how the activity at hand is to be understood, still we must step close enough that no one interpretation satisfies.

Stephen J. Smith

The task is to silence the ready interpretation, and then within this silenc-
ing, encounter things (like slippery slides) with children in mind. The
matter of silence in understanding children's activity is not, therefore,
simply the inaccessibility of the child's experience but rather the meaning
of that which matters both to children and to us as observers of children,
or participants with them. The matter of silence is, on the far side, the
otherness that is evident in our inability to fully account for the child's
activity, and on the near side, the concealedness of that which is the
motive for our interest in the playground. As Bollnow (1974) says: 'we
realize we are on the right track when the subject-matter resists our
interpretation, when it remains independent of our expectations and
forces us to correct our original starting point again and again' (p. 11).
This is what I mean by the farther side of silence. The near side attests to
our complicity in the actions of children. In other words, we identify
ourselves when 'reading' movement texts for this 'reading' is only possible because of a prior complicity in such child-like activity. Hence there
is a tension in our understanding children's activity pedagogically — a
tension of self and other which, because of a common interest, continually
questions the one-sidedness of my view of things. And this questioning,
to the extent that it discloses common ground, allows us to see how we
might be with children in an understanding way.

I think, for example, of four small girls on one of the tire swings at a
local playground. One is seated while the other three stand up by holding
on to the long chains attaching the tire to its supporting beam. Higher
and higher they swing. 'I'm scared', says the one seated on the tire. '*I'm
not scared*', responds one of the others hovering over her. It seems that
the first child is not to be taken literally, for in the next instant she gives a
squeal of delight and calls out 'higher! higher!' Meanwhile a third child,
finding the pitch of the swing a little too much, sits down to face the first
child. The extra space between the chains now allows for greater mobility
on the part of the two girls who remain standing on the tire. One reaches
out with her foot to touch the platform towards which the swing now
revolves. She misses. Next time she manages to make contact with it. On
the third attempt she finds the edge of the platform, and pushing against
it, sends the swing into a much wider orbit than before. 'Stop! I'm scared!'
pleads the girl who registered her fear only a short while ago. 'I want to
get off!' The swing slows down, and for the present the girls seem
content to sit on the tire and talk amongst themselves.

Their talk drifts away from this activity. They see a boy from their
school ride past. 'Jeffrey, Jeffrey', they call out, until the boy spots them
and then self-consciously proceeds upon his way. Inevitably, though,
their thoughts return to the tire swing. And now, as if rested enough, the
swing must once again be set in motion. But who shall they ask to give
them a push? Of course I am standing closeby watching my son Tyler on
the adjacent tire swing. I glance over at the group of girls, thinking they
might request my assistance. Instead, one of the girls calls for her older
sister, Lisa, to come and give them a push. She calls again, and again. It

seems strange to be standing only a pace or two away and yet not be asked. True, they don't know me very well. They have seen me before at the playground, but they don't recognize me as part of their activity. In a sense they don't see me. They only see Lisa who must leave the game she plays with her friends on the far side of the playground in order to give assistance to this little group on the swing. They see Lisa as she wanders over to them while muttering something about 'little brats that can't do anything for themselves'; yet they sense that hers is only a mock annoyance. Lisa is happy to come and help them.

It seems that Lisa is better disposed to give assistance. She knows what the children want. She understands what is required of her by these girls. Lisa is called from a distance, while I who am standing close by get ignored, because Lisa will know how much to push the swing. On the other hand, perhaps I might have offered my help. 'Can I give you a push?' I might have asked. Maybe such an offer would have been accepted; and yet the situation that would then unfold would differ, possibly dramatically, from the situation in which Lisa found herself. Would this adult know how hard to push? Would he know when to stop? In this regard, perhaps there is a time, not so much to mind one's business, but rather to view an activity in what Bollnow (1982) calls 'comprehending silence, a well-intentioned silence' (pp. 43–44). My reluctance to offer help until asked holds out the possibility of seeing the activity at hand even more clearly than Lisa can. In relation to the potential fearfulness of this activity on the swing, this 'well-intentioned silence' holds out the possibility of helping the child in a way that even Lisa is not yet able to understand.

Reminiscence

Here we have an active questioning of what matters to these children. As we watch Lisa push them on the swing we can remember how to play on swings ourselves. We recall the effort of getting the swing started, how far back we must lean in order to thrust the seat forwards, how, by standing on the wooden seat an even greater thrust is possible, and how after a while it seems safer to sit down again. Someone starts pushing us and we go even higher — too high! The supports seem to move in the ground. At the peak of the swing we feel the chains go slack and we drop into a downward arc. Will the swing break? Will we do a complete loop over the bar at the top? Stop pushing, we want to get off!

We see 'the child within us as a way to the child before us' (Lippitz, 1986, p. 58). That which is remembered is not so much the child we once were as the child who stands before us. Our memories of being pushed on swings are caught within an interest in what Lisa is doing with these children on this tire swing — just as our memories of the playground enable us to relate to the following example.

She felt the accuracy with which he caught her, exactly at the right moment, and the exactly proportionate strength of his thrust, and she was afraid. Down in her bowels went the hot wave of fear. She was in his hands. Again, firm and inevitable came the thrust at the right moment. She gripped the rope, almost swooning.

'Ha!' she laughed in fear. 'No higher.'

'But you're not a bit high', he remonstrated.

'But no higher'.

He heard the fear in her voice, and desisted. Her heart melted in hot pain when the moment came for him to thrust her forward again. But he left her alone. She began to breathe.

'Won't you really go any farther?' he asked. 'Should I keep you there?'

'No, let me go by myself', she answered.

He moved aside and watched her.

'Why, you're scarcely moving', he said.

She laughed slightly with shame, and in a moment got down. (Lawrence, 1913/1981, pp. 200 and 201)

There is an empathic quality to such situations. And it registers with what Barritt, Beekman, Bleeker and Mulderij (1985) say is the purpose of educational research, which is to understand situations 'from the point of view of those living through them' (p. 84). In reference to the game of 'Hide and Seek' they ask: 'Is there anyone who does not recognize this experience? Who has either played this game or watched it being played' (*ibid*, p. 143). And who in watching it does not feel the urge to become part of the situation?

Reminiscence can be an occasion for nostalgia and sentimentality; it can also bring us in touch with the present and help us to appreciate what children in front of us are up to. Says Casey (1987) in his phenomenological study of remembering, reminiscence is 'social in origin and operation'; it is 'remembering *with others*' (p. 105). Through reminiscence we recall past events in the company of others, but in doing so we also set the stage for seeing the continuity of our experiences into the present.

Look around with the eyes of your own childhood. Visit the places where you lived as a child . . .

Here is the steep bank from which you first jumped, so that you would not be called a coward. This steep bank did not give you any peace for a long time. You dreamt about it. And even now you look at other small children that are romping around jumping . . . you look and you are filled with excitement, mixed with sorrow, for the childhood years that have irrevocably gone into the past. (Azarov, 1981/83, p. 26)

Look closer still. Attend to the children who can be seen jumping from this embankment. Look at their faces. Hear how they taunt each other. Very soon nostalgia gives way to our own excitement over the quality of *these* children's experiences.

Good Memories

Perhaps we do not even need to try to recall the past ourselves. All we need do is watch a child like Lisa pushing children on a tire swing for certain memories to stir in us of being pushed ourselves. But let us not be content to dwell upon these memories; let us watch how Lisa pushes the swing, how she stands, how she moves to catch the tire and then propels it forward. Let us watch while at the same time we push a child on an adjacent swing. Here we can be drawn fully into the situation, hearing the melody of the past with our hands upon the tire. Our remembering is at this point a kind of 'body memory'. We draw upon 'the body as a memorial container — as itself a "place" of memories — (as that which) furnishes an unmediated access to the remembered past' (Casey, 1987, p. 179).

I think of Tyler who likes to lie on the swings on his stomach. Each time we go to the playground he resists my suggestion that he sit on the swing and let me push him; instead, he takes hold of the seat, pushes it forwards until it rises up to his chest, then he jumps onto it. Too big a jump and he will tip over, too small a jump and he will fall underneath it. It is amusing to watch as he holds tightly to the seat, balancing there, letting himself glide to and fro. Nevertheless, it is not totally satisfying to feel so distant from his swinging. I would like to show him how to really use the swing, not that there is anything wrong with how he is already using it, nor can there be any doubting the pleasure he gains from his preferred position; yet, to sit on the swing going higher and higher — then he would really know what swinging is all about. So I wait. I wait until some time later he sits on the swing of his own volition and asks: 'Can you push me?' I comply with his request, being careful at first not to betray his trust. But I am soon caught up in the activity, remembering the joy this brought me as a child, yet hearing also the excitement at this moment in Tyler's voice, an excitement that cancels out all the swings that made me feel nauseous and all the swings I fell off. Before too long he will want to swing himself, but for the moment it is good to be pushed higher and higher than he has been before.

Through such encounters we can bring back childhood memories, not only to better understand the child but also to deepen our own view of things. As Barritt *et al* (1985) suggest,

> We think that recollections of past experience are a legitimate, and sometimes the only source of information about important events. We believe that these recollections should be used with

the acknowledgment that they are not exactly the same as the original experience. They are not unrelated to it. If the researcher places recollections in the context of the informants' present situation both can be better understood. (p. 66)

These recollections of the playground make us sensitive to the situation of Lisa being called over to lend a hand, sensitive, that is, to what seems best for these children. Just as we remember what it is like to be pushed too hard, so can we now appreciate the children's reluctance to ask us to push their swing; and yet it is this memory which discloses what is best for children, whether it be our silent watching or our offering help. Here we have the advantage over Lisa — the advantage of a maturity which allows us to ask: What is best for these children? You see, imbedded in these memories is a sense of the good of playground activity. In spite of being pushed too high at times, in spite of being fearful and afraid, still we retain a sense of the enjoyment of swinging and a feeling for the good of it. Perhaps it would not be too out of hand to refer to the words of Dostoevsky who, through Alyosha Karamazov, said:

> You must know that there is nothing higher and stronger and more wholesome and good for life in the future than some good memory, especially a memory of childhood, of home (and dare I add, the playground). People talk to you a great deal about your education, but some good, sacred memory, preserved from childhood, is perhaps the best education. (Dostoevsky, 1912, p. 819)

Accordingly, what makes the situation of Lisa and the children on the tire swing so interesting is that it appeals to us as a 'good memory' of childhood. Through Lisa's presence we can question how these children might learn best how to enjoy the activity. In fact we can question even Lisa's ability to help them. And in this questioning, which is much more ours than Lisa's, we can be drawn into the situation in an adult sort of way. Watching Lisa push the swing is not mere recollection, since the question that gave moment for pause — the question of how these children should be helped — is not a remembered one, but rather it is a question of how we, as adults, should help these children on the swing. The remembered experience is more a 'standing-with-oneself, a self-identification with oneself, a process not of introspection but of self-becoming in the action itself' (Bollnow, 1974, p. 17).

Adult recollection signifies on the one hand an attempt to address the child's view of things, and on the other hand the inevitable distance separating adult and child yet a distance that lends significance to what the child does. Marleau-Ponty wrote: 'Do we have the right to comprehend the time, the space of the child as an undifferentiation of our time, of our space, etc . . .? This is to reduce the child's experience to our own, at the very moment one is trying to respect the phenomena' (Merleau-Ponty, 1968, p. 203). As soon as we face the child, his or her experience is in danger of being reduced to our own. Our task is to question this reduction, not to contribute to it, yet to be mindful that whatever we do with children is inevitably a mediation of their experience. Our presence is of itself mediational. Meyer-Drawe (1986) says in reference to the task Merleau-Ponty has laid before us, 'We can only thematize childlike possibilities as specific deviations (of our adult conceptions), and this means that we cannot avoid implicating our own point of view' (p. 50). We are there with the child on the playground. With Lisa we can 'thematize childlike possibilities' which belong neither wholly to them nor to us.

The point we should consider, however, is whether this standing vis-a-vis the child, this methodology of pedagogical understanding, implies a distortion of the child's experience. For Meyer-Drawe the test lies in our capability to be surprised. For me, I would prefer to stay with the notion of silence to the extent that surprise also ushers in silence. Thus we ought to take pains to listen carefully to what the child is saying. We should be silent, if only for a moment, as we try to work out more fully what is the best thing to do for the child who is now before us. And in working out what is best for this child, what can be better than attempting to define this present activity as the stuff of good memories. Such a procedure, I believe, stands a good chance of 'respecting the child's experience', of 'thinking it positively', and thus of seeing its pedagogic significance.

The Domain of Physical Education

What has this concentration on the informal physical activities of young children got to do with the more substantive field of physical education, with games and sports, with dance, gymnastics and aquatics, and with outdoor pursuits? What have experiences with young children in fairly ordinary contexts of physical activity got to do with more formalized and sequenced learning experiences which comprise school physical education programs? Of course we could also turn the question around and ask: what have school physical education curricula really got to do with the memorable physical experiences of childhood? The answer, I believe, lies in the degree to which we can now look at what happens in school physical education programs and see the child more clearly.

Through the examples I have used I hope we might see a connection between the school physical education curriculum and the concrete experiences through which children first come to appreciate physical activity done for its own sake. After all, the playground, from which I have drawn my examples, is not too far distant from the sportsfield, gymnasium or swimming pool; and the pedagogy that is disclosed in our dealings with young children on playgrounds does provide a basis for our thinking about how to teach children in these more formal contexts. By observing closely the nature of children's interactions on the playground we may even see that a good deal of physical education occurs prior to the direct influence of adults. For instance, young children will often look to one another for guidance in how certain activities should be done. They learn from each other how a swing can be manipulated in different directions, how a slippery slide can be made challenging long after the initial satisfaction of sliding down has dissipated, how one can go over, through, around and even stand up on a set of climbing bars. They learn the fundamental actions of climbing, swinging, jumping, leaping and landing (those same actions we want to work on in the gymnasium) by taking their cue from other children on the playground.

As we look more closely at how these physical accomplishments develop we note particular kinds of interactions between children. Often the children will dare each other to try some new activity. There may be a taunt with a malicious tone to it, or there may simply be an entice-ment to try an activity in which other children are already engaged. It depends very much upon who offers the dare — whether it just happens to be another child who is in the vicinity, whether it is someone who is perceived as either a friend or foe, whether it is an older brother or sister, and so on. We note, as well, the recipient of this attention: the timid child, the cautious child, or the child who appears to be a daredevil. We observe how each child responds differently to the words of those around him or her. The question then arises regarding how particular children should be dared, challenged and encouraged, and how each child can be helped to become more thoughtful in that which he or she attempts to do. By considering these different interactions among children we may indeed be in a position to discern the interactional qualities that constitute both a good pedagogy of the playground and a deepened sense of what it means to educate children physically from the playground up.

On this basis, there might be a turn in the teaching of physical education towards an appreciation of 'everyday life concepts' (Hilde-brandt, 1987, p. 17). For instance, the 'skill talk' that has for such a long time legitimated what happens in physical education and which has come under increasing attack from educators at large (for example, Barrow, 1987; Hart, 1978) may be found to hinder the appreciation of a movement language that does resonate with the experiences of children. Here I contend that a 'physical skill' is constituted when we think of children's activity too mechanically, and ignore the experiences which give what children are able to do the appearance of technical proficiency. The language of 'skill' — open and closed skills, psychomotor skill levels, locomotor, non-locomotor and manipulative skills — does not reflect the feelings of reciprocity, familiarity, coexistence and identification which at times characterize a deeply physical experience of the world. Consider, in this regard, a young child bouncing a ball against a wall. Through the actions of sending and receiving (which already suggests a different context of meaning from 'throwing' and 'catching') the child first gains a bodily knowledge of his or her connectedness to the world (see Froebel, 1895, pp. 37 and 38). Or think of older children engaged in a playground game, possibly even a formalized game of soccer or basketball. These children exhibit skills of passing and catching, yet were we to watch them closely we would see that it matters to whom the ball is passed or not passed (and especially to those on the same side); it matters who holds the ball and for how long; and it matters how the ball is thrown, not as judged against some external criterion, but as a function of the children's intensity of activity. The skills of 'passing' and 'receiving', which look different depending upon the game in question, signify in the first instance children's relations to each other and to their collective sense of the playworld. These 'skills' are simply adult shorthand expressions for a language of movement which children themselves articulate in their gestures. Too often such adult movement terminology adulterates a child-oriented language which may potentially give us a better sense of the meaning of young children's physical activity and of the continuity of their physical explorations from the playground to the gymnasium.

A greater pedagogical attentiveness would reveal the 'tricks' that become the focal point of young children's activity. We would see how 'tricks' are learned and how they impinge upon a child's own sense of physical accomplishment. Also, the 'taking of turns' would be seen as much more than an organizational matter. To 'have a turn' is, for the children, an opportunity to put 'into practice' the 'tricks' which they want to learn how to do. Turn-taking is how the children learn from each other how to become physically proficient on the playground. Accordingly, by attending closely to the quality of children's playground experiences we may appreciate how far removed the language of 'skill acquisition' is from the language of the playground. The former can be shown to leave out of account the nature of children's interactions and the sort of peer-group pedagogy that we can discern from their actions. The children's own language of physical competence, the 'tricks' they show one another and the 'turn-taking' that allows them to practice in a very thoughtful way together, should become the focus of our pedagogical inquiries. In place of a technical language of skill development I think we can develop a far more child-oriented conceptualization of how physical competence can be taught (cf. Smith, 1989b).

In this regard I think the language of 'movement education' has been a step in the young child's direction, however any talk of 'what the body does', 'where the body moves', 'how the body moves', and 'what it moves in relation to', still falls short of conveying the child's own sense of how physical competence develops. In fact, the 'movement education' concepts pertaining to space, time, flow and relationship, seem disproportionately placed on the side of adult reasoning . What is needed are everyday life concepts which respect what the child can presently do and yet still link these actions to an adult's sense of what the child might go on to achieve. We need to draw from our observations of children a more inclusive conceptualization of physical education.

Mention should be made at this point of some efforts in this pedagogical direction. Hellison's (1978 and 1985) 'developmental levels' of social responsibility, while not framed as everyday life concepts, have been derived from action research drawing upon his experiences of working with a particular sector of youth. Also, the 'developmental themes' outlined by Hoffman, Young and Klesius (1981) as a structure for physical education programs provide an orientation of sorts to the experiences of children. But for specific research examples of a phenomenological orientation to the lifeworld of physical education which have developed everyday life concepts, I mention Wessinger's (1990) study of the dynamics of physical education games, Connelly's (1990) more encompassing study of how children express a sense of physical accomplishment, and my own work which has been an attempt to develop a child-oriented language of physical education by attending to children's perceptions of the riskness of playground activities (Smith, 1987, 1988 and 1989a).

A Research Agenda

A second hoped-for outcome of this discussion, and the outcome with which I have been most concerned in this chapter, is that from our using a language which tries to keep the child in view we might become more appreciative of those principles which sustain pedagogical research in physical education. In other words, there is a methodology at work in our pedagogical inquiries which has less to do with techniques and procedures and much more to do with the responsibility we have for children's lives and the empathic understanding through which we can remember what is the best thing to do for this child at this particular place and time.

My contention is that we too often ignore the fact that pedagogical understanding is a normative affair, which is to say, that it has to do with studying the right and wrong ways of bringing up children. Pedagogical research, as distinct from psychological, sociological, anthropological, and other detached research stances, carries this very practical ethic. It has to do with articulating the dimensions of those situations in which we already find ourselves responsible for the course of children's activity. Our particular task as pedagogical researchers of physical activity is, however, to see how we might pursue our separate areas of concern in ethically rigorous and methodical ways. We want to study the curriculum of physical education and the didactics of educating physically with a sense of purpose which obliges us to make our methodological assumptions quite explicit and methods of inquiry self-evident. Accordingly, what I am saying is that as we feel ourselves becoming caught up in our research procedures, strategies and techniques, we must continue to keep in mind the normative questions that arise and lend significance to any of our findings.

Our research ought to oblige us to say in what sense we can first look for the child, and then having found him or her, in what sense we are in a position to observe the significance of what it is that the child is doing. It should require an explication of our relation to the child, the child's own relation to his or her world, and a sense of how the child might be brought out of his or her world into the world of responsible adulthood (Langeveld, 1966, p. 97). In so doing, it should raise questions of self-reflection with respect to how we can be in a position to observe the significance of what the child can potentially achieve. For instance, what does it mean for us personally to observe children? Must we settle for the research definitions which have determined many of our inquiries to date? Or might we strive for a research mode of observing children which keeps particular children in view? Can we then justify our research agenda? Can we show that our observations are grounded in some deep and reverent understanding of what it means to be a child and what the good is of being a child? Such questions as these seem to me to disclose the real significance of our pedagogical inquiries. They are questions for remembering children, being mindful of them, and reflecting upon how we might develop their physical competence in ways that are fundamentally in their best interests.

Starting Points

Let me now give some further examples of this type of pedagogical inquiry in physical education. An exercise my undergraduate students undertake as part of a 'designs for learning in physical education' course involves the recollection of a physical activity experience from childhood and the description of this recollection in as much narrative detail as possible. This exercise is intended to be a way of capturing the sense of a pedagogical research question in the realm of physical education. Students are then required to analyze, using phenomenological methods, the meaning of their recollection. Their task is to link their own sense of the significance of physical activity to the diverse situations in which they presently find themselves teaching physical education.

Some students write about gaining confidence and of finding success in physical activity. For instance, Christine relates an episode from her days of swimming competitively.

> Oh Darn! There's the whistle. That means I have to step onto the starting block and in less then fifteen seconds the race, and the pain, will have started. I hate swimming the 200 metre breaststroke; it hurts so much, way more than any other event. Why does this event have to be the one I'm best at? I wish I'd gone slower this morning, then I wouldn't have to swim it all over again in the finals. Everybody here is so fast. What am I doing here? STOP IT!!! I'm being too negative. If Marg knew what I was thinking she would be disgusted. I'm supposed to be psyching myself up. All right, I can do it . . . I can go faster than this morning . . . Marg thinks I can knock two seconds off this morning's time . . . It's only four lengths . . . It will be all over in three minutes . . . Just go for it . . . Do it . . . Do it . . . Arrrrrggg!!!

Second whistle . . . 'Take You're Marks' . . . BANG!

All right! Good start, now keep going, not too fast, stretch it out. This is only the first length, I don't want to burn myself out in the first length. I'm starting to get tired, maybe I should slow down. NO! Keep going. Here comes the first turn . . . Touch . . . Turn . . . Stretch . . . Underwater pull . . . Only three more lengths. Why does this have to be a 50 metre pool, the other end is so far away — I can't even see it. I'm really starting to hurt now, I wish this was my last length.

I hear Marg, 'GO . . . GO . . . GO . . .'.

'Yah, Yah! I hear you. I'm going as fast as I can.' Marg always starts cheering when we start looking tired. Good, here comes the second turn — I'm half way. Third length . . . This is when Marg told me to pick it up. My arms and legs are killing me — how can I possibly pick it up?

What was that? It sounds like Ron's voice. Is Ron really cheering for me. He's the Head Coach of the whole swim club. I don't think he even knows who I am.

'GO . . . GO CHRIS . . . GO . . .'

He is cheering for me! I've got to go faster. Ron coaches all the fastest people on the team, he doesn't want to see someone go slow. Push . . . Go . . . Last turn — only one length left. I don't hear Marg anymore, her voice has blended in with the rest of the screaming parents and shouting swimmers in the crowd. But not Ron's — I can hear every word! He's still watching, don't let him down. Keep stretching . . . Squeeze your arms . . . Extend . . . Push . . . Go!

Here comes the wall, stretch for it . . . and touch! What is my time? Look at the scoreboard — 2:53.59!!! That can't be right, my best time is 2:58. The clock must have screwed up. I look over at Marg — she's got her arms in the air and she's yelling. 'Way to go Chris . . . You made it! That IS my time, ALRIGHT! I qualified for Western Nationals!

I ran over to Marg. For some reason I didn't hurt anymore. She hugged me and got all wet. 'Excellent swim!' she said. Then Ron walked over to us. 'Congratulations Chris, it looks like you're coming to Winnipeg with us', he said. Then he patted me on the shoulder just like he did to his older, faster swimmers. I smiled at Marg and she winked at me. The 200 metre breast-stroke is my favorite event.

Christine goes on to write of the influence that others can have on children's physical accomplishments. She writes of confidence, not simply as something that is acquired or built up, but more fundamentally as experiences of being praised, encouraged, cajoled, challenged, and at times, dared. A real sense of physical competence presupposes a confidence that is held between children and those they look up to.

Others have written of making the team, playing on the team, or being cut from the team. Their recollections provide insight into what makes a team and what makes playing on a team important. Margaret gives the following account.

I stand out in centrefield trying to remember what Roger, our coach, spoke to me about at the end of yesterday's practice. 'We need you out in centrefield. You've got the big arm. You're our last line of defense. You're responsible for every ball that goes into the outfield. You have to be there to cover left and right field, as well as anything that is hit down the middle.' It's a big responsibility, but still, it's hard not to think of going from short-stop to centrefield as a demotion.

Centre-field, how boring! Practices are the worst! I stand out here by myself watching the infield play. The left fielder and right fielder are too far away from me to carry on a good conversation, but sometimes we shout jokes at each other. Nancy is out in left field. She's funny. She is always showing me her latest disco move. I bet she is a good dancer, her moves look pretty cool. The only time I get to touch the ball is when I cover up mistakes the infielders make.

Every once in a while Roger will hit each of us fielders a fly. If he catches us not paying attention he will smash one over our heads and shout 'Stay awake out there!' He does this to me and I dutifully run to the fence, pick up the ball and throw it back in for the infielders to play with. Before I can stop myself I have winged a perfect throw into the catcher. 'Atta girl, Marg!' Roger shouts. I smile inside with pride. Then I remember where I am standing. Marg you fool! Why did you do that! You should have flubbed the throw. That's it. I am doomed to spend my softball career out with the dandelions!

Maybe Maxine will blow it at shortstop. No, look at her zip the ball around — she's right on for today's game. That's the thing with Maxine, she is either hot or cold. When she's hot she can make a diving catch and throw out the runner while still kneeling. When she's cold, she'll make four errors in a row. At these times we all silently pray the ball will just be hit somewhere else, so one of us can make the out. During these frigid moments, Roger usually calls time, to talk with Maxine and settle down his precious infield. Sometimes Maxine won't even join the meeting at the mound or if she does, she walks away early, head down kicking at imaginary clumps of dirt. I wonder why he doesn't pull her? Why doesn't he put me there? At least I'm consistent. Or why doesn't he put Shelley there? She would be great. Shelley has a super arm and a nice even temperament. Then I hear Maxine's mom cheering from her usual spot in the dugout with the scorebook tucked under her arm, (she is our official scorekeeper and takes the job very seriously), 'Come on girls we've got two out. The next one is ours.' Roger says in his no nonsense voice, 'Two in the bucket, girls — shake it up out there!'

I used to wonder what was said during these little infield meetings. I asked my friend Leigh, who plays first base, what goes on. She says all Roger does is tell a joke. When we go to the dugout Leigh always repeats the joke for me. They are always sick. I think Rog has a hard time coming up with material for 13-year-olds. I wonder why Roger never calls a meeting out in centrefield for us? I imagine a big hitter stepping up to the plate with bases loaded. Roger urgently calls time to the umpire. The umpire responds immediately, shouting time with one arm out-stretched, taking off his mask and stepping away from the plate. Roger jogs confidently out to centrefield waving us together. We form a close circle making sure the runners from the other team can't see or overhear anything. The infielders remain in their positions and mill about wondering what secret instructions Roger is giving us. Alas, this never happens. All he ever does during a game is yell our name and wave at us to move over a few steps one way or the other, depending on where that particu-lar batter usually hits. Sigh . . .

Margaret points out the danger in competitive sports that coaches and teachers may get so caught up in their own sense of techniques and skills that they take away the basis of sports enjoyment for the child. Her recol-lection even suggests ways that an adult conceptualization of team play can be more child-oriented. From this starting point she begins to expli-cate those characteristics of children's group play that might be preserved and further developed as children become inducted into more formal, technical, adult, play forms.

Now contrast her recollection with the following situation and see what pedagogic message might be gained.

It had been raining all night, leaving the grass glistening and the air fresh and inviting. Only yesterday, Dad and I had trampled the backyard lawn mercilessly in our joint quest to excel and succeed.

'That was a great pitch Els!'

'Thanks Dad, but it wasn't in the right place.'

'But it was smokin' Kiddo! Aim right in here!' Dad smacked his fist into his worn old catcher's mitt with encouraging empha-sis, and held the mitt low, next to his right knee. Wiggling my toes about in my old soccer cleats, wrapped in hockey tape about my right pitching toe, now ragged and wet from dragging it through the wet grass; I settled my feet firmly upon the muddy plywood pitching rubber. Concentrating on the seams of the softball and staring at Dad's glove that hypnotically beckoned my throw, I released the pitch. It didn't matter that perhaps my pitch was over Dad's head.

Again I laughed with Dad as I tucked my long braid under Dad's Red Sox ball cap which he always let me wear when we practised. Dad smacked his glove and shifted his body about so as not to have me throwing at the basement window, twice broken last month by what Dad called 'untamed pitches'. Turning the Wilson ball about in my right hand, so as to get my fingers in the right position on the seams, and digging my right foot into the pitching hole, I began my windup. Hands together lifted high above my head, right arm, hand and ball swing quickly down and back up behind my head, and back down and around to my right hip, where my wrist snaps the ball out of my hand.

The pitch lands in Dad's glove, perfectly, right above his right shoulder. 'Strike three! You're out!' Dad yells.

Contained within this situation are some messages, not just about desirable parental behavior, but also about how a pedagogic relation is made possible. Elsie's recollection indicates something of the 'tone' of teaching (van Manen, 1986) by alluding to the emotional and affective conditions for effective teaching. But rather than seeing such conditions as separable from teacher-learner behavior, her recollection draws us into a consideration of the 'pedagogic atmosphere' as a composite of 'all those fundamental emotional conditions and sentient human qualities that exist between the educator and the child and which form the basis for every pedagogical relationship' (Bollnow, 1989, p. 5; see also, Vandenberg, 1975).

Other students have written of even less structured physical activities and of the play forms that exist beyond conventional physical activity programs. Catherine tells us of an after-school experience.

We arrived at the fence circling the baseball diamond. Running at the last in our excitement, half thinking that someone might decide to stop us, nervous at the thought that we might be caught, we rejoiced in the risk we were about to take.

In order to get your balance you had to hoist yourself into a kneeling position in one corner of the wooden fence. Then, carefully placing the toe of your runner onto the 2 by 4 used to hold the fence together, you could lift up to a crouched position by holding on to the top of the painted boards with the tips of your fingers. After that it was a matter of slowly rising to full height, trusting your ability to balance motionless on the ball of one foot before carefully placing the other foot beside it on the supporting 2 × 4.

How high it seemed from the ground! The fence trembled under our weight and the task of maintaining balance on the top of the fence increased in difficulty as the others gained their respective positions along it.

Some shuffled along, placing one foot on top of the uprights while sliding the other cautiously along the supporting 2 × 4. Others, more daring or experienced, placed one foot directly in front of the other taking 'baby' steps with arms outstretched at their sides to help them balance.

From time to time the distance from the ground seemed enormous. You would inhale sharply in sudden panic or stop frozen on the fence. Then, as if sensing an ability to control your own body and your own fears, you could lift your head and continue at an increased pace.

The game ended, sometimes when a brother or sister called us in to dinner, sometimes when the farthest and least stable corner was reached, but never as a result of a sudden shaky topple. These awkward descents were never left unchallenged nor unbested. The game was immediately taken up once again.

Catherine asks: How can we as physical educators ensure that children's physical education experiences resemble more closely their experiences during undirected play? Here she is not discounting the significance of adult intervention, for even unstructured play is often conditional upon an adult decision to leave the children be for the moment; on the contrary, her recollection lends itself to an understanding of how the exploratory qualities of unstructured play can be maximized within the context of adult-guided physical activities.

Needless to say, not all the writings vindicate the current practices of physical education (and many of them, like the examples above, are not specifically about what we would normally consider to be a physical education lesson). The students' writings are often about less fortunate physical experiences such as being discouraged in their attempts to come to terms with some activity or experiencing particular fears through their sudden exposure to risky physical education activities. And when they do recall physical education experiences, often they find that what they did in the lesson education runs counter to the implicit pedagogics of those physical activities they might have contrived for themselves. Yet, even the most negative recollection makes a statement with respect to how physical activity might be taught.

The recollections of these students, by the very fact that they are about children's experiences of physical activity, serve to make sense of present courses of pedagogic action. In this regard, it is no accident that certain instances are remembered and not others; in fact, one tends to be most mindful of those past events that provide some sort of interpretation of why one presently acts the way one does. Leman and Carlson (1989) refer to this as the 'Law of Creative Consistency'. In their words, 'people remember only those events from early childhood that are consistent with their present view of themselves and the world around them' (p. 14). But recollections do not simply provide explanations of present conduct; instead, they lend personal meaning to one's actions. Their articulation and subsequent questioning provide, moreover, a basis for assessing the significance of what we do and how we choose to do it. For physical educators, recollections of physical activity bring to mind those formative experiences which enable them to see physical education as a meaningful subject and which expand their sense of what it means to teach physical education well. Recollected childhood experiences provide, in other words, a sense of what should constitute good physical activity experiences for children.

Such recollective accounts are, however, only one kind of starting point when adopting a phenomenological orientation to the lifeworld of physical education. And perhaps it might even be objected that starting here leads to too much introspection, too much nostalgia and naivety with respect to the conditions of children's present lives, too much self and too little world. The advantages of this recollective starting point have mainly to do with the fact that the kind of observation of children which I have talked about earlier in the chapter as orienting us to the lifeworld may not come so easily to those who are still in the business of learning teaching roles and behaviours. On the other hand, for adults who are experienced in being with children one may start by talking to children about their experiences (Barritt *et al*, 1985), developing anecdotal reports while watching children at play (Paley, 1986), or even by going to literary sources and that great pedagogical repository, children's literature. Graduate students who are already comfortable being with children can certainly begin with these more empirical observational procedures (see van Maanan, 1990).

Phenomenological Description

The task of phenomenological description is to ascertain the meaning of those situations that confront us and resonate with our own sense of how things might be. Anecdotes of childhood experience, whether recollective stories or narrative renderings of observed activity, thus become an important means of deliberating on the point of the concrete situation to which they refer. Anecdotes serve to keep the child in view while obliging us to reflect upon not only what a situation once held for onself, but what similar situations might hold for other children. In other words, anecdotes stand between the particularity of once being a child and the more general truth, or the pedagogical theory, which we wish to formulate on the basis of our reflective capacity. It could therefore be said that anecodotes provide a method of phenomenological orientation to the lifeworld of physical education. They are the methodological devices for providing points of attachment, lifeworld attachments, for the somewhat abstract pedagogical theorizing by means of which we give structure to our deliberations on the significance of children's physical activity.

The use of anecdote conforms to the guidelines for lifeworld description which van Maanan (1984, 1989 and 1990) has developed. Here emphasis is placed on writing as the *modus operandi* of the research endeavour. 'Writing is our measure', says van Maanan (1989, p. 188).

> Writing involves a textual reflection in the sense of separating and confronting ourselves with what we know, distancing ourselves from the lifeworld, decontextualizing our thoughtful preoccupations from immediate action, abstracting and objectifying our lived understandings from our concrete involvements . . . and all this for the sake of now reuniting us with what we know, drawing us more closely to living relations and situations of the lifeworld, turning thought to a more thoughtful praxis, and concretizing and subjectifying our deepened understanding in practical action. (*ibid.*, 124)

A text of physical activity results from our writing about remembered experience — a text which suggests how we might see ourselves in the present actions of children. In other words, the anecdotal quality of recollected experience situates us within a 'dialogic textuality' (van Maanan, 1986, p. 90) of physical activity.

The particular application of anecdotal writing to the topic at hand is something that unfolds as each study progresses. Besides, method should not be discussed totally apart from the pedagogical questions and issues we want to raise. At a technical level, such a division of method and substance tends to result in a reconstructed logic of the investigation which, as Soltis (1984) has cautioned, bears little resemblance to the actual conduct of the inquiry. At a phenomenological level, method is as much a way of speaking about our orientation, commitment, and presence of mind as it is about procedures by which we come to understand what children do.

Instead of methods (in the sense of procedures and techniques), perhaps we should speak first of all of steps that might be taken. Barritt *et al* (1985) even suggest attending to what they have done as a guide to undertaking work one might have in mind. Likewise, van Maanan expressed concern when his earlier methodological piece (van Maanan, 1984) was followed too literally, and subsequently he extended this guide into a text of research possibilities (van Manen, 1990). We should also keep in mind that the earlier writers of the 'Utrecht School' wrote very little on method, expecting that phenomenological proficiency would come through a kind of theoretical apprenticeship. There are, nevertheless, some common steps to phenomenological inquiry which have been laid down. As well as the works I have just mentioned, one might look at Giorgi (1985), Spiegelberg (1978), Merleau-Ponty's (1962) wonderful preface to the *Phenomenology of Perception*, as well as the methodological pieces that are published in the North American journal, *Phenomenology and Pedagogy*. One might also seek guidance in the exemplary descriptions contained within the writings of Heidegger, Merleau-Ponty, Sartre, Ricoeur, even Barthes and Levinas, and more particularly, in the translations for key writings by Langeveld, Buytendijk, Bollnow, Luijpen and Beekman.

But in searching for methodological guidance, it is wise to keep in mind Van den Berg's comment that if 'phenomenology is a method; it could be called an attitude' (Van den Berg, 1972, p. 77). Phenomenology is an attitude of attentiveness to the things of immediate experience. For the pedagogically minded, it is an attentiveness to the things that matter to children, to that which brings us in touch with the experiences of children, and ultimately, to the good contained within such experience.

Conclusion

My intention in this chapter has been to describe an orientation to the lifeworld of physical education by calling upon the key tenets of phenomenological inquiry. These are: a suspension of theoretical pre-suppositions; a reflective interrogation of a mode of intentionality; and a description of essential experiential features. I have drawn these tenets from a certain tradition of phenomenological pedagogy (the 'Geisteswissenschaftliche Padagogik' or human-scientific-pedagogical tradition in Europe), taking particular illustrations from the 'Utrecht School' in The Netherlands. However, the general features of phenomenological investigation may still be discerned.

To begin with, the first section of this chapter on *orienting to the lifeworld* deals with the phenomenological 'epoche' — the bracketing of theoretical presuppositions that is necessary for us to begin to attend to what is given in experience. Although I define the point of entry into the phenomenological reduction in terms of a committed observation of children's physical activity, in order to truly observe what is happening to children we need to suspend belief in our observational systems and categories and put out of play the theoretical lenses through which we might presume to know what children are doing. The second section of this chapter, which describes the *grounds for being interested* in the lifeworld of physical education, may now be viewed as a discussion of the 'intentionality' of consciousness which characterizes a pedagogical interest in children's physical activity. Here I have considered the central tenet of phenomenology that we are always in some kind of relation to the world around us, but that the nature of this relatedness, this intentionality, is only retrospectively available to us. Then, in the third section, called *the domain of physical education*, mention is made of the 'essential structures' that begin to map out a domain of lifeworld concern and connect a phenomenological pedagogy of physical activity to a common sense of physical education practice. 'Essences', 'experiential themes', or as I have referred to them, 'everyday life concepts', are the findings of phenomenological inquiry and the terms of our pedagogical connectedness to the lifeworld.

The fourth section of the chapter contains suggestions as to how phenomenological inquiry can be undertaken in a programmatic way. My intention have been to provide some guidance as to how one might begin, and subsequently develop, a phenomenological study of the lifeworld of physical education, by giving the reader a feeling for the work rather than a set of procedures to follow. I realize it is a little presumptuous to call what I have done *a research agenda*; nevertheless, the illustrations provided, in conjunction with the other writings to which I refer in this and earlier sections, ought to suggest the potential impact that phenomenological inquiry can have upon our conceptualizations of physical education. Such work, as it becomes more methodologically sophisticated, points to the possibility of a lifeworld orientation that can enable us to define more clearly the scope and depth of a pedagogy of physical education.

Let me now say something about the relation of this phenomenological orientation to other research orientations which bear upon physical education. First of all, my overriding intent has been to explore in a relatively unfettered manner the implications for researching physical education that arise directly from an attentiveness to the lifeworld. Along the way I have implicitly contrasted aspects of a phenomenological orientation with the current orthodoxy in pedagogical research which bases understanding on systematic, objective, formalized and generally quantifiable, observation. The research orientation I have outlined hopefully provides a significant alternative to this orthodoxy which has come under increasing attack (see especially, Kirk, 1989; McKay, Gore and Kirk, 1990; Schempp, 1987; and Sparkes, 1989). Second, I suggest that the current move towards qualitative inquiry in physical education research (for example, Evans, 1987; Hellison, 1988; Locke, 1989) engenders a tolerance at least for phenomenological methods that appear similar to ethnography, grounded theory, ethnomethodology and other qualitative designs. But it should be kept in mind that the phenomenological orientation I have outlined is imbedded in a scholarly tradition that begins with Husserl, Heidegger and Merleau-Ponty, and then finds pedagogical articulation in the work of Langeveld and the 'Utrecht School'. It is not simply a methodological variant of qualitative research. Third, in taking a phenomenological orientation I remain mindful of the importance of cultural and social critique. I see a need to guard against the naivety of some descriptive analyses and to incorporate in our attentiveness to the lifeworld a suspicion of romanticized descriptions. In this regard, a critical mindedness may well serve to frame one's interest in physical education practice (for example, Kirk and Tinning, 1990), however a good phenomenological study is one in which what is described carries within the description a moral sense of what ought to be. The description orients us to what is critical *within* lived experience.

Finally, we are only now coming to realize the extent to which phenomenological research is essentially a linguistic practice. Sparkes (1991) points out that all our researches are linguistically predicated in terms of 'tacit and explicit' rules governing 'what is said and what remains unsaid' (p. 111); however phenomenological research takes from this insight a methodological imperative. Unlike other forms of research where things are *written down* by way of reporting on events that have taken place, the things of the lifeworld are *written up* in phenomenological research in order to bring their truth into being. To say it another way, our research renders 'meaningful action as text' (Ricoeur, 1971) and in so doing we try to retain a sense of the possibilities that are prefigured in meaningfully lived activities. Methodologically speaking, we are obliged to adopt an animating, narratively rich, description of experience as the method of studying the lifeworld of physical education. But this need not imply that the kind of evocative prose that came out of the 'Utrecht School' should be the goal of all who orient themselves phenomenologically to the lifeworld. That would be too tall an order. Each of us must eventually develop a style of writing that attunes us to the lifeworld of physical education and allows us to catch hold of what it means to be situated there. 'Back to the things themselves', Husserl said over and over again. His admonition carries special force as we are drawn into postmodern discussions of the relativity of differing discourses and each seek to find ways of writing ourselves into a lifeworld that is our personal, pedagogical concern.

References

AZAROV, Y. (1981/83) *A Book About Bringing Up Children*. Moscow, Progress Publishers.

BARRITT, L., BEEKMAN, T., BLEEKER, H. and MULDERIJ, K. (1983) 'The world through children's eyes: Hide and seek and peekaboo', *Phenomenology and Pedagogy*, 1, 2, pp. 140–61.

BARRITT, L., BEEKMAN, T., BLEEKER, H. and MULDERIJ, K. (1985) *Researching Educational Practice*, Grand Forks, ND, University of North Dakota Press.

BARROW, R. (1987) 'Skill talk', *Journal of Philosophy of Education*, 21, 2, pp. 187–95.

BEEKMAN, T. (1983) 'Human science as a dialogue with children', *Phenomenology and Pedagogy*, 1, 1, pp. 36–44.

BEETS, N. (1952) *Verstanding en Onderscheid* (sections translated by Max van Manen) Amsterdam, Boom Meppel.

BOLLNOW, O.F. (1972) 'Existentialism's basic ethical position' in KOCKELMANS, J.J. (Ed) *Contemporary European Ethics*, New York, Doubleday.

BOLLNOW, O.F. (1974) 'The objectivity of the humanities and the essence of truth', *Philosophy Today*, 18, 1/4, pp. 3–18.

BOLLNOW, O.F. (1982) 'On silence — findings of philosophico-pedagogical anthropology', *Universitas*, 24, 1, pp. 41–7.

BOLLNOW, O.F. (1989) 'The pedagogical atmosphere', *Phenomenology and Pedagogy*, 7, pp. 5–76.

CASEY, E.S. (1987) *Remembering: A Phenomenological Study*, Bloomington, IN, Indiana University Press.

CONNELLY, M. (1990) 'Difficulty in physical activity', unpublished PhD dissertation, University of Alberta.

DOSTOEVSKY, F. (1912) *The Brothers Karamazov*, Kingswood, Windmill Press.

DOWLEY, E.M. (1969) 'Cues for observing children's behavior', *Childhood Education*, 45, 9, pp. 517–21.

EVANS, J. (1987) 'Teaching and learning in physical education: Towards a qualitative understanding', *Physical Education Review*, 10, 1, pp. 30–9.

EVERTSON, C.M. and GREEN, J.L. (1986) 'Observation as inquiry and method' in WITTROCK, M.C. (Ed) *Handbook of Research on Teaching* (3rd ed) New York, Macmillan, pp. 162–213.

FLITNER, A. (1982) 'Educational science and educational practice', *Education*, 25, pp. 64–75.

FROEBEL, F. (1985) *Pedagogics of the Kindergarten: Or His Ideas Concerning Play and Playthings of the Child*, London, D. Appleton.

GIORGI, A. (1985) 'Sketch of a phenomenological method', *Phenomenology and psychological research*, Pittsburgh, PA, Duquesne University Press.

HARRISON, J.M. (1987) 'A review of the research on teacher effectiveness and its implications for practice', *Quest*, 39, pp. 36–55.

HART, W.A. (1978) 'Against skills', *Oxford Review of Education*, 4, 2, pp. 205–16.

HEIDEGGER, M. (1962) *Being and Time*, London, Basil Blackwell.

HELLISON, D. (1978) *Beyond Bats and Balls: Alienated (and other) Youth in the Gym*, Washington, DC, AAHPER.

HELLISON, D. (1985) *Goals and Strategies for Teaching Physical Education*, Champaign, IL, Human Kinetics.

HELLISON, D. (1988) 'Our constructed reality: Some contributions of an alternative perspective to physical education pedagogy', *Quest*, 40, 1, pp. 84–91.

HILDEBRANDT, R. (1987) 'The changes of consciousness in the didactics of physical education', *International Journal of Physical Education*, 24, 3, pp. 13–17.

HOFFMAN, H.A., YOUNG, J. and KLESIUS, S.E. (1981) *Meaningful Movement for Children: A Developmental Theme Approach to Physical Education.* Boston, MA, Allyn and Bacon.

HUSSERL, E. (1970) *The Crisis of European Sciences and Transcendental Phenomenology*, Evanston, IL, Northwestern University Press.

KIRK, D. (1989) 'The orthodoxy of RT-PE and the research-practice gap: A critique and alternative view', *Journal of Teaching in Physical Education*, 8, 2, pp. 123–30.

KIRK, D. and TINNING, R. (1990) *Physical Education, Curriculum and Culture: Critical Issues in the Contemporary Crisis*, Lewes, Falmer Press.

LANGEVELD, M.J. (1966) *Some Recent Developments in Philosophy of Education in Europe.* Toronto, Ontario Institute for Studies in Education, pp. 81–114.

LAWRENCE, D.H. (1913/1981) *Sons and Lovers*, Harmondsworth, Penguin Books.

LEMAN, K. and CARLSON, R. (1989) *Unlocking the Secrets of Your Childhood Memories*, Nashville, TN, Thomas Nelson.

LIPPITZ, W. (1986) 'Understanding children, communicating with children: Approaches to the child within us, before us, and with us', *Phenomenology and Pedagogy*, 4, 3, pp. 56–65.

LOCKE, L. (1977) 'Research on teaching in physical education: New hope for a dismal science', *Quest*, 28, pp. 2–16.

LOCKE, L. (1989) 'Qualitative research as a form of scientific inquiry in sport and physical education', *Research Quarterly for Exercise and Sport*, 60, 1, pp. 1–20.

McKAY, J., GORE, J.M. and KIRK, D. (1990) 'Beyond the limits of technocratic physical education', *Quest*, 42, 1, pp. 52–76.

MERLEAU-PONTY, M. (1962) *Phenomenology of Perception*, London, Routledge and Kegan Paul.

MERLEAU-PONTY, M. (1968) *The Visible and the Invisible*, Evanston, IL, Northwestern University Press.

METZLER, M. (1989) 'A review of research on time in sport pedagogy', *Journal of Teaching in Physical Education*, 8, 2, pp. 87–103.

MEYER-DRAWE, K. (1986) 'Kaleidoscope of experiences: The capability to be surprised by children', *Phenomenology and Pedagogy*, 4, 3, pp. 48–55.

PALEY, V.G. (1986) 'On listening to what children say', *Harvard Educational Review*, 56, 2, pp. 122–31.

PLACEK, J. and LOCKE, L. (1986) 'Research on teaching physical education: New knowledge and cautious optimism', *Journal of Teacher Education*, 37, 4, pp. 24–8.

RICOEUR, P. (1971) 'The model of the text: Meaningful action as text', *Social Research*, 38, pp. 529–62.

SCHEMPP, P.G. (1987) 'Research on teaching physical education: Beyond the limits of natural science', *Journal of Teaching in Physical Education*, 6, 2, pp. 111–21.

SCHUTZ, A. and LUCKMANN, T. (1973) *The Structures of the Lifeworld*. Evanston, IL, Northwestern University Press.

SMITH, S.J. (1987) 'Seeing a risk', *Phenomenology and Pedagogy*, 5, 1, pp. 63–75.

SMITH, S.J. (1988) 'Risk and the playground', paper presented at the annual meeting of the American Educational Research Association, New Orleans, April. See also 'Can you push me? A pedagogy of risk-taking', in BERGUM, V. and ROSS, J. (Eds) *Through the Looking Glass*, Ottawa, Canadian Public Health Association.

SMITH, S.J. (1989a) 'Challenges of the playground', *Journal of Learning About Learning*, 1, 2, pp. 36–56.

SMITH, S.J. (1989b) 'Teaching children to take risks on the playground', paper presented at the 8th International Human Science Research Conference, University of Aarhus, Denmark, 18–22 August.

SOLTIS, J.F. (1984) 'On the nature of educational research', *Educational Researcher*, 13, 10, pp. 5–11.

SPARKES, A.C. (1989) 'Paradigmatic confusions and the evasion of critical issues in naturalistic research', *Journal of Teaching in Physical Education*, 8, 2, pp. 131–51.

SPARKES, A.C. (1991) 'Toward understanding, dialogue, and polyvocality in the research community: Extending the boundaries of the paradigms debate', *Journal of Teaching in Physical Education*, 10, pp. 103–33.

SPIEGELBERG, H. (1978) *The Phenomenological Movement*, The Hague, Martinus Nijhoff.

VAN DEN BERG, J.H. (1972) *A Different Existence*, Pittsburgh, PA, Duquesne University Press.

VANDENBERG, D. (1975) 'Openness: The pedagogic atmosphere' in NYBERG, D. (Ed) *The Philosophy of Open Education*, London, Routledge and Kegan Paul, pp. 35–57.

VAN MAANAN, M. (1978/79) 'An experiment in educational theorizing: The Utrecht School', *Interchange*, 10, 1, pp. 48–66.

VAN MAANAN, M. (1984) 'Practicing phenomenological writing', *Phenomenology and Pedagogy*, 2, 1, pp. 36–69.

VAN MAANAN, M. (1986) *The Tone of Teaching*, Richmond Hill, Ontario, Scholastic Publications.

VAN MAANAN, M. (1987) 'Human science and the study of pedagogy'. Unpublished manuscript, University of Alberta.

VAN MAANAN, M. (1989) 'By the light of anecdote', *Phenomenology and Pedagogy*, 7, pp. 232–53.

VAN MAANAN, M. (1990) *Researching Lived Experience: Human Science Pedagogy for an Action Sensitive Pedagogy* London, Ontario, Althouse Press, University of Western Ontario.

WESSINGER, N.P. (1990) '"I hit a homerun!": The shared meaning of "scoring" in games in physical education', paper presented at the 9th International Human Science Research Conference, University of Laval, Quebec, 9–13 June.

Chapter 3

Describing the Experience of Lesbian Physical Educators: A Phenomenological Study

Sherry E. Woods

Introduction

In 1977 Anita Bryant, spokesperson for the 'Save Our Children' organization, targeted one group to justify her efforts to repeal a county ordinance supporting homosexual rights. That group was gay and lesbian teachers. The 'Save Our Children' campaign (as the name itself suggests) triggered people's fear of homosexuality by portraying gays and lesbians as child molesters and proselytizers. By framing these stereotypes in the context of teaching, a profession historically linked to the religious and moral development of vulnerable young minds, Bryant's politically well-calculated crusade capitalized on the legal, religious and psychological stigma associated with homosexuality. This strategy touched the core of the controversy surrounding gay and lesbian teachers: the right of persons stigmatized as immoral to work in a profession rooted in morality.

The ongoing debate regarding the presence of homosexuals in teaching has lacked a critical perspective, that of gay and lesbian teachers. Homosexuals have always been present in the teaching profession, but they have been forced to remain silent and to hide their sexual orientation to avoid jeopardizing their jobs. This chapter explores the perspective of one particular group of homosexual educators: lesbian physical education teachers. Based on a phenomenological study, this chapter focusses on the contextual realities of lesbian physical educators. The intent is to paint a backdrop for understanding their concrete day-to-day experiences from a critical research perspective.

Historically, the teaching profession in the USA has been held to higher standards of conduct than other professions. In colonial times, the main charge of teachers was the religious and moral development of their students. As role models, they were expected to exemplify these teachings and to uphold the behavior standards set forth by their community. Consequently, those who taught were carefully scrutinized both in and outside the classroom; their lives were strictly regulated by community leaders. As public employees, teachers were expected to forego the personal freedoms enjoyed by others for the common good of society. Their function as role models in leading virtuous lifestyles took precedence over their rights as individuals (Harbeck, 1987).

Most of the restrictions placed on teachers' personal lives since colonial times are no longer applied today. Yet many communities have retained their authority to oversee certain aspects of teachers' lives. 'Moral turpitude' clauses in teachers' contracts cover a multitude of behaviors deemed unacceptable for teachers, including criminal behavior and other behavior that falls outside the moral norms of the community. These clauses maintain a community's right to scrutinize a teacher's personal life. In a society that legally stigmatizes homosexuals as 'criminals', religiously as 'sinners' and psychologically as 'mentally ill', gay and lesbian teachers are especially vulnerable to such scrutiny.

The historical connection of teaching to moral development coupled with the fear that lesbians and gay men will molest students or influence them to become homosexual has made the teaching profession a stronghold of anti-gay attitudes. These attitudes force gay and lesbian teachers to remain silent and to keep their sexual orientation a secret, a phenomenon typically referred to as 'being in the closet' (Kingdon, 1979). 'The great hidden minority in education' (Elam, 1977, p. 82), lesbian and gay teachers place their professional livelihood in jeopardy if they publicly disclose their sexual orientation. A review of homosexual teacher litigation in the USA since 1940, for example, portrays a judicial system unwilling to support the employment rights of gay and lesbian educators (Harbeck, 1987). Traditionally, homosexual educators have had little recourse when fired because of their sexual orientation. Although Harbeck argued that some progress has been made, legal discrimination and anti-gay attitudes prevail in the teaching profession.

All gay and lesbian teachers are targets of homophobia, the irrational fear and/or intolerance of homosexuality (Hudson and Ricketts, 1980), but those gay and lesbian teachers whose subject areas are not consistent with traditional gender roles, like the male librarian or the female shop teacher, are particularly vulnerable to homophobic accusations. The lesbian physical educator is perhaps the most vulnerable target of all. She (and all other female physical educators) is frequently assumed to be lesbian whether or not she publicly discloses her sexual orientation (Guthrie, 1982). Within the firmly entrenched male domain of sport and physical education there is an assumed relationship between traditional gender roles and sexuality (Lenskyj, 1986). To put it more simply, to be athletic is equated with masculinity and masculine women are labeled as lesbian. Therefore, athletic women are stereotyped as lesbian.

Allegations of lesbianism are used to intimidate and harass women in physical education and sport (Fields, 1983). As Cobhan (1982) stated, the 'defacto evidence' that sport is the province of lesbians 'will be used as ammunition by those who deny a woman's right to participate in athletics' (p. 179). In addition, just the presence of a female physical educator performing her job results in homophobic allegations. Her teaching responsibilities require her to touch students when instructing a particular physical skill; she also is responsible for supervising locker rooms where girls are changing clothes. Many female physical educators coach after school athletics, and coaches spend a significant amount of concentrated time with a small group of students in a team atmosphere. In a society where homosexuals are stereotyped as child molesters who recruit young children to their so-called deviant lifestyles, female physical educators and coaches are prime targets for homophobic suspicions and accusations.

The negative use of threats and allegations is one form of homophobia. Labeling this kind of behavior as homophobic is a relatively new concept and marks a change from defining homosexual behavior as deviant to defining prejudicial attitudes toward homosexuals as deviant (Weinberg, 1972). Morin and Garfinkle (1978) conceptualize homophobia on two levels: external and internal. Any belief system that maintains and encourages negative myths and stereotypes about homosexuals is defined as external homophobia. Internal homophobia represents a person's acceptance or internalization of negative attitudes and irrational fears about homosexuality.

Both forms of homophobia are a reality for lesbians in physical education and sport. As athletic women, they are negatively labeled by others, and consequently, internalize many of these derogatory stereotypes. They often will change their behavior to avoid the negative stereotypes and labels associated with lesbianism. Felshin (1974) described these behaviors as 'apologetic'; in other words, to 'apologize' for their participation in a traditionally masculine arena, many lesbians, as well as heterosexual physically active women, will act (and are often publicly described) in ways that highlight stereotyped ideas of 'femininity'. They may even go as far as to play less assertively and to sacrifice developing their full athletic potential for fear of appearing too 'masculine' (Lenskyj, 1986). Apologetic behaviors are used by physically active women to diffuse any suspicions regarding their sexual orientation. For lesbian physical educators, these behaviors may protect their jobs.

Allegations of lesbianism pose a special conflict for the lesbian physical educator and place her in a particularly vulnerable position. She is involved in a traditionally masculine activity, in which female participants are stereotyped as lesbians, and in a profession that is perceived by many as unacceptable for homosexuals. To disclose her sexual orientation can jeopardize her job and could reinforce the stereotype that women physical education teachers are lesbians, but there are consequences to silence as well. Silence perpetuates the negative stereotypes associated with lesbianism in sport and physical education. As such, the purpose of my study was to break the silence surrounding the experiences of lesbian physical educators. My goal was to describe, from their perspective, the experience of lesbian physical education teachers who work in the public schools and the meaning they made of their experiences. The focus of this chapter is on one aspect of the research: describing the contextual realities of being a lesbian physical educator. This study was conducted during the mid 1980s, and the twelve participants were public school teachers who lived and worked in northeast USA.

Theoretical Perspective

Much of the research about the experiences of lesbians and gay men in this society uses deviancy theory as a conceptual perspective (Goffman, 1963; Becker, 1963). The focus of deviancy research is the social reactions and interactions that produce the deviant label. Gays and lesbians are attached the deviant label because their lifestyles fall outside the majority's definition of 'normal'. Researchers use this conceptual perspective in gay and lesbian research to study the processes by which that labeling occurs. Another framework that can be used to understand the experiences of lesbians and gay men is oppression theory (Jackson and Hardiman, 1988; Freire, 1972; Baker-Miller, 1976; Memmi, 1965). Although used to understand the same phenomenon, deviancy and oppression theories reflect a different conceptual perspective, and therefore, a different way of viewing the world.

> Oppression is a systematic social phenomenon based on the differences between social groups that involves ideological domination, institutional control, and the promulgation of the oppressor group's ideology, logic system and culture on the oppressed group. The result is the exploitation of one social group by another for its own benefit. (Jackson and Hardiman, 1988, p. 5)

Within an oppressive society, persons in social group 'A' hold a set of negative beliefs about people in social group 'B' and act toward people in social group 'B' based on those beliefs. 'These beliefs and actions are supported, sanctioned, enforced and empowered by cultural ideologies and institutions and result in a privileged existence for social group "A" and a limited existence for social group "B" and the dehumanization of both' (Harro, 1983, p. 1). Oppression theory is used to examine the unequal distribution of power and privilege among various social groups, like males and females, whites and blacks, rich and poor, heterosexuals and homosexuals.

For this research, oppression theory was used as a theoretical perspective for several reasons. First, unlike the social construct of deviancy where the social group membership of deviants and non-deviants is determined by what is socially and culturally defined as 'normal', oppression theory is based on oppressed minorities and subordinates (many of whom are labeled as 'deviants') naming their own oppression. Second, within the deviancy framework, the deviants and their deviant behavior are identified as the problem. Oppression theory asserts that the processes by which oppression operates and the resulting conditions of oppression are defined as the problem. Finally, when applied to understanding the experience of lesbian physical educators, deviancy theory supports and perpetuates the labeling of lesbians as deviants. Some might argue that social researchers who use the deviancy construct to understand deviancy with respect to lesbians and gay men are themselves neutral about homosexuality and are primarily interested in studying the processes by which deviancy is defined and operationalized. The shift by social researchers from defining deviancy as inherent and pathological to defining it as socially prescribed supports this perspective. However, characterizing lesbians and gay men as deviants places them in the same category as other groups labeled as deviant, such as drug addicts, convicts, or rapists. Intended or not, a kind of guilt by association occurs, and with it come all the negative connotations the deviant label carries.

Choosing oppression theory as a conceptual frame in describing the experience of lesbian physical education teachers represents a value perspective. This type of research falls into the category of critical science (Popkewitz, 1981) that provides researchers with a way to understand and respond to changes in Western society and the social problems associated with those changes. Identifying lesbian physical educators as an oppressed minority and using the oppression model as a theoretical perspective from which to make sense of their experiences reflects an underlying goal of this chapter: to be a catalyst for dialogue and change.

Relevant Research

Though there is some research about homosexuality and education (Fischer, 1982; Harbeck, 1987; Griffin, 1989; Olson, 1987; Nickeson, 1980; Sciullo, 1984; Smith, 1985; Squirrell, 1989), there is no research focussing specifically on lesbian physical education teachers. Only three studies were found that directly or indirectly addressed the issue of lesbianism in physical education and sport. Guthrie (1982) examined homophobic attitudes towards females in sport, Beck (1976) studied the lifestyles of 'never married female physical educators' in higher education and Locke and Jensen (1970) explored the heterosexuality of women in physical education. The direct mention of lesbianism was conspicuously absent in these latter two studies. A few writers have addressed the issue of sexual orientation in sport and physical education (Beck, 1980; Bennett, Whitaker, Smith and Sablove, 1987; Boutilier and SanGiovanni, 1983; Cobhan, 1982; Gondola and Fitzpatrick, 1985; Griffin, 1983, 1987 and 1989; Hart, 1974; Lenskyj, 1986), but for the most part, the topic of lesbians in physical education has remained an untouched research area.

Methodology

To describe the experiences of lesbian physical educators and to understand the meaning they make of their experiences, a phenomenological interviewing technique was used (Woods, 1990). Taken from the work of Schuman (1982), the specific interviewing format employed was formally developed by Seidman, Sullivan and Schatzkamer (1983) and consists of three, in-depth open ended interviews. The goal in these interviews was to have the participants reconstruct their experience and reflect on its meaning. An underlying assumption of this approach according to Seidman *et al* (1983, p. 638) is that the meaning people make of their experience is 'crucial to the way they carry out their work'.

One focus question guided each ninety minute interview. In the first interview the participants were asked to provide a personal and professional background for describing their experiences as lesbian physical educators. They were asked in the second interview to recreate the concrete details of their day-to-day work experiences, and the objective of the final interview was to have them reflect on the meaning they made of their experiences as lesbian physical educators.

Participants

The participants in this study were public school physical education teachers who identified themselves as lesbians (Woods, 1990). Twelve elementary and secondary teachers were interviewed. Access to the twelve participants was gained through researcher contacts and from referrals by participants.

The participants ranged in age from 25 to 50-years-old. Five were in their 20s, four in their 30s, two in their 40s and one in her 50s. Eleven were white, and one was African-American. The majority of the participants identified themselves as coming from middle class backgrounds, while two were from upper middle class, one from lower middle class and one from working class backgrounds. (Their parents' occupational status was the criterion used to determine their class backgrounds.) Four of the participants identified themselves as catholic, and the rest were protestant.

Seven of the teachers interviewed were currently teaching in suburban schools, while three taught in rural and two were in urban settings. Five teachers taught at the high school level (ages 14–17), and three taught at junior high or middle schools (ages 11–14). One teacher taught physical education to grades K-8 (ages 5–14) and another taught grades K-12 (ages 5–17). One teacher taught adapted physical education exclusively for a large school system. In addition to her regular teaching duties, one participant served as the athletic trainer for a high school. At the time of the interviews five of the participants were coaching a girls' athletic team, and all but two had coached at some point during their tenure as teachers.

Findings

The interview data for this study was analyzed with two purposes: one, to present profiles of selected participants, and two, to present common themes among the participants. Profiles emphasize the contextually bound uniqueness of participants' stories while common themes reveal the junctures of their shared experience. Both yield valuable information for describing the contextual realities of lesbian physical educators. The underlying purpose of the data analysis was not to make generalizations about the experience of lesbian physical educators. Rather, the goal was to present profiles and themes (in the actual words of the participants) so readers can make connections between their own experience and that of the participants. Using the actual words of the participants instead of paraphrasing communicates more directly the meaning they made of their experience.

The individual profile represents a self-contained, in-their-own-words narrative detailing each participant's experience as a lesbian physical education teacher and the meaning she made of her experience. A profile is more than an expanded anecdote. As Seidman *et al* (1983) commented, 'People's stories — their reconstruction of factors in their life, their bringing order to events, characters and themes — convey knowledge and provide a path to understanding that is grounded in the concrete details of experience' (p. 665). Presenting data in profile form is especially critical at this time because of the silence and denial that surrounds lesbians in physical education. Profiles represent voices that have not previously been heard. However, such data is lengthy and given the space limitations of this chapter, I can not do justice to this form of data presentation. (Please refer to Woods, 1990, for complete profiles.) For present purposes, I have chosen to present three themes which reflect the day-do-day worlds of lesbian physical educators. These themes include: (i) underlying assumptions; (ii) the personal and professional split; and (iii) the identity management techniques the participants used to reveal or conceal their sexual orientation.

Underlying Assumptions

The participants made two assumptions about their experience as lesbian physical educators: (i) as a lesbian teacher, you will lose your job if you are open about your sexual orientation; and (ii) female physical education teachers are often negatively stereotyped as lesbians. These assumptions, shared by all twelve participants, were a consistent theme in their descriptions of their day-to-day worlds and provide valuable insight into choices they made to conceal or reveal their sexual orientation.

Of the twelve participants, eleven believed they would be fired if their sexual orientation was publicly disclosed. (The one participant who did not still engaged in 'passing' behaviors so her colleagues would assume she was heterosexual.) The following statement by Caren reflects the sentiment held by the majority of participants. 'I guess I don't put the two words together, lesbian and PE teacher. Because it means not having a job if I (do), if I was out. My lesbian life is separate. I've kept it, and

I'm trying to keep it very separate from my teaching.' Their 'fear' — as they often described it — of losing their job affected their behavior as teachers and their feelings about themselves.

> I don't think (being a lesbian is) something that even to this day that I would feel comfortable talking to students about. I would wait and talk to them when they were ex-students, but I don't think I would ever talk to them when they were students. There's a real fear in the fact that you can easily lose you job in (this state). It is illegal. If somebody ever had a grudge to hold against you, it could easily be held and that would be immediate grounds for dismissal. That's a fear that's always in the back of my mind, so I wouldn't talk about it in the girls' locker room at school.
> I'm just not willing to risk it. There is that necessity to be separate. And there's times when they definitely feel separate. Conversations come up or jokes come up. I just get really disgusted and usually just walk away. But it's a separate feeling. It's like you look around the room hoping that somebody else might catch your eye and feel the same way, but it doesn't happen very often. (Sara)

Fearing repercussions, the participants often felt powerless to challenge homophobic remarks.

> The head of phys. ed., he's a real nice guy, but he has about as much tact as a steam roller. He's young. And he has his doctorate, but you'd never know it. He always says to me, 'I have no patience with backstabbers and faggots and queers.' It's like you want to say something. Once I said, 'They're people, too.' And he just kind of looked at me, so I dropped it right away,' cause he could get me fired. I just didn't want to have to deal with him. (Pam)

The participants feared losing their jobs if their sexual orientation was revealed, and their love of teaching made their choice to remain silent a simple one. Protecting their employment as a teacher easily outweighed their need to be open about their lesbian identity.

The second underlying assumption expressed by the participants was that female physical education teachers are frequently (and negatively) stereotyped as lesbians by students, teachers, administrators and parents. As Toni stated, 'There's kind of a stigma behind phys. ed. teachers. I don't know what the percentage (is) of women phys. ed. teachers that are actually lesbians, but that's one of those battles that you're constantly fighting.' A common stigma faced by the participants was the labeling of female physical educators as 'locker room peepers'.

> We used to require showers, I remember we did that in the '60s. 'You will take gym. You will sweat, and you will take a shower.'

I didn't really care if the kids smelled or not. But we made them take showers, which none of them did. They just pulled their bra straps down, put their towel around them and walked in the shower, and then they checked off their name, and they just didn't smell any better, but we did our job. We did stupid things back then. Anyway, one of my colleagues overheard (this one young lady say to a friend of hers), 'they make us take showers so they can look at us. They're all queer.' Geez, now who told her that? Somebody must have told her that because it didn't just pop into the kid's head, did it? Most of our ideas come from our parents or from our peers but our peers got those questions and those wise remarks from some place. (Jackie)

Today's students were viewed by the participants as being more aware of the stereotype and willing to confront teachers about it.

I think forever there's been the stereotype that a single PE teacher is a lesbian. When I was in high school you would think that, but I think myself and friends, we really never knew what that meant. That assumption still exists, and kids today are bold enough to confront. I have been asked on two occasions this year by eighth graders (14-year-olds), 'Miss Carlson, you're single, and you don't quite fit the mold. You're not quite like Miss Samanski or Miss Felton. Are you like one of them? Are you a lesbian?' (They asked that) right out, bold as brass.
    'All gym teachers are queer.' 'How do you know?' 'My mother told me.' Her mother told her. It's like that's common knowledge: PE teachers are queer. 'Miss Carlson, are you over 30?' 'Nope, I'm 29.' 'Oh, you're alright, you're still safe.' If you're over 30 and you're a PE teacher and you're single, you're a lesbian. (Susan)

The participants believed that they would be fired if their sexual orientation became known. This threat — a daily reality from their perspective — was compounded by the prevailing stereotype that female physical educators are lesbian. Their worlds and everything they said and did as lesbian physical educators were shaped by these two assumptions.

The Personal and Professional Split

The focus question of the final interview was, 'What does it mean to you to be a lesbian physical education teacher?' Every participant had difficulty with this question; the question assumed an integration of two identities that the participants did not feel. Their difficulty in responding points to the clear separation they made between their identities as a lesbian and a physical education teacher. Although every participant acknowledged making this split, their reasons for doing so differed. Some considered it the norm in their school for teachers to separate their personal and professional lives, while other regarded it as their individual right to do so.

> My private life is my private life. And I don't want to have to answer more questions or add to someone's, 'Is she or isn't she (a lesbian)?' They can say all they want as long as they don't ask questions. I don't really feel like trying to educate them. Even though they're an accepting bunch, I'm not about to go (tell anybody). I might have ten years ago, but I'm not about to now. I'm not willing to get people too close to me. (Jackie)

Many participants justified this individual right on the basis that being a lesbian has nothing to do with their ability to teach.

> Why should people think less of me because I'm homosexual? What does (being homosexual) have to do with teaching? There are bad homosexual teachers just like there are bad straight teachers. What does homosexual have to do with anything? You're a human being. If you have the right moral values, you're not going to put them on other people anyway. (Alice)

Most participants believed making this split was a necessity, that as a lesbian you must keep these two identities separate.

> I think most people have come to the realization that probably I'm going to be an old maid school teacher. So most of the questions that I used to get hit with when I was in my mid-20s were the toughest. 'Boy, Alice, you're 26 and you're not married yet.' By the time you're 36, they don't ask it anymore. But what are you going to do until being a lesbian or being homosexual is accepted, which I really can't see that in the near future, especially teachers? People just feel that teachers have too much influence on children. If they would only realize that straight people influence children, too. And sometimes that's not good either, the way (most people) influence them, but they don't think that way.
>
> But there's a game that you have to play, and you're going to have to play it if you want to be a teacher, if you want to coach. When you're with children, they just assume that you're going to influence them improperly. There's a game we all have to play. It's a game, and it's a lie. You're being a hypocrite. But if you want your job, you probably best do that. I do hate it sometimes. I wish I could tell people. I just want to scream some days, but that's one of those inconveniences, I guess, that I'll have to put up with. It's too bad that it has to be that way, but it is. (Alice)

Like Alice, many of the participants resented not being able to share their personal life.

> (The other teachers) can bring (their personal life) with them (to school). They had a fight with their husband this morning. Or they can be mad about it. Or, 'Damn baby-sitter didn't show up last night.' They are free pretty much to bring theirs with them. I can't go in and say, 'Geez, Jill and I went to a great movie last night.' I can't, so I have to kind of say, 'I saw a great movie' or, 'I went to (town) and went out to eat at this restaurant. Have you ever been there?' But I don't get to say who I'm with really. If I'm really up or down about something, I kind of have to pretty much live it on an even keel. That's why sometimes I'm glad I have a twelve minute ride before I get to school in the morning. I just kind of clear my head. Maybe something went wrong (at home) or maybe something went really right, and I can't really go and say what was good or bad, whereas they can.
>
> That's kind of a bummer. Because there are things I'd like to share. I have to stop myself short sometimes of really saying how I feel. So I feel a little cheated.
>
> Maybe I could go a little bit further and everything would be okay, but I always have the reins on what I'm saying or trying to describe what I've done or what I want to do. I always kind of hold back and not make it sound like I'm gay. (Nancy)

The ride to work was symbolic of the personal/professional split the participants made.

> I would go to school, and it was kind of (a) different situation. You would leave that environment of a bunch of gay women trying to frantically get ready for work, and almost like once you got in your car, you were a different person. You were by yourself, you were going to an environment that was very much different from what you had just left in your living situation. And I played the role. I was good. From the moment I walked in, I was professional. I was a good teacher. I stood my ground. I felt strongly for what I stood for as far as my professional philosophies. But I didn't let my personal life affect my teaching that much. (Toni)

For some participants, however, keeping their two worlds separate was not always possible.

> My lesbian life is separate. I've kept it and I'm trying to keep it very separate from my teaching. It's getting harder and harder. For example, I went to a lesbians' (Alcoholic Anonymous) meeting, and a present student was there. Here you're supposed to go

in and talk and feel good about yourself. Well, I didn't feel good at all. The minute I came into the door, I froze. When I was supposed to speak, I said, 'Well, my name is Caren, and I'd like to listen.' And that's all said for the whole night. You're supposed to admit you're an alcoholic, and no, I just sat there and listened.

I'd rather for [this student] to know that I'm an alcoholic than a lesbian. But I don't feel all that great about anybody knowing anything about me. (Caren)

Unlike Caren, many participants resented not being able to be a positive gay role model for others, especially gay students. They described themselves as being in a 'catch-22' situation. To be a role model they must be out as lesbians, but to be out jeopardizes their jobs, and therefore, their position to be role models.

A few participants contemplated leaving teaching in order to be more integrated personally and professionally, but for most participants, their love of teaching outweighed the personal costs of living a split life.

(Being a lesbian PE teacher is) almost like being a schizophrenic. Because you are one person as a PE teacher and you are one person as a lesbian. Unfortunately, today's society still hasn't gotten to the point where it can integrate the two without giving you a severe pain in the butt for it. Even though they're out there, and we know they're out there, if you are not discreet in certain ways, you're going to lose your job.

But as long as there's been no scandals or locker room peepings, (you'll) get by. But it's frustrating because you give up so many rights just to be gay as it is, and you give up that many more to try to maintain your profession and allow yourself to stay in your own profession. You just have to be very smart. I feel that that's something that I've really learned to look at, that I really have to separate the two. Because I don't want to jeopardize what I enjoy doing. I have to say, okay, for this, I can keep that side closed. In order to be able to teach, I'm willing to give that up. (Traci)

Living a double life was simply accepted as a way of life for a lesbian physical education teacher.

I find myself in that middle, that kind of non-radical kind of lifestyle where I am going to make the least amount of waves. And if it means putting on that different face when I leave my home and what's comfortable to me and going to work to what's professional and what is, quote, 'accepted behavior' for me or what I should be doing as a phys. ed. teacher of young kids, (then) I accept that there is a separation in my life. The least amount of over lapping that happens is going to make things easier.

I'm an okay person. No matter who's looking at me. Whether it's my colleagues at work or my friends from my personal side. I'm Toni King for Toni King. I'm not Toni King because I'm a teacher or because I'm gay or because I'm a gay teacher. I am the person that I am, and how I deal with both of those issues is how I deal with my life. And I think I do an okay job at it. I honestly do. I can say that I can be very comfortable in dealing with either group. But then again, there are situations that I felt very uncomfortable. But overall, I can feel pretty comfortable in both of my lives. And that's what it is, both of my lives. (Toni)

The participants justified their personal/professional split in many ways, describing it as a norm for all teachers, as an individual right, as a necessity, or as a given for lesbians. All experienced conflict around separating their lesbian identity from their teacher identity. This conflict took the form of both resentment and fear: resentment because there was no overlap between their two worlds, and fear because there was. Many of the participants described making this separation as a choice, but in various ways, their words and experiences contradicted this description. As lesbians, they believed disclosure of their sexual orientation would cost them their jobs, and as female physical educators, they assumed they were already stereotyped as lesbians. Both these assumptions shaped the way they experienced being a lesbian physical educator. From their perspective, the only real choices were to conceal their sexual orientation to stay in teaching or to leave teaching altogether. Susan summed it up best when she stated, 'keeping my personal and professional lives separate is by choice. It's very much by choice. If the system changed and said it could be different, then I could see myself taking a step, but until that time, I am a victim of the system. I am making a choice to be a victim of the system.'

The degree to which participants separated their personal and professional identities was reflected in the variety of behaviors they used to manage their lesbian identity within the school setting. These behaviors ranged in intent, from concealment of their sexual orientation to disclosure of it. Primarily, the intent of these behaviors was to conceal their sexual orientation; yet all the participants engaged in behaviors that risked disclosure of their lesbianism.

Lesbian Identity Management Techniques

The majority of participants concealed their sexual orientation much more often than they disclosed it. None of the twelve teachers, however, consistently concealed their sexual orientation; all had disclosed their lesbianism to at least one other teacher, colleague, ex-student, or current student from their school. Two lesbian identity management techniques emerged from the data: (i) strategies to conceal one's lesbian identity; and

(ii) risk-taking behaviors that could disclose one's lesbian identity. All the participants used both management techniques, yet no clear pattern emerged with respect to the choices they made about concealing or revealing their sexual orientation. For example, on one day a participant may have chosen to confront a homophobic remark made by a teacher, but on another day under the similar circumstances, she may have chosen to completely ignore it.

Strategies To Conceal One's Lesbian Identity

All the participants employed strategies to hide their sexual orientation, some more than others, and these strategies were used in their relationships with both heterosexual and gay members of the school community. The strategies the participants employed to conceal their lesbian identity are broken down into three categories: (i) passing as heterosexual; (ii) personal censoring/self distancing from students, teachers and administrators; and (iii) personal censoring/self distancing from any association with homosexuality.

Passing as Heterosexual

A very common strategy used by the participants was to pass as heterosexual. In other words, a participant behaved in ways that led others to assume she was heterosexual. Toni stated, 'There was always a fear that somebody would really pursue what I did (on the weekends). I would say I got together with friends. It was always plural. "I got together with friends." "I went out to a bar", and God forbid anybody would ever question what bar I went to. I'd have a couple of names (of straight bars) I'd pull out of my pocket.' Passing usually took the form of changing pronouns and names from female to male.

> One teacher asked me if I had a boyfriend. It was one of those questions you could say no, but he would think something was wrong with you. I was like, 'Yeah, but we don't see each other that much, 'cause he's at home, and I work all the time. We only see each other on weekends.'
> I have to really remember what I'm saying so I don't contradict myself. (I'd) love to tell him, 'My girlfriend's a trainer.' Tell him about Carrie, but I can't. Especially the kids. Kids are different, though. I'll tell (the junior high kids) stuff about Carrie but just change the name. They'll ask how long I've been going out with my boyfriend, and I just say, 'Oh, for a year,' and be talking about Carrie, but they won't have a clue, 'cause for them, it goes in one ear and out the other. (Pam)

A few of the participants used gay male friends as a heterosexual cover. Alice remarked, 'There's nothing that I keep hidden from my kids except my real personal life. I play games with them. Last weekend I told than I was on a date. I was down at John's who is my gay friend, but I told them I was on a date with John. You've got to play a little game. I have no intentions of my kids knowing that I'm gay.' Many of the participants made reference to the 'games' played when passing as heterosexual.

> The kids would say, 'Oh, you're Miss Johnson. You're not married.' 'No, no, I'm not. I haven't found the right one yet. Prince Andrew is busy.' I'd make up all these things, and they'd laugh. They think I'm having a romance right now with a science teacher, this guy, (Steve). We hang around together in school. So some of the freshman kids started a rumor last year that we were engaged. These kids just thought it was the most wonderful thing, and we let it go. It was kind of fun for a while. And they wanted to be invited to the wedding. So I guess you could say that every once in a while I have all these little games that either I play or a group of kids play, and I just don't push the rumors down that hard. (Nancy)

For some, the passing game almost became second nature.

> Today I was talking with the woman who is the receptionist. She's a really nice person. We've been buddies for years. And she said, 'Are you coming to my party?' She's having this big faculty get together, and I said, 'Gosh, I'm not.' And she said, 'Who are you going out with now?' 'Nobody, that's the problem.' I wish I could have said to her, 'Well, my lover and I really can't come because we're going to a party elsewhere.'
> Things like that happen all the time. I work out in the mornings. And I keep the (weight room) doors open, and the custodians will walk through. This fellow, Charlie, is always saying, 'what are you building up muscles for? Your boyfriend won't like them.' And I said, 'Yes, he does.' It's that banter that has to occur just to keep things going.
> I have to do it. It's just a natural response. I don't even think about it. You have to be quick. I just do it. (Jackie)

For the participants who used them, passing behaviors misled others into believing they were heterosexual. This cover helped counteract the negative stereotype that female physical educators are lesbian and kept suspicions about the participants' own sexual orientation to a minimum.

Personal Censoring/Self-distancing from Students, Teachers and Administrators

The intent of personal censoring was to avoid calling attention to themselves, and therefore, to one's lesbian identity. By distancing themselves from students, teachers and administrators, the participants avoided personal closeness with members of the school community, thus avoiding disclosure of their sexual orientation.

You kind of walk a fine line of how much you want to reveal to these people. I have a tendency not to get too over friendly or warm to my students. I always kind of keep this little front up and sometimes I think the front is sternness. Not that I am a stern teacher, but I hold that front a little bit to kind of keep everybody at arm's length. So that maybe they don't want to pursue too much my personal life. (Toni)

All the participants spoke about distancing themselves from students or colleagues as a way to avoid personal enquiries. They withheld information about themselves or gave vague responses when asked about their personal lives. When choosing to share personal information, many of the participants carefully selected their words, making sure not to reveal too much information at once.

You really have to guard your words. I've gotten so used to saying 'roommate', but I never refer to Kim as my lover. I say something about, 'Well, we went to a craft show on Saturday.' And they'll say, 'Well, who's "we"?' I'll say, 'Well, my roommate and I.' Those kind of things, sure that's fine. I have no qualms with that. In fact if somebody asks, I would certainly more than willingly answer, but I don't know as I would often volunteer it. I don't know whether I dole out pieces at a time and not all at one time so they don't put them all together. I don't know whether I'm being extraordinarily guarded, or I have this real fine line about professionalism, and I have a real fine line about personal life.
    I think (volunteering information is) giving away too much of myself. I'm a little afraid to give that much away of myself. (Sara)

In one-on-one or small group interactions, personal censoring often took the form of silence, denial or even lying.

This is the first year that I am in conflict with becoming a pretty good friend of a (teacher) who is straight and does not know anything about me. The worst part is being so secretive to the point where I am with this new person, Elaine. It is a friendship right now that is based on lying, 'cause I do lie. She'll ask me, 'Who (are) you seeing?' And I say, 'I'm not seeing anyone,' I don't ever make up that I'm dating anyone or anything like that, but instead of saying I'm going to (a gay bar) dancing on a Saturday night, I will just leave it that I've gone to (the city). That's hell for me. (Susan)

The participants distanced themselves from the mainstream of interpersonal interactions within the school to avoid questions about their personal life. By avoiding these situations, they avoided disclosure of their sexual orientation.

Personal Censoring/Self-distancing from any Association with Homosexuality
When confronted directly or indirectly with the issue of homosexuality, the participants employed a variety of strategies to prevent disclosure of their lesbian identity. The most prevalent strategy was to ignore or dismiss homophobic comments made by students, teachers or administrators. Mona stated, 'The boys are into calling each other "faggots" or, "He's queer." I pretend I don't hear those. I try not to make a big deal about it. Kids are into name calling, no matter what they use, they're into name calling. If it's not that, it's something else.' Many believed confronting this form of name-calling would cause students to be suspicious about their teacher's sexual orientation. Even when homophobic comments were directed at themselves, many participants chose to ignore them.

> I was taking my roll this year the first day of class, and the kids (are) kind of gathered around because they're all so eager. I'm checking them off, and I hear in the back, 'Oh, she's the lesbian.' Now, one girl is saying this to another girl. There's no question (but) that they were talking about me. And I'm thinking to myself, whoa. What is this? Already the first day of class, brand new year, and this has happened. The only thing I could think of was somewhere along the line, (a) girl the year before tipped them off. Maybe that's my paranoia about them really and truly knowing it or whether or not they just thought it, and the rumor had just passed around.
>   I didn't acknowledge it. I suspect that they didn't think I heard it, but I didn't acknowledge it. (Sara)

In the teachers' room, many of the participants chose to avoid or ignore conversations or jokes about homosexuals. For some, their avoidance took the form of personally removing themselves in an inconspicuous way from the situation.

> Then you have the problems with the jokes in the teachers' room. My own reaction to that is to pretend that I'm busy, and I'm writing something, and I don't hear what's going on, or I'm not paying attention, or I'm talking to somebody else.
>   You can always be talking to the person next to you while out of your other ear, you're hearing what's going on in this little corner. So you pretend that you don't hear, and you're very interested in your conversation with the person next to you. I'll wait a reasonable amout of time, and then I'll leave. So it isn't too obvious. You know, I've had to do something, I have to make a phone call. It's an escape. I know that. (Mona)

Different forms of personal censoring were used to counteract the lesbian stereotype associated with female physical education teachers. For instance, in the locker room, some participants consciously avoided eye contact with students who were changing clothes while others avoided the locker room altogether. The most common strategy was to avoid physical contact with female students. Even when students initiated physical contact, participants consciously chose not to reciprocate for fear of repercussions.

(The kids) don't feel bad about coming up to me, like some of my hockey players slap me on the back or put their arm around me. But I won't do it to them. That probably will never change. You don't know who's watching or who might go home and say something to their mother. I just wouldn't want any controversy to start when there's nothing to be talked about. But I do worry about it, and I think about it consciously. (Nancy)

Many participants were cautious around a gay or suspected gay student and took extra measures to avoid being alone with students they thought were gay.

You know how you peg kids, this is awful, but you peg them. Like, 'Oh, that kid's going to be gay. I don't want to be near her.' So I never went near (this one) kid. Then she got hurt, she pinched a nerve in her neck. She brought in a doctor's note, and the doctor wanted her to get massages every day. I was like, oh, no. So I always had the doors wide open. I always made sure there were about five kids in the trainer's room. I was real paranoid. I had to massage (her) neck and shoulders. It was for about three weeks, and I was paranoid every single day. (Pam)

Even though they recognized the need to do so, many participants felt counseling gay students or those they thought might be gay was too big of a risk to take. Jody stated, 'There (are some students) that I would love to be able to talk with, but that's one place where I'm afraid. I would not sit down and talk to anyone and give them any counseling about being gay. That's something that's really important that the students have someone to talk to, but unfortunately, I don't feel like I could do that now.' (Jody)

Overall, the concealment strategies used by the participants reflected their need to separate their personal life as a lesbian from their professional role as a teacher. All twelve participants, however, took risks at times to integrate these two identities and actually engaged in behaviors within the school setting that disclosed or risked disclosure of their lesbianism. An examination of these risk-taking behaviors follows.

Risk-Taking Behaviors

Even though concealment strategies were employed much more frequently, every participant engaged in risk-taking behaviors to some degree. The behaviors engaged in by the participants that disclosed or risked disclosure of their lesbian identity fell into three categories: (i) passively overlapping personal with professional; (ii) actively challenging, confronting and supporting in the role of teacher; and (iii) actively overlapping personal with professional. Most of the risks taken were premeditated, yet some were spontaneous. As with the strategies used to conceal one's sexual orientation, a variety of factors played into a participant's decision to take risks that might disclose her lesbian identity.

Passively Overlapping Personal with Professional

This type of risk was characterized by a participant sharing personal information about herself with students or other colleagues. For instance, a participant might have acknowledged that she owns a house with a 'roommate' or brought her partner to school events. She might also have brought students to her home.

The consequences of such risks were not clear; an assumption about the participant being a lesbian might or might not have been made. For example, some participants socialized with heterosexual teachers after school and were not sure how much their colleagues really knew about them.

> We did have a group of teachers at the [school], women that used to get together. For some reason, I was included. They were all either married or living with a man or had been married and have a ton of kids, engaged and have their wedding date planned, etc., etc. And here was Toni in this whole group.
>
> I enjoyed going out with this group, but I felt uncomfortable for several reasons. One being my sexual preference being gay. I was always hoping that nobody ever really talked to me and said, 'Well, are you seeing anybody, are you dating anybody?' And there was never really a time that anybody would delve too deeply into my background. I was always thankful for that, but I could never figure out whether it was really because maybe deep down inside they knew. (Toni)

Another passive way of overlapping one's personal life with professional life was to associate with another gay teacher in the school. Caren stated, 'Lesley is probably my best (contact). She's taught there for four years. She's the other gay person in the office. And I associate with her outside of school and in school. But we're just like a twosome in the building. We do things together, we eat lunch together, we do everything together. And the kids know us for being together. We're the crazies in the office.'

For most participants, avoiding any overlap between their personal and professional identities was impossible and undesirable. Many viewed this kind of limited personal disclosure as a low risk worth taking. Integrating their personal and professional lives, even in a small way, lessened their conflict about maintaining two lives.

Active Challenging, Confronting or Supporting in the Role of Teacher
Many participants took risks as teachers that disclosed or chanced disclosure of their lesbian identity. For example, Susan was willing to challenge her students on their use of 'gay'.

> Other than, 'This sucks', or, 'That sucks', the other most frequently used word is, 'This is gay.' Everything's 'gay' in junior high school. Most often when anyone uses the word gay, I talk to them, and I ask them, 'What does gay mean?' It's really interesting to listen to their definitions. As a matter of fact, under my blotter on my desk, I have a piece of paper saying definitions of gay. And when somebody gives me a new difinition, I write them down. They range from it's just geekish, it's something from being nerdy to two guys that love each other. But it can be anything in between. A lot of lesbian PE teachers would sort of shy away from that stuff, at least ones that I know. If somebody says gay, you sort of just turn your head and make believe you didn't even hear the word. I love finding out what they're thinking. (Susan)

Susan's behavior was atypical of the participant group; yet many participants took other kinds of risks. For instance, some participants chose to counsel students who were questioning their own sexual orientation.

> I had (a) kid that was on my team a couple years ago that came to me, and she said she had something really important to talk to me about, and she didn't know if she could tell me. And I said, 'Well, what is it?' And she wouldn't tell me, and so I said, 'Well, is it about being gay?' She said, 'Yeah, how did you know?' And I just talked to her a lot about it.
> We weren't talking about her. We were talking about gay in general. So I just told her how I felt about people and being different (and that) it doesn't make a difference to me. (Caren)

With ex-students, participants were more willing to come out as a lesbian.

> There was (a) kid my second year as head coach who was a senior. (Jamie) had a lot of problems at home. And I just spent hour on hour, sitting and talking to Jamie and helping her through a lot of situations just (by) talking to her.

Jamie got back in contact to me after her senior year, and she spilled her guts to me. She told me she was in love with me, and she had been. She had evidently spent many emotional evenings and days and weeks and months on end not knowing how to deal with this. Keeping it inside, not knowing who to talk to, so eventually she came back to me. And boy, I'll tell you, I choked on my coffee that day.

I just didn't know what to do. I told her I was flattered. And I told her that in fact I was gay. She asked me. She knew that she had these feelings and attractions toward different women. And she was struggling with what she was feeling. I knew that there was no way I could sit there, looking across the table at this kid and say, no, that I wasn't gay. I couldn't do it. And I didn't want to. I knew that Jamie was having a lot of emotional problems herself, so I knew that I had to be very upfront and honest with her. (Toni)

With homophobic harassment, some participants chose to confront instead of ignore.

One day, I was sitting outside the local pizza place in the car, and Jeannie (my partner) had gone into the restaurant. (These students) were basically saying this to Jeannie, not to me. They called out, 'Hey lezzie.' It was this one girl and two other girls with her. So I watched them, and I got out of the car, and I walked across the street, and I called the girl by her name. I said, 'Becky, come here.' She looked, and then she turned around. So I in a sense threatened her, you know, that she was fooling with the wrong person right now. And if I heard that from her again, she would be dealt with severely. Every time after that I saw her in school, I just gave her this real bad look. I didn't say anything to her. I just stared her right in the eye. I didn't take my eyes off of her, even if she looked. I made her eyes turn away. And I haven't heard anything from her since. (Jody)

The participants often felt torn between their responsibilities as a teacher and their need to protect their lesbian identity (and therefore their jobs). When these two factors came into conflict, participants usually based their decision to risk disclosure on the particulars of the situation. No consistent pattern of risk-taking behavior emerged.

Active Overlapping Personal with Professional
Every participant had revealed or acknowledged their sexual orientation to at least one other member of the school community during their tenure as teachers. Coming out to a teacher, colleague, student or ex-student took many forms; some participants chose to not deny the assumption others made about their sexual orientation.

One funny incident (happened) with this girl Nina who was class president, and I was the class advisor. She spent a lot of time down in my office doing class work. And one day, she's sitting at a desk, and I'm sitting at another desk doing my work, and she says, 'So, are you going out this weekend?' And I said, 'I don't know.' Now she's still looking down, and so am I. And she says, 'Well, if you do go out this weekend, maybe you shouldn't go to P.J.'s,' (which is a gay bar). And slowly my head came up, and I just looked at her. I said, 'What do you mean?' She said, 'Well, Bobbie's going, and she says she can get in.' Bobbie was 16 years old at the time, a junior in high school. I just put my head back down and said, 'Thank you, Nina.'

I spoke to Nina after that one day, and she finally said to me, 'I know,' (referring to me being gay). And I said, 'Well, just keep it to yourself, lady, because this job is kind of nice.' She said, 'I know. Don't worry.' (Alice)

Other participants openly shared their lesbianism.

(When) my relationship with Terri was dissolving, for the first time in my life, I couldn't get a grip on things. I lost probably 20 lbs. So there were some noticeable things that were going on. Teaching, I loved. I was still high energy. As a matter of fact, I hated for the day of teaching to end, because I really put all my energy into it.

At one point I was very close to a guy, the art teacher in this school system. I was in an activity (on the) softball field. I remember him coming out one day specifically and saying, 'Susan, I'm sick because I really think my wife is cheating on me. I think my wife is going to leave me.' And I remember turning and looking at him and saying, 'Larry, I understand that. My wife just left me.' And I remember saying it like that, and I remember him looking at me and him saying, 'Are you gay?' And I said, 'Yeah. And I'm going through hell.' And since then we have developed a great friendship. (Susan)

For some, coming out was considered a better alternative to lying. Others came out to a colleague because they were caught off guard.

In my after school things, I have Sam who's the (athletic director) and this guy, Joey, who's the equipment manager. (Joey) used to tease me once in a while about being gay. And Sam never said a word. Well, Sam and I went one day to pick up some equipment, and he asked me if I was gay. The person who I was seeing, (Carrie), was from the (same town), and he asked around and found out that she was gay. So he just assumed that I was 'cause I was always with her. And he asked me, so I told him, 'Yeah. It's no big deal.'

> He caught me off guard. I didn't know what to do. I was
> going to deny it, (but) it was like, no, why should I? I've never
> lied to him before, why should I now? So I didn't. I figured he
> wouldn't say anything 'cause he had hired me and that would
> make him look like a fool, according to his standards. (Pam)

A participant who was willing to take more risks that disclosed or
risked disclosure of her lesbian identity did not necessarily employ fewer
concealment strategies. In addition, the longer a participant had been a
lesbian or the more accepting she was of that identity had no bearing on
the degree to which she protected her lesbian identity. In other words, a
consistent pattern with respect to how and when participants concealed
or revealed their lesbianism did not emerge from the data. Rather, the
participants' decisions were made on a case-by-case, day-to-day, person-
to-person basis and were contingent upon numerous factors (Woods,
1990). A participant could have behaved differently from one day to the
next, and the difference in her behavior could be attributed to something
simple, like whether or not she was having a good day to something
more complex, such as how deeply the negative stereotypes associated
with lesbian physical education teachers affected her acceptance of her
own lesbian identity.

Discussion: Lesbian Physical Educators as an Oppressed Minority

One purpose of critical research is to be an impetus for dialogue and
change, and using oppression theory in research about lesbian physical
educators facilitates this goal by framing their day-to-day work lives in a
broader social context and analysis. The participants' experiences, when
viewed through the lens of oppression, demonstrate the pervasiveness of
their oppression as women and as lesbians. Although the participants did
not use the phrase 'oppressed minority' to describe their experiences, their
stories reveal the homophobia, sexism and heterosexism that enveloped
their worlds as lesbian physical educators.

Individually as lesbians in physical education, the participants challenged the underpinnings of their oppression. As women, they defied
stereotypical definitions of femininity and as athletes, assumed roles that
women historically have been barred or discouraged from assuming. As
physical educators, they broke new ground for young girls and boys,
teaching and modeling the athletic potential of females. As lesbians, they
silently, but visibly rejected women's dependence upon men for economic support and emotional validation. Consequently, their presence
alone challenged the foundations upon which homophobia, sexism and
heterosexism are built.

Yet as individual lesbians, they felt powerless to change the institutional and social forces that maintained their status as subordinates

in a dominants' world. The conditions of oppression the participants encountered as lesbian physical educators — the negative labeling imposed upon them by others, their internalized homophobia, the harassment and discrimination to which they were subjected and the acceptance of their socialized roles as subordinates — all served to maintain and perpetuate an oppressive system in four basic ways (Jackson and Hardiman, 1988). One, the participants were silenced. Two, they feared being discovered as lesbians. Three, they isolated themselves, and four, they felt powerless. Their sense of powerlessness can be further described in three ways: (i) the participants blamed themselves; (ii) they accepted their oppression as unchangeable; and (iii) they formed no collective identity as an oppressed minority. These outcomes are typical consequences for subordinates who attempt to survive and live within a successful system of oppression.

The function of negatively labeling lesbians was to instill fear in the participants. The fear of exposure, of harassment and intimidation and of being fired rendered participants powerless to challenge their oppression. Consequently, they remained silent about their sexual orientation, they were discouraged from 'making waves' and upsetting the status quo, and they felt powerless to change the conditions of their subordinate status.

In a larger context, stereotyping physically active women as lesbians succeeds in keeping sport a male domain and in relegating female sport participants to a marginal status. Many women choose not to participate in sport for fear of being labeled a lesbian. If they do participate, some apologize for their physical ability by not playing to their full potential on the court or by emphasizing their femininity off the court. If they participate fully (as most participants did in this study), they are faced with consequences. One consequence for the participants was isolation. To alleviate the effects of negative labeling, most participants isolated themselves from male colleagues, heterosexual female colleagues and the general school community. Some even isolated themselves from other gay teachers. This isolation was a key component in maintaining a system of oppression. Isolated from other gay and lesbian teachers and potential heterosexual allies in school, the participants had little power (or support) to change their status.

The negative labeling of gay and lesbian educators as child molesters or locker room peepers also disempowered the participants. To avoid accusations, the participants remained silent about their sexual orientation, or they engaged in behaviors that led others to assume they were heterosexual. To protect themselves from being accused of improper relationships with students, the participants emotionally and physically distanced themselves from students. Maintaining silence and distance are common survival strategies among subordinates who feel powerless to interrupt a system of oppression.

Like negative labeling, internalized homophobia has similar functions in maintaining oppression. Internalized homophobia is a form of self-blame and self-hatred. Gearhart (1989) stated that internalized homophobia affects lesbians and gay men in several ways: 'it silences us, it intensifies our fear of discovery and it isolates us' (p. 8). Consequently, individuals with similar experiences stay separated from one another and do not develop a collective identity as an oppressed minority. The participants' stories revealed their internalized homophobia and for some, their non-acceptance of their lesbian identity. The silence, the fear of discovery and the isolation were common themes in each participant's description of her individual experience as a lesbian physical educator. These lesbian physical educators did not share a collective identity as an oppressed minority, and therefore, had no collective strength to challenge their status as subordinates.

The harassment and discrimination directed at the participants also intensified their fear, silence, isolation and sense of powerlessness. Whether blatantly threatened by administrators or subtly discouraged from bringing partners to faculty gatherings, the participants learned (and to some degree accepted) that, as lesbians, harassment and discrimination were everyday occurrences. The participants learned to accept as normal the homophobia and heterosexism that overshadowed their worlds. This acceptance is reflective of their fear and their belief that their oppression was unchangeable. For example, if an individual participant challenged the harassment and discrimination she encountered, she believed she would be subjected to additional harassment and would possibly have to reveal her sexual orientation. If she acknowledged her lesbianism, however, she believed she jeopardized her employment as teacher. Most participants chose the 'safe' route and remained silent in the face of harassment and discrimination. Their fear, their sense of powerlessness and their silence are clear indications of a successful system of oppression in operation.

Another clear indication is the participants' acceptance of their subordinate roles. This group of lesbian physical educators acknowledged the widespread homophobia that is present both inside and outside school settings, but most participants felt powerless to change the oppression they experienced on a daily basis. They communicated this powerlessness in many ways, sometimes in the form of tolerance. For example, they expressed the belief that society, family, friends and colleagues should not be forced to openly deal with sexual orientation issues and argued that the less open they were, the more likely their lesbianism would be tolerated. They dismissed the generic, negative use of 'gay' as meaningless, characterizing it as just a word students currently use instead of 'jerk'. They restricted their behavior as teachers to avoid accusations.

Moreover, they described sexual orientation as a personal and private matter that does not need to be publicly acknowledged. They relegated their lesbianism to the private realm of the individual. When sexual orientation is viewed from this perspective, the institutional forces that shape and define oppression are not questioned, and 'progress is defined by accommodating to the inducements of present institutional arrangements and forces' (Boutilier and SanGiovanni, 1983, p. 250). The onus of change is placed on the individual and not the system. One consequence of a person-change perspective is person-blame. A few participants blamed themselves for being lesbian and grudgingly described their lesbianism as a personal reality they had to accept. These same participants expressed a desire to be heterosexual so they could assimilate into the dominants' world.

In summary, the conditions of oppression present in the participants' worlds succeeded in keeping them silent, fearful, isolated and powerless. Pointing out their role in maintaining their subordinate status is not to blame them. In fact, the participants challenged their subordinate status by taking risks that disclosed or risked disclosure of their lesbian identity. Although cautious and unpredictable, their risk taking behavior should not be minimized. Given the homophobic climate of their work worlds, their willingness to come out to students and colleagues as well as to participate in this study represent courageous acts of defiance. However, the message communicated by these acts was often veiled in secrecy and caution: 'It is okay to be gay or lesbian, but don't be open about it and be selective in whom you tell.'

The participants' role in maintaining their subordinate status reflects the complex and overwhelming nature of oppression. Together, the silence, fear and isolation they experienced reinforced their sense of powerlessness and prevented the participants from seeing the broader social context of their experience and from believing change is possible. This, in turn, deterred them from developing a collective identity as an oppressed minority. A collective identity is critical in eliminating a group's oppression as subordinates.

One purpose of this research has been to break the cycle of silence, isolation and fear that currently exists among lesbian physical educators. By openly acknowledging their presence to each other, lesbian physical educators can begin the process of developing a positive collective identity. This collective identity is essential for interrupting the effects of homophobia and heterosexism within physical education and sport.

> For lesbians to experience freedom, individually and collectively, we have to free ourselves both from within and without. Freedom does not come from the struggles of a few leaders in isolation . . . Great strides for freedom come when large groups of oppressed people come to believe that they deserve freedom and then work together to achieve it. (Pharr, 1988, pp. 82–3)

I have often referred to the interviews with the twelve participants as the 'gems of their lives'. Their stories and experiences are precious gems and represent a history, a present and a future that must be claimed with collective pride and not rejected with individual silence. More stories need to be heard, but given the risks at this time, most lesbian physical educators choose not to publicly come out and talk about their experiences. For that reason, this research serves a critical role. Even though the number of participants in this study is small, going public with these twelve women's stories, with the gems of their lives, begins the process of dialogue and change.

References

BAKER-MILLER, J. (1976) *Toward a New Psychology of Women*, Boston, MA, Beacon Press.

BECK, B. (1976) 'Lifestyles of never married women physical educators in institutions of higher education in the US', *Dissertation Abstracts International*, 37, p. 2715A. (University Microfilms No. DA 76-24, 936).

BECK, B. (1980) 'No more masks! A feminist perspective on issues and directions in professional preparation', *Proceedings of the National Association for Physical Education in Higher Education (NAPEHE) Annual Conference*, 2, pp. 126–35.

BECKER, H.S. (1963) *Outsiders: Study in the Sociology of Deviance*, London, Free Press of Glencoe.

BENNETT, R.S., WHITAKER, G., SMITH, N. and SABLOVE, A. (1987) 'Changing the rules of the game: Reflections toward a feminist analysis of sport', *Women's Studies International Forum*, 10, 4, pp. 369–79.

BOUTILIER, M.A. and SANGIOVANNI, L. (1983) *The Sporting Woman*, Champaign, IL, Human Kinetics.

COBHAN, L. (1982) 'Lesbians in physical education and sport' in CRUIKSHANK, M. (Ed) *Lesbian Studies: Present and Future*, Old Westbury, NY, Feminist Press, pp. 179–86.

ELAM, S.M. (Ed) (1977) 'Gay teachers: Yea or nay?', *Phi Delta Kappan* (special issue), 59, 2.

FELSHIN, J. (1974) 'The dialectic of women and sport' in GERBER, E. *et al* (Eds) *The American Woman in Sport*, Reading, MA, Addison-Wesley, pp. 179–210.

FIELDS, C. (1983) 'Allegations of lesbianism being used to intimidate, female academics say', *The Chronicle of Higher Education*, 26 October, pp. 1 and 22.

FISCHER, T.R. (1982) 'A study of educators' attitudes toward homosexuality' (doctoral dissertation, University of Virginia), *Dissertation Abstracts International*, 43, p. 3294A.

FREIRE, P. (1972) *Pedagogy of the Oppressed*, New York, Herder and Herder.

GEARHART, S. (1989, April) 'Treason in the delivery room: A feminist analysis of the social construction of gender', paper presented at the annual meeting of the American Alliance for Health, Physical Education, Recreation and Dance, Boston, MA.

GOFFMAN, E. (1963) *Stigma: Notes on the Management of Spoiled Identity*, Englewood Cliffs, NJ, Prentice Hall.

GONDOLA, J.C. and FITZPATRICK, T. (1985) 'Homophobia in girls' sports: "Names" that can hurt us . . . all of us', *Equal Play*, 5, 2, pp. 18–19.

GRIFFIN, P.S. (1983) 'How can a female sports performer avoid, diminish, or disarm treats to her own sense of femininity?', Paper presented at the New Agenda for Women in Sport Conference, Washington, DC, November.

GRIFFIN, P.S. (1987) 'Gender as a socializing agent in physical education' in TEMPLIN, T. *et al* (Eds) *Socialization in Physical Education: Learning to Teach*, Champaign, IL, Human Kinetics.

GRIFFIN, P.S. (1989a) 'Using participatory research to empower gay and lesbian educators.' Paper presented at the annual meeting of the American Educational Research Association, San Francisco, April.

GRIFFIN, P.S. (1989b) 'Homophobia in physical education', *Journal of Canadian Alliance for Health. Physical Education and Recreation*, 55, 2, pp. 27–31.

GUTHRIE, S.P. (1982) 'Homophobia: Its impact on women in sport and physical education', unpublished master's thesis, California State University, Long Beach.

HARBECK, K. (1987) 'Personal freedoms/public constraints: An analysis of the controversy over the employment of homosexuals as school teachers, Vol. I and II' (doctoral dissertation, Stanford University), *Dissertation Abstracts International*.

HARRO, R.L. (1983) 'Heterosexism 101: Content for an educational experience', unpublished manuscript, University of Massachusetts, Amherst.

HART, M.M. (1974) 'Stigma or prestige: The all-American choice' in McGLYNN, G. (Ed) *Issues in Physical Education and Sports*, Palo Alto, CA, National Press Books, pp. 214–20.

HUDSON, W.W. and RICKETTS, W.A. (1980) 'A strategy for the measurement of homophobia', *Journal of Homosexuality*, 5, 4, pp. 357–72.

JACKSON, B. and HARDIMAN, R. (1988) 'Oppression: Conceptual and developmental analysis', manuscript submitted for publication.

KINGDON, M.A. (1979) 'Lesbians', *The Counseling Psychologist*, 8, 1, pp. 44–5.

LENSKYJ, H. (1986) *Out of Bounds: Women, Sport and Sexuality*, Toronto, Ontario, The Women's Press.

LOCKE, L.F. and JENSEN, M. (1970) 'The heterosexuality of women in physical education', *The Foil*, Fall, pp. 30–4.

MEMMI, A. (1965) *The Colonizer and the Colonized*, Boston, MA, Beacon Press.

MORIN, S. and GARFINKLE, E. (1978) 'Male homophobia', *Journal of Social Issues*, 34, 1, pp. 29–47.

NICKESON, S.S. (1980) 'A comparison of gay and heterosexual teachers on professional and personal dimensions', *Dissertation Abstracts International*, 41, p. 3956A. (University Microfilms No. DA 8105601).

OLSON, M. (1987) 'A study of gay and lesbian teachers', *Journal of Homosexuality*, 13, 4, pp. 73–81.

PHARR, S. (1988) *Homophobia: A Weapon of Sexism*, Inverness, CA, Chardon Press.

POPKEWITZ, T.S. (1981) 'The study of schooling: Paradigms and field-based methodologies in educational research and evaluation' in POPKEWITZ, T.S. *et al* (Eds) *The Study of Schooling*, New York, Praeger, pp. 1–26.

SCHUMAN, D. (1982) *Policy Analysis, Education, and Everyday Life*. Lexington, MA, D.C. Heath.

SCIULLO, A.A. (1984) 'Tolls at closet doors: A gay history for teachers', *Dissertation Abstracts International*, 45, p. 497A. (University Microfilms No. DA 8412076).

SEIDMAN, E., SULLIVAN, P. and SCHATZKAMER, M. (1983) *The Work of Community College Faculty: A Study Through in-depth Interviews* (Grant No. NIE-G-81-0056). Washington, DC, National Institute of Education.

SMITH, D. (1985) 'An ethnographic interview study of homosexual teachers' perspectives', *Dissertation Abstracts International*, 46, p. 66A. (University Microfilms No. DA 8506864).

SQUIRRELL, G. (1989) 'Teachers and issues of sexual orientation', *Gender and Education*, 1, 1, pp. 17–34.

WEINBERG, G. (1972) *Society and the Healthy Homosexual*, New York, St. Martins Press.

WOODS, S.E. (1990) 'The contextual realities of being a lesbian physical educator: Living in two worlds', (doctoral dissertation, University of Massachusetts, Amherst), *Dissertation Abstracts International*.

Chapter 4

Life Histories and Physical Education Teachers: Exploring the Meanings of Marginality

Andrew C. Sparkes and Thomas J. Templin

It is an evening in January 1991. Outside the weather is very cold and the warmth of the open coal fire is welcomed. Two people sit on cane chairs positioned on either side of the fire. Both consume numerous cups of coffee. A conversation with a purpose is taking place between one of the authors (Andrew Sparkes) and Helen, a 22-year-old probationary teacher of physical education (PE) at a comprehensive school in the South West of England. A tape recorder is in operation and rests on a nearby table. The two individuals are relaxed, they knew each other before this meeting, and the topics focussed on in the conversation are wide ranging with both contributing to the ebb and flow of the exchange. For example, in the first of many of these life history interviews that took place in Helen's house we talked about the problems that PE faces in her school regarding time constraints in the National Curriculum, the views that other teachers and pupils have of her in her dual roles as PE teacher and maths teacher, the fatigue of teaching, her likes and dislikes about her school, and the financial problems of running a car on a teaching wage, to name but a few. Subsequent interviews explored, amongst other things, Helen's family background, experiences of her own schooling, her reasons for choosing a career in PE, critical incidents and key people in her life, the problem of ageing for the PE teacher, her life outside of school, and her hopes for the future.[1]

But why engage in such conversations? In short, our answer is we believe that to understand Helen as a teacher we need to understand her as a person in a holistic sense, that is, as someone who has a past, a present and aspirations for the future. Such a stance is far from original. As Beynon (1985) argues 'Unless we first understand teachers we can hardly claim to understand teaching' (p. 158). He warns that teachers in the past have too often been treated as though they were cardboard cut-outs which denies that behind the act of teaching there are embedded a range of attitudes, motives and emotions. Likewise, Connell (1985) notes how many sociological studies have 'tended to ignore the personal dimensions of teaching and often give an oddly inhuman account of this most human of jobs' (p. 4). However, as Ball and Goodson (1985) have reminded us, the previous career and life experiences of teachers will shape both their views on teaching and the manner in which they set about it. They also note that teachers' lives outside of school, their latent identities and cultures will also have an impact upon their work — all of which are located within a particular historical period.

More recently, Goodson (1991, p. 138) has drawn upon lessons learnt from folk music to suggest that those who sing the songs are more important than the songs themselves which cannot be understood without knowing something about the life of the singer. He comments 'to understand teacher development and curriculum development and to tailor it accordingly, we need to know a great deal more about teachers' priorities. We need in short to know more about teachers' lives'. Goodson (1990) emphasized, 'Above all, we should understand more about teachers' lives, precisely because we currently know so little: for teachers play such a central role in the complex conundrum of schooling' (p. 3).

The Life History Approach

One very good way to gain a greater understanding of teachers' lives is to listen to what Bertaux (1981) has called their life stories. Such stories, as Corradi (1991) notes, focus exclusively upon oral accounts.

> In sociology, the term 'life stories' refers to the results of a research approach that consists of collecting an individual's oral account of his or her life or of special aspects of it; the narrative is initiated by a specific request from the researcher and the ensuing dialogue is directed by the latter towards his or her field of inquiry. A life story thus involves a dialogical interactive situation in which the course of an individual's life is given shape: by reason of the request that stirs and orientates them, and the subsequent analysis to which the researcher subjects them, life stories aim to explain and give meaning to social phenomena. (p. 106)

Life stories are very often incorporated within a more diverse approach that comes under the umbrella term of life history which includes as sources of data autobiographies, personal documents, human documents, life records, case histories, etc. Clearly, there is no one single life history method or technique but rather a range of strategies. This point is emphasized by Faraday and Plummer (1979, p. 786) who in their own study drew upon data from a range of sources that included: letters (solicited and unsolicited), interviews (focussed and unfocussed), observations (covert and overt), books (autobiographical, pornographic, novels and books authored by their subjects), and diaries. These strategies can be used to focus upon an individual or upon groups. In the latter an attempt is made to explore the commonalities that often emerge across many life histories. Neither is the life history approach exclusive to any one theoretical domain and it has been used in recent years by a wide variety of researchers for different purposes. For example, the studies presented in Bertaux's (1981) *Biography and Society* draw upon diverse theoretical frameworks ranging from symbolic interactionism to structuralist Marxism.[2] Consequently, the term 'life history' can take on different meanings depending upon the discipline of the individual and their particular perspective within that discipline.

The life history approach has deep historical roots that are explored elsewhere.[3] For our purposes it needs to be recognized that, having been established as a *bona fide* research method in the 1920s and 1930s by Robert Park and his colleagues at the Chicago School of Sociology, its popularity peaked in the 1930s. After this the life history approach fell from grace and was largely abandoned by social scientists. According to Goodson (1988), 'This was firstly because the increasingly powerful advocacy of statistical methods gained a growing number of adherents among sociologists, but perhaps also because among ethnographically-inclined sociologists more emphasis came to be placed on situation rather than on biography as the basis for understanding human behavior' (p. 74). Likewise, Butt (1989) comments 'Given the power of empirical, behavioral, positivistic approaches in teacher education, it is not surprising that biography faded almost to oblivion during the last ten or more years' (p. 147).

While it is beyond the scope of this chapter to consider in detail the demise of the life history it needs to be remembered that its fate, both then and now, is inextricably bound to the historical emergence of sociology as a discipline and in particular its quest for academic respectability. As Goodson (1983) recognizes, life history studies often appeared to be only 'telling tales' and this was seen as a low status exercise in 'scientific' or 'academic' terms, 'Set against the life history of the aspirant academic we clearly see the unattractiveness of the life history method' (p. 137). He also argues:

> the pervasive drift of academic disciplines towards abstract theory has been irresistibly followed: in this evolutionary imperative, it is not difficult to discern the desire of sociologists to gain parity of esteem with other academic disciplines . . . Alongside the move towards abstract academic theory, sociological method became more 'professional'. Essentially this led towards a model of *single study* research . . . But this dominant experimental model, so fruitful in analogies with other *sciences*, and hence so crucial in legitimating sociology as an academic discipline, led to the neglect of sociology's full range of methodology and data sources . . . life history and biography have remained at the sidelines of the sociological enterprise. (Goodson, 1988, pp. 76–7)

However, in recent years various scholars have done much to rehabilitate the life history approach and initiate its revival in the domain of educational research (for example, Ball and Goodson, 1985; Goodson, 1981, 1983, 1988 and 1990; Goodson and Walker, 1991; Sikes *et al*, 1985; Woods, 1987). Between them these scholars have presented a strong case for the use of life histories and they have begun the complex task of overcoming some of the key methodological problems associated with this approach, such as, those of representativeness and typicality along with the major time commitments required for life history research. In particular, attention has been given to an issue raised by Faraday and Plummer (1979) who warned that while life histories may provide the 'truth' about immediate experience, they need not necessarily provide 'the truth' about 'the location of that immediate experience in the wider structure' (p. 779).

This issue has been an ongoing dilemma for those drawing upon the symbolic interactionist perspective that so often informs the life history approach. As Marsick (1989) comments 'Life history as a qualitative research methodology highlights the concerns of the interpretive tradition in which it is rooted for reporting the perspectives of people in the situation being studied' (p. 1). Illuminating the insider perspective is of great importance in any attempt to explain why people act in certain ways rather than others. Indeed, the ability to explore the subjective reality of individuals in a way that respects their uniqueness and allows them to speak for themselves is a major strength of life histories which cannot, and should not, be ignored. However, focussing too intently on the individual can result in a kind of blindness that divorces personal experience from the wider socioeconomic and political structures that shape them. This danger is particularly acute when we attempt to conceptualize a career in teaching. As Ball and Goodson (1985) remind us, there are both subjective and objective dimensions to a career in teaching:

> By definition individual careers are socially constructed and individually experienced over time. They are subjective trajectories through historical periods and at the same time contain their own organizing principles and distinct phases. However, there are important ways in which individual careers can be tied to wider political and economic events. (p. 11)

More recently Acker (1989) suggests that, 'individuals called teachers face a structure of opportunities outside of their control. Their chances of achieving the rewards offered by these structures, should they want them, are significantly altered at different times in history' (p. 9). Equally she emphasizes the structural dimension of a career by stating 'Historical, demographic, economic and political structures are part of the context in which teaching careers are constructed. We can see their operation around us only dimly' (Acker, 1990, p. 3). Clearly, it is limiting to simply view teachers as calculating individuals who make their decisions in a sociopolitical vacuum. Equally, it is inappropriate to view teachers simply as cogs in a machine who are unable to influence the circumstances that shape their work (Sparkes, 1991). As Giddens' (1979) notion of structuration suggests, social structures are both constituted by human agency, and at the same time are the very medium of that constitution. He argues:

> Power relations therefore are always *two-way*, even if the power of one actor or party in a social relation is minimal compared to another. Power relations are relations of autonomy and dependence, but even the most autonomous agent is in some degree dependent, and the most dependent actor or party in a relationship retains some autonomy. (p. 93)

In order to gain a sense of the dialectical process that exists between the agency of individuals and the constraints of social structures, there is a need to integrate situational forms of analysis with those that focus upon biographical and historical strands. Such an integration, according to Goodson (1981) would move studies away from a position where 'the human actor is located and studied in a manner contrively divorced from the previous history of both the actor and the situation' (p. 69). In this sense the study of life histories can actually assist in illuminating and throwing into sharp relief the wider social formations. As Faraday and Plummer (1979) comment:

> When one conducts a life history interview the findings become alive in terms of historical processes and structural constraints. People do not wander round the world in a timeless, structureless limbo. They themselves acknowledge the importance of historical factors and structural constraints . . . The analysis of life histories actually pushes one first of all to the problem of constraints bearing down upon the construction of any life. (p. 780)

This potential of life histories needs to be developed in order to guard against the production of accounts that focus exclusively upon personal process and experiences at the expense of any consideration of sociohistorical structures. In relation to this, Goodson (1988) warns, 'The life historian must constantly broaden the concern with personal truth to take account of the wider sociohistorical concerns *even if these are not part of the consciousness of the individual*' (p. 80). With these points in mind we began to explore the lives and careers of PE teachers.

A Focus on Careers

For us, the first step towards locating individual lives in a wider context begins with a focus on the former. We were interested initially to know what it meant for those involved to have a career in PE and what it felt like to be a PE teacher in schools. That is, we were concerned to see careers from the individual's point of view. Sikes *et al* (1985, p. 1) outline several important characteristics of this perspective on careers, for example, it is subjective; it takes a whole life view (a longitudinal dimension); it takes a whole personal world view (a latitudinal dimension); it is concerned with ongoing development; and it is concerned with a person's identity. To explore this subjective dimension we wanted to hear PE teachers at different stages in their life cycle and careers tell their life stories, in their own words, and at their own pace. As a consequence, each of us interviewed at least[4] one male and one female PE teacher from the following categories.[5]

(a)   Student teachers
(b)   Inductees-probationers (in first year of teaching)
(c)   Early career (two-seven years)
(d)   Mid-career (eight-nineteen years)
(e)   Late-career (twenty years and still teaching PE)
(f)   Retirement
    (i)   retired from PE but employed in schools;
    (ii)   retired from career in teaching/school employment;
    (iii)   career change (held a teaching position, then decided to leave teaching for another profession).

These interviews were 'reflexive' (Hammersley and Atkinson, 1983) in that we did not decide beforehand on the questions we were going to ask although we had developed a provisional list of themes for framing some questions based on our previous contacts with PE teachers, our own experiences as physical educators, and our previous research into this subject area. Later interviews often focussed upon issues raised by the teacher in previous interviews or they followed new lines of development initiated by both the teacher and us. Importantly, throughout the process our own experiences were often shared as part of the ongoing dialogue in what Woods (1985, p. 13) has called a 'mutual endeavour'. As Corradi (1991) comments:

> there is the fact that the narrative is engendered by a question on the part of the researcher, and it takes shape in a dialogue that places narrator and researcher on an equal footing. In fact, very soon after the beginning of the interview there will no longer be a questioner and an answerer, one who understands and one who is understood. Instead each of the participants is understood by the other and altered by the interaction with each other. This face-to-face relationship directs the life story and makes it the product of an intersubjective process of knowledge. The life story contains the narrator and the researcher; through dialogue the latter becomes a constituent element of his or her own object of study. (p. 108)

The flow of the interview, its direction and pace were predominantly controlled by the teachers themselves. For us, this issue of control was important. Our choosing to focus upon the lives of teachers, rather than directly upon their practice in the classroom, gave much greater control to the teachers. In relation to this Goodson (1991) has expressed concern over those who wish to develop collaborative modes of research that give full equality and stature to the teacher but who then focus upon the practice of teachers as the initial and predominant focus. He argues that for the researcher this focus may seem quite uproblematic. However, for the teacher it may seem to be the maximum point of vunerability. For him a more valuable and less vunerable entry point would be to examine teachers' work in the context of their lives since this focus potentially allows the teacher greater authority and control over the research process.

> Talking about her or his own life the teacher is, in this specific sense, in a less immediately exposed situation; and the 'exposure' can be more carefully, consciously and personally controlled. (This is not, it should be noted, to argue that once again 'exploitation' might not take place, nor that there are no longer major ethical questions to do with exposure.) But I think this starting point has substantive as well as strategic advantages. (*ibid*, p. 148)

Where possible other sources of data, such as, written documents were incorporated to supplement the life stories and to provide further insights into the life history of the individual.[6] Once again the availability of such documents was controlled by the teacher. These various data sources are informing a study that is still ongoing so the following is based on a provisional analysis of the data so far regarding the life histories of PE teachers in England. This provisional analysis has raised our awareness of the multidimensional nature of marginality and the impact it can have for those who work as PE teachers in schools. Consequently, the data for this chapter has been selected with a view to fleshing out several of these dimensions and this selection needs to be recognized as we attempt to move beyond the consciousness of individuals to locate their voices in the wider sociohistoric landscape that they inhabit. In doing so we hope to illustrate the potential of the life history approach to illuminate both our understanding of individual lives and the manner in which these are intimately related to and shaped by the lives of others in society.

Living with a Low Status Image

Various writers have commented on the status problem that is associated with the subject of PE in schools. For example, Hoyle (1986) comments, 'As a profession, teaching is prone to status concerns and, within teaching, physical educationists are particularly given to pondering status issues . . . we also know that there is a subject hierarchy but there is little comparative data on this. What one suspects is that physical education is universally lower rather than higher in the pecking order of school subjects' (p. 43). Status itself is a multifaceted concept involving prestige, wealth and authority (Biddle and Thomas, 1966; Biddle, 1979). Many of the PE teachers we spoke to saw it in a similar manner but placed an emphasis on the prestige and wealth criteria. As a male, mid-career departmental head commented, 'I gauge status, I suppose it's status in the eyes of other people in the school. Obviously, the most important people in the school are the hierarchy'. In terms of the status of their subject in the eyes of other staff there was an awareness across generations that physical educators had a poor anti-intellectual and non-academic image.

I mean everybody is moaning about the lack of time because of the National Curriculum. But it's systematically been taken away from us over the last five years. We're down to three hours a fort-night for the first-years. That was something like five periods just five years ago . . . It's low status as regards PE in the school. It's an area that just gets taken from, as does music, and art and drama. We are all shoved into one faculty, the Faculty of Performing Arts. It makes me feel resentful . . . The Head of PE, Harry, he's resentful. He's always pushing all the time to get more of a profile for PE . . . just to get more recognition . . . the fact that what we are contributing to the curriculum is something worthwhile. It's not just a time filler . . . In terms of PE they just see me as somebody who does a lot of sport . . . They don't see us as intellectuals . . . I don't think anybody does it deliberately but a lot of the time I feel like I'm being patted on the head and put in the corner . . . going into the staffroom on my maths days they sort of say 'Oh, you've got your maths hat on', and they don't talk about PE things like house matches. I'm addressed as a normal human being I suppose. (Female, probationary teacher)

It annoys me that I see subjects that are afforded status because of certain qualifications. Like people say 'Oh, he's an English teacher'. The fact is that he is afforded status because English is seen as a priority subject, purely because he's an English teacher — nothing about what he brings to the subject . . . It just niggles me. You get the impression of people, because they are dealing in what everyone recognizes as an academic subject, that what they are bringing to it is better than what I am bringing to PE, purely by virtue of the qualification and course I followed. But because it's academic, I mean in the National Curriculum you get English, maths and science (core subjects). It's good that PE is in there obviously (as a foundation subject) but it's afforded less of a status because it's not an academic subject. That's the impression I get. (Male, early career).

Physical educators from different generations were also aware that other staff did not see theirs as an important subject. A 46-year-old late-career PE teacher made the following comments based on her experiences at the grammar school she first taught in during the mid 1960s and the comprehensive she was teaching in at the end of the 1980s.

> In some ways it could have been described in the grammar school days as an awful job because the status of PE was so low anyway. I was only one of about four non-graduates on a very academic staff and such people actually sort of regarded you as an inferior being . . . PE as a whole had a bad name in the school. We were rather tolerated and PE people were seen as a bit incompetent. I remember I gave out the wrong 'O' level papers, which is unheard of, and I think that the Deputy Head was a bit sort of strict. I think the reason she was so nice about it was a bit, 'Well, it is only the PE department, perhaps we shouldn't have asked them to do something as important' . . . The important thing was 'O' levels. And it (PE) was useful because they let off steam . . . I mean we had a very good name for modern languages. Now some of them actually did three and that came out of PE time.
>
> (In the comprehensive school) It's a bit of a joke. We're useful for controlling less able kids. Until next year the less able kids in the lower part of the school get more PE than the others . . . They think it is good for them to let off steam . . . They're sort of more worn out and a bit more manageable. And the fact that we are filling up the timetable. But as far as making any serious contribution it's not deemed important. I mean one of the hardest things to take when I came back off secondment is that nobody could actually accept that I was going to get a degree out of it . . . I think the term is 'cerebral PE teacher'. But they just don't accept that there's any need for them or that they exist at all. And I'm quite sure that the ways things are going that our head does not see the need to have a head of a PE department who can do anything in the way of curriculum development — just keep the kids happy and keep winning the matches . . . Basically the status of PE is a joke. There is only one bigger joke than PE and that's TVEI (laughs). No, but that's true and that's one of the very difficult things when you are trying to get out (of PE) — you are regarded as 'all brawn and no brains'. People make generalizations and you have to work really hard to dispel them.

Others, who continued to teach PE throughout their career in school but have now retired also recall indicators of marginality. Danny, now 60-years-old remembers examples of institutional neglect at several points in his long career.[7] Another retired PE teacher of 63 years of age recalls that there were subject divisions when she started teaching in the 1950s, and how PE was considered on a slightly lower level than home economics.

The same teacher recognized that while PE was defined as a low-status subject in both the selective grammar school and the non-selective secondary modern school she had taught at, in the latter it was viewed more favourably:

> You had to fight for time. You fought for time more in the grammar school than you did in the secondary school. You didn't have to fight for time so much in the secondary school so much. Yes, I think the staff valued PE more . . . it was a two-way thing. They were happy to get rid of kids perhaps. That's sometimes the case isn't it, they are happy to get rid of their lower-band kids, they're delighted that somebody wants them . . . Some of the academic staff (in the grammar school) would not rate it very highly I think and begrudge the time spent on it, and expect that the top-band kids wouldn't have as much PE on their timetables as the lower-band kids.

It would seem that for both male and female PE teachers across generations working in a variety of schools that their subject is seen as less important than others.[8] On those occasions where it is granted some esteem it is for reasons that are questionable, for example, providing a form of catharsis to tire less-able students and make them more placid and controllable during classroom lessons. Such personal troubles as described by these physical educators, however, have their referents in wider social, political and economic issues that need to be signalled in order to contextualize their individual concerns.

Locating the Personal in a Historical Landscape[9]

The comments made earlier by the PE teachers have deep historical roots that go back throughout recorded history as people have debated the nature of the mind and its relationship to the body. The ancient Greeks assumed that the physical and mental aspects of the whole being formed two distinct entities, with the former in the service of the latter. This stance was reinforced in Roman times by Juvenal's apophthegm, *mens sana in copore sano*, which implied that a healthy body was indispensable to a healthy mind. Physical activity was seen as an important contributor to mental processes of the highest order. The mind-body split was further emphasized by Descartes during the seventeenth century. According to Turner (1984) 'The Cartesian revolution gave a privileged status to the mind as the definition of the person . . . and an underprivileged status to the body which was simply a machine' (p. 49). These beliefs have permeated Western thought and have been influential in the development of educational theory and practice. Commenting on this Entwistle (1969) cited by Viant (1989), notes 'The intellectualist theory biased schools of Western Europe appear to reflect the Cartesian Doctrine of Western thought: "I think, therefore I am". They reflect the assumption that thought is the primary category of experience and that practice is the step-child of intelligent theorizing' (p. 117). Consequently, the physical continues to be regarded as something apart from and somewhat inferior to the mental. That is, in Arnold's (1988) terms, propositional knowledge of the know-that kind is valued more than procedural knowledge of the know-how kind.

Braverman (1974) has also drawn our attention to the prevailing mental-manual dichotomy in our society and the manner in which intellectual labour is taken to be superior to physical labour. Saunders (1982) makes a further distinction and emphasizes that leisure is still conceived as subsidiary to work, the latter being seen as a means of acquiring the treasured symbols of our society. Similarly Kirk *et al* (1986) talk of the work-play relationship and the manner in which work-like activities are elevated to the realms of seriousness and significance just as play-like activities are marginalized and trivialized. These deep-rooted beliefs contained in the wider society are legitimated and reproduced in schools. Commenting on this Giroux (1983) argues that one of the dominant features of the school is the manner in which it recognizes and rewards mental labour while at the same time denigrating manual labour. Likewise, Evans and Williams (1989) point out that 'Teachers in schools, like society at large, tend to celebrate and reward general knowledge work rather than technical knowledge, the work of the mind rather than the work of the hand and the body' (p. 247).

A study by Apple (1979) illustrates some of the above points. His work revealed that objects often used in the work of PE teachers tend to be defined as 'play things' by the wider society and are assigned low status in schools. In observing the introduction of a group of young children to school in North America, Apple found that one of the first lessons they were taught was that in school there were 'work things' and 'play things'. 'Work things' included books, paper, writing instruments and the like. 'Play things' included balls of all sorts, jump ropes and bean bags, etc. That is, all the objects found in a typical PE class were classified as 'play things'. A second lesson the children learned was that one never played with 'work things' and one never worked with 'play things'. The children were also taught that play was appropriate only after the work had been completed. This reinforced the message that work is more important than play. In particular, it reinforced and expressed the commonly held assumption identified by Kirk (1988) that 'physical activity is antithetical to cognitive development, that educational activities are essentially about developing cognition, and so physical education ought to play a minor role in the pupil's educational experience, with less timetable time than "real" subjects' (p. 40). As such, the hidden curriculum of the formal curriculum transmitted the powerful and disturbing message that the very concept of ability is intimately linked to the intellectual-cognitive domain (cf. Hargreaves, 1982). These assumptions, messages and practices have serious implications for the subject area of PE, whose curricula draw upon a range of play-like physical activities, such as, sports, games and health-related exercises.

Physical education, and subjects like art, music and drama are engaged in teaching a particular bodily skill or set of skills. As a consequence, they find difficulty gaining acceptance within what Connell (1985, p. 87) describes as the 'hegemonic academic curriculum' that is devoted to self-referring, abstract bodies of knowledge. He suggests that this form of curriculum 'has pride of place in the schools, it dominates most people's ideas of what real learning is about; its logic has the most powerful influence on the organization of the school, and of the education system generally; and it is able to marginalize and subordinate the other curricula that are present'. The continuing marginalization of these curricula manifests itself in the low status and prestige given to them in schools, which in turn influences their positioning in relation to the allocation of power, resources and funding between subject areas. Therefore, the experiences of marginality and subordination expressed earlier by the PE teachers is located in a wider web of constraints that shapes their lives and career opportunities in schools.

Individual Feelings and Structured Implications

How others think and feel about a subject has important implications for those who teach it. Teachers in other subject areas may be happy to interact with PE teachers on a social level but be less convinced regarding their potential to contribute to curriculum design and educational debate. Certain forms of in-service courses may not be deemed appropriate for those teaching in practical areas, and this has a direct bearing upon teachers' professional development. For example, Jeff an early career teacher commented that it was more difficult for PE staff to get on in-service courses, 'like the provision of INSET and staff. Money this year went to maths and science . . . nothing provided for PE at all . . . So they weren't prepared to fund us, even though PE is coming to the fore in terms of National Curriculum development and stuff. They weren't prepared to offer us any money for cover so that we could go on the course and keep up to date with it all'. This in turn has implications for children's learning in PE classes: continually having to fight for time on the curriculum and for money to go on courses can lead to low morale and can affect what the teacher chooses to teach and how he/she teaches it. Furthermore, teachers who continue to feel devalued are unlikely to remain committed to their subject and will divert their energies into other areas of school life and their personal lives in order to gain both psychic and material rewards (see Sparkes, 1988 and 1989; Templin, 1988 and 1989).

In combination, these issues, along with those mentioned earlier, interact in subtle ways to structure career opportunities and development in a marginal subject that are, for the most part, beyond the control of the individual. For example, it is generally assumed that the so-called academic subjects, which are taken to contain within their boundaries some form of examinable knowledge, are more suitable for the 'able' students, while other subjects are not. More resources are given to able students and hence to the academic subjects. Therefore, as Goodson (1984) reminds us, the conflict over the status of examinable knowledge is above all a battle over the material resources and career prospects available to each subject community or subject teacher. In its simplest form, the higher the status of the subject the better the prospect for the teachers involved with regard to staffing ratios, higher salaries, more graded posts and better career prospects. Consequently, status means strength and strength means greater bargaining power for the finite resources available within the individual school and the educational system as a whole. Pollard (1982) notes how these finite resources set parameters for activities in the school and the manner in which these are dependent 'on the particular policies or patterns of allocation which exist in each school. These will reflect the institutional bias, in particular the influence of the headteacher, and the relative power and negotiating skills of the staff as they bid for resources' (p. 32).

How significant others regard a subject and how the teachers who teach it regard their subject, together act to structure the careers of individuals. Many PE teachers are acutely aware of such issues. As a female probationary teacher commented prior to the introduction of the new pay structure in 1987[10] 'Low status in the school would be how the hierarchy viewed the subject . . . If you are given a scale point in the school, looking around at the departments, who would you give it to first? It wouldn't be PE, it would be an academic subject . . . I don't think that he (the headteacher) sees it on a par with academic subjects'. Others agree.

I think that probably teachers in the academic subjects have an easier time in getting incentive allowances . . . I don't know, it's just an impression I get . . . So in a sense it's more difficult for you to get on if you are a PE teacher. If you are in competition with other subjects then it is more difficult. There are accepted routes for promotion for PE people in that you go off into the pastoral system . . . But promotion against teachers in other subjects I think we have got a more difficult job. I mean it is a competition now with LMS — you've definitely got a more difficult job. (Male, early career)

I think the major thing (the lack of promotion) it's all based on, I think she (the headteacher) doesn't rate PE. I'll emphasize that again — we needn't bother being there. If she had her way I think that PE would be removed from the timetable. She sees PE as just a complete and utter waste of time. That's how she views it. You can't get on in this school if you are PE. As a PE teacher I'm wasting me time. Sally's (female member of PE department) wasting her time, and everyone else is wasting their time. (Male, early career)

What these comments connect each individual to are patterns of disadvantage that operate within the educational system and the wider society. Historically, Ball (1987, p. 174) reminds us, certain patterns of structural advantage and disadvantage have been institutionalized in our schools. He argues that these ingrained career patterns extend across schools and that 'The most significant of these structures is the organization and differential status of subject departments'. More recently, Evans and Williams (1989) emphasize this point and note 'Teachers' careers are structured (limited or facilitated) by ideologies in the school work place that influence and differently define the position and status of both men and women and the academic and the "nonacademic" (practical) curriculum; and that these ideologies have their bases in wider society' (p. 237). They go on to argue that competition between subject groups and individuals is a fundamental feature of school life and an inescapable aspect of individual advancement through teaching. However, they point out that the competition is not equal in that teachers do not have the same status, social, or professional resources on which to base their claims.

In terms of the objective dimension of a career, Hilsum and Start (1974) indicate that 'If headship is the target, then *for teachers of equal experience* the best chances of achieving that goal lie with history, physics, French and maths' (p. 52). Similarly, figures provided by the Department of Education and Science (1982, p. 9), analyzing teachers qualified in each subject by salary scale, indicate that PE teachers have a lot less chance than those in other subjects to rise above the level of a scale 3 position within their subject department. Commenting upon their findings, the DES remark 'Nevertheless there are marked differences between subjects, with physical education, art/craft, craft, design and technology, home economics and music having a lower proportion of senior posts and scale 4 posts than the more 'academic' subjects' (p. 3). Apparently, those who choose to teach the more practical subjects are unable to compete with other subjects and are destined to remain on the lower rungs of the managerial ladder.

Women Physical Education Teachers and Experiences of Double Marginality

Choosing to teach a practical subject brings the problems associated with marginality to all those who make such a choice. However, the problems and dilemmas associated with marginality are not experienced by all PE teachers in the same way. That is, subject status alone does not account for the many difficulties that some teachers experience when they attempt to gain promotion or look for a job. Acker (1989) emphasizes that teachers need to be seen as a heterogeneous group.

For those belonging to particular groups there are blockages and barriers making their passage more difficult. Individuals possess different currencies (qualifications, length and type of experience, subject specialities) but their probabilities of holding these also depend on their class, sex, race, age and other identifications and memberships. Even qualities like motivation and personality may be differently received and interpreted by others according to who displays them. (p. 19)

In this sense, Ball (1987) argues, 'Women teachers may validly be regarded as a distinct interest group within the school if only because the overall pattern of their career development is so clearly different from that of men teachers . . . Women are severely disadvantaged in career terms by the male dominance of schools' (p. 191). As Helen, a probationary teacher, noted.

It's different for women. One of our deputy heads is a woman and there are two male deputies. The two male ones are in charge of timetabling and various other important type jobs. And Hilary is in charge of students, probationary teachers, and records of achievement. Things that are important but don't get the same status as organizing the timetable and INSET . . . of all the roles that are covered with deputies, she has got the ones with less status . . . I think she knows that's as high as she is going to get . . . I was just trying to think how many female heads of department there are in the school. I think there are only two . . . Men seem to get the good positions.

Helen, of course, is right. Drawing upon survey data of career patterns of PE teachers in a county in England, Evans and Williams (1989, p. 238) found that some striking patterns emerged between men and women when the distribution of responsibilities, rewards, and status were examined. Although most of the teachers in their study operated in schools with a male and a female in charge of boys' and girls' PE, they found that in 84 per cent of these schools it was a male teacher who held responsibility as overall head of the PE department. Furthermore, 88 per cent of the men in their sample, as compared to 38 per cent of the women had achieved scale 3 or 4 positions, that is, the top salary scale before moving onto senior management positions. Commenting upon these differences these authors suggest they have much to do with the fact that 'the language and structure of schooling and the subject departments inside them are often deeply shaped by patriarchy. The gatekeepers to jobs are predominantly held by men and they do not always believe women are either capable or suitable, because of their competing family and work roles, for advancement into senior positions'.

Similar disparities pervade the educational system. For example, contributors to Acker's (1989) *Teachers, Gender and Careers*, and De Lyon and Migniuolo's (1989) *Women Teachers: Issues and Experiences* draw upon qualitative and quantitative data to illustrate that while the teaching profession is dominated in the numerical sense by women, the positions of real power remain the domain of men (also see Spencer, 1986). Drawing upon DES (1989) statistics Acker (1990) indicates that while women make up 60 per cent of teachers in England and Wales, they are better represented in the primary than the secondary phase. Women make up 46 per cent of primary headteachers and 16 per cent of secondary headteachers. Both figures indicate a significant underrepresentation of women at senior levels compared to their presence in the occupation. Essentially, as Grant (1989) in making use of DES (1987) statistics argues:

> for although teaching is a career highly associated with women
> . . . and one in which levels of femininization are likely to increase
> over the next few years, it is a career in which women tend to be
> found in some roles and not others and in receipt of certain
> responsibilities rather than being represented across the range . . .
> Thus, as the proportion of men increase, women's representation
> at headship level decreases . . . Women are disproportionately
> underrepresented at management levels in all schools in which
> men form a significant group. (pp. 36–7)

The dynamics and complexities of the processes that socially construct and maintain such inequalities are beyond the scope of this chapter to discuss. However, in relation to this process we want to draw upon some strands of one PE teacher's life history to indicate how this approach can illuminate and help to explain the dilemmas that many women face in the context of a patriarchial system. Jenny is now in her early 50s and has recently left the teaching profession having accepted early retirement along with a redundancy payment in a school with falling rolls. Looking back Jenny remembers being an active and committed young PE teacher at a school in London during the late 1950s. Sharing a flat with friends, spending long hours after school running school teams, and still finding time for her own sporting activities. During this period Jenny went for a holiday in the West Country where she met her future husband who worked in that area. They got married at the start of the 1960s and, in keeping with many married women who end up teaching in the areas where their husbands are employed, Jenny moved away from London to be with her husband.

Having gained temporary teaching positions for a while she gained full-time employment as a PE teacher in a secondary modern school. At this stage of her life Jenny loved teaching and felt as though she wanted a career and 'get on' in teaching. Jenny did become departmental head towards the end of the 1970s but a range of events acted to disillusion her and make her happy to leave teaching in 1987. However, in terms of her career progression several points are noticeable that revolve around her marriage and her children. Talking about her marriage which ended in divorce Jenny notes:

The getting married in the first place was a key point that changed my life (laughs). By picking a wrong marriage. Because I knew I'd done that not long after I got married . . . I knew it wasn't right, we were totally different. We just weren't compatible at all . . . Being a PE teacher didn't fit in with being married. He objected to the Saturday morning business and the after school clubs . . . He didn't think much of me earning more than he did . . . I started on £520 a year, I can remember that (laughs) . . . my husband made it known to me in sarky remarks. The reasons for it all (the divorce), well, mainly I think it was because he wasn't as well educated as I was and he couldn't accept it. He couldn't accept that I was getting on in my job, especially when I was made head of department in the 70s . . . I think that was the way it was in those days, that men were in charge. I think that was even more so in the South West . . . The time I gave to PE created tensions. He would say 'You spend more time at school than you do at home'. It got to the stage when he began to say 'But you're not really doing all this sort of thing. It wasn't all work'. Hinting as some affair. He'd just got hang-ups about it. He knew he was marrying a PE teacher but whether he knew what was entailed I don't know. I don't know if he realized how much out of school time is involved in PE. He certainly couldn't accept it.

In 1963 Jenny had her first child. Four years later her second child was born and eighteen months after this came her third. With the divorce in 1974 Jenny gained custody of the three children. She notes, 'The divorce was a major upheaval in my life . . . I have basically brought up the three kids by myself. That obviously has affected my life in a pretty big way'. Jenny felt that her choice to have children, regardless of the divorce, had a dramatic impact upon her career aspirations because it meant her being out of full-time teaching for six years.

In those days you just had to leave and that was the end of your job. You had to apply for another job if you wanted to go back. So all those years, like when I was off I lost that pension. I lost those years for pension rights. There was no way around it. It was a big factor for women and their jobs and their careers. I couldn't have sort of had the kid and then gone back to work putting him with a baby sitter like they do now. You just couldn't do it, you had to leave the job . . . It was accepted. That was what happened up till then, there had never been any choice so you just accepted it . . . it was unfair especially if you were a woman. It affects your career. Not only that, it affects you later on in life as well. I would probably have had a bigger pension. I would have had a bigger redundancy payment, but time out for three kids reduces all that doesn't it.

There was no maternity leave . . . so I had no choice . . . I ended up picking up work wherever it came along. Sometimes it was PE, sometimes it was English or maths (laughs), women coming back into teaching then were the equivalent of supply teachers . . . My husband was happy with that at the time . . . I saw a career at first in teaching. When I first started I thought I would stay in PE for ever so I was aiming for head of department but that got put back when I had children . . . (when second and third children born close to each other) I decided I would have to wait until they went to school and then see what develops. Fortunately, this head of department did develop just after I'd gone back full time. At Marshlane they took me back without any question as an ordinary scaled teacher. Then within a year the head of department left and I got it, but it was all luck. You can't plan if you have kids.

It's different trying to have a career if you are a woman. When a woman has children anyway it mucks up her career. As I say, not so much nowadays but I think it did for me speaking personally. But, I mean, now the systems different, so if you really are career minded you plonk your kids with a child-minder and go straight back. I don't know, but having kids does make a difference. Having said that, women don't tend to get to the top do they. I don't understand it. After a woman's had a family and she's gone back, she should be able to make it then. But then again do we go back to this age thing. Is she by then too old? Or has she missed out on all those years in between to get experience behind her to get those jobs? . . . I suppose if you wanted a career when I started you just had one (child) and got back as quick as you could.

They built a new sports hall at the school and they offered me the manager's job. I felt I just couldn't take it because of the time involved, it was evenings. That was one of the main things that made a difference, having to turn down that job, because there was no way I could have coped with it . . . That was just before we broke up . . . He didn't think much of it.

Having the divorce limited what I could do after that in many ways. Career wise and otherwise . . . I chose to keep the kids, I didn't want to give them up. Life would have been easier for me if I had but no way, no, I took them with me. I was committed to them after that. I felt that they shouldn't suffer any more after that so I tried to make life as normal for them as possible . . . Once I was divorced I had to concentrate quite a bit of time on the kids . . . I suppose that's why my career came to a halt at that stage because I was thinking about them mainly rather than myself . . . If I hadn't had the kids to worry about and think about what was best for them I could probably have moved to somewhere different. But with them having moved house and they'd already moved school because of it, I just felt they wanted some stability somewhere. So rather than look at my own career then and see a job somewhere else and go for it, which would mean uprooting them again, I tended to think of them first.

I suppose I had to lead two separate lives.

Jenny, as a mother and a PE teacher, is not alone in attempting to lead two separate lives as a means of coping with the role conflicts that arise when individuals are faced with simultaneous, yet contradictory, sets of expectations from self and others. Many of the women in our study spoke of the tensions and strains, both physical and mental, of running a home, trying to be a good mother, and trying to be a good teacher. Acker (1990) talks of women 'who juggled domestic and work commitments with the finely honed skills of circus performers' (p. 18). Likewise, as Evans and Williams (1989) found in their study 'Many women had to manage two careers, one in the paid educational work place, the other in the unpaid context of family life; still they have to bear the main responsibility for child rearing and servicing other family member needs' (p. 241). Indeed, Spencer (1986) talks of women teachers having a 'triple day' of work, 'They taught all day, did most of the housework (including child care), and then did more school work, such as grading papers' (p. 13).

Evans and Williams (1989) suggest that performing these multiple roles often has important implications for how women are perceived in schools and concomitantly for their occupational careers. Furthermore, we would argue, these dual pressures act in important ways to shape the expectations and perceptions that women have about themselves that has consequences for the way they function as people both in and out of school. As Connell (1985) argues 'the way one responds to the emotional demands of teaching becomes decisive for one's whole emotional economy' (p. 151). While many teachers would like to compartmentalize their life at home and school it remains impossible for most to do so since relationships in one facet of a teacher's life are interrelated to relationships in other areas. According to Spencer (1986) in her study of contemporary women teachers:

> Home and school events were ever-present realities, regardless of differing situational contexts. For example, teachers' salaries and working conditions affected their life-styles and limited or broadened their choices for options or change. At the same time, marital choices, husbands' incomes and job locations, and the number of children in their families also limited or broadened their alternatives for teaching jobs. Dissatisfaction with teaching influenced personal and marital relations, and personal problems influenced teaching effectiveness. The effects of home and school were inextricably interrelated. (pp. 185–6)

Women in other walks of life also experience a range of contradictions between being a mother and maintaining some form of independence in the outside world. Gieve (1989, pp. x–xi) in the introduction to her edited book, entitled *Balancing Acts: On Being a Mother,* comments on the dashed hopes of many women who began their working lives within the groundswell of the women's movement in the 1950s and 1960s, who aspired to be able to have children and also be their own persons, earning a living and playing a part in the public world. She notes, 'It does not seem too much to ask. Yet as things are now it is a great privilege to do so without exhaustion and desperation, and a sense of shortchanging one world for another . . . There are many contradictions to understand and come to terms with in coping with the emotional stresses of motherhood and reconciling them with the rest of life'. For her, such reconciliations would be facilitated by major changes in the public world that include: a willingness to restructure work conditions for those with domestic responsibilities; a willingness to use collective resources to provide better care for children outside their homes; and a willingness to provide an environment that is more friendly to those who look after children. Unfortunately, 'Neither the political rhetoric nor the practice of the 1980s has shown this willingness. The opposite is true'.

It is within this sociohistorical landscape that the experiences of Jenny as a working mother have been shaped and connected to the experiences of other women in similar situations. In order to make sense of her experiences we need to be aware of this landscape. For example, Ball (1987) comments 'Negotiations over the issue of female labour will be resolved differently in different households according to whether tradition (patriarchy) or rationality (maximization of economic interests) prevail' (pp. 198–9). He goes on to argue that where both models have equal or similar importance for household members in explaining their social world that negotiations are likely to lead to conflict, 'The costs arising from such a conflict may be high; working wives may find that they face difficult decisions in weighing up their marriage and family against their career'. At times this can lead to breakdowns in the marital relationship. However, even where resolutions within the household are achieved, he emphasizes 'the organization of family life alongside work life may prove problematic . . . the contemporary conditions of employment continue to be orientated to the male employee. Married women find they must adapt themselves to the conditions based upon a male norm'. As Cunnison (1985) cited in Ball (1987), bluntly puts it 'The world of work is made-to-measure for men who do not get pregnant and have family responsibilities' (p. 32).

Of course, we do not wish to suggest that all women, whether married or divorced, experience teaching in the same way as Jenny. Women in similar situations may have very different stories to tell. Stories will also vary for those in different situations. For example, Templin (1988 and 1989) provides examples of two female PE teachers, one single and one with a supportive partner willing to enter into a symmetrical relationship, who chose not to make their occupational careers secondary to a 'career' as wife or mother. The availability of other stories, however, does not detract from the importance of the one told by Jenny as it helps to illuminate and explain the strands of oppression that structured her life chances and experience along with those of many other women.[11] This exposure can assist in the ongoing critique of the dominant structures in our society that has been mounted by feminist scholars in recent years (see chapter 6 in this volume). Ultimately, as Benn (1989) argues:

> Ending the old divisions, however, cannot be limited to balancing the proportion of the sexes in the traditional spheres of male and female teaching influence. This superficial approach ignores the deeper structural factors that account for so many of the problems women teachers meet in any part of the education and training . . . Inequality and discrimination for women teachers is only partly a matter of gender; ultimately it is a matter of power . . . Challenging for equal power in teaching means challenging power throughout society. (pp. xxiii–xxv)

In this sense, exploring the life histories of women (and other oppressed groups) provides a powerful form of engagement that is able to widen women's awareness about the structural realities of their lives that would include the ways in which the socializing process conditions them to accept masculinized images of schooling, accept/tolerate discrimination and to undervalue themselves in teaching. Furthermore, their stories invariably raise the issue of the division of labour in the home which for many is the key to changing male perception and participation. As Al-Khalifa (1989) notes in her consideration of the benefits of single-sex training in terms of empowerment and creating change for women wanting to enter management positions, 'no major change is possible without a significant reorientation in training and management practice which affects mens's attitudes and behaviours as well' (p. 96). Within her framework, life histories could be used to support anti-sexist training for men in teaching and encourage such reorientations to take place.

Comment

In providing a brief rationale for the life history approach and the kind of data it draws upon, we hope that we have been able to illustrate the richness and explanatory power of this approach and the manner in which it can encompass the universal within the particular by anchoring the subject in larger social, historical, political and economic contexts that have a general influence on an individual life. While a major strength of this approach lies in its ability to explore the subjective reality of the individual in a way that respects the uniqueness of people, it also promotes an identification of the commonalities between them and the way these

commonalities are linked to wider socioeconomic and political circumstances that effect people at the micro level of their lives. Since life
histories are able to give meaning to the overworked notion of *process*
they can, for those teachers and researchers engaged in constructing them
or reading them, assist in making connections between personal troubles
and social issues (Mills, 1959). As Woods (1987) notes 'Life histories can
also inform our thinking about the personal engagement with social structure, with implications for some of the most prominent public issues of
the day' (p. 130).

In its ability to highlight the links between private and public issues
life history work with teachers is able to provide important insights into
the nature of teaching, for example, teaching as a gendered profession (cf.
Goodson, 1990). Furthermore, because life histories enable individuals to
explore how their self was constructed this approach has the potential to
raise teacher consciousness with respect to a range of other closely related
issues that involve forms of oppression in educational institutions based
on race/ethnicity, sexual orientation, social class and disability. Such
consciousness raising illuminates for both teacher and researcher the
interrelationship of thought, action and experience. Importantly, it can
facilitate critical reflection, development and growth on the part of the
teacher, enabling her or him to become aware of a range of dimly lit
problems, so that they can be challenged and transcended (see Sparkes
(*et al* 1990; Sparkes, 1991). Therefore, as Butt and Raymond (1987) realize,
biography has the potential to be emancipatory, 'not only for the teacher
and researchers' knowledge and growth, but also in terms of liberating
them from the dysfunctional structures of previous roles and relationships'
(p. 79)[12] They outline another important strength of the life history
approach and suggest that as a form of collaborative research, involving
collegial rather than vertical relationships, that the teacher's voice is able to
be heard.

> It provides a vehicle for recording and interpreting the *teacher's
> voice*. The notion of the teacher's voice is used in several literal
> and metaphorical senses ... In a political sense, the teacher's
> voice attests to the *right* of speaking and being represented. It can
> represent the views of both unique individuals and a number of
> people — a collective voice. 'Voice' also connotes that what is
> said is *characteristic* of teachers, as distinct from other potential
> voices. (*ibid*, p. 77)

According to Elbaz (1990) a concern with voice is implicit in the work of
all those who are committed to the empowerment of teachers and that
where the notion of 'voice' is used, 'the term is always used against the
background of a previous silence, and it is a political usage as well as
an epistemological one' (p. 17). In relation to this Goodson (1991) points
out that with regard to the world of teacher development, 'the central

ingredient so far missing is the *teacher's voice*', and that strategies need to be developed which 'facilitate, maximize and in a real sense legislate the capturing of the teacher's voice' (pp. 141–2).

By creating knowledge that carries the teacher's voice the life history approach has the potential to overcome several of the problems that have been associated with much of the previous research *on* teachers. In summarizing these problems Woods (1987, pp. 121–22) suggests amongst other things that much of this research has not produced knowledge for teachers but for others in a way that is remote from the practical concerns of teachers. Furthermore, such knowledge is not under their control, 'It is produced "out there" and "up there" on an apparently superior plain in forms and terms with which they cannot engage . . . teachers are small cogs in the mighty wheel. Their own views on the matter do not appear to count'. Likewise, the input of a teacher's own personal resources and the degree to which teachers can change situations as well as themselves are largely left out of the account. In view of all this it is hardly suprising that many teachers define much educational research as irrelevant. In contrast, while not a panacea for all the problems associated with educational research, the life history approach offers teachers access to research, control over it, and it can provide results that have personal meanings in their lives.

Therefore, as Woods (1987) argues, life histories have a definite part to play in the 'construction of a meaningful, relevant and living teacher knowledge' (p. 132). Importantly, in relation to this construction, Goodson (1990, p. 11) believes that because in the development of life histories, teachers are involved in work that is able to illuminate and feed back into the practice, conditions and understandings of their working lives, 'We might then develop a paradigm where research and teacher understanding move forward in harmony . . . an extended paradigm of educational inquiry where teachers could become both a central focus for and active agents in the undertaking of educational inquiry'.

In drawing this chapter to a close we hope that we have been able to indicate some of the strengths and potentials of the life history method. We believe it to be a worthwhile and justifiable approach in and of itself. However, we do not just value its analytical power in isolation and recognize its complementary relationship with other forms of research, such as, critical theory and phenomenology, as well as with more 'experimental' and positivistic approaches. All are taken to be legitimate epistemologies that are able, both individually and in suitable combination, to provide a rich understanding of educational life. This is not to deny the fundamental tensions that exist between several of these approaches. These exist and they are important issues (see chapter 1 in this volume). However, we believe that each has its story to tell. In this sense the research enterprise should not be viewed as monolithic but as multi-faceted. Goodson (1988) draws upon the imagery of the mosaic and the jigsaw to locate the place of life histories and suggests that 'By rehabilitating the life history the jigsaw puzzle might finally fall into place, for there is always a better chance if all the pieces are used' (p. 80). We could not agree more.

Notes

1   Tom Templin (Purdue University) and Paul Schempp (Oregon University) were having similar conversations with PE teachers in the USA.

2   The range of contributions in Bertaux (1981) suggests that the life history approach is appropriate for the study of macrosociological issues as well as for illuminating issues at the microsociological level.

3   More detailed histories of the life history approach are available in Beynon (1985) and Goodson (1983 and 1988). For a detailed consideration of the contribution of the Chicago School see Bulmer (1984).

4   The term 'at least' is used to indicate that each researcher was not constrained and was free to seek interviews with teachers who provided interesting cases within the defined categories. That is, snowball sampling was encouraged. This was seen as important in providing rich contrasts both within and between categories.

5   These categories are in themselves problematic in that they were initially constructed in terms of an idealized career in PE for the purposes of sampling. However, as the realities of negotiating a career in this subject in different cultures emerge from the data the categories are likely to be modified. Therefore, these categories should not be seen as discrete entities with rigid boundaries.

6   For example, one PE teacher made available an essay that she had prepared for a course on the topic of her experiences with school governors. These experiences were then located in the context of increased governor power in the last decade. See Sparkes (1990a, 1990b and 1992).

7   Further details of Danny's life are provided elsewhere in Templin *et al* (1991).

8   We have discussed the typical reactions to this marginality elsewhere (Sparkes *et al*, 1990). We suggest that the dominant response is that of strategic compliance which further devalues PE in relation to the competitive academic curriculum. Teacher education programmes are seen to reinforce a sense of restricted professionality that excludes critique and disempowers physical educators on entry into school. The call was made for a more politicized teacher education programme for those who teach marginal subjects.

9   This section of the paper draws upon a paper previously published in the *Journal of Education for Teaching* (see Sparkes *et al*, 1990). We are grateful to Professor Edgar Stones for his editorial permission to use this material.

10 Prior to 1987 most teachers in England and Wales were paid within a salary structure that contained four scales and a senior teacher scale (headteachers and deputy heads have a separate scale). A rise to a higher scale was in effect a promotion and at the discretion of the headteachers. Since then a new system has been introduced that combines scales 1 and 2 into a main professional grade that teachers move up in annual increments. There is also a series of incentive allowances. Headteachers and school governors have considerable influence over who will receive these allowances. It remains to be seen how PE teachers will be positioned under this new system.

11 Other strands that operate within associated webs of oppression include race/ethnicity, sexual orientation, age, disability and social class.

12 Life histories have been utilized in initial teacher education courses (see Sikes and Troyna, 1991; Sparkes *et al*, 1990) and in-service teacher education (see Butt, 1989).

References

ACKER, S. (1989) 'Rethinking teachers' careers' in ACKER, S. (Ed) *Teachers, Gender and Careers*, Lewes, Falmer Press, pp. 7–20.

ACKER, S. (1990) 'Women teachers at work', paper presented at the Canadian Teachers' Federation, Women in Education Conference, Vancouver, BC, November.

AL-KHALIFA, E. (1989) 'Management by halves: Women teachers and school management' in DE LYON, H. and MIGNIUOLO, F. (Eds) *Women Teachers: Issues and Experiences*, Milton Keynes, Open University Press, pp. 83–96.

APPLE, M. (1979) *Ideology and Curriculum*, London, Routledge & Kegan Paul.

ARNOLD, P. (1988) *Education, Movement and the Curriculum*, Lewes, Falmer Press.

BALL, S. (1987) *The Micro-Politics of the School*, London, Methuen.

BALL, S. and GOODSON, I. (1985) 'Understanding teachers: Concepts and contexts' in BALL, S. and GOODSON, I. (Eds) *Teachers' Lives and Careers*, Lewes, Falmer Press, pp. 1–26.

BENN, C. (1989) 'Preface' in DE LYON, H. and MIGNIUOLO, F. (Eds) *Women Teachers: Issues and Experiences*, Milton Keynes, Open University Press, pp. xiii–xxvi.

BEYNON, J. (1985) 'Institutional change and career histories in a comprehensive school' in BALL, S. and GOODSON, I. (Eds) *Teachers' Lives and Careers*, Lewes, Falmer Press, pp. 158–79.

BERTAUX, D. (Ed) (1981) *Biography and Society*, London, Sage.

BIDDLE, B. (1979) *Role Theory: Expectation, Identities and Behaviours*, London, Academic Press.

BIDDLE, B. and THOMAS, E. (1966) *Role Theory: Concepts and Research*, New York, Wiley.

BRAVERMAN, H. (1974) *Labour and Monopoly Capital: The Degredation of Work in the Twentieth Century*, London, Routledge & Kegan Paul.

BULMER, M. (1984) *The Chicago School of Sociology: Institutionalization, Diversity and the Rise of Sociological Research*, Chicago, IL, University of Chicago Press.

BUTT, R. (1989) 'An integrative function for teachers' biographies' in MILBURN, G., GOODSON, I. and CLARK, R. (Eds) *Re-Interpreting Curriculum Research: Images and Arguments*, Lewes, Falmer Press, pp. 146–59.

BUTT, R. and RAYMOND, D. (1987) 'Arguments for using qualitative approaches in understanding teacher thinking: The case for biography', *Journal of Curriculum Theorizing*, 7, 1, pp. 62–94.

CONNELL, R. (1985) *Teachers' Work*, London, George Allen & Unwin.

CORRADI, C. (1991) 'Text, context and individual meaning: Rethinking life histories in a hermeneutic framework', *Discourse and Society*, 2, 1, pp. 105–18.

CUNNISON, S. (1985) *Making It In a Man's World: Women Teachers in a Senior High School*, University of Hull, Department of Sociology and Anthropology, Occasional Paper No. 1.

DE LYON, H. and MIGNIUOLO, F. (Eds) (1989) *Women Teachers: Issues and Experiences*, Milton Keynes, Open University Press.

DEPARTMENT OF EDUCATION AND SCIENCE (1982) 'The secondary school staffing survey', *Statistical Bulletin*, 5/82, March, London, HMSO.

Department of Education and Science (1987) *Statistics of Education: Teachers in Service 1985*, London, HMSO.

Department of Education and Science (1989) *Statistics for Education: Teachers in Service 1986*, London, HMSO.

ELBAZ, F. (1990) 'Knowledge and discourse: The evolution of research on teacher thinking' in DAY, C., POPE, M. and DENICOLO, P. (Eds) *Insight into Teachers' Thinking and Practice*, Lewes, Falmer Press, pp. 15–42.

ENTWISTLE, H. (1969) 'Theoretical and practical learning', *British Journal of Educational Studies*, XVII, 2, pp. 117–28.

EVANS, J. and WILLIAMS, T. (1989) 'Moving up and getting out: The classed and gendered career opportunities of physical education teachers' in TEMPLIN, T. and SCHEMPP, P. (Eds) *Socialization into Physical Education: Learning to Teach*, Indianapolis, IN, Benchmark Press, pp. 235–49.

FARADAY, A. and PLUMMER, K. (1979) 'Doing life histories', *Sociological Review*, 27, 4, pp. 773–98.

GIDDENS, A. (1979) *Central Problems in Social Theory*, Berkeley, CA, University of California Press.

GIEVE, K. (1989) 'Introduction' in GIEVE, K. (Ed) *Balancing Acts: On Being a Mother*, London, Virago, pp. vii–xii.

GIROUX, H. (1983) *Theory and Resistance in Education*, London, Heinemann.

GOODSON, I. (1981) 'Life histories and the study of schooling', *Interchange*, 11, 4, pp. 62–76.

GOODSON, I. (1983) 'The use of life histories in the study of teaching' in HAMMERSLEY, M. (Ed) *Ethnography and Schooling*, Driffield, Nafferton, pp. 131–54.

GOODSON, I. (1984) 'Beyond the subject monolith: Subject traditions and sub-cultures' in HARLING, P. (Ed) *New Directions in Educational Leadership*, Lewes, Falmer Press, pp. 325–41.

GOODSON, I. (1988) *The Making of Curriculum: Collected Essays*, Lewes, Falmer Press.

GOODSON, I. (1989) 'Teachers' lives' in ALLEN, J. and GOETZ, J. (Eds) *Qualitative Research in Education: Teaching and Learning Qualitative Traditions*, Proceedings of the second annual conference of the Qualitative Interest Group, Athens, Georgia, January, pp. 150–9.

GOODSON, I. (1990) 'Studying teachers lives: Some answers to the questions, why? and how?', paper presented at the annual meeting of the American Educational Research Association, Boston, April.

GOODSON, I. (1991) 'Teachers' lives and educational research' in GOODSON, I. and WALKER, R. (Eds) *Biography, Identity and Schooling: Episodes in Educational Research*, Lewes, Falmer Press, pp. 137–49.

GOODSON, I. and WALKER, R. (Eds) (1991) *Biography, Identity and Schooling: Episodes in Educational Research*, Lewes, Falmer Press.

GRANT, R. (1989) 'Women teachers' career pathways: Towards an alternative model of "career"', in ACKER, S. (Ed) *Teachers, Gender and Careers*, Lewes, Falmer Press, pp. 35–50.

HAMMERSLEY, M. and ATKINSON, P. (1983) *Ethnography: Principles in Practice*, London, Tavistock.

HARGREAVES, D. (1982) *The Challenge of the Comprehensive School*, London, Routledge & Kegan Paul.

HILSUM, S. and START, K. (1974) *Promotion and Careers in Teaching*, Windsor, National Foundation for Educational Research.

HOYLE, E. (1986) 'Curriculum development in physical education 1966–1985' in *Trends and Developments in Physical Education*, Proceedings of the VIIIth Commonwealth and International Conference on Sport, Physical Education, Dance, Recreation and Health, London, E. & F.N. Spon, pp. 35–48.

KIRK, D. (1988) *Physical Education and Curriculum Study: A Critical Introduction*, London, Croom Helm.

KIRK, D., MCKAY, J. and GEORGE, L. (1986) 'All work and no play? Hegemony in the PE curriculum', in *Trends and Developments in Physical Education*.

Proceedings of the VIII Commonwealth and International Conference on Sport, Physical Education, Dance, Recreation and Health, London, Spon, pp. 170–77.

MARSICK, V. (1989) 'Learning to be: Life history and professionalization', paper presented at the annual meeting of the American Educational Research Association, San Francisco, March.

MILLS, C. (1959) *The Sociological Imagination*, Oxford, Oxford University Press.

POLLARD, A. (1982) 'A model of classroom coping strategies', *British Journal of Sociology of Education*, 3, 1, pp. 19–37.

SAUNDERS, E. (1982) 'Sport, culture and physical education', *Physical Education Review*, 5, 1, pp. 4–15.

SIKES, P., MEASOR, L. and WOODS, P. (1985) *Teacher Careers: Crises and Continuities*, Lewes, Falmer Press.

SIKES, P. and TROYNA, B. (1991) 'True stories: A case study in the use of life history in initial teacher education', *Educational Review*, 43, 1, pp. 3–15.

SPARKES, A. (1988) 'Strands of commitment within the process of innovation', *Educational Review*, 40, 3, pp. 301–17.

SPARKES, A. (1989) 'Towards an understanding of the personal costs and rewards involved in teacher-initiated innovations', *Educational Management and Administration*, 17, 3, pp. 100–8.

SPARKES, A. (1990a) 'The changing nature of teachers' work: Reflecting on governor power in different historical periods', *Physical Education Review*, 13, 1, pp. 39–47.

SPARKES, A. (1990b) 'The emerging relationship between physical education teachers and school governors: A sociological analysis', *Physical Education Review*, 13, 2, pp. 128–37.

SPARKES, A. (1991) 'The culture of teaching, critical reflection and change: Problems and possibilities', *Educational Management and Administration*, 19, 1, pp. 4–19.

SPARKES, A. (1992) 'The changing nature of teachers' work: Physical education, school governors and curriculum control' in ARMSTRONG, N. (Ed) *New Directions in Physical Education (Vol. 2): Towards a National Curriculum*, Champaign, IL, Human Kinetics Press, pp. 1–31.

SPARKES, A., TEMPLIN, T. and SCHEMPP, P. (1990) 'The problematic nature of a career in a marginal subject: Some implications for teacher education programmes', *Journal of Teaching in Education*, 16, 1, pp. 3–28.

SPENCER, D. (1986) *Contemporary Women Teachers: Balancing School and Home*, London, Longman.

TEMPLIN, T. (1988) 'Settling down: An examination of two women physical education teachers' in EVANS, J. (Ed) *Teachers, Teaching and Control in Physical Education*, Lewes, Falmer Press, pp. 57–81.

TEMPLIN, T. (1989) 'Running on ice: A case study of the influence of workplace conditions on a secondary school physical educator' in TEMPLIN, T. and SCHEMPP, P. (Eds) *Socialization into Physical Education: Learning to Teach*, Indianapolis, IN, Benchmark Press, pp. 165–97.

TEMPLIN, T., SPARKES, A. and SCHEMPP, P. (1991) 'The professional life cycle of a retired physical education teacher: A tale of bitter disengagement', *Physical Education Review*, 14, 2, pp. 143–56.

TURNER, B. (1984) *The Body and Society*, Oxford, Basil Blackwell.

VIANT, R. (1989) 'Physical education, justification and style in the secondary school', unpublished MEd dissertation, University of Exeter.

Woods, P. (1985) 'Conversations with teachers: Some aspects of life-history method', *British Educational Research Journal*, 11, 1, pp. 13–25.
Woods, P. (1987) 'Life histories and teacher knowledge' in Smyth, J. (Ed) *Educating Teachers: Changing the Nature of Pedagogical Knowledge*, Lewes, Falmer Press, pp. 121–35.

Learning the Language? Discourse Analysis in Physical Education

Chapter 5

Learning the Language: Discourse Analysis in Physical Education

Gill Clarke

This chapter focusses on the language of teaching within the domain of physical education (PE) and draws upon data from a case study of language use in a secondary school (Clarke, 1987). In particular, my attention is given to a series of mixed gymnastics lessons in order to explore the process of teaching and the manner in which it is accomplished through the central medium of language. Encounters between teachers and pupils are taken to be social encounters and my interest is in how meanings are constructed and maintained in such encounters. Consequently, my gaze is directed towards the patterns and composition of classroom talk between teachers and pupils along with the outcomes and consequences of these interactions. In doing so I engage in a form of discourse analysis.

I use the term discourse in its most open sense to include all forms of talking and writing (see Potter and Wetherell, 1990). Like these writers when I talk of discourse analysis I too mean analysis of any of these forms of discourse. Hence, it follows that this research process involves looking critically at language and 'texts' in order to understand the meanings, social relations and cultural practices that underly them. To dwell further on definitions would serve only to illustrate the terminological confusions and lack of definitional consensus that abounds and be in danger of oversimplifying a complex area of research. For me, then, discourse analysis rests upon a number of assumptions, namely that language is central to all social actions and that through this medium a vision of the world is both constructed and conveyed. However, it should not be assumed that meanings are fixed since they may well vary according to who holds the power and the context of the exchange (see Sparkes, 1991). Indeed, I would go further and say like Fairclough (1989) that discourse is a vehicle for ideology and thus for social control. In connection with this it is axiomatic that different discourses carry different weights and the evaluation of their worth may vary according to who does the evaluation. It is worth noting too that there may be many meanings within a single utterance. Thus, it is important not to take meanings for granted. For language serves multifarious functions, and its use has polymorphic consequences. Like Weedon (1989) I support the claim that 'language is not an abstract system, but (that it) is always socially and historically located' (p. 41).

This analysis rests upon the above beliefs and the premise that 'actors' make sense of their world through language, and the statements that they make indicate not only how they perceive the situation to be, but also where they are in the world. Though the reality of the situation may lie behind the actual words and action used it is through speech that we impose our view of the world upon others and our identities are constructed. Consequently, while I acknowledge the contribution to our understanding of PE based on studies that have employed systematic observation schedules that facilitate the recording of quantitative data, I would suggest that by themselves they are ill-suited to describing and understanding life in PE. In particular, the restricted nature of many of these coding schemes denies the richness and complexities of teaching and learning (Delamont and Hamilton, 1986; Walker and Adelman, 1975). In view of this I would agree with Evans (1986) who suggests that:

> . . . if we are to begin to understand the nature and quality of teaching in the physical education curriculum and its impact upon the identities of both children and teachers, then we now need research which is sensitive not only to the patterned activities of classroom life, but also to the intentions, interpretations and actions of teachers and pupils and to features of the social and organizational contexts in which they are located. (p. 30)

The assumptions that undergird my study of language are consistent with those of the interpretive paradigm in that I was concerned to explore the subjective meanings of teachers and pupils as they interacted in PE lessons (see Carr and Kemmis, 1983; Sparkes, 1989 and 1991). In particular, I drew upon two major traditions within this paradigm, these were, symbolic interactionism and ethnomethodology. Both have played their part in refocussing the manner in which the language of teaching has been studied. Denzin (1969) highlights how both focus on some way on the individual and posit a link between the person and the social structure that rests on the role of symbols and common meanings. He further suggests that another area of mutual concern is the language of interaction, 'If interaction involves both languages[1] then ethnomethodology and interactionism provide a perspective for analysing the contingencies of face to face encounters' (p. 931).

In choosing to study language in use I accept the views of Graham *et al* (1986) who argue that PE classes are active communication environments in which academic and social goals are pursued. The four assumptions that underlie their own social interactionist research into the teaching-learning process are germane to my own study and they had a major impact upon the research. In brief these assumptions are as follows.

1 The physical education class is a dynamic communicative environment in which interactions between and among participants have multiple outcomes and meanings. . .

2 The teaching-learning context is actively created and multiple levels of context co-occur as the teacher and students interact . . .

3 Meaning is situation-specific . . .

4 Interpretation is required for understanding of the instructional conversation and related actions . . . (*ibid*, pp. 50–1)

Graham *et al* (1986) draw upon the concept of 'frame' to assist in the analysis of the teaching-learning process in PE. They describe how, as teachers and students work together, they engage in a process that develops several frames of reference that include expectations of behaviour and appropriate forms of participation. Since the concept of frame is such a powerful tool in the study of language I will now consider it in more detail.

Frame Factors and the Interpretation of Classroom Discourse

The idea of frames has been conceptualized in a variety of ways both by sociologists and educational researchers. Lundgren (1972 and 1977) has sought to explain the teaching process through the image of frame. He believes that if we are to understand, study, analyze or change the teaching process, it is necessary to see it as a process occurring within limits. Thus, he sees frame factors as being constraints on the teaching process and his model incorporates three types of frame factors all of which are seen to be interrelated. The first refers to the goals or objectives of teaching; the second factor refers to the sequence of the content units; the third factor is the time needed by a student to master the content and, hence, achieve the goals. Frames, according to Lundgren (1977) are regarded as limitations, in that 'they define certain allowable "outer limits" seen as necessary for the fulfilment of that process' (p. 3). A frame then, is any factor that limits the teaching process.

Bernstein (1971) also writes about the concept of frame although in contrast to Lundgren he uses the term 'frame' to refer to the strength of the boundary between what may be transmitted and what may not be transmitted in the pedagogical relationship. In this view then, strong frames reduce the power of the pupil over what, when and how they receive knowledge and increases the teacher's power in the pedagogical relationship. Evans (1985) draws upon the work of Bernstein and Lundgren and uses the concept of frame in his study of mixed ability grouping. His frame analysis indicates 'how specific factors of classroom life and the outside are interrelated' (p. 10). Evans delineates three major aspects of framing at the school organization level. The first is the curriculum, the second is the timetable, and the third is schooling. Further to this, he states:

> We can thus look at the classroom as a context of transmission which is constituted by the interrelation of related frame factors — what is made available to pupils (content frame), how it is made available (transmission frame), when it is made available (pacing frame) and the relationships between teacher and pupil (disciplinary or schooling frame) along with those of resource (physical and human). These factors constructed by and for teachers define the parameters for teacher-pupil interactions. (*ibid*, p. 11)[2]

The frames then that Evans (1985) describes which pertain to this study are those of content, transmission and pacing. These are closely related and exert considerable influence over the form the verbal encounters between pupils and teacher. Essentially, they determine what is to be taught, how it is to be taught and when it is to be taught.

The analysis that follows draws upon the work of the aforementioned writers in so far as this concept of frame provides a useful backdrop with which to begin to demystify the language of teaching in PE. It is against these interrelated frames of reference that participants' utterances are constrained and meaning assigned.

Context of Transmission and Competence

If we are to provide more holistic accounts of life within PE then the social context within which classroom discourse occurs needs to be considered. A conceptual framework to help us understand and explore the nature of context and its relationship to action is therefore necessary. This view is echoed by Edwards and Furlong (1978) who comment that making sense of what is said depends on locating language in the contexts in which it is used. Lundgren (1977) writes that few educational researchers have recognized the necessity of analyzing the social structure which forms the context for the communication pattern. He argues that the social structure of communication is as important as the content of communication in determining its meaning. For to interpret research without reference to this, is to render the interpretation inadequate. Stubbs (1986) echoes this claim:

> . . . a failure to study context reifies the object of study, by neglecting the interpretative procedures by which situated meanings are constructed, and by failing to treat as problematic the ways in which social order is successfully accomplished by members. . . . context free studies of language are reductionist. (p. 66)

Erickson and Schultz (1981) raise interesting questions about 'when' a context is, as well as asking 'what' it is. They ask how persons assess what context they are in and what features of context they seem to be attending to. These questions can be asked about pupils; how do they learn what social behaviour is appropriate within different contexts? How do they learn to become competent pupils? These are important issues because in PE the context of the gymnasium and the games field may be quite different and they may place contrasting demands upon the pupil both linguistically and behaviourally.

Within the context of the classroom a pupil needs to be able to monitor the different situations so as to know what behaviour, skills and knowledge are deemed to be appropriate for the given context. Thus, for effective classroom participation the pupil must display both situational and social competence. The concept of social competence appears to have grown out of Mehan's (1974) and Cicourel's *et al* (1974) earlier interest in the problem of how teachers and pupils acquire the ability to interpret rules and categories. This procedural settling-down involves learning rules on getting started with work, working on one's own, talking and paying attention (see Stebbins, 1981). Saville-Troike (1982) interestingly speaks not of social and procedural competence but of communicative competence. This, she claims, involves knowing not only the language code, but also what to say to whom, when to say it, and how to say it appropriately in any given situation. She identifies this as embracing three components of communication which include, linguistic knowledge, interaction skills and cultural knowledge.

This concept of communicative competence provides a useful tool for the analysis of the communicative skills demanded of pupils, and for identifying the contrasts and continuities between the contexts of home and school. Unfortunately, there are large gaps in our knowledge about *how* pupils actually learn to become competent members of a group and also how they learn to locate themselves within the world of the classroom. A vital question that needs addressing relates to what do they as pupils need to know in order to produce competent interaction. In the analysis that follows I attempt to illuminate the ways in which social competence is acquired.

Discourse Analysis in Action: An Example from Gymnastics Lessons

Forest Edge School opened in 1969 as a mixed comprehensive catering for pupils from 11–16 years. At the time of the research in 1986 there were 1300 pupils on roll. The PE Department had five full time members of staff, three male and two female, and there is also one part-time member of staff. The Department was headed by Mr. Jones who had been at the school since promotion to the post from another school in the area in January 1982. Mrs. Smith was in charge of the girls' PE, a post which she has held since 1979. She joined the school from college in 1977. It was from their lessons that data was gathered.

The curriculum was deliberately planned and developed since the arrival of Mr. Jones, 'To be pupil centred rather than activity centred and to reinforce the unique and essential part the subject plays in the balanced curriculum' (PE Syllabus, p. 1). All the staff acknowledged that their work[3] had realized a number of critical changes in both the content and methodology of their PE programmes. A development that they claimed had hopefully made PE more relevant to *all* pupils, with less emphasis on the product — skills, skilful performers, winning teams et cetera especially — in the junior section of the school. This then, was the broader school context in which the PE Department was set. It defines a framework of rules relating to behaviour, the schooling frame, (Evans, 1987) and it sets a curriculum frame of time and space in which teachers attempt to realize their aims and objectives.

The main research technique employed was participant observation of two first year mixed ability and gender classes. I use the term 'participant observation' here to refer to several techniques; it involved participating in the activities of the group, interviewing, analyzing documents and observing what was going on. These classes were selected as one of my research interests was in studying initial encounters between teachers and pupils; thus it was important to be there to observe their first meetings. These observations began in September 1986 and finished at the end of November 1986.

During observations detailed field notes were written and audio tape recordings of the teachers' talk were made. I also had informal discussions with the staff and pupils about what was about to take place or conversely about what had just occurred in the gym. Documents were collected in order to gain further information about the school and the PE Department.

In order to contextualize this analysis a description of the pattern that the gymnastics lessons followed is included. The lesson, once 'set up', had clearly definable features, and the structure unfolded sequentially through time. Both teachers assembled their lessons into similar component parts. Prior to the formal commencement of the lesson, both supervised the changing rooms while the pupils changed and both called a register of the pupils present. In this context, Mrs. Smith called the girls by their Christian names and Mr. Jones the boys by their surnames. Jewellery, valuables and notes explaining the pupils' reasons for non-participation in the lesson were collected at this time. These mixed lessons then followed fairly similar patterns.

The opening of the lesson frequently involved the teacher in an extended soliloquy, telling or informing the pupils about the form that the lesson and future lessons would follow. The children were then required to complete the next phase of the lesson, commonly referred to as the 'warm up'. For Mrs. Smith, this intially involved the children in copying a series of exercises demonstrated by her at the front of 'the stage'. In subsquent lessons, the children were allowed to take responsibility for their own individual warm up. Both teachers expected the children to complete a timed run as part of their preparation for the work to come later on health-related fitness. Mr. Jones' warm up activities were different to Mrs. Smith's. He engaged in a variety of games such as 'stick in the mud'. The next phase tended to involve the teachers in questioning the pupils about previous work. The following phase could be described as the instructional part of the lesson. Here, movement tasks were set for the children to solve. The children commenced work on the floor, then transferred this to benches and finally to the apparatus. This stage was seen by both teachers and children as the climax to the lesson. The final component of the lesson was its closure. This involved bringing the pupils together so that the teachers could either recap on what they had done in the lesson or asking them to recall the salient points or topic of the lesson. Directives might be given for the following lesson and or administrative tasks completed. Finally, the children were dismissed by the teacher to their changing rooms where they were expected to shower. Jewellery and valuables were then handed back by the teacher. In many ways then, the closure of the lesson mirrored the opening of it, since the procedures were quite similar. The phases of the lessons were quite distinct and they served different purposes. For example, the warm up was designed to prepare the children physically for the work that was to follow. The instructional stage of the lesson required the children to answer movement tasks such as: 'I want you to show me five different methods of travelling across the mat. Alright, five different methods of travelling across it.' (Mrs. Smith, Lesson 1)

Nevertheless, this description of the sequential nature of the lesson is merely that; it neither reveals how the lesson is organized nor accomplished. Consideration, therefore, needs to be given to what teachers and pupils have to do and know, in order to achieve this. Central to this quest is an understanding of the concepts of context and competence as referred to earlier in this chapter. In order for a pupil to perform successfully within the classroom, they need to know within which context they are working so as to display social, procedural and linguistic competence as defined by the teacher. In order to highlight these issues I want to turn my attention to the initial encounters that pupils have with teachers.

Initial Encounters

These initial encounters have been described by Beynon (1985) as special occasions. It is here that the teacher has to establish rules and routines for the future conduct of lessons; it is indeed a truism that 'lessons just don't happen' (Payne, 1976). The teacher at this juncture is unable to hide behind a variety of routines as they have not been constructed. In relation to this, Ball (1980) describes the interaction process between teacher and pupils during these initial encounters as exploratory. He argues that from these meetings a more or less permanent, repeated and highly predictable pattern of relationships and interactions emerges. He refers to this as the process of establishment. The teacher in these encounters must establish order and routine, it is they who generally lay down the rule structures and implement them. In doing so they define the situation, which in turn fixes the behavioural and transactional possibilities.

Clearly it would be an oversimplification, and indeed misleading, to believe that this defining is totally a one-way process. Pupils are not plastic and as Stebbins (1977) shows, definitions are not necessarily consensual. Pupils endeavour to test or 'suss' out the teacher, they try to discover the level of their tolerance and managerial competence. Furthermore, pupils observe how a teacher interprets and applies norms and whether they are consistent and even-tempered (Beynon, 1985). It is at this stage that they have to learn to listen and talk on demand. There is during this process of induction-tight organization of both the content and action frames; pupils must rapidly learn how to code and decode messages and judge what is appropriate behaviour for the given situation (Edwards and Furlong, 1978).

Much of this behaviour follows clear patterns which are guided by the existence of certain normative rules and the notion that orderliness must be maintained within the classroom. The following extracts indicate how these concepts and rules were established by the teachers during their initial meetings with their classes and the manner in which this process shaped the transactional possibilities for future lessons (see Bellack *et al* 1966). In particular they show how certain rules are publicly and explicitly announced and implemented as pupils learn to make sense of the new activities and demands of their environment.

Mrs. Smith in her first gym lesson with 1A made this explicitly clear during the warm up phase of the lesson: 'Start with heads first, just nod at me. Not too fast just slowly, 'a No'. You won't say 'No' very often I hope.' Both teachers in these early encounters made other rules evident. The children have to sit down where and when the teacher tells them to. 'Teacher: Right, let's have you sitting up. I know I say 'sit down', but when I say 'sit down' I also mean sit up. (Mrs. Smith, Lesson 1). Pupils also have to demonstrate their work publicly on request from the teacher and they are consistently reminded that the teacher is: 'Looking for a nice one to show everybody'. (Mrs. Smith). Not only do they have to show their work to their peers but they have also to watch each other's work. Doing nothing is not permitted and both teachers were concerned to keep the pupils 'busy, happy and good' (Placek, 1983). For example: 'Don't just sit and watch, it's not a spectator sport, everybody should be involved and doing things what you know you are capable of' (Mr. Jones, Lesson 1).

As well as behavioural expectations being stated, physical expectations for the pupils were also established. Mrs. Smith makes it clear that she is: 'A bit fussy in gymnastics and when I say straight roll I mean legs straight, arms straight.' (Lesson, 1). She makes her demands known again to the pupils when she tells them how she expects their feet to be positioned, 'These things at the bottom of your legs they're called feet. A lot of them looked a bit like kippers, wet fish at the bottom of your legs cos they are all sort of floppy. What I'd like you to be doing with them is to be getting them nice and stretched'. (Lesson 1)

The word 'kippers' was used in later lessons without any further explanation. Its usage subsequently meant that feet must be stretched and pointed, its meaning had become routinized. Mr. Jones also exhibited this kind of idiosyncratic and symbolic language. He too used words to convey a multitude of meanings in the context of his lessons. For example, '. . . Sit down. We've got five Southern Softies six Southern Softies, we need all the luxury don't we for the Southerners? We need to be sitting on something comfortable we can't be sitting on boards' (Lesson 2). Decoded this meant that the children were not to sit on the mats whilst either the teacher was talking or someone in the class was demonstrating their work. Importantly, the pupils have to learn to interpret and decode ambiguous instructions. The pronoun 'we' used by the teacher in reality meant 'you' the pupils. They also had to distinguish between questions proper that required an answer and pseudo-questions which did not. The latter were intended as statements, a pupil answer would not have been sanctioned.

Both teachers stressed certain words and concepts as prerequisites for the successful conduct of future lessons. Cooperation and trust were two concepts.

Teacher: Cooperation, that word is going to crop up again and again, even in that run certain individuals were not cooperating. (T. pauses.) Who were doing things to make it awkward for others. I would like to be able to say that 1A can cooperate with one another but at the moment I can't, but I would like to be able to. (Mrs. Smith, Lesson 2)

Competence involves knowing the rules about when to talk. These rules were stated explicitly by both teachers: 'Can I remind you that when I do the Register I don't expect anybody to chatter.' (Mrs. Smith, Lesson 1). Mr. Jones, in his second lesson with 1B, frequently told his class after giving them instructions: '. . . don't talk, do it.' A further example of this is the way that the teacher abruptly stops their speech when a pupil is talking at an incorrect time, 'Invasion, means games like hockey and rugby, netball, basketball and soccer, we shall be using — (Teacher stops as two boys are chatting) — If you've got any comments to make would you like to make them to me at the end, alright'. (Mrs. Smith, Lesson 2).

The pupil is required not to talk whilst the teacher is talking nor to question what they are told to do. The teacher determines who the pupil is allowed to talk to and in this situation it is no one, other than the teacher. Further, if they, the pupils, have any comments that they wish to make then they must do this at the appropriate time as defined by the teacher. Therefore, the pupil needs to know when and who to talk to and that this talk can also be dependent upon the nature of the work that they are involved in. It was permissable for the pupils to talk whilst working on the movement tasks set but not when they were involved in the warm up phase or the timed run: 'Don't talk, don't waste your breath'. (Mr. Jones, Lesson 2). Therefore the pupil has to constantly interpret the situation in order to know when talk is and is not permitted. They must also know how to state their replies. In order to respond to the Register being called they must answer in the required manner i.e. 'Yes Miss'. The teacher, through the use of statements as shown previously, is steering the pupil towards their definition of the situation.

The teacher's task is to keep the pupils there and to maintain their attention. This is achieved through strategies such as interrupting the speech pattern to draw attention to the fact that pupils are talking when they should not be and by reminding them of the rules previously laid down about when talking is permitted. Linked with this is the requirement that the pupil knows when to be attentive. The pupil has to learn to listen to the teacher on demand and to follow instructions correctly i.e. they have to be procedurally competent. This was particularly evident when the children were taught how to handle and manoeuvre the apparatus, for they had to listen in silence to lengthy explanations about precisely how this was to be done. Nothing else will suffice if they are to know what to do in order to engage in a competent performance after the teacher had finished talking. A competent performance in gymnastics requires physical as well as social competence and this is well illustrated in the lesson Mr. Jones taught. He stopped the class whilst they were working to make the following observations: 'Right, 50 per cent, that was excellent, 50 per cent absolute disaster. . . . That group there, I think you've got the wrong idea . . . I think some of you have got to listen much more carefully to instructions. Listen to what you've been told'. (Lesson 1.) Listening is a skill that the pupils must develop if they are to successfully complete their work.

These extracts begin to illustrate what competent membership of a classroom demands. A pupil must display through their behaviour that they understand what is involved and required of them in particular situations in order to achieve this competency. The notion of competency is perhaps more complex than this initial analysis suggests. Indeed, this may be central to an understanding of what it means to be a successful pupil. For if a pupil is unable to correctly follow procedures as determined by the teacher, then they are unlikely to conform to the teacher's expectations of what makes a competent or successful pupil.

Introducing Subject Specific Language

As part of the initial encounters aspects of subject specific language are introduced to pupils. That is language which meets the particular requirements of gymnastics. A specialist vocabulary and terminology is used by the teacher to describe certain aspects of gymnastics. It is important both for the communicative and learning process that the children share a reciprocity of meaning with the teacher. In gymnastics words such as 'travelling' take on highly specialized meanings and the pupils have not only to learn to understand these new concepts but they must also be able to employ them correctly during verbal encounters in the classroom.

> *Teacher:* Right, now the first thing we are going to talk about is travelling and that doesn't mean going down to the bus stop and catching a bus. Right, it's different sorts of travelling. Can you tell me what sort of travelling we could do in here, different methods? (Mrs. Smith, Lesson 1)

Edwards and Furlong (1978) suggest that the special language of school subjects can been seen as a mixture of intellectual necessity and group solidarity. Pupils are thus inducted into the use of 'subject languages' (see Cohen and Manion, 1980). The pupil also has to recognize the existence of other set words whose meaning must be correctly understood and interpreted. The teachers' use of words such as 'right', 'well', 'good' and 'OK' for example were often used to denote boundaries between various parts of the lesson and/or changes of topics.

Later Lessons

As the lessons progressed from these initial exploratory encounters so it became apparent how teachers control the communicative process and allocate pupils talk opportunities or turns.[4] For it is widely recognized that the teacher is the dominant force in the classroom and that communication is centralized and controlled through them (see Young, 1984). They decide who talks when, about what and for how long. Teachers, through this power, control the allocation of turns thereby enabling the lesson to proceed in an orderly fashion. A turn may be allocated by name to a pupil, this means that they have the floor and are allowed to speak on the topic asked; a teacher may also select a pupil once they have put their hand up. Pupils may sometimes reply in unison to a question asked and then the teacher has to decide whether to accept their response. The teacher also has to decide how to cope with unsolicited replies. They may choose to ignore them or where there is no other answer forthcoming, they may accept them rather as a matter of expediency. It is likely that an incorrect answer in terms of procedure is likely to be rejected and the proper way of answering or bidding described. Nevertheless, on many occasions the rules for turn taking remain tacit — they are not publically stated every week. Instead, they eventually become implicitly incorporated into classroom life and are no longer stated explicitly except for when they appear to have been forgotten by the participants.

Progressive teaching has been seen to place great importance on questioning as a means of stimulating pupil thought and discussion and if we are to understand the nature and impact of 'discursive weaponry' (Edwards and Mercer, 1987) the analysis of this aspect of discourse is vital. The lesson transcripts illustrate the vast amount of time spent in questioning the pupils by the teacher. In fact Brown and Edmondson (1984) found that teachers spend about 30 per cent of their time asking questions. Pupils are asked questions by the teacher for a number of contrasting reasons. The data reveals that typically the process of questioning provides slots for pupil participation within the lesson (Maclure and French, 1980). In the lessons observed; the teacher asked questions mainly of the whole class, and on these occasions the class were expected to listen to both the question and then the reply:

> *Teacher:* Right everybody come over here and sit down. (Pupils come and sit down, Teacher asks them a question.) Right, what can you tell me about gymnastics, what is it?
>
> *Caren:* It's a kind of movement of the body doing different kinds of athletics and movement.
>
> *Teacher:* Right, yes. (Pause) Can we use music?
>
> *Pupils:* (Chorus) Yes.
>
> *Teacher:* Yes we could do, sometimes we might, sometimes we might not . . . (Mrs. Smith, Lesson 1)

These questions might also be addressed to named individuals:

> *Teacher:* . . . What's the important thing when you've set that up? Matthew?
>
> *Matthew:* Put the things up on top.
>
> *Teacher:* Right, just check, it's obviously important to get the bolt in the bottom, but also check (Teacher rattles bars) bolts in at the top and exactly the same when you put it away again . . . (Mr. Jones, Lesson 2)

Many of the questions asked by both teachers functioned to test the pupils' factual knowledge about the topic being discussed:

> *Teacher:* What's the bone going down the middle of your back called?
>
> *Girl:* Spine.

> *Teacher:* Yes, it's called the spine, do you know what it looks like? (Mrs. Smith, Lesson 1)

and,

> *Teacher:* Right, can anybody tell me what's happening to your heart when you start to run for a long time or when you are doing any type of exercise, what's happening to your heart?
>
> *Simon:* It speeds up.
>
> *Teacher:* It speeds up. What actually happens then? (Mr. Jones, Lesson 2)

The teacher then, not untypically (see Mehan, 1979a) also evaluates the answer and follows this up with a further question if they require additional information. Thus it may be seen that it is sometimes only after the question has been asked and initially answered by a pupil that what the teacher really wants to know becomes clear to the class.

Questions were also asked to see how much the pupil could recall either about the previous work undertaken or about what they have just done in the lesson.

> *Teacher:* Right, what sort of theme were we working on? (Mrs. Smith, Lesson 2)
>
> *Teacher:* Right, what did we do last week on the floor? What did we do? (Mr. Jones, Lesson 2)

The teacher can also ask questions for a totally different purpose. They can be used as a check on whether the class or pupil is doing as they have been requested:

> *Teacher:* . . . what did I ask you to do?
>
> *Colin:* Get across the mat, doing rolls and that.
>
> *Teacher:* . . . Prove to me that you can do it now. (Mrs. Smith, Lesson 2)

Finally, questions were also used to test or check a pupil's understanding:

> *Teacher:* Now another word that's going to keep cropping up, I'm going to use, is the word 'originality'. Anybody tell me what that means? (Mrs. Smith, Lesson 2)

The examples given illustrate that teachers use questions for a variety of reasons: to get pupil participation, to test factual knowledge, to recall or revise work, management (doing as asked) and to check understanding.

Question format varied according to what the teacher wanted to know. It is the teacher who sets the boundaries or parameters in which the answer must fall it is they who control this discourse. The unique feature of classroom discourse is the fact that the teacher knows the answers to the questions asked (Mehan, 1979b). Questions tended to be closed, that is to say, there was only one particular answer possible and demanded. Through this process pupils were expected to display under-standing, memory and competence.

Teacher:	Stop, O.K., right just sit down where you are. Right, what sort of theme were we working on?
B.:	Travelling.
Teacher:	Travelling, what's your name?
B.:	Tim.
Teacher:	Travel, right. This morning so far we've been travel-ling . . . (Mrs. Smith, Lesson 2)

A more open format was also used wherein the response might take on several forms. But always the teacher knows the answer. For example, it might require the pupil to give an opinion on a sequence or movement that they have just observed:

Teacher:	Right, let's see Jenny's first of all. (Jenny shows her sequence to the class.) Very nice, give her a clap, well done, excellent. What was the most noticeable thing about Jenny's? Jack.
Jack:	It flowed.
Teacher:	Sorry, it flowed, it flowed nicely. Something else you noticed about it? Something that I'm always pestering you all about. Amy.
Amy:	Tension.
Teacher:	Tension, very neat and tidy. I don't think I saw her feet apart from that shape at all, lovely, well done. (Mrs. Smith, Lesson 3)

The above illustrates how the teacher already knows the answer to the question asked. The scenario exemplifies how the teacher steers the communicative process so that eventually she receives the answer that she wants, even when outwardly a more 'open' type of question has been posed to the class.

It is evident though that the pupils' responses are very brief. They may serve as an indication as to whether or not the pupil is operating within the teacher's frame of reference (see Edwards, 1980). While it might be argued that the giving of correct answers is an indication that learning has occurred, this is rather a simplistic view and one which denies the reality that may lie behind what is actually said. However, it appears that most pupils quickly learn how to answer the teacher's questions in the desired fashion. That is, they give the answer in a way that they know the teacher wants to hear. The following incidents illustrate this:

Teacher: I think there are one or two things that we've got to think about 1A (Pauses) and one of them which will crop up in the next two or three weeks is the word co-operation. (Pauses) Who can tell me what it means? . . .

Girl: When you co-operate with somebody you help them and you join in with what they're doing and you

Teacher: (Interrupts) Right, yes when you co-operate with somebody you do things that will help them . . .

When Mrs. Smith concluded that lesson, her question required that the pupils gave her the answer that she wanted to hear.

Teacher: Right, give me two words that we've concentrated on a bit today. What's your name?

Girl: Rose — co-operation.

Teacher: Co-operation, that word is going to crop up again and again . . . (Lesson 2)

Questions may constrain a pupil's thinking since the way they are posed and phrased can limit replies. Not only does the teacher seek the correct responses but they also expect that the pupil answers the question or takes the floor in the appropriate manner. This too is learned early on in the classroom. The pupil is required to put up their hand if they wish to answer the question:

Teacher: Right, hands up who can tell me what a sequence is? (Waits) Every hand in this room should go up. Every single hand. (T. selects pupil to answer.) Ali. (Mrs. Smith, Lesson 5)

The pupils are also told that they must put their hands up if they require help.

Teacher: If you're not very confident, put your hand up and I'll come and see you. (Mrs. Smith, Lesson 1)

Mrs. Smith stated that she tended to ask the pupil who put their hand up first. Both teachers agreed that when nominating children to answer the questions asked, they tried to ask an equal number of boys and girls.

A pupil has to claim the right to answer a question (see Edwards and Furlong, 1978). Sacks (1976) argues that the teacher owns the conversation and that children have restricted rights to it. There is some evidence of this in the transcripts for the teacher decides who is to answer and these rights appear limited. It is the teacher who accepts or rejects the answer. An answer that is shouted out may well be ignored as the pupil has not displayed procedural competence. They have not put their hands up and waited their turn. For example:

Teacher: (T. to all class.) Right, sit down. What was I rather fussy about last week?

Pupil: Kippers. (Desmond calls out.)

Teacher: Mark. (Teacher ignores Desmond's comment.)

Mark: Feet.

Teacher: Your feet, right I call them kippers cos they're all floppy and horrid. I hope you've been practising stretching those old toes, let's have a look, see if you can feel the muscles in your legs. (Mrs. Smith, Lesson 2)

Teachers also have to cope with the absence of replies.

Teacher: So there's lots of different sorts of rolls. We'll go through them in a minute. Anything else? (No answers from the class.) I saw some lovely jumps right over the mat. Anything else? (Pupil answers.)

Boy: Walking sideways.

Teacher: Yes, walking sideways. (Mrs. Smith, Lesson 1)

They may, as shown in the example above, choose simply to carry on and then ask the question again, or they may offer the pupil clues or cues to help them answer it. Equally they may decide to simplify the form of the question so that the pupils are able to answer it. At times they seemed to be engaged in a form of piloting (see Lundgren, 1972 and 1977). The process of questioning, serves also as a means of demonstrating the teachers' authority, since they control the rights of the respondent and the parameter in which their replies are to fall. Being able to give the right answer to the teachers' question also:

> . . . requires a knowledge of the conventions governing a particular kind of teaching and the ability to 'read the signs' in the teacher's structuring of the lesson. Together, these are both a necessary and a sufficient condition of answering the question. (Hammersley, quoted in Atkinson, 1981, p. 111)

The teacher is very much in control of these verbal interactions. The discourse is centred or channelled through them and they reserve the right to interrupt answers at will. The pupil is not accorded the same rights. This is indicative of the heirarchical nature of the teacher/pupil relationship, that is, it is the teacher who holds the power. Questions can be a means of exercising this power (Young, 1984). The very fact that questions can serve so many purposes illustrates the complex and problematic nature of classroom talk and this brief incursion into their use barely scrapes the surface of our understanding about their use. What it does show us is how questions become means of socializing pupils into learner roles and the retaining of teacher initiative. (Beynon, 1985).

Concluding Remarks

Successful classroom lessons are the result of the joint actions between teacher and pupil that are situated within specific frames of content, transmission and pacing (see Evans, 1985). These do not just happen, they must be accomplished through collaborative enterprise (Mehan, 1979a). Order must be maintained by the teacher if this is to occur. This is achieved by the teacher since they control the classroom environment. This orderliness comes about through the induction of children into the way of life of the classroom. It is not something that is random or haphazard, rather it develops over a period of time as teacher and pupil meet and interact. Teachers are largely responsible for and have the power to establish the behavioural frame (Evans, 1987); though this is not to say that pupils do not have a say in this process. However, this study has not been able to explore the details of the negotiation process (see Pollard, 1979).

The meaning of language as used and understood by teacher and pupil is not solely conveyed through the grammatical form; often the reality may lie behind the obvious features of the speech act. Each act can indeed have a range of potential meanings. The task for the pupil is to select the appropriate one for the discourse that is currently taking place. A pupil, therefore, has to display that they possess this knowledge and that through this behaviour they are a competent member of the group. They must know how to communicate and interact with others. The teacher is the hub of these processes, communication is centralized through them. They control this discourse through their power to select speakers at will and to terminate conversations at random. Thus, they control the classroom floor. The relationship between teacher and pupil is very much an hierarchical one. The teacher controls the knowledge to be transmitted and the pupil must receive it. Little opportunity is given for the pupil to question this. Indeed it could be argued that this is positively denied by the teacher in order to preserve both the orderliness of the lesson and the status quo within it. The gulf between teacher and pupils remains a vast one, even in the liberal and intentionally all embracing practices of gymnastics. Teaching even in this progressive environment remains characterized by the dominance of the teacher.

Central to an understanding of how interaction is accomplished and maintained within the classroom is the concept of competency. To be a competent pupil, that is one who is able to give a successful performance in the classroom requires that pupils display certain behaviours and skills as determined by the teacher. They have to learn how to interpret the teacher's language and to take account of the customs that are associated with their rights to talk and act. Thus they have to correctly integrate both social and academic knowledge, to assess the situation and determine what behaviour is appropriate.

The gymnasium demands particular competencies from the pupil, they must know and follow the correct procedures for the handling of apparatus, they have therefore to display situational competence. The pupil must also understand matters of form that is they must know the rules for speaking. The teacher controls these through the machinery of turn allocation. Further to this the pupil has to know when they must attend to the teacher; when they are allowed to move and commence work; when they must remain silent and also when they must reply or provide information. These rules are not always explicitly communicated to the pupil so they have to learn to interpret what is being said for hidden meanings. They learn the structures of the classroom as they participate in it, they learn accordingly how to participate in it competently as defined by the teacher. It would be naive to assume that the pupils are totally passive in all this or that the rules for classroom discourse are static. Indeed, the pursuit of common knowledge and shared understanding remains both problematic and a mystery for some pupils. Over a period of time though these rules become incorporated into the very fabric and structure of classroom life and so appear to be implicit and tacitly understood by the participants therein. We need more studies to examine the process by which pupils differentially accomplish classroom interaction.

This analysis has provided some insight into the complexity of classroom life and the nature of discourse within it as well as illustrating the kind of pupil competence that is a crucial prerequisite for successful interaction to occur. We have seen too the need for knowledge about the context and the speaker if we are to begin to understand and explain this process. Future work needs to consider the location of discourse within gender power relations. For, although it is now well established that in mixed sex classrooms females receive less attention from the teacher (see French, 1984) few attempts have been made to explain this phenomenon (Spender, 1982). It has been argued that within schools, girls are quickly made aware that their talk is evaluated differently from the boys. Spender (1982) comments perceptively that one of the consequences of girls not talking in class is that their interests do not need to be accommodated. Could the same be experienced within PE? There is room for development of our knowledge about this aspect of interaction. Wright and King's (1991) analysis of gendered discourse in PE and the effect that differences in meanings have on the production of different social realities for boys and girls looks promising, for I believe we have underestimated the significance of language in reproducing and maintaining male hegemony. Language by virtue of its social and historical construction can be the medium for social control and the playing out of gender power relations. Discourse analysis has the potential to unveil the nature of these power relations and the ideology that underpins and pervades these speech acts.

Post-structuralism and post-modernism may also have the capacity to help further our understanding of these issues (see Sparkes, 1991; Weedon, 1989) Unfortunately the language of both is difficult to comprehend. However, since they have the potential to inform our theoretical purchase on language in classrooms and schools, I would agree with Giroux (1988) and argue that the conceptual struggle is worthwhile and that to dismiss such perspectives as new code words and theoretical fashions would be too easy and a waste of the possibility of a new and startling vision.

Acknowledgment

I should like to thank Sarah Gilroy for her help and advice with the writing of this chapter.

Notes

1 Here Denzin (1969) is referring to 'two languages, one silent and one vocal, which characterize the interaction process' (p. 931).
2 Evans and Cook (1985), Evans (1987), along with Evans and Clarke (1988) consider these factors within the classroom context of PE.
3 Their 'work' describes the recent innovatory programmes that they have developed in health-related fitness, mixed PE and the foundation type games courses that the pupils follow. The latter refers to courses which are not game-specific but instead the pupils are involved in the learning of (i) ball skills; (ii) games-centred games (here their attention is focused upon the understanding of tactics and principles); and (iii) games-making (pupils devise their own games to establish their understanding and the need for basic rules).
4 Edwards and Westgate (1987) define 'turn' as: 'One person's turn at speaking; anything from for example, a single exclamation to a long series of utterances' (p. xi).

References

ATKINSON, P. (1981) 'Inspecting classroom talk' in ADELMAN, C. (Ed) *Uttering, Muttering*, London, Grant McIntyre, pp. 98–113.
BALL, S. (1980) 'Initial encounters in the classroom and the process of establishment' in WOODS, P. (Ed) *Pupil Strategies*, London, Croom Helm, pp. 143–61.
BELLACK, A., KLIEBARD, H., HYMAN, R. and SMITH, F. (1966) *The Language of the Classroom*, New York, Teachers College Press, Columbia University.
BERNSTEIN, B. (1971) 'On the classification and framing of educational knowledge' in

YOUNG, M. (Ed) *Knowledge and Control*, London, Collier MacMillan Pub. Co., pp. 47–69.

BEYNON, J. (1985) *Initial Encounters in the Secondary School*, Lewes, Falmer Press.

BROWN, G. and EDMONDSON, R. (1984) 'Asking questions' in WRAGG, E. (Ed) *Classroom Teaching Skills*, London, Croom Helm, pp. 97–120.

CARR, W. and KEMMIS, S. (1983) *Becoming Critical: Knowing Through Action Research*, Lewes, Falmer Press.

CICOUREL, A., JENNINGS, K., JENNINGS, S., MacKAY, R., MEHAN, H. and ROTH, D. (Eds) (1974) *Language Use and School Performance*, New York, Academic Press.

CLARKE, G. (1987) 'Towards an understanding of the language of teaching in physical education: An ethnographic study', unpublished MA dissertation, University of Southampton.

COHEN, L. and MANION, L. (1980) *Research Methods in Education*, London, Croom Helm.

DELAMONT, S. and HAMILTON, M. (1986) 'Revisiting classroom research: A continuing cautionary tale' in HAMMERSLEY, H. (Ed) *Controversies in Classroom Research*, Milton Keynes, Open University Press, pp. 25–43.

DENZIN, N. (1969) 'Symbolic interactionism and ethnomethodology: A proposed synthesis', *American Sociological Review*, XXIV, 6, pp. 922–34.

EDWARDS, A. (1980) 'Patterns of power and authority in classroom talk' in WOODS, P. (Ed) *Teacher Strategies*, London, Croom Helm, pp. 237–53.

EDWARDS, A. and FURLONG, V. (1978) *The Language of Teaching*, Oxford, Heinemann.

EDWARDS, A. and MERCER, N. (1987) *Common Knowledge*, London, Routledge.

EDWARDS, A. and WESTGATE, D. (1987) *Investigating Classroom Talk*, Lewes, Falmer Press.

ERICKSON, F. and SCHULTZ, F. (1981) 'When is a context? Some issues and methods in the analysis of social competence' in GREEN, J. and WALLAT, C. (Eds) *Ethnography and Language in Educational Settings*, New York, Ablex Publishing Corporation, pp. 147–60.

EVANS, J. (1985) *Teaching in Transition*, Milton Keynes, Open University Press.

EVANS, J. (1986) *Physical Education, Sport and Schooling*, Lewes, Falmer Press.

EVANS, J. (1987) 'Teaching and learning in physical education towards a qualitative understanding', *Physical Education Review*, 10, 1, pp. 30–9.

EVANS, J. and CLARKE, G. (1988) 'Changing the face of physical education' in EVANS, J. (Ed) *Teachers, Teaching and Control in Physical Education*, Lewes, Falmer Press, pp. 125–43.

EVANS, J. and COOK, S. (1985) 'Teacher strategies and pupil indentities in the physical education curriculum: Towards a qualitative understanding', paper presented to ICPHER Congress, West London Institute of Higher Education, July.

FAIRCLOUGH, N. (1989) *Language and Power*, London, Longman.

FRENCH, J. (1984) 'Gender imbalances in the primary classroom — An interactional account', *Educational Research*, 26, 2, pp. 127–36.

GIROUX, H.A. (1988) 'Post-modernism and the discourse of educational criticism', *Journal of Education*, 170, 3, pp. 5–30.

GRAHAM, K., GREEN, J. and EARLS, N. (1986) 'A multi-faceted approach to systematic discovery and documentation of teaching — learning processes, *Journal of Teaching in Physical Education*, 6, 1, pp. 50–65.

LUNDGREN, U.P. (1972) *Frame Factors and the Teaching Process. A Contribution to Curriculum Theory on Teaching*, Stockholm, Almqvist and Wiksell.

LUNDGREN, U.P. (1977) *Model Analysis of Pedagogical Processes*, Stockholm, Stockholm Institute of Education, Department of Educational Research, C.W.K. Gleerup.

MACLURE, M. and FRENCH, P. (1980) 'Routes to right answers on pupils' strategies for answering — teachers' questions' in WOODS, P. (Ed) *Pupil Strategies*, London, Croom Helm, pp. 74–93.

MEHAN, H. (1974) 'Accomplishing classroom lessons' in CICOUREL, A. *et al* (Eds) *Language Use and School Performance*, New York Academic Press.

MEHAN, H. (1979a) *Learning Lessons*, Harvard, MA, Harvard University Press.

MEHAN, H. (1979b) '"What time is it, Denise?": Asking known information questions in classroom discourse', *Theory into Practice*, XVIII, pp. 285–94.

PAYNE, G. (1976) 'Making a lesson happen: An ethnomethodological analysis' in HAMMERSLEY, M. and WOODS, P. (Ed) *The Process of Schooling*, London, Routledge & Kegan Paul, pp. 33–40.

PLACEK, J. (1983) 'Conceptions of success in teaching: Busy, happy and good?' in TEMPLIN, T. and OLSEN, J. (Eds) *Teaching in Physical Education*, New York, Human Kinetics, pp. 46–56.

POLLARD, A. (1979) 'Negotiating deviance and "getting done" in primary school classroom' in BARTON, L. and MEIGHAN, R. (Eds) *Schools, Pupils and Deviance*, London, Driffield Nafferton.

POTTER, J. and WETHERELL, M. (1990) *Discourse and Social Psychology*, London, Sage.

SACKS, H. (1976) 'U.C.L.A. lecture notes, spring in M. Speier, the child as conversationalist: Some cultural contact features of conversational accounts between adults and children' in HAMMERSLEY, M. and WOODS, P. (Eds) *The Process of Schooling*, London, Routledge & Kegan Paul.

SAVILLE-TROKE, M. (1982) *The Ethnography of Communication — An Introduction*, Oxford, Basil Blackwell.

SPARKES, A. (1989) 'Paradigmatic confusions and the evasion of critical issues in naturalistic research', *Journal of Teaching in Physical Education*, 8, 2, pp. 131–51.

SPARKES, A. (1991) 'Toward understanding, dialogue, and polyvocality in the research community: Extending the boundaries of the paradigms debate', *Journal of Teaching in Physical Education*, 10, 2, pp. 103–33.

SPENDER, D. (1982) *Invisible Women: The Schooling Scandal*, London, Writers' and Readers' Cooperative.

STEBBINS, R. (1977) 'The meaning of academic performance: How teachers define a classroom situation' in WOODS, P. and HAMMERSLEY, M. (Eds) *School Experience*, London, Croom Helm, pp. 28–55.

STEBBINS, R. (1981) 'Classroom ethnography and the definition of the situation' in BARTON, L. and WALKER, S. (Eds) *School Teachers and Teaching*, Lewes, Falmer Press, pp. 244–63.

STUBBS, M. (1986) 'Scratching the surface: linguistic data in educational research' in HAMMERSLEY, M. (Ed) *Controversies in Classroom Research*, Milton Keynes, Open University Press, pp. 62–78.

WALKER, R. and ADELMAN, C. (1975) *A Guide to Classroom Observation*, London, Methuen.

WEEDON, C. (1989) *Feminist Practice and Post-structuralist Theory*. Oxford, Blackwell.

WRIGHT, J. and KING, R. (1991) 'I say what I mean', said Alice: An analysis of gendered discourse in physical education', *Journal of Teaching in Physical Education*, 10, 2, pp. 210–15.

YOUNG, R. (1984) 'Teaching equals indoctrination: The dominant epistemic practices of our schools', *British Journal of Educational Studies*, XXXII, 3, October, pp. 220–38.

Chapter 6

Feminist Research and Physical Education

Sheila Scraton and Anne Flintoff

Introduction

One of the most recent and prolific critiques within the social sciences has been that of feminism (Harding, 1987; Smith, 1987). Feminists have criticized much of current social theory, arguing that it is male orientated, distorts girls' and women's experiences, or alternatively, ignores them completely. Within education, feminists have attempted to show, both theoretically and practically, how schooling and the education process operate to reinforce and perpetuate gender inequalities and the strategies that are necessary to resist oppression and enforce institutional and personal change (Arnot and Weiner, 1987; Spender, 1982; Stanworth, 1983). The debates continue in feminist theory with a concern to establish how feminism not only influences the research process, but also raises ontological and epistemological questions concerning the nature of feminist knowledge and feminist consciousness (Stanley and Wise, 1983; Stanley, 1990).

This chapter focusses particularly on *feminist research*, introducing the key debates and considering how these debates *can* and *should* inform and challenge current research in PE (physical education). In the latter part of the chapter we will discuss one particular research project within the field of PE which was derived in, and attempted to work through, a feminist standpoint. Initially, however, the chapter considers the key debates surrounding the feminist research process in relation to theory, 'method', 'methodology' and 'epistemology'. It is important to distinguish between these latter three terms as one of the distinguishing features of early feminist writing on the research process has been the tendency to subsume 'methodology' and 'epistemology' under the umbrella term 'method' (Harding, 1987). Stanley (1990) provides a succinct definition of terms:

> . . . we see 'method' as 'techniques' or specific sets of research practices, such as surveys, interviews, ethnography and the like. 'Methodology', however, is a 'perspective' or very broad

theoretically informed framework, such as symbolic interactionism or functionalism within sociology . . . And 'epistemology' is
a theory of knowledge which addresses central questions such as:
who can be a 'knower', what can be known, what constitutes and
validates knowledge, and what the relationship is or should be
between knowing and being (that is between epistemology and
ontology). (p. 26)

As this chapter will discuss, there are many different conceptions of
feminist research. However, there is one issue which continually re-
emerges in the literature and provides a common framework for our
discussion: *feminist research is fundamentally linked to feminist politics.* Its
primary aim is to create change and improvement in women's lives.
Feminist research, therefore, is research *for* women, rather than simply
research *on* women. Research *on* women may provide information about
women but could be produced from any methodological position and
may not have the overt political intention of fundamental social change.
In her discussion of 'feminism', Roberts (1981) comments that it is 'in the
first place an attempt to insist upon the experience and very existence of
women' (p. 15). In agreement, we suggest that feminist research places
women at the centre of the process, recognizes that women are oppressed
and are subordinated to men in many aspects of their lives, and seeks to
change this through a feminist research process.

Before focussing our attention on what constitutes a 'feminist
research process', it is important to look at the complex relationship
between theory and practice.

Theory — Praxis

The relationship between theory-practice or theory-research is con-
troversial. Feminist theories have developed since the 1960s with the
resurgence of a strong and committed feminist movement, with gender
inequalities receiving sustained, analytical and political attention.[1] The
relationship between practice and theory has been strong as women, in
the consciousness-raising groups of the mid-1970s through to the political
campaigns around abortion, childcare and violence, have attempted to
place their experiences and positions at the centre of analysis and political
action. This has been extended to the development of intense theoretical debates geared to historical, political, social and economic analyses of women's
positions. Importantly, women have developed theoretical frameworks
around their *practice*, recognizing a dialectical relationship whereby theory
can inform practice just as practice must be the cornerstone of theory.

However, this relationship between feminist research and theorizing
is complex and remains a key area of debate. Stanley and Wise (1979)
identify two traditional approaches to this relationship. They argue strongly against the first position that theory initiates any process of enquiry,
coming before both experience and research. Stanley (1990) develops this

argument further when she discusses the difference between theory with a capital 'T', which she regards as having become part of 'academic feminism', divorced from, and considered superior to, the experiences of 'mere women', and feminist theory with a small 't', which is grounded in experience, reflexive, self-reflexive and accessible to everyone. In the latter relationship between theory and research, theory develops out of the research experience and thus is 'grounded theory'. These discussions concerning the theory-research relationship do not exist solely within feminism. They have been addressed, for example, within phenomenology and have been central to ethnomethological challenges to traditional positivist methods. Feminists, however, have furthered these debates by raising fundamental questions about the researcher-researched relationship, objectivity, reflexivity, etc. These issues will be discussed more fully later in the chapter when we consider the research process. However, our experiences of attempting to conduct research in PE suggests that there is no clear dichotomy between theory with a capital 'T' and 'grounded theory'. The theoretical work of both feminist academics and practitioners (although we are not convinced that there *ought* to be a distinction here as feminism *is* politics) has informed our research. We did not begin with an 'empty head' devoid of theoretical thinking. We had been immersed in feminist writing and had formulated our own understandings with the benefit of the intense and complex debates that we had read and engaged with. However, theory is not static, nor neatly compartmentalized. Thus, as our research developed, grounded both in the experience of the researcher and researched *and* our theoretical understanding, so theory emerged and developed within and out of the research process. As Harding (1987) argues:

> The ability to go beneath the surface of appearances to reveal the real but concealed social relations requires both theoretical and political activity. Feminist theorists must demand that feminist theorizing be grounded in women's material activity and must as well be a part of the political struggle necessary to develop areas of social life modelled on this activity. (p. 175)

Both investigation (research) and explanation (theory) help to illuminate our understanding of inequality and oppression and contribute to political change. What is apparent is that the questions that some researchers attempt to answer have developed out of their own feminist theoretical standpoint. It is important, therefore, to briefly consider the different feminist theoretical positions and some of the research in PE that has been informed by a 'feminist' approach.

Feminist Theories and Their Application to PE

Critical questions relating to the primary source of women's oppression have resulted in several strands of feminist theory giving primacy to different factors. While there is no space in this chapter to do justice to the intense and complex debates between the different feminist perspectives, it is important to briefly outline the major theoretical standpoints.[2] Acker (1984) makes a useful distinction between 'implementary' approaches and 'fundamental' approaches (p. 64). She suggests that implementary approaches 'do not address questions about the underlying reasons for the domination/subordination patterns; instead, they ask how individuals in a given culture go about learning and perpetuating such arrangements'. These approaches tend to be categorized as 'liberal' or 'equal opportunities' feminism and are concerned with issues around socialization, stereotyping and challenging discriminatory practices. There is no analysis of the broader social context as a power structure which prevents women gaining equality with men. The liberal feminist perspective assumes that the social arrangements within 'democratic' societies are fundamentally sound but that certain adjustments — such as gender equality — need to be made, thus removing the aberrant and outdated discriminatory practices.

It is easy to identify these emphases in liberal feminist research approaches to PE. Attention is centred on the differentiation of activities — the socialization of girls into 'female' activities, for example, netball and gymnastics, and boys into 'male' activities, for example, football and cricket (ILEA, 1984). Discriminatory practices relating to clothing for PE lessons, stereotyping of girls and boys by PE teachers, unequal access to facilities and extra-curricular time, and differential career structures of female and male teachers have all received attention (*ibid*; Leaman, 1984, Evans and Williams, 1989).

Although this remains the dominant perspective and approach within feminism there has been a challenge from feminists arguing for a more 'fundamental' approach defining, locating and challenging the roots of women's oppression within power relations. These are usually categorized as radical, Marxist and socialist feminist perspectives.

Radical feminists concentrate on the power relations between men and women using the concept of *patriarchy* to develop a systematic explanation of the structural relations of oppression whereby men dominate women in a complex arena of power relations.[3] It is thus the notion of patriarchal power relations which places radical feminist theory in a much more critical framework than that of liberal feminism.

Probably the most influential work from a radical feminist perspective applicable to PE is that which focusses on sexuality as fundamental to the subordination and oppression of women. The links between physical activity (central to PE) and sexuality are examined by Lenskyj (1986). In her extensive historical research, she focusses specifically on male control of sexuality by and through sport, the importance of the female reproductive function in medical-physiological restrictions on girls' and women's participation in sport and PE, and the emphasis on traditional sex stereotyping in the legitimization of women's subordinate sporting and physical position. Radical feminists argue that male sexuality (what

Connell, 1987 refers to as 'hegemonic masculinity') functions to control women in work, leisure, school, social space, etc. (Coveney *et al* 1984). Thus, radical feminist research in PE emphasizes the means and processes by which PE reinforces and reproduces female and male heterosexuality. Girls and young women learn through PE a female 'physicality' which emphasizes appearance, presentation and control (desirable 'femininity') while their brothers are encouraged to develop physical strength, aggression and confidence in their physical prowess (desirable 'masculinity'). It is the connections between physical activity, sexuality, physicality and gender power relations which are central to this approach (Scraton, 1987a and 1989).

Marxist feminist theoretical explanations are part of the broader Marxist framework which situates gender relations within the context of the social reproduction of class relations.[4] The primary focus of this analysis places relations between men and women within the context of the dominant exploitative relations between the owners of the means of production and wage labour. The sexual division of labour is crucial to explaining women's subordinate position in the context of capitalist class relations, in that women are concerned with the reproduction of the labour resources, both by servicing and supporting the male breadwinner and by producing the next generation of workers (Barrett, 1988; Gardiner, 1975).

In PE, the stress is placed on the part it plays in the reproduction of capitalist values (Hargreaves, 1986). PE for girls is seen to be premised on the relationship between physical health and motherhood. Historical analysis is fundamental to Marxist feminist explanations. Girls' PE is seen to have developed out of the desire to ensure that the mothers of future generations were physically fit to produce healthy workers (Scraton, 1989). There is little empirical evidence developed within this framework although theoretically, the sexual division of labour is identified as a very real constraint on the sporting lives of many girls and young women (Talbot, 1980).

The criticism of Marxist feminism, that it is overdeterministic, fails to pay sufficient attention to the importance of resistance and agency and ignores or undertheorizes the concept of *patriarchal* domination and control, has led to an attempt to provide an integrated or dual analysis which identifies the importance of both capitalist social relations *and* patriarchy as structural determinants of women's oppression (Cockburn, 1983; Eisenstein, 1984; Young, 1981). These socialist feminist positions, as with much neo-Marxist analysis, stress the significance of culture, ideology and history. However, gender is not simply added to the analysis (as in much neo-Marxist theory) but is situated centrally alongside class (recognizing a *dual* system of oppression — capitalism *and* patriarchy) or incorporated with class as a unified, integrated system which recognizes the universality of patriarchal social systems (capitalist patriarchy).

Social feminist analyses and research in PE emphasizes the importance of identifying the roots of contemporary teaching. Ideologies of femininity and masculinity, particularly relating to physicality, motherhood and sexuality, are central to an understanding of the relationship between gender and PE. However, the experiences of girls in PE are seen to be dependent, also, on their class location. There is a concern to situate analysis within the context of the reproduction of a sexual division of *leisure* fundamental to any analysis of advanced capitalism in the late twentieth century (Scraton, 1986, 1987a, 1987b and 1989).

Finally, a criticism that has been levelled at all the feminist theoretical positions that have been discussed, is that 'race' continues to be ignored or marginalized. Black feminists[5] have identified the ethnocentrism of much feminist analysis *and* research (Amos and Parmar, 1984; Carby, 1982; Hooks, 1981). Research into gender and schooling/PE is no exception. There is little theoretical work in PE that considers 'race', and the limited amount of research that does investigate gender, 'race' and PE has tended to concentrate on a cultural approach (for example, Carrington *et al* 1987; Carrington and Williamson, 1988). This work is problematic in that it focusses on how gender differences in school PE and community leisure activities may be heightened by *ethnicity*. There is an identification of stereotypical perceptions held by many teachers that South Asian boys are particularly good at cricket and enthusiastic about weight training and self-defence. This confirms other racial stereotyping which assumes that Afro-Caribbean children *naturally* excel at certain athletic and sporting events. Furthermore, there is an emphasis on the cultural pressures on Asian girls, exerted by parents, which restrict their participation in co-educational activities (especially swimming), their involvement in extra-curricular pursuits and the problems associated with 'suitable' dress for PE.

However, what is missing in this research is a thorough analysis of 'race' and racism, and the complex relationship of gender and race within the contextual framework of structures of patriarchy and neo-colonialism. It is this neglect that has been identified and criticized by black feminists. In PE research (as in other research into 'race') there is a danger that research and analysis identifies a 'problem' which is seen to relate to cultural 'difference'. Yet in relation to PE, the issue of pupils and teachers from culturally distinct backgrounds centres not only on stereotyping and teacher-parent expectation, but also on the reinforcement and reproduction of institutional racism through PE teaching. The 'problem' is the ethnocentrism and racism of schooling rather than the cultural diversity of the pupils.

Girls and young women who experience racism (Afro-Caribbean, South Asian, Irish, Chinese, etc.) experience gender inequalities and oppression mediated by 'race' and racism. Many aspects of gender cut across racial inequalities, but the extent to which racial inequalities and oppression intersect with gender remains under-researched and under-theorized.

The Feminist Research Process

Epistemological Questions

Epistemological questions centre on the nature of knowledge. Feminism has been concerned not only to critique and correct the *context* of much sociological knowledge, which has either ignored or distorted the experiences of women, but also to criticize the conventional modes of *establishing* social knowledge (Ramazanoglu, 1989b). Harding, a feminist philosopher, has been interested in looking at the epistemological questions raised by a feminist research process (Harding, 1986 and 1987). She identifies two feminist epistemologies which she defines as 'feminist empiricism' and 'feminist standpoint'.

Feminist empiricism, she argues, is a response to sexist biases and prejudices in traditional research disciplines. It has developed out of a feminist critique of the social sciences which has identified and challenged their androcentrism. The result has been to focus attention not only on selection of research projects but also the content of the research *process*. In doing this feminists have challenged many existing assumptions and practices relating to research relationships, ethics and objectivity. Feminist empiricism has developed out of, and in line with, liberal feminism. As with liberal feminist theory, research based on this approach emphasizes the identification and elimination of stereotyping, bias and discrimination using a research process that is 'girl/woman friendly'.[6] However, critics argue that this leaves intact the bases of 'scientific' enquiry and such research lacks a radical challenge to the 'nature' of knowledge itself (Stanley, 1990). Feminist research needs to identify what constitutes 'feminist knowledge' and thus be girl/woman *centred*.

Feminist standpoint epistemology aims to do this by a more radical attempt to explore feminist knowledge through a focus on women's experiences and understandings. In order to achieve this, Smith (1987) suggests that feminist research must be located in the 'everyday world' which provides a problematic where the subject of the research is 'always located just as she or he is actually located in a particular material setting' (p. 99). Research investigation and enquiry is focussed on 'the knower in the everyday world'; rather than being separated out with the researcher seen to be the 'expert' or holder of knowledge. Thus, research from a feminist standpoint,

> preserves the presence of subjects as knowers and actors. It does not transform subjects into the objects of study or make use of conceptual devices for eliminating the active presence of the subjects. Its methods of thinking and its analytical procedures must preserve the presence of the active and experiencing subject (*ibid*, p.105).

Returning to the relationship between theory and research this would seem to suggest that research from a 'feminist standpoint' actually starts from the 'grounded theory' of women's material experience. However, in agreement with Smith, we would argue that:

> investigating the problematic of the everyday world does not involve substituting the analysis, the perspectives and views of the subject, for the investigation by the sociologist. Though women are indeed the expert practitioners of their everyday worlds, the notion of the everyday world as problematic assumes that disclosure of the extralocal determinants of our experience does not lie within the scope of everyday practices. We can see only so much without specialized investigation, and the latter should be the sociologists' special business. (*ibid*, p. 161)

We will return to this point in the next section on methodological issues.

Finally, in relation to a 'feminist standpoint' it is important to acknowledge that if feminist research is to start with, and centre on, women's experiences then there can be no, one, universal 'feminist standpoint'. The accepted universality of such concepts as 'women' and 'feminist standpoint' has been a criticism of much feminist theory, particularly the early writings of radical feminists. It is important to recognize that women are different and cannot be categorized without regard for determining relations other than gender, such as class, race, age, disability, etc. Thus epistemologically, there must be a plurality of 'feminist standpoints' which need to be acknowledged within feminist research. As researchers, our own experience is grounded in our realities as white, middle class, heterosexual women and the experiences of the women with whom we conducted our work will depend on their particular locations and realities.

Methodological Issues

There are a number of issues relating to the research process which have been the focus of debate within feminist enquiry. We have selected out some of the central concerns which are raised throughout the literature and have implications for any research from a feminist standpoint. The debate about methodology is best seen as a concern for the production of principles and ethics for the doing of feminist research rather than the search for an 'ideal' type of feminist research process (Cook and Fonow, 1986; Mias, 1983; Smart, 1984).

A key issue of concern for feminists is the way in which 'conventional' social science has reinforced the 'norm of objectivity' (Westcott, 1979). It has been argued that the replacement of the researcher's own particular viewpoint with a disinterested, unattached stance, guards against the bias of 'subjectivity' entering the research process, allowing for the production of more valid, 'objective' data. Feminists argue, on the contrary, that a real understanding of women's lives and their experiences is impossible if such a stance is maintained, and that we need to recognize that all research is political and value laden. Rather than abdicating the responsibility for the ethical and political concerns of the research 'subjects', by writing the 'self' out of research reports — thereby creating the illusion of 'objectivity' — the researcher must be prepared to situate herself *reflexively* in the research account, providing an analysis of the social relation underpinning the research process (Nebraska Feminist Collective, 1983; Harding, 1987; Stanley and Wise, 1983). It is suggested that it is only by minimizing the power differentials between the researcher and the researched, that the research will be able to capture the subjective feelings and experiences of women. A number of strategies have been adopted by feminists attempting to reduce the hierarchy between themselves and their objects of research; these have included using unstructured interviewing or life histories which allow the interviewee to control the direction and pace of the interview (for example, Acker *et al*, 1983; Graham, 1984), sharing information about their own lives with the women being interviewed (for example, Finch, 1984), answering interviewee's questions and providing them with helpful information (for example, Oakley, 1981; Roberts, 1981) and trying to make the interview less formal by using first names and memorizing questions to avoid taking in threatening interview schedules (for example, Davies, 1984; Griffin, 1985).

However, despite these attempts, it does seem impossible to eliminate such power differentials totally, for as Ramazanoglu (1989a) notes, 'since, by and large, people do not choose to be investigated, they are logically the objects of research chosen by the feminist for purposes defined by the feminist' (p. 55). As previously discussed, the very real differences between women researchers and 'ordinary' women — of age, of class, of race and of culture for example, may be far more important that the notion of our 'shared femininity' (McRobbie, 1981). As the discussion in the opening section of this chapter indicated, black women's critique of (white) feminism, has moved the issue of difference to the forefront of feminist debate (see, for example, Amos and Parmar, 1984; Brah, 1988; Carby, 1982). Any feminist research needs to be sensitive to the power differences between women, and the part these power differences play in the research process.

The process of involving the interviewee as subjects in the research, and attempting to minimize the power relationships between the researcher and the researched becomes even more problematic when the focus of the research is 'powerful' men or 'powerful' women. In Smart's (1984) study of the legal system, for example, she was involved mainly in interviewing male magistrates and lawyers. This meant that far from sharing her feminist views and opinions, she had to endure the frustrating and alienating experience of sitting and listening to sexist views, with men controlling much of the research process. Arguing along the same lines, Cain (1986) suggests that it would be difficult to see how a feminist research project focussing on police officers, for example, could do anything other than *deny* them access as subjects of the research. Any critical research faces similar problems in relation to the researcher-researched relationship. However, feminists have highlighted the need to seriously question this relationship and to challenge the traditional power relations in the research context.

Some feminists (for example, Davies, 1985; Mias, 1983) have argued that these problems will be eliminated by moving towards a position where women and girls can undertake research for themselves — that the study of the oppressed should be carried out not by experts, but by the objects of the oppression. This stance, too, seems problematic, for research cannot *just* be descriptions of women's lives given by themselves. As Smith (1987) argues, and as we discussed earlier, what is important — if we are to produce research knowledge which will change women's lives for the better — is the analysis of these accounts within their wider context of economic, social and political dimensions. The question becomes one of 'how to produce an analysis which goes beyond the experience of the researched while still granting them subjectivity' (Acker *et al*, 1983, p. 429), or what Ramazanoglu (1989b), has called the 'problem of transcending women's expression of their experiences' (p. 434).

Consciousness raising has been suggested as an important part of including women as subjects in a feminist research process (Cook and Fonow, 1986). While this is important and is an aspect of the research that 'gives back' to the research subject as well as having clear political intentions, it can prove problematic. It is important to recognize that in raising consciousness for some women it could put them in a difficult position if there is no comparable change in their lives. In Acker *et al*'s (1983) research on housewives and mothers, the issue of whether or not to confront groups and individuals with interpretations of their lives which were radically different to their own was a major ethical question. Indeed, the researchers found that they could only do this with some women, with those who, to a large extent, shared the same world views.

What becomes clear in relation to 'subjectivity', power differentials, consciousness raising etc., is that there can be no blueprint for all feminist research. Just as there are many 'feminist standpoints', there must be a plurality of research processes dependent on specific situations. However, feminist methodology has challenged many taken-for-granted assumptions of the research process and heightened *our* awareness of these issues.

Method — Is There a Distinctive 'Feminist' Method?

In their criticisms of sociological research, feminists differ in their acceptance of traditional research methods or techniques. Many argue, as the previous section has discussed, that the emphasis should not be on adopting either quantitative or qualitative techniques but rather on the intent, practice and language of research (Roberts, 1981). However, some feminist researchers (for example, Stanley and Wise, 1983) conclude that the most appropriate methods for feminist work are those which maximize the ability to explore the experiences of women's lives, and as such, are necessarily qualitative. This is in contrast to others who support the use of a variety of methods, suggesting that whilst quantitative methods are useful for uncovering the nature and extent of the structural dimensions of women's lives, qualitative methods are necessary to discover the social processes by which such structures operate and work (Graham, 1983; Green *et al*, 1990; Jayrantne, 1983). There is no definitive answer to the question as to whether there is a distinctive feminist method of research. In agreement with Harding (1987) we would conclude that 'my point here is to argue against the idea of a distinctive feminist method of research. I do so on the grounds that preoccupation with method mystifies what has been the most interesting aspects of feminist research processes' (p. 1). It is the epistemological and methodological debates raised by feminists interested in the research process that have contributed most to questions relating to both theory and practice.

Feminist Research in Action

Many of the qualitative studies of schools, which have used ethnographic methods, have chosen to exclude PE, as a specific subject area, from their analyses (for example, Ball, 1984). Knowledge of PE in the social sciences has been confined largely to data gathered from quantitative methods, either from large scale curriculum surveys (for example, ILEA, 1988; Kane, 1973; Physical Education Association, 1987) or classroom observational research aimed at improving teacher effectiveness (for example, Bailey, 1981; Spackman, 1986). As in many areas of research, this has resulted in a concentration on male PE with male definitions of knowledge and 'truth' which has been validated, on the whole, by male researchers and theorists. Although there is a growing amount of feminist research in the wider area of leisure (for example, Deem, 1986; Dixey and Talbot, 1982; Woodward *et al*, 1987) there remains very little empirical feminist research which has focussed on PE. Having introduced some of the key debates in feminist theory and research, the second part of the chapter will focus on an attempt by one of the authors to apply a feminist research process to research in PE in a study entitled, *Shaping Up to Womanhood: A Study of the Relationship between Gender and Girls' Physical Education in a City-based Local Education Authority* (Scraton, 1989).[7]

The Research Context

The research did not develop from a desire to investigate a specific problem that was 'out there' requiring explanation and proof. It developed out of the personal experience of teaching girls' PE, work with adolescent girls and a growing personal commitment to feminist politics. Immediately this challenges the basis of positivistic methodology which claims neutrality and 'hygienic' research (Graham, 1983; McRobbie, 1982; Smith, 1974; Stanley and Wise, 1979 and 1983). My research started from the acceptance that all research is 'grounded in consciousness' and that the personal and political commitments and experiences of the researcher inform and are integral to the research methodology. This accepts the feminist arguments that research cannot, and should not, be value free and recognizes the link between research and politics and the relationship between the researcher and researched (Stanley and Wise, 1983; Stanley 1990). Thus the research project developed within a feminist framework which recognized women's oppression and the need to investigate an important aspect of girls' and young women's lives in order to challenge gender divisions and inform future policy. This complements Harding's (1987) views that 'the researcher appears to us not as an invisible, anonymous voice of authority, but as a real historical individual with concrete, specific desires and interests' (p. 6).

The aim of the research, therefore, was to examine how images of 'femininity' and the social construction of gender-appropriate behaviour are reinforced or challenged by the structure, content and teaching of girls' PE in secondary schools. It began from an awareness of gender power relations and identified the need to examine PE both in the institutional, structural form and in the practices of those who hold power, for example, advisers, heads of department etc. Studying the structures of PE alone would not necessarily reveal ideological positions and the aim, therefore, was to examine structures and practices which might sustain or reproduce gender inequalities as well as the ideological underpinnings of this institutional form.

Methods and Methodological Issues

In order to understand the structures, policies and practices of PE a variety of research techniques were necessary. The adoption of quantitative techniques which reduce the analysis to a discussion of organizational 'facts' was seen to be inadequate and inappropriate for feminist research, which was attempting to situate gender inequalities in schooling in wider structural and ideological contexts. While it was important to know what was taught to girls in their PE lesson, how often they had curricular and extra-curricular activities etc, this could only identify inequality at an overt level. It was necessary, also, to look more deeply and qualitatively at the ideas of those who were the decision makers (i.e. advisers, heads of department) and at their practices in the everyday situation of PE teaching.

Thus, a range of research methods were adopted in order to obtain a full and complete 'picture' of girls' PE. In agreement with Woodward *et al* (1987) who were engaged in a large research project on women's leisure in Sheffield, I accepted that there was no distinctive feminist method and that in many situations the most fruitful approach is to adopt a range of methods involving both quantitative and qualitative techniques. The techniques used included library research (historical and contemporary), semi-structured interviews and sustained observation in selected case study schools.

Therefore, the research did not use a 'feminist' method, but was based on a feminist methodology which acknowledged the need for research on women and gender relations, was grounded in the experience of the researched and researcher, and developed out of a feminist political and theoretical commitment. Furthermore, it was reflexive in that it was subject to 'on-going attempts to understand, explain, re-explain what is going on' (Stanley and Wise, 1983, p. 46). Most importantly, throughout the research process there was a continual link between theory, empirical research and political response.

Access

Having selected a research LEA (Local Education Authority), the first step in the research process was to gain access to the heads of departments of girls' PE. It was at this initial stage that my previous experience, rather than being ignored or denied, became valuable. This stage of the research, although time consuming, presented few difficulties. The primary reason for this was that I had been a teacher of PE within the research LEA. This confirmed the value of selecting a locality for the research which was not only known to the researcher, but also where the researcher was known to the LEA. There exists a well established suspicion within the teaching profession of researchers who are seen to live in a privileged world, with little real understanding of the 'chalkface' reality of everyday life in front of pupils. As I was a qualified teacher who had taught in city comprehensive schools, there developed an immediate bond between researcher and researched. This relationship existed throughout all stages of the research and was important to the gathering of material. Official access to educational research in schools is negotiated through the LEA office via specialist advisory staff. At this stage of the access procedure, the PE adviser was of central significance to the teaching of PE throughout the authority. Therefore, it was decided that an initial structured interview would be carried out with the female adviser. This interview was conducted as a preliminary to the interviews with the heads of PE and the case study observations.

The Interviews

Traditionally, interviews are viewed as a one-way process, where the interviewer gathers information but there is limited personal interaction between the interviewee and interviewer. Within this process there is a clear and intentional hierarchical relationship between interviewer and interviewee, with the former holding the expertise and the latter being the passive respondent. As discussed earlier in the chapter, feminist work has developed a critique of this traditional text book approach which challenges many of these basic assumptions (Finch, 1984; Oakley, 1981; Stanley and Wise, 1983). This critique argues strongly that there can be no objective distance between the interviewer and interviewee, and that *all* research is political, whether it is investigating personal situations, state institutions or is carried out by large scale research organizations.

Oakley (1981) argues that in interviewing women she is putting her feminist politics into practice which, through necessity, must involve a two-way process. For this two-way process to evolve there must be interaction and response between the interviewer and the women interviewed. In agreement, Stanley and Wise (1983) suggest that the interviewer must attempt to make herself 'more vunerable' by responding to questions and contributing her own personal experiences to the interview — although Smart (1984) points out the limits of this when interviewing the powerful, as discussed earlier. As can be seen, this is in direct contrast to the 'hygienic' research prescribed in classic methodology on interviewing techniques.

My interviews were initiated from a position sympathetic to these feminist critiques. However, there were certain problems when I attempted to apply a feminist process of interviewing women to my research. Smart identifies an area which she found crucial to her research into the law and the practices of solicitors, magistrates etc. She comments:

> One important element in all this vetting was how the researcher presented herself and a vital element of that was dress. Discussions on doing research rarely consider dress and yet this was experienced as a subtle but important aspect of doing the research. (*ibid*, p. 153)

In this quotation, Smart identifies an aspect of research which was a constant consideration throughout my project. As my historical research showed, the traditions of PE centre around the 'correct' appearance and presentation of both pupils and teaching staff (Fletcher, 1984). Dress is a fundamental aspect of PE and is emphasized throughout PE teacher education. In this research situation, therefore, it was important that I dressed in what would be considered as an 'acceptable' style in order to retain credibility, particularly with the PE adviser. In agreement with McRobbie (1982):

> If the research has to change the way people look at things, to challenge structures which determine the conditions of existence, which in this case women and girls inhabit, then it has to be convincing. (p. 54)

This raises a further issue which creates problems with Oakley's analysis of interviewing women. She considers that in her interviewing of women she is putting her feminist politics into practice. In her argument there is an assumption that both the interviewer and the interviewee share the same or similar values (Smart, 1984). However, in my research there was a clear discrepency between the feminist politics of the researcher and many of the attitudes held by the adviser and the heads of department. This posed a dilemma, in that at times it was necessary to listen and record sexist comment and opinion. In this situation to respond as a 'feminist' would suggest challenging opinions rather than sharing ideas in a two-way process. Smart (1984) found when faced with a similar dilemma in her research:

> This meant that in order to express a dissenting view the interviewer not only had to find an opportunity but would have, in the process, shattered the inferential structure within which the interview was carried out. In other words the interview would have become impossible. (p. 155)

This latter point of Smart's is crucial and is applicable to any critical social research which involves research into state institutions. To place feminist politics to the forefront of my research would have created an immediate barrier and, potentially, distrust between the interviewee and the interviewer. Therefore, feminism could provide the theoretical basis for the research, influence the direction and methodology, but overtly could not be part of the practice of carrying out the research.

Oakley (1981) and Stanley and Wise (1983) discuss the need to break down the power relation between the interviewer and interviewee with the assumption that the researcher holds the power in the situation. Again there are problems with this assumption when researching key figures of authority, decision-makers or the 'locally powerful' (Bell and Newby, 1977). While the experience of being a former PE teacher proved invaluable for access it influenced my relationship with the PE adviser. In this situation, it was the adviser who perceived herself as being the 'expert' in relation to the research focus and this placed me in a more vulnerable position. I had to strive continually to present an acceptable, inquiring yet almost deferential manner in the interview situation. My experiences suggest that there is not one, universal feminist interview technique to be adopted for every situation. Whilst feminist research acknowledges the centrality of feminist politics, is grounded in experience and is intent on using research to help create political action and change, the methods of carrying out this research are many and varied and must be adopted with regard to each specific research need.

Critical research, by its definition, represents a fundamental challenge to the 'status-quo' or the established order and practices of a social system. The interviews were carried out, in this research, within the context of feminism. Unlike traditional positivistic research there was no attempt to guarantee a mythical 'neutrality' or 'objectivity'. However, in contrast to the arguments of Stanley and Wise (1983), there was no attempt to be 'open' or 'up front' about feminist politics as this would have created a barrier that would have at best inhibited and at worst endangered the project. However, this did not mean that the interviews were simply a one-way hierarchical process in keeping with the methodological traditions. The interviews were conducted with as much sensitivity to the teachers' situation as possible. I responded to any questions asked and there was a commitment to 'give back' to the research authority rather than simply extracting the information and data required.

Observation

Approximately half-a-term (six weeks) was spent full-time in each of the four case study schools (a total of two terms observation). In each school, written information was collected on the stated policy and organization of both the school in general and PE in particular. Once again, previous experience as a PE teacher made it easier for me to 'fit' into the department and a knowledge of PE conventions and traditional ethos proved invaluable in many situations. Being aware of the general routines of PE teaching helped make full use of the research time in each school with little time needed to familiarize myself with the research situation. Apart from gathering written policy statements, daily observations were recorded in a field diary. It was essential that a 'systematic reflection' (Wright Mills, 1970) was carried out by careful documentation of events, discussions and observations.

The period of observation presented less difficulties in relation to equalizing the relationship between researcher and researched. My experiences as a PE teacher meant that I soon blended into the background and, in most instances, quickly became part of the department. I found, also, that researching in an all-female environment reduced some of the problems faced by other feminist researchers particularly in relation to sexual harassment etc. However, I was faced constantly with the situation of observing sexist practices between teachers and pupils and listening to sexist comments. It was a difficult decision as to whether simply to record and gather material or whether I should actively intervene. If consciousness-raising is a key feature of feminist research then I was faced with whether I should challenge individual teachers or suggest alternative practices. Ultimately in most situations I remained as an 'outsider' recording, observing and listening. My decision was that it was important not to intervene in the actual process in order to ensure as 'natural' a research setting as possible. Intervention could have resulted in teachers feeling threatened and thus withdrawing and behaving as they felt I wanted, rather than their normal practice.

Conclusions

The fieldwork in this research project involved a number of research techniques and attempted to adopt a feminist approach. As has been shown, feminist research is not always straightforward, and there is no blue-print for a 'correct approach'. Feminism influenced the choice of research, how the research was carried out, and the analysis and evaluation. Although the research was selected within a particular theoretical framework, there was a constant reflexive process and theory grew out of the experience of the research. It did not 'prove' a particular theoretical question or position, but informed and helped develop feminist theoretical thinking. Furthermore, hopefully, it has contributed to political change. Practical action and policy recommendations were the key to the analysis and conclusion. Finally, although I felt unable to intervene during the research process, I felt it important not only to 'take' from the research situation. Thus, having made contacts throughout the schools, I tried to 'pay back' by becoming involved in various anti-sexist/equal opportunities initiatives that began to develop in the following years in several of the LEA schools. This involved taking part in, and contributing to, meetings arranged by working parties (equal opportunities/anti-sexist) within some of the schools and spending some time discussing policy initiatives with equal opportunities coordinators who were appointed in the authority following reorganization in the year after the research was completed.

Overall, this chapter has considered some of the key issues and debates in feminist research. As has been shown there is no straightforward means of applying a feminist approach to research in PE. However, we would like to conclude with three major points.

Firstly, there is a need for *all* research in PE to adopt a feminist empiricist approach i.e. to remove bias, discrimination, and prejudice from all aspects of the research process. At a minimum, all research in PE must be non-sexist, must acknowledge the experiences, ideas, understandings of girls and women, and this must be reflected not only in the selection of research problematics, but also in the practice of doing the research.

Secondly, the issue of gender relations must be centralized in far more research projects. This involves making research girl or woman/centred with an emphasis on research which explores both ontological and epistemological questions. As we have argued throughout this chapter, feminist research is political, and in PE, the aim must be to contribute to an informed knowledge and understanding which will help alter policies and practices.

Finally, we should add that although feminist research is *for* women, this does not, and should not, limit the focus of research solely to women, or indeed to research *by* women. Research which focusses on boys' and men's experiences of PE — carried out by both men and women — is also vital if we are to widen our understanding of the

Sheila Scraton and Anne Flintoff

contribution PE makes to the reinforcement of ideologies of masculinities, and the role of men in gender power relations.

Notes

1 See Eichler (1980) for an interesting discussion on the complex definitions of 'sex and gender'. In this chapter we use the most commonly accepted definitions: 'sex' refers to the biological aspects of being female and male, and 'gender' as the social/cultural construction of femininity/masculinity.
2 We have limited our discussion here to the four major feminist theoretical positions. See Tong (1989) for a comprehensive overview of feminist theory.
3 The major debates concerning patriarchy can be found in Beechey (1979).
4 Marxist feminist work draws on the work of Engels on the family.
5 We are using the term 'black' in the same way as Maynard (1990) does, as a political label 'which acknowledges that the political, social and ideological force of racism creates a gulf between white people and those whom they oppress, on both a face to face and an institutional level' (p. 250). It is not meant to refer to a fixed cultural identity and it does not deny the existence of diversity between, and within, each cultural group.
6 'Girl-friendly'/'girl centred'. These terms originated from feminist teachers' working on the development of gender policy initiatives in schools. For a discussion of the differences between the two, see Weiner and Arnot (1987).
7 The following discussion focuses on the research methodology and methods involved in the project. For a full account of the research findings and conclusions, see Scraton, 1986, 1987a, 1987b, 1989, 1992.

References

ACKER, J., BARRY, K. and ESSEVELD, J. (1983) 'Objectivity and truth: problems in doing feminist research', *Women's Studies International Forum*, 6,4, pp. 423–35.
ACKER, S. (1984) 'Sociology, gender and education' in ACKER, S., MEGARRY, J., NISBET, J. and HOYLE, E. (Eds) *World Yearbook of Education: Women and Education*, London, Kogan Page, pp. 64–78.
AMOS, V. and PARMAR, P. (1984) 'Challenging imperial feminism', *Feminist Review*, 17, pp. 3–19.
ARNOT, M. and WEINER, G. (Eds) (1987) *Gender and the Politics of Schooling*, London, Hutchinson.
BAILEY, L. (1981) 'Systematic observation of activities in physical education: Need for research', *Physical Education Review*, 4, 2, pp. 96–103.
BALL, S, (1984) 'Beachside reconsidered: Reflections on a methodological apprenticeship' in BURGESS, R. (Ed) *The Research Process in Educational Settings: Ten Case Studies*, Lewes, Falmer Press, pp. 69–96.
BARRETT, M. (1988) *Women's Oppression Today; Problems in Marxist Feminist Analysis* (2nd edn) London, Verso.
BEECHEY, V. (1979) 'On patriarchy', *Feminist Review*, 3, pp. 66–82.
BELL, C. and NEWBY, N. (Eds) (1977) *Doing Sociological Research*, London, Allen & Unwin.
BRAH, A. (1988) 'Extended review', *British Journal of Sociology of Education*, 9, 1, pp. 115–21.

CAIN, M. (1986) 'Realism, feminism, methodology and the law', *International Journal of the Sociology of Law*, 14, pp. 255–67.

CARBY, H. (1982) 'White women listen! Black feminism and the boundaries of sisterhood' in CENTRE FOR CONTEMPORARY CULTURAL STUDIES (Eds) *The Empire Strikes Back*, London, Pluto Press, pp. 215–35.

CARRINGTON, B. and WILLIAMSON, T. (1988) 'Patriarchy and ethnicity: The link between school physical education and community leisure activities' in EVANS, J. (Ed) *Teachers, Teaching and Control in Physical Education*. Lewes, Falmer Press, pp. 83–96.

CARRINGTON, B., WILLIAMSON, T. and CHIVERS, T. (1987) 'Gender, leisure and sport: A case study of young people of South African descent', *Leisure Studies*, 6, 3, pp. 265–79.

COCKBURN, C. (1983) *Brothers: Male Dominance and Social Change*, London, Pluto Press.

CONNELL, R. (1987) *Gender and Power*, Cambridge, Polity Press.

COOK, J.A. and FONOW, M.M. (1986) 'Knowledge and women's interests: Issues of epistemology and methodology in feminist sociological research', *Sociological Enquiry*, 56, 1, pp. 2–29.

COVENEY, L., JACKSON, M., JEFFREYS, S., KAY, L. and MAHONY, P. (Eds) (1984) *The Sexuality Papers: Male Sexuality and the Social Control of Women*, London, Hutchinson.

DAVIES, L. (1984) *Pupil Power: Deviance and Gender in School*, Lewes, Falmer Press.

DAVIES, L. (1985) 'Ethnography and status: Focussing on gender in educational research' in BURGESS, R. (Ed) *Field Methods in the Study of Education*, Lewes, Falmer Press, pp. 79–96.

DEEM, R. (1986) *All Work and No Play? The Sociology of Women and Leisure*, Milton Keynes, Open University Press.

DIXEY, R. and TALBOT, M. (1982) *Women, Leisure and Bingo*, Leeds, Trinity and All Saints College.

EICHLER, M. (1980) *The Double Standard: A Feminist Critique of Social Science*, London, Croom Helm.

EISENSTEIN, H. (1984) *Contemporary Feminist Thought*. London, Unwin.

EVANS, J. (Ed) (1986) *Physical Education, Sport and Schooling — Studies in the Sociology of Physical Education*, Lewes, Falmer Press.

EVANS, J. and WILLIAMS, T. (1989) 'Moving up and getting out: The classed and gendered career opportunities of physical education teachers' in TEMPLIN, T. and SCHEMPP, P. (Eds) *Socialisation into PE: Learning to Teach*, Carmel, CA, Benchmark Press, pp. 235–85.

FINCH, J. (1984) ' "It's great to have someone to talk to someone to talk to": The ethics and politics of interviewing women' in BELL, C. and ROBERTS, H. (Eds) *Social Researching: Politics, Problems, Practice*, London, RKP, pp. 70–87.

FLETCHER, S. (1984) *Women First: The Female Tradition in English Physical Education 1880–1980*, London, Athlone Press.

GARDINER, J. (1975) 'Women's domestic labour', *New Left Review*, 89, pp. 47–58.

GRAHAM, H. (1983) 'Do her answers fit his questions? Women and the survey method' in GARMARNIKOV, E., MORGAN, D., PURVIS, J. and TAYLORSON, D. (Eds) *The Public and the Private*, London, Heinemann, pp. 132–46.

GRAHAM, H. (1984) 'Surveying through stories' in BELL, C. and ROBERTS, H. (Eds) *Social Researching: Politics, Problems, Practice*, London, RKP, pp. 104–24.

GREEN, E., HEBRON, S. and WOODWARD, D. (1990) *Women's Leisure, What Leisure?*, London, Macmillan.

GRIFFIN, C. (1985) *Typical Girls: Young Women from School to the Job Market*, London, RKP.

HARDING, S. (1986) *The Science Question in Feminism*, Milton Keynes, Open University Press.

HARDING, S. (Ed) (1987) *Feminism and Methodology*, Milton Keynes, Open University Press.

HARGREAVES, J. (1986) *Sport, Power and Culture*, Cambridge, Polity Press.

HOOKS, B. (1981) *Ain't I a Woman?: Black Women and Feminism*, London, Pluto Press.

ILEA (1984) *Providing Equal Opportunities for Boys and Girls in Physical Education*, London, ILEA.

ILEA (1988) *My Favourite Subject: A Report of the Working Party on Physical Education and School Sport*, London, ILEA.

JAYRANTNE, T.E. (1983) 'The value of quantitative methodology for feminist research' in BOWLES, G. and DUELLI KLEIN, R. (Eds) *Theories of Women's Studies*, London, RKP, pp. 140–61.

KANE, J.E. (1974) *Physical Education in the Secondary School*, Schools Council Studies, London, Macmillan.

LEAMAN, O. (1984) *Sit on the Sidelines and Watch the Boys Play; Sex Differentiation in Physical Education*, York, Longman for the Schools Council.

LENSKYJ, H. (1986) *Out of Bounds: Women, Sport and Sexuality*, Toronto, Women's Press.

MCROBBIE, A. (1982) 'The politics of feminist research: Between talk, text and action', *Feminist Review*, 12, pp. 46–51.

MAYNARD, M. (1990) 'The re-shaping of sociology? Trends in the study of gender', *Sociology*, 24, 2, pp. 269–90.

MIAS, M. (1983) 'Towards a methodology for feminist research' in BOWLES, G. and DUELLI KLEIN, R. (Eds) *Theories of Women's Studies*, London, RKP, pp. 17–139.

NEBRASKA FEMINIST COLLECTIVE (1983) 'A feminist ethic for social science research', *Women's Studies International Forum*, 6, 5, pp. 535–43.

OAKLEY, A. (1981) 'Interviewing women: A contradiction in terms' in ROBERTS, H. (Ed) *Doing Feminist Research*, London, Routledge, pp. 30–61.

PHYSICAL EDUCATION ASSOCIATION (1987) *Physical Education in Schools*, London, Ling House.

RAMAZANOGLU, C. (1989a) *Feminism and the Contradictions of Oppression*, London, Routledge.

RAMAZANOGLU, C. (1989b) 'Improving on sociology: The problems of taking a feminist standpoint', *Sociology*, 23, 3, pp. 427–42.

ROBERTS, H. (1981) *Doing Feminist Research*. London, Routledge.

SCRATON, S. (1986) 'Images of femininity and the teaching of girls' physical education' in EVANS, J. (Ed) *Physical Education, Sport and Schooling: Studies in the Sociology of Physical Education*, Lewes, Falmer Press, pp. 71–94.

SCRATON, S. (1987a) 'Gender and physical education: Ideologies of the physical and the politics of sexuality' in BARTON, L. and WALKER, S. (Eds) *Changing Politics, Changing Teachers*, Milton Keynes, Open University Press, pp. 169–89.

SCRATON, S. (1987b) 'Boys muscle in where angels fear to tread: The relationship between physical education and young women's subcultures' in HORNE, J., JARY, D. and TOMLINSON, A. (Eds) *Sport, Leisure and Social Relations*, London, Kegan Paul, pp. 160–86.

SCRATON, S. (1989) 'Shaping up to womanhood: A study of the relationship between gender and girls' PE in a city based local education authority', unpublished PhD thesis, Education Department, Open University.

SCRATON, S. (1992) *Shaping Up to Womanhood; Girls and Physical Education*, Milton Keynes, Open University Press.

SMART, C. (1984) *The Ties that Bind; Law, Marriage and Patriarchal Relations*, London, RKP.

SMITH, D. (1974) 'Women's perspective as a radical critique of sociology', *Sociological Enquiry*, 44, pp. 7–13.

SMITH, D. (1987) *The Everyday World as Problematic*, Milton Keynes, Open University Press.

SPACKMAN, L. (1986) 'The systematic observation of teacher behaviour in physical education', *Physical Education Review*, 9, 2, pp. 118–34.

SPENDER, D. (1982) *Invisible Women: The Schooling Scandal*, London, Writers and Readers Publishing Company.

STANLEY, L. (Ed) (1990) *Feminist Praxis*, London, Routledge.

STANLEY, L. and WISE, S. (1979) 'Feminist research, feminist consciousness and experiences of sexism', *Women's Studies International Forum*, 2, pp. 359–74.

STANLEY, L. and WISE, S. (1983) *Breaking Out: Feminist Consciousness and Feminist Research*, London, RKP.

STANWORTH, M. (1983) *Gender and Schooling: A Study of Sexual Divisions in the Classroom*, London, Hutchinson.

TALBOT, M. (1980) *Women and Sport: A Leisure Studies Perspective, Working Paper (77)*, Birmingham, Centre of Urban and Recreational Studies.

TONG, R. (1989) *Feminist Thought: A Comprehensive Introduction*, London, Unwin Hymen.

WEINER, G. and ARNOT, M. (1987) 'Teachers and gender politics' in ARNOT, M. and WEINER, G. (Eds) *Gender and the Politics of Schooling*, London, Hutchinson, pp. 354–70.

WESTCOTT, M. (1979) 'Feminist criticism of the social sciences', *Harvard Educational Review*, 49, 4, pp. 422–30.

WOODWARD, D., GREEN, E. and HEBRON, S. (1987) *Leisure and Gender: A Study of Women's Leisure in Sheffield*, London, Sports Council/ESRC.

WRIGHT MILLS, C. (1970) *The Sociological Imagination*, Oxford, Oxford University Press.

YOUNG, I. (1981) 'Beyond the unhappy marriage: A critique of dual systems theory' in SARGENT, L. (Ed) *Women and Revolution: The Unhappy Marriage of Marxism and Feminism*, London, Pluto Press, pp. 43–69.

Chapter 7

Action Research as Epistemology and Practice: Towards Transformative Educational Practice in Physical Education

Richard Tinning

Action research has a limited history in physical education research yet a considerable history in the broader fields of education and social psychology. Although there has been a rigorous debate about the nature of action research within educational discourse for over a decade (see for example Elliott, 1978; Carr and Kemmis, 1986), the debate seems to have eluded the world of physical education.

Within this chapter action research will be explained and placed in a brief historical context. The epistemological assumptions underpinning various interpretations of action research will be discussed, together with different forms of knowledge and human interests which such interpretations favour or reflect. Three different examples of action research in physical education will be outlined with particular reference to the knowledge and interests they represent. Some emergent problems for action research will be presented and the potential for its contribution to transformative educational practice in physical education discussed.

What is this Thing Called Action Research?

It seems reasonable that before any discussion of action research can proceed we need to have some shared understanding of what action research is meant to be. But herein lies the first problem for, as we will see shortly, it means different things to different people. So in that sense this question is the essence of this chapter and it cannot be answered in a paragraph or two. However, we can at least begin with the claim that when people talk about action research they are all referring to a process which, at face value at least, has been variously described as a cycle of phases or moments which include *planning*, *acting*, *monitoring*, and *reflecting*.

A simplistic example may help to understand this process. A teacher discusses with a colleague a particular issue of her/his educational practice which s/he wishes to improve. Together they: plan a strategy for change and a way in which the colleague can monitor and collect data on the nature of the issue; implement the strategy and monitor the practice; discuss (reflect) on the success or otherwise of the change strategy based on the data collected from the monitoring; plan a subsequent change strategy and the cycle starts over again.

Of course if action research were as simple as that there would hardly be any debate over its nature. In fact, the simple process outlined above leaves many important questions unasked . . . and the answers to these questions are the major points of contestation. For example: is it possible to have action research when the issue of focus is determined by someone other than the practitioner?; must there always be a colleague (or other 'critical friend') to monitor and discuss the issue with?; is it ok if the colleague is the school principal or a faculty member from a local university, or even a parent or a student teacher?; what counts as educational practice?; what counts as data?; what is the nature of knowledge which is privileged by asking certain questions of practice?; what assumptions of professional practice of teachers are embedded in action research? In the discussion which follows some of these questions will be addressed or at least explored. The important meta-issue which will be emphasized in this account is that action research is itself problematic and that physical educators who engage with action research must recognize the limitations and assumptions embedded in their particular interpretations.

Action Research isn't a New Idea! A History of Contestation

At the outset it is important to realize that educational action research is not a new 'invention' and, although it developed originally in the United States it also has a substantial history in the United Kingdom (for example Elliott, and Adelman 1973; Bell, 1985) continental Europe (Finger, 1988; Brock-Utne, 1980) and Australia (Grundy and Kemmis, 1981; McTaggart and Garbutcheon-Singh, 1988).

There is no doubt that action research is now coming of age within the official discourse of physical education as is evidenced by the 1991 AIESEP/NAHPE convention in Atlanta devoting an entire section to the issue of 'Building bridges through action research'. This recognition of action research has not materialized out of nowhere. In Great Britain there has been a relatively long history of working with the ideas of action research within physical education but little has found its way into the journals of the profession. In the United States the first report of an action research project to be published in the *Journal of Teaching in Physical Education* appeared in 1988 (see Martinek and Butt, 1988).

Although there has been a strong history of action research in continental Europe, for the purposes of this account I will concentrate only on its development in the USA, Britain and Australia. Such a limitation is necessary given the brief nature of this account but also because the English speaking tradition is more accessible and relevant to the recent developments in physical education. The beginnings of discussion of action research in the English speaking world is often associated with the writings of the American social-psychologist Kurt Lewin, sometimes known as the 'father of action research'. Apparently, as McTaggart (1991) informs us, Lewin's work was preceded by that of Collier (1945) who wrote about action research as the way to improve the circumstances of oppressed American Indians, but it is Lewin's work which represents the conception of action research which became popularized after the Second World War.

Lewin's work stood out as an example of a new emphasis among a major group of social-psychologists working on the social problems of prejudice, authoritarianism and dogmatism. His work was a direct challenge to the orthodox conception of the role of the social scientist as a disinterested 'objective' observer of human affairs. Moreover, the notion of action research he advocated reconceptualized the relationship between theory and practice and between researcher and researched. The conventional wisdom of social science conceived theory as something to be applied to practice but for Lewin practical and theoretical problems were to be investigated together as if they were one. Action research was to be a group process which always involved a collaboration between researcher and researched (the social actors). As McTaggart (1991) says, 'Action research was not then considered a process which could be identified primarily as the property of people who were not professional researchers' (p. 8). This is an important point of divergence from much of the later work in action research in both the UK and Australia during the 1980s in which it was important that the action research be 'owned' by practitioners; that practitioners conduct action research as part of their professional practice as teachers.

Given that the concept of educational research which was embodied in action research as conceived by Lewin challenged head-on the assumptions of the dominant research paradigm it became evaluated in terms of the criteria which were set by that paradigm. Hence Lewin's ideas were reinterpreted increasingly from a positivist interpretation and defined in terms of the dominant scientific paradigm (McTaggart, 1991). A consequence of this contestation, this challenge to the dominant paradigm, was the reinterpretation and cooption of action research. The beginnings of this re-interpretation began with Chein *et al*'s paper entitled 'The field of action research' (1948) which was a key paper in the popularization of action research in the 1950s. But while the paper 'disavowed the objectivism of the prototypical social scientist' (McTaggart, 1991, p. 9) it also began a fragmentation of the original Lewinian idea.

The writings of Stephen Corey (1949, 1952 and 1953) from the Horace Mann Lincoln Institute at Teachers College, Columbia University, introduced and developed the idea of action research with many teachers in the United States. However, as McTaggart points out, his efforts to popularize and legitimize action research actually made it more vulnerable to its critics. In contrasting the idea of action research with 'fundamental' research and in his efforts to argue that action research was a way of achieving 'generalization' Corey was unwittingly paying deference to the prevailing dominant research ideology which in turn 'owned' the criteria by which action research was to be judged. Thus 'action research was not to find and assert its own criteria for legitimacy' (McTaggart, 1991, p. 11).

Thus, during the 1950s, a time in which educational research was increasingly under the dominance of positivistic social science, action research failed to achieve legitimacy and its popularity declined. In this climate Hodgkinson (1957) regarded action research as a common-sense rather than a scientific approach and judged it against the criteria necessary for valid scientific experimentation. He concluded that it was 'only problem-solving ('easy hobby games for little engineers'); was statistically unsophisticated; did not lead to defensible generalization; did not help to create a system of theory; and was practised (and not very well) by amateurs' (McTaggart, 1991, p. 15).

By the 1960s in the USA the significant educational problems were deemed to be national rather than local or individual. In a context in which educational research was to provide and verify the principles by which nationwide educational improvement could be achieved, the idea of researching one's own practice seemed trivial and of little importance. It was not until into the 1970s that action research was to regain some respectability. According to McTaggart (1991) this was linked to the emergence of curriculum as a field of enquiry and the struggle to make that field distinctive and relevant to the solution of curriculum problems. It was in this context that the work of Schwab (1970) proved particularly significant. Schwab introduced to the field of curriculum what he called the 'language of the practical' which articulated a central position for an epistemology of practice. However, Schwab's notion of the practical was different from the original ideas of Lewin (and the subsequent ideas of Stenhouse and Carr and Kemmis as we will see shortly) in that his focus was on curriculum development and the 'search for data' rather than on the notion of collectively and strategically planned change to improve certain social practices.

The 'new age' of interest in curriculum development and theorising during the 1970s in Britain spawned the notion of 'teacher as researcher' coined by Lawrence Stenhouse. Stenhouse's work, particularly the influential *Introduction to Curriculum Research and Development* (1975) located action research as the process in which educational ideas, which were first translated into curriculum materials or guides, were put to the test of practice. His ideas were very influential in Britain and Australia but not so in the USA. It was a one time colleague of Stenhouse, Len Almond from Loughborough, who introduced the notion of action research and teacher-as-researcher to the physical education world. Almond's early work with physical education teachers in curriculum development and action research was somewhat marginalized, however, perhaps owing to its limited availability in published form, from most curriculum and research discourse within physical education until the current (late 1980s/early 1990s) interest in action research as mentioned above.

Two other British educationalists who were also strongly influenced by the work of Stenhouse and who were associated with the popularization of action research in the UK and Australia were John Elliott and Clem Adelman, through their work in the Ford Teaching Program. Elliott in particular strongly supported Schwab's notion of the practical and he articulated (as did Grundy in Australia) the links between action research and the Aristotelian notion of practice informed by self-reflection (I will return to this important association later).

During the 1970s another set of discourses began to be foregrounded in the attempt to explain and justify action research as *educational* research. These discourses, collectively called critical theory, have been championed in Europe by Klafki (1970 and 1975) and Brock-Utne (1980) and by Carr and Kemmis (1986) in the UK and Australia. The critical theory discourses are strongly influenced by the work of the German philosopher of critical theory, Habermas (1972 and 1974). However, Habermas' ideas (which will be discussed shortly), although dominant, represent only one lineage of the critical perspective in action research. According to McTaggart (1991) a more broadly-based critical perspective is present in the writings of action research (often called participatory research) in the Third World and cross cultural settings (for example, Freire, 1982; Hall 1979 and 1981; and Fals Borda 1979).

Within Australia action research has been greatly influenced by the work of a group of scholars at Deakin University who initially received inspiration from Stephen Kemmis who had moved to Deakin from the Centre for Applied Research in Education (CARE) at the University of East Anglia in the mid 1970s. *Becoming Critical: Knowing Through Action Research* (1986) a book written by Wilf Carr (then of the University College of Wales at Bangor) and Kemmis became the most articulate account of what came to be known as the 'Deakin view' (McTaggart, 1991, p. v) of action research. Although this 'view' is actually much more diverse than that presented in Carr and Kemmis and has undergone considerable change since the early 1980s, it does nonetheless locate itself clearly as a critical perspective which identifies itself as 'emancipatory' action research in contrast to what have been characterized as either technical or practical versions of action research.

This characterization of action research as technical, practical and emancipatory (or critical) came from the work of Grundy and Kemmis (1981), Carr and Kemmis (1986) and Tripp (1984) whose work was substantially influenced by each of these sources. The importance of these characterizations was much more than heuristic. It actually became for some a framework to judge what was 'authentic' action research and what was not.

Aristotle, Habermas and Ways of Viewing Human Action

At this point I want to return to the idea I mentioned above that the conception of action research can be linked back to the Aristotelian tradition of practical philosophy. Aristotle's work must be understood in the context that the ancient Greeks distinguished between three forms of discipline, the 'theoretical', the 'productive' and the 'practical'. The purpose (or *telos*) of the theoretical disciplines was knowledge for its own sake, such as we might claim of pure mathematics. The productive disciplines were associated with craft and skill such as that practised by an artisan. The practical disciplines were concerned with what the Greeks called *praxis* or critically informed action.

Aristotle distinguished between different dispositions which inform human action. The first disposition which informs action is that of *techne* or skill. The knowledge associated with the productive disciplines requires craft or skill (*poietike*) which embody the disposition of techne in which instrumental reasoning applies certain preordained criteria or rules by which practice can be judged. Aristotle identifies this disposition as that associated with the craftsman (sic) and this is certainly a view of teachers which is popular among some circles.

The disposition of *phronesis* gives rise to practical action. According to Grundy (1987), the term phronesis is often translated as 'practical judgment' but the concept is more complex than that and really no single English word is capable of capturing the true spirit of the word as it was used by the ancient Greeks. However, we can recognize that the disposition of phronesis is unlike techne in that it is concerned not with what is correct in terms of pre-specified rules but rather it involves a moral judgment concerning action. Thus phronesis as 'practical judgment is a disposition towards "good" rather than "correct" action. It possesses an aspect of moral consciousness which the disposition of techne lacks' (*ibid*, p. 62). Action, therefore, which is motivated by the disposition of phronesis, is of a different kind to that motivated by techne. Whereas the idea (*eidos*) which guides techne is the efficient or correct accomplishment of a particular end, the eidos which guide phronesis are those associated with choice and deliberation about the means to achieve the 'good life', which for the ancient Greeks was a concept which combined aesthetic, moral, and intellectual meanings. It is concerned with how we ought to act. It is a form of reflection concerned with translating universal ethical values into concrete forms of action in a particular situation. In this context phronesis was not a form of instrumental reasoning about the most efficient way to achieve a particular end, rather it was concerned with *praxis* or moral action. It was the Greeks who introduced the term 'praxis' to denote the idea of critically-informed practice.

A necessary association or link now needs to be drawn between the Greek concepts of knowledge and the relationship between and human interests as defined by Habermas. It is possible to match Aristotle's notions of kinds of discipline with the Habermasian concepts of knowledge and human interest; namely 'technical'; 'practical'; and 'critical'.

In their book *Becoming Critical: Knowing Through Action Research*, Wilfred Carr and Stephen Kemmis (1986) provide a useful representation of the Habermasian concept of knowledge and human interests which helps to locate the critical social science perspective with respect to other traditions of enquiry.

Interest	Knowledge	Medium	Science
Technical (prediction and control)	Instrumental (causal explanation)	Work (instrumental action)	Empirical-analytic or natural sciences
Practical (interpretation and understanding)	Practical (understanding)	Language	Hermeneutic or 'interpretive' science
Emancipatory (criticism and liberation)	Emancipation (reflection)	Power (dominance and subordination)	Critical sciences
			(adapted from Carr and Kemmis, 1986)

Habermas's theory is that different kinds of knowledge serve different human interests. Moreover those forms of knowledge are shaped by the particular human interests they serve. According to Gibson (1986) Habermas contrasts the interests (the concerns and purposes) of critical theory with the interests of two other major modes of understanding: positivism and hermeneutics. Said another way, 'three types of knowledge arise from three interests: technical control, interpretation and the struggle for freedom' (Gibson, 1986, p. 37).

Action Research, Knowledge and Human Interests

According to Tripp (1984) it is possible to identify different forms of action research which can be characterized as emphasizing different knowledge and human interests. He defines *technical action research* as:

> Other-directed (that is, directed by others, where the educational or social practitioner is the implicit 'self'), individual or group, generally aimed at improving existing practices, but occasionally

at developing new ones, within existing consciousness and values with an unproblematized view of constraints'. (p. 12)

In Habermasian terms the human interests of this form of action research are technical (they focus on prediction and control) and the knowledge form is instrumental (concerned with means-end efficiency). The Aristotelian notion embedded in such action is techne.

While such action research may result in improvements in practice, the fact that the knowledge and human interests served are first and foremost those of the facilitator or outsider, has led to sharp criticism from action research theorists. Carr and Kemmis (1986) took a cautious view of such work and claimed that such action research (to the extent that it is action research at all) 'often create circumstances under which project control is not in teacher's hands . . . and facilitators have coopted practitioners into working on externally-formulated questions which are not based in the practical concerns of teachers' (p. 202). Some recent critiques by McTaggart and Garbutcheon-Singh (1986 and 1988) have claimed that such practice should not be regarded as action research at all. '*Practical action research*' according to Tripp (1984) is:

Self-directed (that is, directed by practitioners), individual or group, aimed as much at developing new practices as at improving existing ones, within consciousness and values from which a sense of what is 'right' is utilized to guide action, with an unproblematized view of constraints. (p. 12)

Thus the interests are practical (they focus on interpretation and understanding) and the knowledge form is practical (concerned with understanding and with moral judgments in action). Here we see the action research embodiment of the Aristotelian notion of phonesis. In a practical action research project the aim is the ultimate autonomy of the teachers themselves to conceive and implement such projects on their own; to be critically informed self-reflecting practitioners. As Carr and Kemmis (1986) claim, 'the facilitators role is Socratic: to provide a sounding-board against which practitioners may try out ideas and learn more about the reasons for their own action, as well as learning more about the process of self-reflection' (p. 203).

Continuing with Tripp's definitions, '*emancipatory action research*' is the activity of a 'self-leading group, aimed at developing new practices and/or changing the constraints, with a shared radical consciousness and problematized values' (Tripp, 1984, p. 12). According to McTaggart (1991), 'emancipatory action research extends beyond the interpretation of meanings for participants to an understanding of the social, political, and economic conditions which cause and allow meanings to be as they are' (p. 30). In terms of knowledge and human interests, emancipatory action research is clearly aimed at criticism and liberation (from restrictive thoughts and practices) through a process of critical reflection. The human interest served by such practices is that of 'collective emancipation' (McTaggart, 1991, p. 30). Praxis (which embodies informed committed action) is the desired outcome of such action research. Thus, emancipatory action research is more than simple radical critique — it demands action.

For the critical theorist action research which is based on the notion of phronesis, while accepted as addressing the shortcomings of techne, falls short of providing a critical basis for rendering practice problematic in ways which have the potential to create the conditions for emancipation. They claim that '"critical social science" . . . is the science which serves the "emancipatory" interest in freedom and rational autonomy' (Carr and Kemmis, 1986, p. 136).

A Consideration of Action Research as Represented in Physical Education

In order to consider the ways in which action research has been interpreted within physical education I want to describe three examples of action research which are located in the official discourses of the profession (namely in journals and books). Of course there will be other cases of action research not recorded in such form but for the purposes of this chapter these three highlight different interpretations.

Action Research Projects as Collaboration Between Teachers and University Faculty

As mentioned above, the earliest reported reference to action research in the physical education literature is that by Len Almond from the University of Technology, Loughborough, England. Almond, who was heavily influenced by the work of Stenhouse, has worked for over twelve years in action research projects with teachers in the UK.

In an early account of action research Almond (1983) outlines how he and a project team from Loughborough worked with teachers on a project relating to 'teaching games for understanding'. He claimed that 'An action research perspective was selected because it attempts to involve teachers in developing an understanding and self awareness of what their practice entails in order to improve both their practice and the situation in which the practice takes place' (p. 145). The procedure of the project was described by Almond as follows:

> A number of teachers and advisers had already expressed an interest in 'teaching for understanding' in games so they were contacted and invited to join the project. After preliminary meetings a course was arranged for all the teachers to examine the basis for games teaching and to explore a range of ideas that required

teaching for understanding. This was followed by meetings in each local education authority to discuss and examine classroom research. In addition to conducting and documenting their research, the teachers were asked to write a diary of problems that they faced in trying to incorporate a research task and adopt a research attitude to their teaching. (p. 145)

Later he went on to explain that 'the research task for the teachers is to test diagnostic hypotheses about teaching for understanding in games. However, the research task for the project team is somewhat different but logically related to it. The project team is doing research into effective ways of supporting teachers' theorising about their practice' (p. 146). Almond claimed that the teachers' study was 'first-order' research whereas the project team was engaged in 'second-order' research.

This categorization of first and second order research is useful in separating the interests of the members of the project team and in recognizing that there are separate human interests being served in such a project. However, I think that it is clearer to recognize the work of the teachers as a form of action research while that of the project team from the university as an evaluation type study which just happens to be of an action research project.

Almond recognizes that action research is conceived differently by different people who use the term to describe their work with teachers and cites the difference between the interpretation of action research articulated by Grundy and Kemmis (1981) and that of Hustler (1986). For Hustler 'Their (teachers) prime concern is to improve their own practice in a particular situation from the standpoint of their own concern or worry. For them action research seems to be a practical way forward . . .' (cited in Almond, 1987, p. 3). For Grundy and Kemmis however, action research 'aims at improvement in three areas: (i) the improvement of a practice; (ii) the improvement of the understanding of the practice by its practitioners; and (iii) the improvement of the situation in which the practice takes place' (*ibid*). According to Almond, the difference between the two accounts of action research is significant for there 'is a qualitative difference in the focus' (*ibid*, p. 4). For Grundy and Kemmis the emphasis is on understanding. He goes on to claim that 'one way round this problem is to call Hustler's account an example of a "weak", case, whereas both Stenhouse and Grundy are "strong" cases of action research' (*ibid*). We can see how Almond's version of weak and strong action research is similar in spirit to the notions of technical and practical action research discussed above.

Commenting on his own work with teachers Almond admits that he recognizes many examples of 'weak' action research but he has not seen examples of 'strong' action research. He claims further that the writings of Stenhouse, Grundy and Kemmis, although persuasive, conflict with his own practical knowledge of teacher involvement in action research projects (what he calls teacher-based research projects). He says 'All the time I come in contact with teachers who want to be told what to do, how to do it, and they ask for recipe-based guidelines' (p. 4).

The examples which Almond cites for action research cannot be clearly located as either technical or practical. They embody aspects of both. Indeed, from his accounts it seems that the projects were initiated *by* the university faculty and then organized *for* the teachers. This is clearly what Tripp (1984) was calling 'other-directed'. On the other hand it seemed that when the project 'got up and running' the teachers themselves had more input into the direction of the research. Perhaps it is the case that in such large scale projects the interests and agendas of teachers always become subservient to the dominant agendas of the organizers of the project. Another factor is that the written accounts of projects often give a limited version of the teacher perspectives of their involvement in the project. There are many reasons for this including the allowed length of published papers, the foregrounding of issues of 'scholarly significance' etc. The point is that it is difficult to get a real sense of the extent to which teachers have gained more than merely improved technical practice from their involvement in a project. It is difficult to find examples of teachers becoming (or even claiming to be) emancipated through their involvement in such projects.

Certainly the language used in Almond's accounts of his work with teachers reflects more of what we might recognize to be an interest in interpretation and understanding rather than of prediction and control. However although his work is best located in the framework of the hermeneutic or interpretive sciences rather than the empirical or natural sciences it does not represent emancipatory action research. In all of Almond's work there is little sense of the dialectical relationship between agency and structure (Giddens, 1976) which would help teachers to locate their own attempts at change within the broader social and structural context. In this sense Almond's work is best located as a form of interpretive science which reinforces, through its liberal discourse, individualism and ignores issues of power and dominance. If action research is to claim to be emancipatory then it must, in my view, address such issues.

The first report of an action research project by American physical educators to be published in the *Journal of Teaching in Physical Education* is that of Martinek and Butt (1988). This paper, titled 'An application of an action research model for changing instructional practice' begins with a general account of the failure of applying research-based recommendations to instructional practice in school settings. They suggest that action research is a research methodology which has the potential to make research relevant to practitioners because it

> advocates a team concept whereby teachers, researchers, and administrators engage concurrently in the formulation and conduct of the research. The primary focus is on resolving the concerns of the practitioners. It is designed to yield results that are immediately applicable to the practitioner's situation. (p. 215)

Their account of the project is predicated on the collaboration between faculty from the university and teachers from a local school district. They claim that their case study reveals how, through the action research process, the teachers became the researchers and the university faculty became consultants and resource persons.

The project involved 'the development, delivery, and assessment of a middle school physical education program' and represented 'a unique model whereby university and public school combine resources to provide effective physical education instruction for children' (p. 215). The process of action research, as they defined it, involved working through a number of stages which were outlined by Tikunoff, Ward and Griffin (1979). These stages consisted of:

(i)   identifying a solvable problem;
(ii)   the action research team assists the teacher in developing a plan of action for researching the problem;
(iii) implementation of the project;
(iv) teacher and the AR team discuss and analyze the results;
(v)   overall evaluation and recommendations and a new cycle begins.

In this particular project, Martinek and Butt (1988) outline how 'the teacher decided to design an action research strategy that would work on increasing the time-on-task of three of his most disruptive students in a specific class' (p. 216). Baseline data on time-on-task was then collected. An intervention strategy was then implemented and results pre and post-intervention displayed in bar graph form for analysis. Substantial increases in on task pupil behaviour were observed and the teacher felt that the project goals had been met.

It is worth noting that Noffke (1990) considers that the guidelines for action research presented by Tikunoff *et al* (1979) which are used as the model for this project do include 'some of the same characteristics present in other action research work' but there are also 'some important differences' (Noffke, 1990, p. 33). The focus on teaching skills, while ignoring curriculum development, was one criticism levelled at the conception of action research articulated by Tikunoff *et al* (1979). Moreover, Noffke (1990) considers that the conception of teaching as a matter of discerning and acquiring a set of specific competencies or techniques is a position rejected by the earlier action researchers in the United States. She concludes by stating that '. . . the focus seems to be less on teachers producing research and more on the likelihood that teachers would become more willing and able to be "consumers" of the research of others' (p. 33). This concern finds legitimacy in the Martinek and Butt (1988) comment that

An important extension of this research model (AR) is that the university researcher and teachers use their findings to help support or refute relevant instructional theory and research. This provides verification of past research findings and a data base from which new theories can be developed. (p. 215)

Clearly the teachers had a say in determining the issues of focus of this project, however there was little sense of problematizing the constraints to improved practice and importantly no apparent shift in the prevailing consciousness of the teachers or the university researchers with respect to the problematic nature of the chosen focus (namely time-on-task) or the nature of professional knowledge. Instead, the project seemed intent on confirming the wisdom of the knowledge generated in previous research studies (presumably those which studied teaching as an 'objective reality'). Although, the teachers did have a say in determining the focus of the study (a criterion for the Tripp account of practical action research) the project was more technical in its orientation.

When considered in the Habermasian framework of knowledge and human interests it is clear that the Martinek and Butt account of action research represents more of a technical interest with emphasis on instrumental knowledge and an application of empirical-analytical sciences. The focus is with the instrumental action of determining if certain means (strategies for reducing time off task) are effective in achieving the non-problematic end (more on-task time). Let me state quite clearly that I consider such projects to be of considerable significance to teachers and improvement in the technical skills of teaching is often both necessary and laudable. Certainly such an interpretation of action research within the physical education profession in the United States is entirely under-standable given the widespread acceptance of technocratic rationality as the dominant logic of professional practice within physical education (see Kirk, 1986; Bain, 1990; Tinning, 1990). However, although it is understandable, it is I believe, limited in its vision of the nature of action research for it offers no possibility for emancipation. In limiting attention to techne, it not only does not foreground understanding and inter-pretation, it gives no consideration to the material and ideological condi-tions which constrain educational practice and the way it is informed and hence does not develop praxis.

Action Research in Physical Education Teacher Education

Over the last ten years I have attempted to use action research as a way of improving the educational practice of pre-service and in-service teachers who enrol as students in degree courses at Deakin. In 1985 at a conference in New York, in a paper titled 'Beyond the development of a utilitarian teaching perspective: An Australian case study of action research in teacher preparation' I presented an account of a project in action research in pre-service teacher education (Tinning, 1987a). The paper began with a critique of what Ken Zeichner (1980) had first called the utilitarian teaching perspective which is facilitated by student teaching. The use of action research as a form of 'teacher-as-researcher' (in this case student teacher as learner teacher-researcher) was then advocated and a case study of the use of action research with my own student teachers presented.[1]

The project involved student teachers working in pairs for the duration of their school experience practicum during which time they were expected to act as 'critical friends' (a term used in the action research literature) for each other with respect to the teaching of physical education. Each student teacher was expected to teach a certain number of lessons and have their critical friend monitor and record certain data which was predetermined by discussion within the pair. This process was part of the action research spiral of plan, act, monitor, reflect which was outlined earlier. Student teachers were required to submit a paper detailing the way they worked through the action research process over the series of lessons and to include reactions to the process itself and what they felt they had learnt in the process. As I will outline shortly, the notion of action research within an award bearing course is itself problematic and the experience of this project bore this out.

Analysis of this paper reveals the discourses of critical theory were those which were foregrounded. The following quote from Kemmis and McTaggart (1988) firmly located the supporting discourse for the argument of the paper: 'In the long term, these propositions (being tested) will develop into a perspective on education itself, becoming a critical theory . . .' (p. 10). Other examples of language used in the account included 'critical friend'; 'systematic self-study'; 'critical reflection'; 'epistemology'; 'dialectic'; 'just, rational and moral'. Within that paper the argument was put that action research

> will involve more than counting the number of positive reinforcement statements or determining the amount of academic learning time. Whereas these data may indeed be important with respect to certain issues of concern for teachers, in and of themselves they represent technical questions that represent part of the current problem in trying to improve schooling in general and physical education specifically. (Tinning, 1987a, p. 117)

In emphasizing the ideas of critical theory, I was attempting to argue a case for emancipatory action research. It was hoped that the student teachers would, as a consequence of their experience with action research, not only improve their practice of physical education teaching but also their understandings of the practice and the conditions in which the practice took place — namely primary schools.

As such, I have required my students to become teacher-as-researcher, to self-reflect on their own physical education practice (or that of a friend or colleague) informed, in part, by ideas contained within a text titled *Improving Teaching in Physical Education* (1987b). However, given that the assessment requirements were 'built around' the submission of a report on the action research project a particular problem emerged. Action research can as McTaggart (1991) has claimed be reduced to a form of iconic simplicity in which the cycles of the process are treated as technical steps, the completion of which are seen to represent action research. Given the degree of instrumentalism which characterizes much undergraduate education (Kelly, 1990) it was no real surprise that for some students at least the idea of action research was simply an assessment requirement which was to be completed in the most efficient, but least engaging manner. At worst this might have involved the slavish following of the cycles of action research and the writing of 'self-reflective' comments which might be thought to be 'in sympathy' with what the lecturer wanted. Fitzclarence (1983) called this 'picking the bias of the lecturer'.

While I would claim that for some students in the pre-service program, the action research project afforded the opportunity to work collaboratively with another student, and to reflect and analyze their teaching of physical education in a systematic and informed manner, for others it was an exercise in 'going through the motions' to get the assignment done. In terms of the forms of action research outlined above, some students engaged only 'technical action research'. They wanted to be told what to 'research' (that is they didn't have an issue of their practice which was of interest to them in a problematic sense), and were happy to locate the power for determining action to remain with either myself as lecturer or the teacher in whose class they were teaching. Of course such practice is entirely understandable given that as Kelly points out:

> various discursive practices, for instance, accreditation and assessment throughout their educational histories, serve to position student teachers in an instrumental fashion. Student teachers have this instrumentality reinforced in an accreditation process which is marked by progression through a series of 'hoops' (assignments/tasks/teaching rounds). (Kelly, 1990, p. 78)

On the other hand I am aware also of some examples of exceptionally insightful and thoughtful work done by many students over the last ten years or so. Action research however, at least in forms which might approach the sentiments of emancipatory action research, clearly can't be mandated for either within the context of teacher education courses or in any forms of authorised in-service education for teachers.

Action Research for Praxis

As action research has become popular, its proponents have, because of their different positions with respect to knowledge and human interests, interpreted action research differently. Working from the perspective of action research as critical social science, McTaggart and Garbutcheon

Singh (1986) reported on an action research seminar held at Deakin University the purpose of which was 'to critique action research theory and practice as it has evolved over the past decade . . .' (p. 1). They claim that 'In many instances action research had been *stripped of its fundamental values, reduced in meaning to a variety of techniques and spiral iconic representations, and given an individualistic emphasis*' (my emphasis).

The Deakin seminar was concerned with the way certain key concepts had become reified and no longer considered as problematic. In particular the term 'practice', for example, was considered as too narrowly understood. The idea of facilitation in action research was 'now seen as an essentially technical notion which may create dependence in groups of action researchers where it aimed (mistakenly) to "transfer" power from a "facilitator" to the participants themselves' (p. 1).

Probably the most concise account of the nature of action research as articulated by these Deakin scholars is represented in *The Action Research Planner* (Kemmis and McTaggart, 1988). In defining action research Kemmis and McTaggart list four things which they claim action research is NOT.

(i) It is *not* the usual thing teachers do when they think about their teaching. Action research is more systematic and collaborative in collecting evidence on which to base rigorous group reflection.

(ii) It is *not* simply problem solving. Action research involves problem-posing, not just problem solving. It does not start from a view of 'problems' as pathologies.

(iii) It is *not* research done on other people. Action research is research by particular people on their own work with and for others.

(iv) It is *not* the 'scientific method' applied to teaching. Action research is not just about hypothesis-testing or about using data to come to conclusions. It adopts a view of social science which is distinct from a view based on the natural sciences.

When defined as a critical social science, action research is centrally concerned with the concept of emancipation, which in turn is a key feature of the discourse of critical theory. As Gibson (1986) has claimed 'Action research receives the attention of critical theorists because it embodies the latter's central principle: emancipation' (p. 162). Since action research is a democratic mode of research in that the participants work out their own solutions to their own problems (and that they employ their own language and concepts rather than those of the 'expert') action research affords teachers the opportunity to gain greater control over their own teaching lives (Gibson, 1986).

But improvement in practice is not *necessarily* emancipatory for according to McTaggart (1989) the improvement of practice should be linked to an understanding of the material and ideological conditions which constrain practice and the way it is informed. Certainly it is possible for teachers to improve their practice through a process which embodies the cyclic attention to planning, teaching, monitoring, and reflecting as was evident with the Martinek and Butt example. However, although improvements in practice can be facilitated by 'weak' or technical forms of action research, unless understanding is given a central place in the dialogue about practice then it is not possible to claim that the improvement in practice is emancipatory.

However emancipation is an illusive concept and I believe it is possible to have different forms of emancipation. As I have argued elsewhere (Tinning, 1987b) it is possible, as a result of involvement in action research, to develop a heightened sense of the limitations of one's practice within certain agency/structure relationships but still be constrained by those relationships and hence unable to improve certain practices. In this case I would say that there has been what might be called 'cognitive emancipation'; a form of consciousness raising. 'Complete' emancipation (if there really is ever such a thing) must involve not only consciousness raising but also practical action which is informed by such consciousness. In this sense emancipation must involve praxis as informed committed practice. Therefore it is not possible to claim that improvement in practice (such as the improvement of pupil on-task behaviour) is itself emancipatory.

Commenting on the development of action research at Deakin in the 1980s McTaggart (1989) claimed that there was 'The need to specify minimum requirements for action research — the axiomatics of action research praxis'. However, in the process of seeking the axiomatics the 'language of action research became more sophisticated, and more conscious of the concepts drawn from social theory.' (p. 3) McTaggart went on to suggest that while foregrounding the discourses of social theory may have made action research more defensible (to some academics) on the one hand, it apparently (and predictably) became more esoteric to teachers. It is the language of social theory used in the discourses of critical theory foregrounded in the Deakin perspective on action research which has attracted the strongest criticisms from teachers and other teacher education professionals.

Goodson and Walker (1991) have a different reaction to action research. They make a general claim that it 'does not follow logically or psychologically that to improve practice we must initially and immediately focus on practice' (p. 141). Their point is that 'to place the teachers' practice at the centre of the action for action researchers is to put the *most exposed* and problematic aspect of the teachers' world at the centre of scrutiny and negotiation' (p. 141, my emphasis). They go on to argue that the use of teacher biographies, examining the nature of teachers' work in the context of teachers' lives is a more appropriate and productive place to start. Perhaps this makes even more sense when we consider the suggestion made by Lortie (1975) that an important condition of teaching is 'privacy'; privacy in the way in which the physical geography separates teachers into private spaces; and privacy in that teachers do not readily discuss their teaching openly among themselves.

Recognizing the possible validity of Goodson and Walker's claim does not, however, decrease the validity of the claim made by McTaggart (1991) that action research has become

> dislodged from its cornerstone of critical self-reflection, and diverted from its goals of social and educational reform through making existing practice problematic. Action research so coopted lost its essential epistemological character — the formation and extension of critical theorems and the development of theoretically informed practice through personal but shared engagement in the struggle to change. (p. 42)

In terms of the history of action research, and in terms of action research for praxis, he is absolutely correct.

Of course, one may argue that action research necessarily will change over time and that it is entirely appropriate that it will have different meanings for different people. Considered as a text, action research will be read differently by different individuals because of their own discursive histories. However, in claiming that action research can have multiple meanings I am not suggesting that any reading is possible or indeed defensible. The fact that a form of cultural practice is recognizable *as* action research is because there is a limited number of possible readings given the set of discourses which make up the text. As I have argued elsewhere (Tinning, 1990) individuals will foreground certain discourses and background others as a result of their own particular set of human interests. The Deakin 'view' clearly foreground the discourses which relate to the ideals of emancipation and praxis, whereas others, for example Martinek and Butt (as representatives of the dominant current conception of action research in the United States) foreground the discourses of technocratic rationality which underlie more technical readings of action research as a process to improve practice.

From my own perspective and experience I consider that action research has much potential for improving the lives of teachers (but so will teacher biographies and life histories (see Goodson and Walker, 1991; Sparkes *et al* 1990) or critical ethnographies (see Walker, 1987)). Recognizing, but not in spite of, the valid criticisms of the epistemological foundations claimed for action research by the critical theorists and the vested human interests of those critical theorists (see Lather, 1990; and Ellsworth, 1989), I still believe that only action research which aspires to be emancipatory warrants the term action research. The four points of Kemmis and McTaggart (1988) outlined earlier which develop from the original spirit of action research for praxis seem to me to rule out more technical conceptions such as those described in the Martinek and Butt account.

My claim is that collaborative research which utilizes the cycle of action research but which embodies techne as the dominant disposition is best described as something other than action research. I think that the essence of action research should be recognized as a spirit or disposition which clearly locates itself within the notion of praxis. Projects which foreground prediction and control rather than praxis can be pursued by numerous forms of positivistic research which need not be confused with action research. We should consider action research as a way of transforming educational practice based on a recovered (from Aristotle) form of phronesis located in an contemporary ethic of emancipation which enables not only improved educational practice but also greater control over the what is defined as good practice and the constraints which militate against its attainment. Only in this sense action research will be for praxis.

Note

1   The version of the paper which appeared in Barrette *et al* (eds) *Myths, Models and Methods in Sport Pedagogy* (1987) was published, for reasons of its length, without the details of the case study.

References

ALMOND, L. (1976) 'Teacher involvement in curriculum planning' in KANE, J. (Ed) *Curriculum Development in Physical Education*, London, Crosby, Lockwood & Staples, pp. 96–121.

ALMOND, L. (1983) 'Action research: The challenge to improve professional practice' in TELAMA, R. *et al* (Eds) *Research in School Physical Education*, Finland, The Foundation for Promotion of Physical Culture and Health, pp. 123–9.

ALMOND, L. (1987) 'Action research in England since 1970', paper presented at the AIESEP World Convention, June, Universite du Quebec a Trois-Rivieres, Canada.

BAIN, L. (1990). 'Visions and voices', *Quest*, 42, 1, pp. 2–12.

BARRETTE, G., FEINGOLD, R., REES, C. and PERION, M. (1987) (Eds) *Myths, Models and Methods in Sport Pedagogy*. Champaign, IL, Human Kinetics.

BELL, G. (1985) 'Can schools develop knowledge of their practice?', *The Action Research Reader* (1988) Geelong, Deakin University Press, pp. 227–35.

BROCK-UTNE, B. (1980) 'What is educational action research?', *The Action Research Reader* (1988) Geelong, Deakin University Press.

CARR, W. and KEMMIS, S. (1986) *Becoming Critical: Knowing Through Action Research*, Lewes, Falmer Press.

CHEIN, I., COOK, S. and HARDING, J. (1948) 'The field of action research', *American Psychologist*, 3, 1, pp. 43–50.

COLLIER, J. (1945) 'United States Indian administration as a laboratory of ethnic relations', *Social Research*, 12, pp. 265–303.

COREY, S. (1949) 'Action research, fundamental research and educational practices', *Teachers College Press Record*, 50, pp. 509–14.

COREY, S. (1952) 'Action research by teachers and the population sampling problem', *Journal of Educational Psychology*, 43, pp. 331–8.

COREY, S. (1953) *Action Research to Improve School Practices*, New York, Teachers College Press.

ELLIOTT, J. (1978) 'What is action research in schools?', *Journal of Curriculum Studies*, 10, pp. 355–7.

ELLIOTT, J. and ADELMAN, C. (1973) 'Reflecting where the action is: The design of the Ford Teaching Project', *The Action Research Reader* (1988) Geelong, Deakin University Press, pp. 189–95.

ELLSWORTH, E. (1989) 'Why doesn't this feel empowering? Working through the repressive myths of critical pedagogy', *Harvard Educational Review*, 59, 3, pp. 297–324.

FALS BORDA, O. (1979) 'Investigating reality in order to change it: The Columbian experience', *Dialectical Anthropology*, 4, pp. 33–55.

FINGER, M. (1988) 'Heinz Moser's concept of action research', *The Action Research Reader* (1988) Geelong, Deakin University Press, pp. 259–69.

FITZCLARENCE, L. (1983) 'When the 'crunch' came: A two-dimensional view of school experience', *Australian Journal of Teaching Practice*, 3, 2, pp. 11–17.

FREIRE, P. (1982) 'Creating alternative research methods: Learning to do it by doing it' in HALL, B. *et al* (Eds) *Creating Knowledge: A Monopoly?* New Delhi, Society for Participatory Research in Asia.

GIBSON, R. (1986) *Critical Theory and Education*, London, Hodder & Stoughton.

GIDDENS, A. (1976) *New Rules for Sociological Enquiry: A Positive Critique in Interpretative Sociology*, London, Routledge & Kegan Paul.

GOODSON, I. and WALKER, R. (1991) *Biography, Identity and Schooling: Episodes in Educational Research*, Lewes, Falmer Press.

GRUNDY, S. (1987) *Curriculum: Product or Praxis?*, Lewes, Falmer Press.

GRUNDY, S. and KEMMIS, S. (1981) 'Educational action research in Australia: The state of the art (an overview)' *The Action Research Reader* (1988), Geelong, Deakin University Press, pp. 321–37.

HABERMAS, J. (1972) *Knowledge and Human Interests* (translation J. SHAPIRO), London, Heinemann.

HABERMAS, J. (1974) *Theory and Practice* (translation J. VIERTEL), London, Heinemann.

HALL, B. (1979) 'Knowledge as a commodity and participatory research', *Prospects*, 9, 4, pp. 393–408.

HALL, B. (1981) 'Participatory research, popular knowledge and power', *Convergence*, 14, 3, pp. 6–19.

HODGKINSON, J. (1957) 'Action research — A critique', *Journal of Educational Sociology*, 31, 4, pp. 137–53.

HUSTLER, D. (1986) *Action Research in Classrooms and Schools*, London, Allen & Unwin.

KELLY, P. (1990) 'Subjectivity in teacher education: A study of discursive self production in critical pedagogy', unpublished honours thesis, Deakin University.

KEMMIS, S. and McTAGGART, R. (1988) (Eds) *The Action Research Planner*, Geelong, Deakin University Press.

KIRK, D. (1986) 'A critical pedagogy for teacher education: Toward an inquiry-oriented approach', *Journal of Teaching in Physical Education*, 5, pp. 230–46.

KLAFKI, W. (1970) 'Pedagogy: Theory of a practice' *Suid-Aafrikaanse Tydskrif vir die Pedagogiek*, 4, 1, pp. 23–9.

KLAFKI, W. (1975) 'Decentralised curriculum development in the form of action research', *Council of Europe Information Bulletin*, 1, pp. 13–22.

LATHER (1990) *Getting Smart! Empowering Approaches to Research and Pedagogy*, London, Routledge.

LAWSON, H. (1984) 'Problem-setting for physical education', *Quest*, 36, pp. 48–60.

LORTIE, D. (1975) *Schoolteacher: A Sociological Study*, Chicago, IL, University of Chicago Press.

McTAGGART, R. (1989) 'If action research is an "innovation", its advocates have all failed', paper presented as part of the workshop 'Action research: Projections and reflections' at the Biennial Conference of the Australian Curriculum Studies Association, Canberra, July.

McTAGGART, R. (1991) *Action Research: A Short Modern History*, Geelong, Deakin University Press.

McTAGGART, R., ROBOTTOM, I. and TINNING, R. (1990) 'Action research in Australian teacher education' in STEVENSON, R. and NOFFKE, S. (Eds) *Action Research and Teacher Education: International Perspectives*, Buffalo, Graduate School of Education Publications, Buffalo Research Institute on Education for Teaching, State University of New York at Buffalo.

McTAGGART, R. and GARBUTCHEON-SINGH, M. (1986) 'New directions in action research' *Curriculum Perspectives*, 6, 2, pp. 42–6.

McTAGGART, R. and GARBUTCHEON-SINGH, M. (1988) 'A fourth generation of action research: Notes on the Deakin seminar', *The Action Research Reader* (1988) Geelong, Deakin University Press, pp. 409–29.

MARTINEK, T. and BUTT, K. (1988) 'An application of an action research model for changing instructional practice', *Journal of Teaching in Physical Education*, 7, pp. 214–20.

NOFFKE, S. (1990) 'Action research and the work of teachers' in STEVENSON, R. and NOFFKE, S. (Eds) *Action Research and Teacher Education: International Perspectives*, Buffalo, Graduate School of Education Publications, Buffalo Research Institute on Education for Teaching, State University of New York at Buffalo, pp. 113–24.

RIZVI, F. (1986) 'Bureaucratic rationality and the democratic community as a social ideal', paper presented at the annual meeting of the American Educational Research Association, San Francisco, April.

SCHON, D. (1984) *The Reflective Practitioner: How Professionals Think in Action*, New York, Basic Books.

SCHWAB, J. (1970) 'The practical: A language for curriculum', mimeo, Washington, DC, National Education Association.

SPARKES, A., TEMPLIN, T. and SCHEMMP, P. (1990) 'The problematic nature of a career in a marginal subject: Some implications for teacher education programmes', *Journal of Education for Teaching*, 16, 1, pp. 3–28.

TIKUNOFF, W., WARD, B. and GRIFFIN, G. (1979) *Interactive Research and Development on Teaching: Final Report* (Report IR & DT-79-11). San Francisco. Far West Laboratory for Educational Research and Development.

TINNING, R. (1987a) 'Beyond the development of a utilitarian teaching perspective: An Australian case study of action research in teacher preparation', in BARRETTE, G., FEINGOLD, R., REES, C. and PERION, M. (1987) (Eds) *Myths, Models and Methods in Sport Pedagogy*, Champaign, IL, Human Kinetics, pp. 113–23.

TINNING, R. (1987b) *Improving Teaching in Physical Education*, Geelong, Deakin University Press.

TINNING, R. (1990) 'Pedagogy in teacher education: Dominant discourses and the process of problem-setting', keynote address to the Sport Pedagogy section of the AIESEP World Convention, Loughborough University, UK, July.

TRIPP, D. (1984) 'Action research and professional development', discussion paper for the Australian College of Education Project, Perth, Murdoch University.

WALKER, J. (1987) 'Knowledge, culture and the curriculum: Implications of a five year ethnographic study of transition from school' in SMYTH, J. (Ed) *Educating Teachers: Changing the Nature of Pedagogical Knowledge*, Lewes, Falmer Press, pp. 95–107.

ZEICHNER, K. (1980) 'Myths and realities: Field based experiences in pre-service teacher education', *Journal of Teacher Education*, 31, 6, pp. 45–55.

Chapter 8

Curriculum History in Physical Education: A Source of Struggle and a Force for Change

David Kirk

The Australian journalist and social critic, Phillip Adams, recently wrote an article on Clive Wearing, the subject of a British television documentary called *Prisoner of Consciousness*. Wearing suffered from a condition brought about by the 'herpes simplex' virus which destroyed a large section of his brain. As a result, he suffered loss of long-term memory, and apart from a miscellany of competencies, could not retain information for more than a few minutes. Inspired by the documentary, Adams drew an analogy between Wearing's condition and the state of consciousness in society at large in an age of mass media.

> There's tendency to live, more and more, in a world of vivid, lurid immediacy, a present tense made more tense by the magnifying glass of the media. A present so powerful that it obliterates the past. That's simply something to be plundered for counterfeit nostalgia — its nothing but a quarry for pastiche music and 'fashion'. 'Now' becomes NOW, a succession of over-bright, hyped presents, more like sequins than sequence . . . We are constantly confronted and astonished by events without precedent or context, yet imagine ourselves to be well-informed. That's how we buy tired, second-hand goods like the New Age or the New Right and imagine them to be revelations. Our lives are feverish, superficial and, for all our wondrous communications technologies, ignorant. (Adams, 1989, p. 2)

Adam's journalese is colourful to be sure, but his point is nevertheless clear. Like Clive Wearing, society at large has an increasing tendency to live in the present tense, in such a way that each experience seems to be a new experience, and each is intensified out of proportion by the magnifying effect of the electronic media. The implications of this imprisonment in the present are for Adams ominous. Since our awareness of anything more than the immediate past is limited to sentimental nostalgia, we are unable to learn from our previous experiences.[1] As a consequence, we are willing, indeed, ethusiastic, consumers of tired old ideas wrapped up in the bright tinsel packaging of the New Right and other forms of simplistically reductive political rhetorics.

The cultural shift Adams points to, which has been underway in earnest since at least the 1950s, has been characterized by some writers as the postmodern era.[2] Over the last twenty to thirty years or so there has been a qualitative shift in culture, initiated and in large part sustained by a conglomeration of new electronic technologies we rather indiscriminately describe as the media. There have, of course, been many critiques of television, film and the glossy magazine as purveyors of culturally undesirable values and practices. But Adams' comments move beyond this debate. His point, and in this he is echoing much recent literary and cultural analysis, is that the various mass media have been influential in creating a more profound shift in the ways in which we perceive the world. As a consequence, our sense of ourselves, of others, of the material world, and of time itself has also begun to change. According to Adams, we are fast on the way to being permanently imprisoned in the lurid present, trapped in a world of surface appearances, where 'the look' is all important and, eventually perhaps, all there is.

The purpose of this chapter is to develop a position on curriculum history and its value to physical educators, in light of this apparent cultural shift which threatens to trap us in the present tense and in a world of surface appearances. First of all, I want to explain relatively briefly what is distinctive about *curriculum* history compared with other historical work in education and physical education, and to offer a particular view of curriculum history. Following that, I hope to show something of the kind of material curriculum history produces and the sources of struggle it illuminates by drawing on some of my own research. And finally, building on this section, I want to locate curriculum history within curriculum research more broadly and, returning to the points about imprisonment in the present made by Adams, to say what its significance might be within a critical pedagogy.

I need to make clear at the outset that my interest in curriculum history is far from 'academic'; it has a very practical, strategic and political source. As the title of this chapter states, curriculum history can be 'a source of struggle and a force for change'. Put less cryptically, by exposing the ways in which change in physical education has occurred over time, through struggle, conflict and contestation, historical material provides one means (among several) of generating critical and reflective self- and collective-awareness among physical educators. In an era marked by cultural upheavals associated with continuing saturation of everyday experience by electronic mass media, I believe this quality is an essential precondition to teaching physical education programmes which are sensitive to matters such as social justice, gender and racial oppression, environmental degradation and non-violence (to name only a few).

Matters such as these infuse the work of all teachers in schools. In addition, reflective awareness is an essential dimension of a profession which is able to critique its own practices in the light of changing circumstances and to adapt or modify these practices accordingly.

With this perspective in mind, I will attempt, in the next section, to say something about the relationships between curriculum history and what I will call traditional history, and through this to present a particular view of curriculum history.

Curriculum History and Traditional History

Interest in history among curriculum researchers and in the curriculum among historians has been growing since the early 1980s. Curriculum history embraces a diverse range of studies which can be identified broadly by their use of historical methods to investigate the processes of selecting, organizing and distributing knowledge through educational institutions; by an emphasis on the socially contested nature of these processes; and by a concern to illuminate the deep, sedimented structures of contemporary conflict by locating struggles temporally. Studies which have been identified by the label curriculum history have tended to focus on either the emergence and decline of school subjects (for example, Goodson, 1983), or the etymology of terms associated with schooling such as curriculum, class, and instruction, and the process of social editing that the use of these terms entails (for example, Hamilton, 1989).

This interest in curriculum history has arisen at a time of crisis for humanities disciplines generally in universities. The same process has also been noted in teacher education courses, where studies of culture, society and history have been increasingly marginalized. The alleged lack of relevance of history to teacher education in particular is, perhaps, symptomatic of our throwaway culture, where news from the past is no news at all, except as some commentators have pointed out, in the form of curios, nostalgia and pastiche (Adams, 1989; Postman, 1985). Indeed, history of education as it has been conceived and practised traditionally presents an exemplary case of this crisis. In his critique of the ways in which history of education had traditionally been done in Britain, Goodson (1988) has suggested that while the institutionalized form of history of education has been, like every other curriculum topic, far from 'monolithic', it has tended to retain what he calls an acts and facts flavour. In this form, history of education deals mainly with institutionalized and formal 'progress' but rarely with the social detail of change, thus presenting historical information as at best a partial account of change, and at worst as inert and irrelevant to contemporary projects.

The effect of this treatment of history in teacher education courses has been two-fold. First, it has had the effect of presenting history as of little concern to teachers' and schools' current needs, and second, by working back on the teaching of history of education courses, it has

resulted in their omission from teacher education because of this perceived irrelevance. Much of the work in curriculum history of late has
attempted to counter this problem explicitly. In his book *Learning About
Education*, Hamilton (1990) demonstrates clearly that contemporary
notions like education, schooling, curriculum and teaching cannot be
understood outside the social, cultural and temporal contexts in which
they are used. Goodson (1988) has argued more explicitly and at some
length that historical studies of the school curriculum form as essential
component of any research effort that seeks to understand the ways in
which contemporary efforts to bring about change can be accomplished,
since without a detailed sensitivity to what he calls the internal nature of
schooling and its changing forms over time, attempts to effect change are
likely to be unsuccessful. In Australia, Musgrave (1988) has similarly
argued that the recent upsurge in interest in curriculum history has been
marked by a shift in motivations from a need to simply understand the
past, to a desire to participate more effectively in complex practical
situations in the present.

Hamilton, Goodson and Musgrave have not been alone in their
separate claims that curriculum history has immediate relevance to contemporary projects. In a recent and comprehensive review of curriculum
history research, Seddon (1989) remarked that, following a period of
neglect by curriculum researchers in the 1950s and 1960s, studies of
the history of school subjects and pedagogy, and of the curriculum field
itself, have proliferated in the 1980s. She claims that despite a degree of
unevenness across countries in terms of numbers of studies and active
researchers, the sub-field of curriculum history has now reached a stage of
self-conscious reflection, in which issues of purpose, method and theory
have begun to be worked through by exponents. As a result of this reflective effort, Seddon has been able to map a number of key issues which she
has proposed as an agenda for future curriculum history research. In
particular, she claims (following Americans Kliebard and Franklin) that
the substantive focus of this sub-field

> centres curriculum in the selection, organisation and distribution
> of *knowledge*; sited in *educational institutions* and hence, implying
> that curriculum is oriented to *learners*. Additionally, it indicates
> that curriculum is the consequence of people's activity which
> constitutes social and political processes over time, that is, there is
> a relationship between *people and things*. (*ibid*, p. 3)

According to Seddon, this statement provides a useful means of identifying the central concerns of curriculum history as a sub-field of curriculum and educational research more broadly, though a number of other
key issues continue to present themselves as in need of resolution by
curriculum historians; she stresses especially the issues of the boundaries
of curriculum history, the nature of historical research, and the place of
theory in curriculum history as matters which are currently under debate

by researchers in the field. Despite varying opinions on these matters among curriculum researchers, a common thread running through most of this recent curriculum history work has been the explicit use of history to inform contemporary projects for change, and thus an acknowledgment that curriculum research is, as Reid (1978) clearly indicated, an inherently political activity that is interwoven with the pragmatics and practicalities of educating and schooling.

In contrast to curriculum history as it is described by Seddon and as I wish to use the term here, historical research in physical education has sometimes tended to be concerned exclusively with the achievements of Great Men (and less often Great Women) and their contributions to 'progress'. Much more historical work has taken its (apparently straight-forward) task to be describing and cataloguing facts and events. Most history in physical education has generally taken the form of the pro-duction of chronologies, narratives and descriptive accounts of changes. Evans and Davies (1986, p. 27) have argued, however, that taken together, the net effect of this historical work is to project an unproblematic image of the development of school physical education as a single and uncontested line of evolution and progress from drill through physical training to the comprehensive programmes of today. They have stressed the point that 'conflict and disagreement within the ideas and attitudes (towards physical activity, the body and sport) of middle class males or females, and between their aspirations and other social and ethnic groups, remain largely unexplored'.

Despite these charges, which I believe are accurate in the main, there has been research of exceptional quality carried out on topics such as sport and the competitive games tradition.[3] While the theoretical complexity and sophistication of these studies has varied greatly, much of the material they have produced is invaluable for the practical, strategic and political purposes I have in mind here. However, historical work in physical education in general stands in stark contrast to the recent curric-ulum history work, in two senses. First, even in the best historical work, there has been little explicit concern for the processes of selecting, organizing and distributing knowledge in school and tertiary level phy-sical education programmes. Second, little of this research has been concerned with locating contemporary trends within the temporal flow, or with utilizing such research as part of contemporary struggles over definitions of 'really useful knowledge' in physical education.

In saying this, I do not mean to convey the impression that existing historical work in physical education is of little value for studying con-temporary events. On the contrary, I believe this historical material to be of immense importance. What I am suggesting is that, in distinguishing between historical study in physical education as it is commonly done, and the notion of curriculum history I am presenting here, there are significant differences in purposes and assumptions. In curriculum his-tory in contrast to traditional history, I have suggested that concerns to illuminate contemporary events and inform future action are of central importance. Whereas work in traditional history tends to restrict itself to particular time periods, curriculum history often attempts to begin with contemporary problems and trace these back across time; in other words, to foreground *processes* of change. A key task in curriculum history is to question how current orthodoxies have come to be, and to search the past as a means of understanding the present and the future in a more explicit fashion than traditional history has tended to do.

Moreover, there is no claim to political neutrality in the version of curriculum history I am arguing for, where the selective and interpretative nature of research is not merely acknowledged, but is actually celebrated as a source of purpose and guidance. As James Hexter (1971) has pointed out, doing history is an interpretative exercise. There is no such thing as an objective primary record of facts and artefacts, there is only, in effect, the historian's second record of interpretations of events. Facts only make sense — indeed, they only exist as facts — within the context of any one person's current understanding, within their socially generated frames of reference.[4] It is this understanding or perspective which organizes information, which identifies some data as admissible and relevant, and other data as unworthy of attention. And since historians each come to the (so-called) primary record with different levels of understanding and different social-biographical experiences, their second records, their interpretations of events, often differ, sometimes quite considerably.

There are some important implications in this line of argument for understanding the status of curriculum history as research, and the products of this research. One of these is that since our biographies shape our understanding and purposes, it is important that curriculum historians provide readers with some insights into their perspectives, understandings and motivations for carrying out a particular piece of research. It is only by doing this that a reader can make a judgment about the coherence of an account. And if an account makes little or no sense to a reader, there is very little chance of it being persuasive. This is not to say that scholarship or respect for the compelling weight of evidence are any less important in curriculum history than traditional history. But it is to say that notions like 'scholarship' and 'the compelling weight of evidence', and what actually counts *as* evidence, only make sense within a person's biographically produced frame of reference, and the matrices of cultural norms, beliefs and values in which such frames of reference are embedded.[5]

In light of these comments, I need to make one point very clear. By arguing that curriculum history is motivated by a concern to act in an informed way in the present is not to commit the methodological sin of presentism, which is the reading — and distortion — of past events through contemporary lenses. Neither am I suggesting that we 'raid the past' (Young, 1975) in order to legitimate our current activities and aspirations. The error of presentism is to assume that contemporary events closely resemble in some way or other events in the past, so that by studying the outcomes and consequences of previous actions we can find ready-made strategies for actions in the present.

One example of this use of history is occurring in relation to the revitalized interest within the physical education profession in matters of health and fitness. Contemporary protagonists for a health-related orientation to the curriculum cite historical precedent as a means of legitimating their current concerns; 'physical educators', so the rhetoric runs, 'have since the earliest days of the subject's entry into the curriculum, had a major concern for health and physical fitness'.[6] The dangers of such comparisons are that current social conditions and the interventive measures they inspire have changed a great deal since the late nineteenth century. Physical activity at that time was viewed as a response to fears for the physical deterioration of the race, and one component of health alongside adequate food, clothing, shelter and fresh air. This was a therapeutic use of exercise, an after-the-event cure, or at least treatment, for particular manifestations of poor health such as poor posture, pigeon chests and bad feet, created by the conditions of that time. The contemporary rhetoric linking physical activity and health is quite different. In the sedentary, consumer-oriented and leisured present, the concern is for prevention rather than therapy. Exercise is no longer seen as a compensatory treatment for illnesses brought on by deprivation, but rather as an integral part of modern lifestyle, as an antidote to overconsumption and its end-products.

The error of presentism, as illustrated through this example, is to cite one set of circumstances which have an apparent similarity to present events so that it is assumed 'history is repeating itself'. The difficulty with such a move is that it assumes the context in which the events occurred are either similar or worse, irrelevant, and that the intervening period has merely caused the prior set of events to be forgotten, only to be rediscovered anew and reincarnated intact, ready to be picked up from where our ancestors left off. In short, the superficial similarities are noted without any acknowledgment of underlying differences.

Curriculum history, on the other hand, begins with concerns about present events and asked the questions 'why is this happening here and now?', and 'what are the preconditions of this series of events?'. Both of these questions draw attention to the (often forgotten) fact that all human activity takes place in time and in specific geographical and material sites or locations (see Hamilton, 1990). It is important to bear in mind that time and space do not merely form a inert backdrop to social interaction, like the scenery of a stage play. In a play, scenery provides visual support for the make-believe world the actors construct according to the script; it is, literally, a backdrop. But in most cases, the play could continue whether the scenery was there or not, and in some cases, it does. In contrast, real life as it is experienced unifies time and space so that they are not two separate, interacting phenomena, but one phenomenon, 'time-space' (cf. Giddens, 1984). Moreover, time-space *constitutes* social interaction; it forms the stuff, the fabric, of social life quite unlike inert stage scenery.

So, just as sociocultural studies of the present require events to be properly contextualized in time-space, so it is necessary to situate past events (which have become the pre-conditions of contemporary events) in their geographical, temporal, social, cultural, political and economic contexts. Curriculum history does this by accepting as its starting point the proposition that school knowledge is given form and substance through the interactions of individuals and groups of people in particular time-space localities. It accepts, in addition, that since these interactions take place in particular time-space localities, they will be in the form of struggles over limited material and ideological resources. The error of presentism is thereby avoided, since studies in curriculum history are studies of social interaction in time-space locations which demand that interpretations of events take place in this context. Rather than commit the error of presentism by making comparisons between past and present, curriculum history attempts to understand how it is contemporary events came to be the way they are. In so doing, it becomes possible to see how the values, practices and interests of some sections of the community come to infuse and shape the lives of the majority, how particular notions become orthodoxies, and how specific definitions of physical education itself come to be accepted without demur as *the* definitions.

In the next section, before moving on to offer an account of a curriculum history study in physical education, I want to preface this example with a brief outline of my own biography in physical education and the leading concerns I carried into my study.

Biography as Social Editing

Our biographies are a kind of screening device. In the most general sense, through our experiences and accumulated learning, we are able to identify with increasing accuracy and expertise what information is worthy of attention in any particular situation. The same process is at work in carrying out a research project. The major difference between more general everyday situations and research is that in the case of the latter, we are attempting to collect evidence about particular issues, following (relatively) systematic procedures and incorporating reflectivity as a means of generating insights into these issues. My own biography played an important part in shaping the study I eventually carried out, particularly in terms of issues I thought worthy of serious attention, and the evidence I considered to be admissible in relation to these issues.

I trained as a physical education teacher and taught physical education in a large comprehensive school in Scotland in the late 1970s, early 1980s. Since that time, I have been involved with the pre- and in-service education of physical education teachers. I began using historical material within my undergraduate curriculum courses in 1984. Over a number of years, this material has taken increasingly larger portions of time in these courses until by 1988 most of my teaching was framed by three meta-questions about the curriculum and physical education: where are we now? how did we get here? and, where are we going? Increasingly too, the notion of change became an organizing concept for these courses. Overall, this pedagogy seemed to resonate strongly with my students' experiences, many of whom were disorientated by the sheer pace and extent of change in physical education from month to month and year to year. By explicitly locating the analysis of physical education in time-space, the processual nature of social life, of which physical education is a part, seemed to be less awesome and intimidating and also more coherent.

As a physical education teacher, teacher educator and researcher, increasingly I have come to see physical education as a profession enamoured with a view of itself as scientific, or at the very least, as a profession which draws on a body of scientific knowledge as the basis of professional practice. This claim to scientific status is not a problem in a range of fields which are relevant to the professional preparation of physical educators. There are no difficulties with the idea that some problems are entirely appropriately tackled using scientific methods and sophisticated technologies. But a problem in physical education arises when the logic which informs the study of appropriately scientific phenonema of interest to physical educators begins to define other realms of activity also of interest to physical educators. More than this, it is when biophysical phenomena which are amenable to scientific treatment are judged to be of *greater relevance* to the work of physical educators than studies of history and culture that problems are compounded. As Andrew Sparkes' introductory chapter reveals, the physical education research community is riven by epistemological and methodological disputes that arise out of this very problem (see, for example, Kirk, 1990b; Lawson, 1990; McKay, Gore and Kirk, 1990; McKay, 1986; Sparkes, 1989 and 1991; Whitson and MacIntosh, 1990).

When the importance and relevance of scientific methods are inflated out of proportion, science becomes scientism, a belief system and a way of looking at the world rather than a collection of methods and techniques for understanding the world. On the basis of my own experience of preparing students to become physical educators, which have been confirmed by the experiences of a sizeable number of my colleagues around the world, I have to say that physical educators as a professional group are becoming more and more saturated in scientistic ways of seeing the world (see for example, Tinning, 1988; Dewar, 1987; Gore, 1990 and Hellison, 1988). And when students are fed a diet of scientized knowledge and when they receive the powerful message that biophysical, scientific knowledge is of most relevance to physical educators, their motivations to approach the study of cultural phenomena that is of crucial importance to their work is low, notwithstanding their abilities to even perceive its relevance in the first place.

This is not to join in the chorus of arrogant and ignorant ridicule which has often accompanied physical educators' attempts since the 1950s to develop the field as a discipline in tertiary institutions. It is to say nothing derogatory at all about the intellectual capacities of physical educators in general and as a physical educator, I am well aware that any criticism of current orthodoxies can compound the often cited marginality of physical education as a field of study. Indeed, I recognise that the enthusiatic adoption of science by physical educators has been part of this very status problem. However, the more general arguments presented by Adams and others (cf. Postman, 1985; Aronowitz and Giroux, 1985) that people's abilities to think abstractly and reflectively across time and space are being steadily eroded by electronic mass media (which we are all affected by) reinforce for me the present imbalance of power and knowledge in physical education which not only elevates the importance of scientific and technological ways of thinking, but applies these ways of seeing the world to the whole of physical education. And if physical education teachers themselves are unable to reflect critically on the ways in which the body, fitness and health and institutionalized forms of sport are implicated in the production of cultural practices, then what chance do they have of engaging in meaningful communication around these issues with children and adolescents?

As I became more convinced of the appropriateness and importance of historical research as a key component of curriculum studies, I decided in 1987 to begin some research of my own, focussing on what seemed to me to be a series of interesting and important events in British physical education. In the next section, I want to provide an example of curriculum history from my own research, focussing on some of the major substantive themes as a means of illustrating the kinds of material such a study might produce.

Defining Physical Education

The two years in British physical education preceding 1987 had been unusual. All of a sudden, it seemed, school physical education was being debated and discussed in the tabloid and 'serious' press, and professional (non-physical education) teaching journals. The crowning glory of this public interest was a one hour television documentary presented by Richard Lindley for *Panorama* in March 1987. Never before, even in times of national crisis such as war, had school physical education received such public attention. And while the insatiable appetite of the mass media for material certainly had much to do with the way in which this debate proceeded, this was a new experience for physical educators. Briefly and much simplified, the cause of the (at times) heated exchanges flying through the airwaves and the pages of newspapers and journals seemed to be an alleged decline in interest in sport among physical educators, and its replacement by (again allegedly) trendy left-wing ideas about non-competitive, individualized health and fitness programmes.

Given the unprecedented and public nature of these events, it seemed to me that the questions 'why are these events happening here and now?' and 'what are the preconditions of these events?' could throw some light on the debate itself, but just as importantly, on the process of curriculum and sociocultural change more broadly. Guided by these initiating questions, I began the study in August 1987 armed with a particular way of viewing change in physical education adapted from Goodson's work (see Goodson, 1983 and 1984), which was that the aims, content and pedagogy of a curriculum topic (or school subject more specifically in this case) changes through conflict, struggle and contestation centred around material resources and interests, a framework I subsequently elaborated to suit my own purposes.

Two factors emerged almost immediately which were of crucial importance to shaping my research.

The first was that the two decades which followed the end of the Second World War were a watershed period for physical education in British schools. Along with the many other changes in social life experienced after the war, physical education began to take on its contemporary form during the 1950s and into the 1960s, stimulated considerably by some of the new technological ideas produced by the war, and by the introduction of mass secondary schooling. With this latter innovation, physical education almost overnight presented itself as a more attractive profession to men; from the 1890s until the 1940s, the profession had been dominated by women who had taught mainly in girls' grammar and private schools. Along with this influx of men came new ideas and practices, and it wasn't long before the female and male sections of the physical education profession were at loggerheads.

The second factor was a more substantive issue and it emerged as significant early in the study. The phrase 'traditional physical education' was used frequently in the 1985–1987 debate, and it commanded a great deal of respect and emotive force, particularly among physical education's critics. While the meaning of the term was rarely articulated, most people who used it seemed to assume that competitive teams games such as rugby union, football (soccer), cricket, field hockey and netball were the core components of physical education *and always had been.* 'Traditional physical education' was, in effect, a definition of physical education, of its aims, content and pedagogy. More than this, to judge by the reactions of physical education's critics, it was a sacred and sacrosanct definition, one that wasn't under any circumstances to be challenged.

These two factors gave rise to a range of more substantive questions. How, in the first place, were these two factors connected, if at all? What did the arrival of males in physical education, and the subsequent demise of a distinctively female influence in the two decades following the war, have to do with the current crisis? How traditional, in fact, were competitive teams games as a form of physical education? And why were the critics *so* upset, even though it was apparent early in the piece that the accusations about the demise of games and sport were in reality false, or at least, greatly exaggerated? As the study progressed, answers to these and other questions began to suggest themselves. Readers interested in the whole story can refer to the published accounts of the study (Kirk, 1990a and 1992). Here, I want to try to show, very briefly, how the social construction of the meaning of physical education in the post-war period provides us with some insights into how and why physical education was positioned in the way it was during the debate, as the arch-villain of the piece, as the purveyor of dangerously misguided left wing ideals.

I want to begin by suggesting that the 1985–1987 debate arose as part of a general crisis within Conservative politics in Britain in the lead-up to the 1987 General Education. As Evans (1990) has so cogently argued, the debate wasn't really about school physical education and competitive team games at all; or at least, only in so far as competitive team games could be seen to represent, symbolically, a range of values such as competitiveness, controlled aggression, team spirit, a particular form of masculinity, elitism, excellence and so on, values which have considerable power for particular sections of society. The 'crisis' reached the proportions it did because, at that particular time in specific places in Britain (time-space), it provided a means of articulation of these values. 'Traditional physical education' was a magical litany, three words which evoked patriotic emotion and pride in some sections of the community, and the debate attacking alleged trendy left-wing undermining of competitive team games in schools assisted Conservatives at a time of crisis within their own ranks (Evans, 1990; Johnson, 1989). The litany served as a rallying call to flag, queen and country.

However, the alleged demise of 'traditional physical education' would not have been able to provoke such moral outrage among Conservatives and other right-wing critics unless school physical education had already been practiced in such a way as to permit it to be used in this manner, symbolically representing some key right-wing values. Prior to the war, competitive team games were played in many types of schools, urban and rural, rich and poor, secondary and to a lesser extent primary (elementary) schools too. But by far the most numerous and enthusiastic exponents of this form of physical education were the boys' private and state high schools. It was to the private schools that competitive team games were *traditional*; indeed, as Mangan (1981) has shown, upper class male pupils began to organize their own games at these schools from the 1830s. Some games, such as rugby football, were even invented in these schools, or at least, were given their recognizable contemporary form.

But it wasn't just games playing in itself which created the 'tradition' to which right-wing critics in the 1985–1987 debate could so blithely refer. It was the cluster of very powerful sentiments, values and rules of conduct in which games playing was embedded and which gave the games social meaning and significance for these upper class males which made this tradition. Even though, as Mangan points out, this games ethic and the cult of athleticism of which it was a part, was on the decline in the upper class schools following the end of the first world war, this very powerful system of values associated with games playing had by the 1920s already found a firm foothold in popular culture (see, for example, McIntosh, 1968, p. 222). The advent of universal secondary schooling in the late 1940s in Britain was simply the final step in this process of massifying and popularising, not so much team games, which were already part of popular culture, but the upper class games ethic, and persuading the general populace that this was a national, not a sectional, system of values. Mass secondary schooling more than any other medium in the 1950s spread and consolidated the word, and it was during this period in time, on the playing fields of the many new secondary schools around Britain, that the *myth* of 'traditional physical education' was born and nurtured.

I say myth of 'traditional physical education' quite intentionally, and I am using the term in much the way that Barthes (1957) has suggested. Barthes means by myth an unproblematic way of seeing the world, a perspective we are not fully conscious of and which seems, for all intents and purposes, to be 'natural'. A myth is a way of thinking which is so deeply buried in our collective consciousness that it is, most of the time, invisible. 'Traditional physical education' is a myth, not only because it was unproblematically accepted as *the* definition of physical education by the critics in the recent debate, but also because it is not quite what it seems to be. It is a fact that *the value systems* competitive team games projected were not traditional to the culture of the majority of the British population. Moreover, the games ethic didn't even represent women within the social groups from which it was generated (McCrone, 1988). Games playing and the games ethic represented one particular view of the world, of what is valuable, of the correct way to behave, or how society is or should be organized and governed, a view that belonged to an elite, wealthy and predominately Anglo-Saxton, Protestant, male minority.

When men began to enter the physical education profession after the Second World War, team games formed a relatively minor part of physical education programmes for the majority of the school-age population. Swedish gymnastics *was* physical education, and had been since the late 1800s. Moreover, this definition of physical education was the hallmark of the women physical educators, and it had dominated thinking about school physical education until the 1940s, when educational gymnastics began to challenge its pre-eminent position. Indeed, for over a decade, between the early 1940s to the early 1950s, the women argued vociferously amongst themselves over which form of gymnastics should constitute physical education (Kirk, 1990a). But this debate was swept away to the margins of the profession's concerns, and almost completely out of its collective memory, by the rise to prominence of the male physical educator and competitive team games. Within a remarkably short space of time after the war, team games usurped gymnastics to become the core of physical education, first in boys' secondary programmes, then in girls', and only much later, in the 1970s, in primary school programmes also.

On their entry to secondary schools after the war, the male physical educators had faced two major problems relating to status, and team games helped them begin to deal with these problems. First, since physical education had been a predominately female profession until this time, it was perceived as such by other secondary school teachers; this meant second-class citizen status straight away. To compound this problem, the women physical educators were almost exclusively from the middle classes and were trained in private, fee-paying colleges, whereas many of the male physical educators were from lower middle and upper working class backgrounds. So even within physical education, the men were perceived to be socially and professionally inferior to their female counterparts. And second, physical education was a practical subject in a secondary school curriculum dominated by academic disciplines, and physical educators were diploma, not degree qualified, in the case of women, and only one year trained (on top of a general degree) in the case of the men. In the 1940s through to the late 1960s, this meant lower salaries, restricted promotion, and such humiliations in some cases as non-access to the teachers' common rooms.

Unsurprisingly, the male physical educators used whatever means that were to hand to improve this inferior status both inside the profession and out. The games playing tradition of the private schools and its associated values had already achieved public prominence, mainly through the participation of upper class men in international sports contests such as the Olympic Games and other annual events such as the Oxbridge boat race, and it supplied a ready-made means of enhancing their social and professional position. This is not to suggest that this was an intentionally planned strategy. While some benefits may have been consciously anticipated, the effects of such intentional action would always have been limited to particular localities in time-space. It is simply to point out that the circumstances were ripe for male physical educators to adopt a version of physical education which resonated with their personal experiences of sport, formed an already prominent cultural institution, and was embedded within an existing system of values originating from upper class males which projected a particular version of masculinity, ethical conduct and social organization.

Moreover, the male physical educators very quickly saw the potential benefits for sports performance of scientific analysis, and in the 1950s there was an flood of interest in exercise physiology and the mechanics of sports skills and techniques. Later, in the 1960s, this rapidly evolving body of scientific biophysical knowledge formed the basis for physical educators' claims to academic status in Britain through the Bachelor of Education degree, a movement that was dominated by men (Fletcher, 1984). And later still, in the 1970s and 1980s, this body of knowledge, growing progressively more complex and intricate by the minute, found its way into school physical education programmes. At this stage though, in the 1950s, this scientific knowledge and the technologies of fitness and skill development which were honed by the Armed Services during the war were quickly applied in teacher training courses, but as a means of assisting the teaching of competitive team games rather than as a body of knowledge for study in its own right.

The Contribution of Curriculum History to
Understanding the 1985–1987 Physical Education Debate

This story of the males' rise to prominence and power in physical education over the female influence, which finally succumbed to 'traditional physical education' and the pervasive world-view of biophysical science at the end of the 1960s when resistance crumbled almost completely, is not as straightforward as this very abbreviated account suggests. There were setbacks, there was opposition to change (from both women *and* men), there were pressures exerted and opportunities presented by changes to other parts of the educational, political, economic and cultural systems, there was coherence and contradiction in just about equal measure. But while this is an incomplete and much simplified account of the events which became the preconditions of the 1985–1987 debate, it provides us with some clues to how 'traditional physical education' could be used as a powerful symbol of right-wing values, and more generally is an illuminative example of how the curriculum changes.

In the first place, this example from the study provides some sense of the very complex ways in which curriculum change happens, and highlights the central place of struggle and contestation in this process. Indeed, physical education has been a veritable battleground over attempts to define the subject, especially since 1945, with the profession riven by acrimonious debate mainly between females and males. I don't believe the strength of this language at all exaggerates the depth of feeling such conflict aroused, as those who experienced the debates of the 1950s and 1960s first-hand will testify. None of this suggests, however, that there was ever a conspiracy to usurp women physical educators, or that these struggles were ever intentionally conceived beyond local geographical regions and within relatively short time spans. The male physical educators did not author a grand plan to take-over physical education, though there are many examples of males and females acting intentionally towards specific ends in particular circumstances. In these cases, people had to make the best of their circumstances as they found them and as they understood them, and act accordingly. The fact that the males had the dice weighted in their favour in this process was not a situation the physical educators of the 1950s created, but their actions took place within a patriarchal social system and were greatly assisted by this form of social organization.

Secondly, I hope this example shows that physical educators as a profession are not the sole authors of the cultural meanings infusing their subject. These meanings have been formed by their predecessors over time, and by others at other times and in other places. As such, physical educators individually and collectively have only limited control over the sense other people or they themselves can make of physical education. The study convinced me that leading up to the recent debate, physical educators as a professional group have had only a limited sense of their role as authors of the meanings in which their subject is embedded, and have done little to attempt to extend their control over the process of defining their subject. Or to put this in more straightforward terms, they have paid little attention to what other people thought of physical education, and on the whole have not been particularly skilful public relations people for themselves as a profession.

Thirdly, it is quite clear that the ideas which inform physical education practices, and which as I've suggested were at the bottom of the characterisations of physical education by its critics, have been rooted in questionable and contestable views of masculinity, femininity, competitiveness, etc., and the value of physical education. There is no suggestion here that physical educators are any more chauvinist or elitist or conservative than anyone else. But, nevertheless, there is a problem. Physical education explicitly deals with the body and thus has implications for body image and sexuality; it draws its content from a prominent and important cultural institution, that is, sport; and, if the popular press are anything to go by, commands broad public support for its existence mainly on the basis of its ability to supply skilled performers for the international sports business and, in the process, fuel patriotic zeal (cf. Williams, 1985). For physical educators to be so (apparently) ambivalent towards issues of nationalism, racism, sexism, consumerism and social justice is quite astonishing. It suggests an absence of critical awareness of social and cultural phenomena which are of direct relevance to the work we do.

The precise effects of the 1985–1987 debate on the cultural significance attributed to physical education have yet to become clear. At this point in time we can only guess at what these might be. If anything can be said with certainty, it does seem that the notion of 'traditional physical education', aided and abetted by biophysical science, has received a considerable boost through this debate. At least, it has confirmed for the general public that physical education is mainly about competitive team games, which are excellent vehicles for fostering particular versions of masculinity and femininity, competitiveness, patriotism and so on. In circumstances such as this, physical educators not only risk losing what little control and authorship they have had over the process of defining their subject, but may be forced to accept and work within the myth of 'traditional physical education' (with all of its sedimented biases and distortions), as it is understood by the general public, including vote-conscious politicians, journalists, elite athletes and other sports personalities and celebrities, and commercial sponsors.

The purpose of this section has been to provide an illustration of the kind of material curriculum history can produce and the process of struggle it can begin to illuminate, struggle which is relevant to the here and now. In the final section, I want to return to the argument outlined in the introduction to this chapter, and to suggest how curriculum history might be located within curriculum research more broadly and within a critical pedagogy in physical education to become a force for change.

Curriculum History, Curriculum Research and
Critical Pedagogy

Through the example of 'traditional physical education' in the previous sections I hope to have illustrated, albeit in a much abbreviated fashion, something of the complexity of constructing and conducting the sociocultural process we call physical education. While the account given attempts to simplify the circumstances and preconditions of a recent extraordinary public debate over physical education in Britain, an adequate explanation of this series of events is unavoidably complex. It is for this reason that curriculum history, as a dimension of curriculum research more broadly, is particularly useful. Because the material such research produces permits a degree of analytic distance from contemporary events, allowing us to see beyond the surface appearance of things in the lurid present. It reveals the ways in which powerful ideas, like 'traditional physical education' are constructed by people interacting at particular times, in specific locations, in response to their immediate circumstances, and infused with their interests, preoccupations and values. It shows how these ideas over time become orthodoxies, taken-for-granteds, assumptions. And as it was used by physical education's critics in the debate, the specific notion of 'traditional physical education' is revealed as a myth, a cluster of sectional interests and values of considerable symbolic and emotive power parading as the common interest.

But the example given here of a recent debate in physical education is merely the tip of the iceberg of contemporary social problems and issues which are of pressing relevance to physical educators' work and which could be illuminated through historical treatment. Media images of sport, physical activity more generally, and the body in its many shapes and forms, each project cultural values which affect the teaching of physical education. But because these bombard us primarily through television, a medium which we watch for pleasure, as Phillip Adams and others argued, we rarely problematize these images. Its almost as if the visual image numbs our critical faculties, our abilities to see beyond surface appearances. Curriculum history sharpens this critical edge, however, by removing the comfortable familiarity of our commonsense perspectives, and by literally moving us beyond the range of our vision, of what we can see here and now.

In a sense, the attempt to separate curriculum history from curriculum research more generally is artificial. This is because, as I have argued throughout the paper, historical material is of interest to curriculum researchers for particular contemporary purposes. It is just one dimension of what C Wright Mills (1970) has called 'the sociological imagination' applied to the study of physical education. Integrated with this historical dimension, Mills argues that the sociological imagination requires 'anthropological insight' or, to say this another way, a concern for the meaning-making activities of a society, and a critical edge or political consciousness. Expressed in this way, the sociological imagination is at the heart of what I mean by the term critical pedagogy (Kirk, 1986). A critical pedagogy, whether applied to the teacher education process or to school physical education programmes, requires students to combine these three dimensions of the sociological imagination to see beyond the obvious, surface image.

It is within this broader context of curriculum research and critical pedagogy that curriculum history is indispensable. As a dimension of research and as a substantive component of pedagogy in both teacher education and school physical education, curriculum history, in summary, makes the following contribution. First, it supplies an antidote to the tendency in contemporary culture to imprisonment in the lurid present through our absorption of electronic media and the visual image, by distancing us from the present. Second, it specifically exposes the contested nature of the processes of selecting, organizing and distributing knowledge, and the ways in which these processes are part of, and contribute to, the production of circuits of power in society. Third, by revealing the contested nature of curriculum, historical research highlights the ways in which schooling intersects with power relations in society and their substantiations through relations of class, race, sex and age. And fourth, the unveiling of the political nature of knowledge production and the ways in which human agency is circumscribed and structured over time, feeds into and informs contemporary struggles over definitions of 'really useful knowledge' in physical education, and assists combatants in these struggles to identify the broad terrain of ideological contestation and the specific sites of struggle.

In conclusion, it is on these sites of contestation and struggle that physical educators need to become active, in an attempt to control the process of defining their subject. Curriculum history provides a source of information which can feed into such struggle. Nevertheless, there are limits to knowledge and the uses to which it can be put as a force for change. Knowledge and understanding by themselves cannot create a good and just society. This is only possible through the uses to which the knowledge gained from historical study are put. It cannot empower and it cannot bestow wisdom, but can only provide some of the means by which empowerment and wisdom might, under particular circumstances, be possible.

Notes

1   When I began writing this paper in September 1990, there was a major conflict taking place in the Persian Gulf. The day before I came across an article suggesting that jingoism is on the rise again in Britain, this time targeted at Saddam Hussein. The writer of the article asked the question, what kind of image of the Falklands debacle has remained in popular memory? Have people forgotten already the horror and revulsion felt at the time for so many needless deaths and so much personal tragedy?

2　I don't want to encumber the present discussion with an exposition of what post-modernism is or might be, or to debate its desirability or otherwise here. For readers unfamiliar with this term who wish to know more about postmodernism, a readable text is Harvey (1989).

3　A number of notable examples are Mangan (1981); Flecher (1984); Hargreaves (1986); McCrone (1988).

4　See Chalmers (1982) for this argument applied to scientific research, especially the notion of the theory dependence of observation, chapter 3.

5　In relation to a curriculum history study of my own (Kirk, 1990a and 1992), which examined how the meaning of physical education was socially constructed in Britain during the post-war period, I was interested in the ways in which vying individuals and groups represented their understandings of physical education. Since I was centrally concerned with the process of meaning-making, the main sources of evidence for the study were any public or private texts (book, journal article, speech, lesson plan, school program, or an account of events or actions) which articulated a particular view of physical education. These texts were treated as discursive formations, as linguistic systems (Hall, 1985), since each projected a definition of physical education. Consequently, the notion of language, of discourse, was a key concept in this curriculum history study. It could be argued that a more comprehensive approach to this question of evidence would also include the oral accounts of people who lived through the time in question (for example, physical educators in the 1950s and 1960s in Britain). Practical and financial constraints made the inclusion of oral histories impossible for my study. However, Andrew Sparkes' work has begun to add this crucial dimension to our understanding of the social construction of physical education since the end of the Second World War (see, Sparkes, Templin and Schempp, 1990).

6　One example which comes close to this line of argument is Williams (1988).

References

ADAMS, P. (1989) in *The Australian Weekend*, 19–20 August, p. 2.

ARONOWITZ, S. and GIROUX, H. (1985) *Education Under Siege*, London, Routledge & Kegan Paul.

BARTHES, R. (1957) *Mythologies*, New York, Farrar, Straus and Giroux.

CHALMERS, A. (1982) *What Is This Thing Called Science?* (2nd edn) St Lucia, University of Queensland Press.

DEWAR, A. (1987) 'The social construction of gender in physical education', *Women's Studies International Forum* 10, 4, pp. 453–65.

EVANS, J. (1990) 'Defining the subject: The rise and rise of the new PE?', *British Journal of Sociology of Education* 11, 2, pp. 155–69.

EVANS, J. and DAVIES, B. (1986) 'Sociology, schooling and physical education' in EVANS, J. (Ed) *Physical Education, Sport and Schooling: Studies in the Sociology of Physical Education*, Lewes, Falmer Press, pp. 11–37.

FLETCHER, S. (1984) *Women First: The Female Tradition in English Physical Education, 1880–1980*, London, Althone Press.

GIDDENS, A. (1984) *The Constitution of Society*, London, Macmillan.

GOODSON, I. (1983) *School Subjects and Curriculum Change*, London, Croom Helm.

GOODSON, I. (1984) 'Subjects for study: Towards a social history of curriculum' in GOODSON, I. and BALL, S. (Eds) *Defining the Curriculum: Histories and Ethno-graphies*, Lewes, Falmer Press, pp. 25–44.

GOODSON, I. (1988) *The Making of Curriculum: Collected Essays*, Lewes, Falmer Press.

GORE, J. (1990) 'Pedagogy as text in physical education teacher education: Beyond the preferred reading' in KIRK, D. and TINNING, R. (Eds) *Physical Education, Curriculum and Culture: Critical Issues in the Contemporary Crisis*, Lewes, Falmer Press, pp. 101–38.

HALL, S. (1985) 'Signification, representation, ideology: Althusser and the post-structuralist debates', *Critical Studies in Mass Communication* 2, 2, pp. 91–114.

HAMILTON, D. (1989) *Towards a Theory of Schooling*, Lewes, Falmer Press.

HAMILTON, D. (1990) *Learning About Education: An Unfinished Curriculum*, Milton Keynes, Open University Press.

HARGREAVES, J. (1986) *Sport, Power and Culture*, Cambridge, Polity Press.

HARVEY, D. (1989) *The Condition of Postmodernity*, Oxford, Blackwell.

HELLISON, D. (1988) 'Our constructed reality: Some contributions of an alternative perspective to physical education pedagogy', *Quest*, 40, 1, pp. 84–90.

HEXTER, J. (1971) *The History Primer*, New York, Basic Books.

JOHNSON, R. (1989) 'Thatcherism and English education: Breaking the mould or confirming the pattern?', *History of Education*, 18, 2, pp. 91–121.

KIRK, D. (1986) 'The curriculum and physical education: Towards a critical perspective, in *Trends and Developments in Physical Education*, London, E. & F.N. Spon, pp. 279–87.

KIRK, D. (1990a) 'Defining the subject: gymnastics and gender in British physical education', in KIRK, D. and TINNING, R. (Eds) *Physical Education, Curriculum and Culture: Critical Issues in the Contemporary Crisis*, Lewes, Falmer Press, pp. 43–66.

KIRK, D. (1990b) 'Knowledge, science and the rise and rise of human movement studies', *ACHPER National Journal*, 127, autumn, pp. 8–11.

KIRK, D. (1992) *Defining Physical Education: The Social Construction of a School Subject in Postwar Britain*, Lewes, Falmer Press.

LAWSON, H. (1990) 'Beyond positivism: Research, practice and undergraduate professional education', *Quest*, 42, 2, pp. 161–83.

McCRONE, K. (1988) *Sport and the Physical Emancipation of English Women*, London, Routledge.

McINTOSH, P.C. (1968) *Physical Education in England Since 1800*, London, Bell.

McKAY, J. (1986) 'Sport science: the study of elites by elites for elites?', paper presented to the XXIII FIMS World Congress of Sports Medicine, Brisbane.

McKAY, J., GORE, J. and KIRK, D. (1990) 'Beyond the limits of technocratic physical education,' *Quest*, 42, 1, pp. 52–76.

MANGAN, J.A. (1981) *Athleticism in the Victorian and Edwardian Public School*, Cambridge, Cambridge University Press.

MILLS, C. WRIGHT (1970) *The Sociological Imagination*, Harmondsworth, Pelican.

MUSGRAVE, P.W. (1988) 'Curriculum history: Past, present and future', *History of Education Review*, 17, 2, pp. 1–13.

POSTMAN, N. (1985) *Amusing Ourselves to Death: Public Discourse in the Age of Show Business*, London, Heinemann.

REID, W. (1978) *Thinking About the Curriculum: The Nature and Treatment of Curriculum Problems*, London, Routledge & Kegan Paul.

SEDDON, T. (1989) 'Curriculum history: A map of key issues', *Curriculum Perspectives*, 9, 4, pp. 1–16.

SPARKES, A. (1989) 'Paradigmatic confusion and the evasion of critical issues in naturalistic research', *Journal of Teaching in Physical Education*, 8, 2, pp. 131–51.

SPARKES, A. (1991) 'Towards understanding, dialogue and polyvocality in the research community: Extending the boundaries of the paradigms debate', *Journal of Teaching in Physical Education*, 10, 2, pp. 103–33.

SPARKES, A., TEMPLIN, T. and SCHEMPP, P. (1990) 'The problematic nature of a career in a marginal subject', *Journal of Education for Teaching*, 16, 1, pp. 3–28.

TINNING, R. (1988) 'Student teaching and the pedagogy of necessity', *Journal of Teaching in Physical Education*, 7, 2, pp. 82–98.

WHITSON, D. and MACINTOSH, D. (1990) 'The scientization of physical education: Discourses of performance', *Quest*, 42, 1, pp. 40–51.

WILLIAMS, A. (1985) 'Understanding constraints on innovation in physical education', *Journal of Curriculum Studies*, 17, 4, pp. 407–13.

WILLIAMS, A. (1988) 'The historiography of health and fitness in physical education', *Physical Education Association Research Supplement*, 3, pp. 1–4.

YOUNG, M.F.D. (1975) 'Curriculum change: limits and possibilities', *Educational Studies*, 1, 2, pp. 129–38.

Chapter 9

A Short Paper About People, Power and Educational Reform. Authority and Representation in Ethnographic Research Subjectivity, Ideology and Educational Reform: The Case of Physical Education

John Evans

Preface

This paper was written for the conference on Ethnography and Education held at the University of Warwick in September 1990. Preparing conference papers *post facto* for publication in books or academic journals, in my experience at least, usually involves some re-working of the paper, a process in which the uncertainty, the disorganization, the 'draft quality' of the original is carefully omitted, written out, in the interest of bringing greater coherence, clarity and authority to the text. On this occasion, however, for reasons which hopefully will become clear in the discussion below I have as far as possible resisted making such editorial interventions, a process which would inevitably impose yet another level of editorial order and organization on the social world that the text purports to describe. The paper thus remains in its original form but for the addition of some sub-headings and minor alterations, changes which hopefully improve the clarity of the paper without either jeopardizing its conceptual uncertainties or obfuscating the sense of intellectual insecurity which I felt at the time of its preparation. The introductory comments in particular may seem inappropriate for the context of this book written as they were with thoughts of a more personal, face-to-face audience encounter in mind. However, they are retained in order to convey something of the personal, emotional and intellectual processes involved in writing research reports or papers. My hope is simply that the questions raised in this paper (many of them still unanswered in my mind), now increasingly debated in the discourse of ethnographic research (see, Atkinson, 1990; Kutz, 1990), will similarly trouble the imagination and interests of others who like me might endeavour to apply sociology and ethnographic methods in educational research.

Introduction

I suppose some sort of explanation is really in order. One does not often find a paper offering three titles! We anticipate that our own and other papers along with the conceptual structures which help produce them are too tidy, too organized, too systematic for that. But then it's the end of term, three days in advance of me departing for cooler and welcoming Welsh parts. My energies are minimal and my capacities for precision as always are suspect; but I am bothered by this indecision, bothered by the inclusions and exclusion that my title will imply. Together the above titles signify roughly what I want to do and have to say, but each alone captures neither the untidiness of my thinking, the variety of data which I have to deal with and call on, nor the confounding complexity of the world and of the people that I am going to try and represent and describe. Yet I have to start this enterprise, I have to organize, order and manage my text and therefore, or is it thereby, reduce and distance myself from the social world I am trying to describe. Atkinson (1990) is right, titles do contribute to the self-presentation of the text, they do help establish a framework and a set of reader expectations. The title, as he says, 'has rhetorical force'. It not only helps signify what the author wants or has to say, it begins also to implicitly and subtly convince the reader of claims which are about to be made.

This paper is about authority and representation in educational ethnographic research, it is about ideology, subjectivity and authorial power. My data are about a particular case of innovative teachers of physical education, though my titles suggest (see *ibid*) that the paper is about something more and beyond, of wider significance than the boundaries of my local study. They signal that this story enters wider debates in sociology and education about how we researchers conceptualize and characterize the thinking and actions of those whom we study, and how we go about the business of conducting and reporting ethnographic educational research. Of course, it is not only titles that have rhetorical force. As Sparkes (1991) and others have pointed out, rhetoric operates, albeit rather differently in the *texts* of both qualitative and quantitative researchers; rhetoric which can take the form of a 'persuasive discourse' (Nelson *et al*, 1987; see Sparkes, 1991). Indeed it is difficult, if not impossible, to conceive of a text which does not either implicitly or explicitly contain an argument; an argument in which the values of the researcher are inevitably embedded. Yet this may not always be acknowledged. The author's rhetoric and value position may be obfuscated either by claims of objectivity or value freedom, or by appeal to 'naturalism' (see Hammersley and Atkinson, 1983) and the claim that the researcher, by sharing and documenting the culture and experiences of a people under study, is only *describing* the social world as it 'really' is.

In the discussion below I will comment on the way in which a researcher's voice and values can dominate, suppress or even replace the voices and interests of his/her research subjects. Although my critique centres on ethnographic research which I have carried out on the physical education curriculum, the questions raised, I contend, might also be asked of the many other sociologically informed ethnographic studies of education which have been conducted in Britain in recent years and of other forms of research which have been applied to aspects of physical education in schools.

Seeing Red or Blue: Interpreting Educational Change

In March 1987, Jan Gordon and Philip Taylor, along with the rest of their colleagues in the PE Department at Forest Edge School, achieved, or more accurately were imputed, the collective identity of 'radical teachers'. That is to say they were defined, by others, as teachers engaged in innovative practices that were putatively as damaging to the nation's economic wealth as they were to its children's fitness and health. This came as something of a surprise to these teachers. Previously they had not thought of themselves as either politically radical (left wing) or subversive. Yes they were innovative, they were engaged in developing new health education, co-educational and games teaching initiatives. But in their view these developments were grounded in neither left wing nor radical action or intent. Yet this was how the practices of other teachers like them, and by implication they too, were represented to the public by the media and other political spokespersons of the conservative New Right (Evans, 1990).

What happened to these teachers and others like them, in my view, illustrated very well indeed many of the social and political pressures and processes which have acted upon educational practice of every sort in schools in the last ten years. What we saw in the particular case of PE was not only a struggle over particular definitions of what were to count as valid PE and as culturally legitimate conceptions of the body but also an instance of a much broader attack on the teaching profession and purportedly the progressive elements in it. That struggle goes on. The battle isn't yet over though one could hazard a guess at the direction it is taking with a glance at the constitution of the working party which has been appointed to prescribe the content of the National Curriculum for PE in schools.[1]

The PE curriculum achieved a high public profile because of its important representational qualitites. It was used by the political right in Britain to illustrate much broader curricular and ideological trends in the education system and to signify all else that was wrong with state education provision and to vilify and negate progressive elements within it. Because many people equate PE with sport any discussion on this subject was likely to have widespread popular appeal.

Meanwhile, the PE teachers at Forest Edge and others like them were being attacked from both flanks. While the voices of the conservative right attacked them for being too egalitarian or too progressive in their actions, those from the political left claimed that they were neither progressive nor radical enough. Some PE teachers, it was claimed (see Evans, 1988; Sparkes, 1987) had acquired a new language, a new discourse of PE and as a result they were now offering a different and better 'rhetorical justification' (see Sparkes, 1987) for their unchanged subject in the secondary school curriculum. Beneath the linguistic carapace, the deep and conventional structures of communication between teachers and taught, between pupils and knowledge remained largely unchanged Sparkes and others argued.

My own descriptions of PE innovations have been very much of this latter order. The claims I have made have been based on data from an ethnographic study of PE at Forest Edge School, which I have been conducting, on and off, for the last five years. Teachers and pupils have been interviewed, engaged in casual conversation, their lessons have been observed, and curriculum materials have been collected and subjected to documentary analysis, reporting and review. My appraisal of their work has, like that of the conservative Right, been almost entirely negative, mainly because my values, my interests are at one and the same time both present and deviously silent in the production of a text which putatively captures and analyzes the reality of the situation described.

As the project has developed, however, (indeed it now has to be drawn to a close) I've become increasingly dissatisfied with my role in the research, with the way in which I have conceptualized and represented the thinking and actions of the teachers in the study and with my inability to convey the diachrony and complexity of either the social and intellectual changes, or the educational reform processes which these people have experienced. My problems are both methodological and theoretical and below I will try reflexively to allude to them both.

Theorizing Curriculum Change

In trying to make sense of the data which the research has generated and in particular of the processes of production of educational knowledge and the special character of that knowledge, I have drawn heavily on the theoretical work of Basil Bernstein (1986a and 1986b). I have long found Bernstein's ideas and concepts both challenging and useful, particularly as they prompt and aid an examination of the relationships between different sites of knowledge production and reproduction and of processes of teaching and learning in schools. In his recent work Bernstein distinguishes between three crucial, interdependent contexts of knowledge production, reproduction, interdependent contexts of knowledge production, reproduction, educational discourse, practice and organization. The first of these he calls the primary context and the process whereby an educational text is developed and positioned in this context, primary contextualization. This is a process:

> whereby new ideas are selectively created, modified and changed and where specialized discourses are developed, modified or changed. This context creates, appropriating Bourdieu, the 'intellectual field' of the educational system. This field and its history are created by the positions, relations, and practices arising out of the production rather than the reproduction of educational discourse and its practices. Its texts today are dependent partly, *but by no means wholly,* on the circulation of private and state public funds to research groups and individuals. (Bernstein, 1986b, p. 226)

The second is the 'secondary context' with its various levels of agencies, positions, and practices. This context, in Bernstein's view, refers to the selective reproduction of educational discourse within the tertiary, secondary, primary and pre-school levels. 'This context structures the field of reproduction' (*ibid*, p. 226) Bernstein goes on to argue that from these two fundamental contexts can be distinguished a third context, a 'recontextualizing context' in which agents and practice are concerned:

> with the movements of text/practices from the primary context of discursive production to the secondary context of discursive reproduction. The function of the position, agents, and practices within this field and its subjects is to regulate the circulation of texts between the primary and secondary contexts. (*ibid*)

The recontextualizing context entails a number of recontextualizing fields which include, in Bernstein's view, not only a variety of specialized educational departments and agencies (for example, the LEAs, university departments, specialized media of education) but also fields not specialized in educational discourse and its practices but which are able to exert influence both on the state and its various arrangements and/or upon special sites, agents and practices within education. The non-educational media might well fit this definition/category. At the heart of Bernstein's argument is the claim that when a text produced in the primary context by educationalists of one sort or another is appropriated ('read', received and used) by recontextualizing agents (educational or non-educational), it usually undergoes transformation prior to its relocation in the secondary context. In the process of appropriation (which he refers to as delocation and relocation) the text may 'be modified by selection, simplification, condensation and elaboration or it may be repositioned and refocussed' (*ibid*, p. 227). The process of appropriation is crucial and critical, because as Bernstein states

> the major activities of recontextualizing fields is creating, maintaining, changing and legitimizing discourse, transmission and organizational practices which regulate the internal orderings of pedagogic discourse. (*ibid*)

In other words it is within the recontextualizing field that definitions and principles are created and issued and these together define how and what education ought to be.

There are, however, limits to Bernstein's conceptual model. As Kirk (1990) has pointed out it does tend to privilege one particular site (the primary context) as producer and others as reproducers of knowledge and this does 'obscure the potential that groups at all three sites of meaning production have to appropriate and make their own use of texts' (p. 419). Although Bernstein seems well aware of this shortcoming in his text (see footnote, 1986b, p. 230) because his structuralism (see Atkinson, 1985) is overly concerned with the 'relationships between' particular social phenomena, with the impersonal structures and processes that work 'behind peoples backs', it does in my view provide us with very little scope for either confronting or interrogating human agency (the capacity of people to act upon and influence their social worlds), or the complexity of the subjective dimension in the policies and politics of schooling and wider social life in a very detailed or coherent way. It is perhaps partly for this reason that the subjective element, mine and the teachers, is underplayed in my work. Perhaps the most critical reading I can give my own research is that my accounts (research reports) are peopled almost entirely by what Atkinson (1990) refers to as 'anonymous individuals' (p. 133). Their 'authenticity is warranted not by the presentation of intimate knowledge of individuals but by the aggregated accumulations of the outside observer'. People involved in the study are not presented as 'rounded characters' and there is little or no psychological text. To this matter I will return below.

The Ethnographer's Arrogance

The strength of Bernstein's conceptual model, however, is that it helpfully allows us to explore the processes of both knowledge production and reproduction in each of the contexts he describes, and to examine the linkages in what Kirk (1990) calls 'the chain of socially patterned activity that produces knowledge' (p. 419). This is something that my investigation of developments in the PE curriculum attempted to achieve. I have examined and analyzed the way in which PE texts emerging from the primary context of knowledge production have been regulated and recontextualized (by the media and conservative spokespersons) then reproduced in the secondary field (see Evans, 1987 and 1990). In this sense, it might be argued, in the fashion of good ethnography, my analyses have been properly holistic (Lutz, 1986), comprehensive in their focus, all embracing and multi-levelled, but they are also hardly reflexive.[2] It's as if my sociological discourse, my professional work activities (producing texts), my politics and subjectivity have somehow operated outside of, or above, the contexts of knowledge production and reproduction that I have tried to describe. This position now seems to me to be both arrogant and sociologically and politically naive; but it's a position which isn't untypically found in ethnographic research.

Finch (1985) has pointed out that the act of defining oneself as a provider of knowledge upon which others (teachers or policy makers) can act, without being a direct or active participant in the policy making process, is a not an uncommon stance for sociologists to take. In 'ethnographic' research style the genre has been with us for twenty years or so. Finch cities Lacey's Hightown Grammar study, reported in 1970, as an early example of this. Lacey writes:

> It was not the intention of the researcher to be directly interventionist . . . but to provide teachers and students in general with an insight into their own world that would lead to further debate, redefinition of problems and the development of new solutions. (quoted in Finch, 1985, p. 121)

The implication here, as Finch points out, is that the researcher is the provider of knowledge, the purveyor of *insights* which invite the participants to reconceptualize their own world and therefore possibly to devise ways of changing it. The researcher's aim is that of the 'enlightenment' of the research subject. It's a stance in which the relationship between the researcher and the subject is diffuse, complex but essentially asymmetrical with the sociologist providing what Janowitz (1970) has called 'a sophisticated form of intelligence, by charting complex trends and conceptualizing social processes so as to help society to clarify or even alter its social and political goals and objectives' (p. 122). The intelligence provided rarely includes terms which assist possible implementation of change in its light.

For me, however, the issue here is not that of how or whether we ethnographic researchers intervene in the social world (all research is inevitably interventionist) but rather how we document, describe and represent it in a way which is both democratic and does justice to the complexity of the thinking and actions of those whom we study[3]. For Clifford (1988) the limited consideration which researchers have given to this issue of representation can be partly explained with reference to a methodological stance long established in anthropological and ethnographic research. He claims that by the mid 1930s there was a developing international consensus within anthropology which prescribed that valid anthropological observations were to be based, wherever possible, on intensive cultural descriptions by qualified scholars. The researcher visited other (foreign) cultures, made fieldnotes and documented the way of life before removing him/herself from the field to reproduce the social and cultural scene in an authoritative text. The processes involved in reporting and writing ethnographies were not a matter of major concern. Only recently has this attitude been contested (Atkinson, 1990; Hess, 1989). Clifford (1988) for example asks,

> if ethnography produces cultural interpretations through intense research experiences, how is unruly experience transformed into an authoritative written account? How precisely is a garrul-ous, overdetermined cross-cultural encounter shot through with power relations and personal cross purposes circumscribed as an adequate version of a more or less discrete 'other world' com-posed by an individual author? (p. 25)

Clifford's claim is that in anthropology, and I would add in educational ethnography too (and in my research at Forest Edge in particular) we frequently find (see, hear and read) what he refers to as the 'monological authority' of the researcher. The author's voice is active while those of the subjects is passive. This, as Marcus and Fischer (1986) state, is itself 'an exercise in power, in effect denying subjects the rights to express contrary views by obscuring from the reader recognition that they might view things with equal validity' (p. 1), but from an entirely different (value laden) point of view.

Let's return for a moment to the voices of the teachers at Forest Edge School, or more accurately to my representation of them in my critical account of their everyday curriculum work. In my view, changes in the thinking and actions of these teachers, while innovatory, were neither radical nor progressive because the 'new' curriculum which they had generated did not challenge or confront the ideology of possessive in-dividualism which I and others (Hargreaves, 1986) claim is endemic in PE and the wider school curriculum.

My critical reading of their texts is built not only on a limited interrogation of teachers' thinking but also on an ideological mix of Methodism, Socialism, Bevanism and their recent reconstructions in the literature of the left. Mine is an appeal for a rejection of Thatcher's materialistic individualism and for the sort of democratic individualism which Leadbetter (1989) outlines. This places stress on collective and co-operative action, on universal rights and responsibilities and on policies which would foster individuality, diversity and plurality both in and through the curriculum of schooling and in wider society.

These are neither the ideological starting points nor the goals of the teachers in the study. To assume that curriculum change (if it's to be called 'radical') necessarily either involves or requires changes in an individual's domain assumptions or fundamental ideologies, (in the direc-tion of those held by the researcher) is both arrogant, undemocratic and profoundly misconceived. Once we set the curriculum changes at Forest Edge against the teachers' own ideological beliefs and curriculum starting points, their actions can in some respects seem radical indeed.

Reconceptualizing Subjectivity

Both Jan and Philip had received their professional training in single sex PE colleges in the early and mid 1970s. Each had been professionally socialized within a discursive field in which the dominant discourse had emphasized the development of their own sports performance and that of the children who would be in their care. Theirs was the 'sporting perspective' to which Sparkes (1987) has referred; a perspective which is subject centred, concerned with the development of physical skills and maintaining standards within a meritocratic system, and with fostering enjoyment and a love of sport amongst all children while securing the potential of elite performers and the more physically able child. Jan describes her college training like this:

> In fact our training wasn't even geared around the schools because it was so much geared to your own personal performance, on what you could do yourself.
>
> We went through all these grade systems and you know, you had to pass these grades for every single thing at a certain level . . . we needed more help on teaching really.
>
> I suppose it was just enjoying playing the games really, that was the philosophy, enjoyment . . .

Philip too had experienced a training programme which was similarly sports orientated:

> I mean the hockey, the rugby, the soccer or . . . the doctrine was all very traditional. Perhaps, perhaps slightly non-conventional in that there was this move afoot to involve the whole class regardless of ability but it was still taught in a very traditional way, you know, three groups of five with a ball each and we're going to practice the skill and at the end we'll go into a game situation.

Both these teachers saw the introduction of new initiatives to the PE curriculum at Forest Edge as exciting developments but also as a process which had left them initially feeling insecure and deskilled. Jan for example had:

> felt very much under pressure . . . I felt a bit inadequate because he (the Head of Department) had all these new ideas and I felt 'oh am I going to cope with this' and we'd come to every lesson . . . whereas before, before you'd obviously got into a rut and . . .

right you go out for netball and you know exactly what you are
doing for the first years and exactly what you are doing with the
second years and so on. I suppose every lesson we didn't have to
think about it and it obviously was a rut . . .

Both teachers, however, celebrated the skills of the Head of PE and the
quality of social relationships within the department, which, in their
view, had together generated a secure and supportive environment in
which their new curriculum and pedagogical skills could develop gradually over time. In Philip's perspective the changes he had experienced
were significant but almost imperceptible because they had occurred so
gradually:

there was no one week where I had to take a whole timetable that
involved these new concepts. In the beginning it may have been
two or three first year lessons. I think one of the good things
about this department is that nobody is right and if the lesson is
wrong and it's our fault there's no one who's afraid of walking
back into the office and saying 'that was an absolute disaster'. Its
been developmental, I mean, I think our teaching approach has
changed so gradually that I would find it difficult to say categor-
ically that I have changed but I accept the fact that I must have.
My approach . . . is so completely different now to what it was
twelve years ago.

In the perspectives of these teachers the changes that they had instituted
were both substantial and profound; in fact they felt that within the
school, they were in the vanguard of curriculum development and
change. As Philip remarked:

In many respects PE has been far ahead in initiatives . . . what
people are worrying about in the academic side of the school
we've been doing for years. I mean many of the concepts of TVEI
and the National Curriculum, we've been moving in that direction for years and a lot of things that they're talking about . . .
pupil centred learning is the classic example, working in
groups . . . People in the classroom are threatened by that concept
and they stand back in amazement at how we have managed to let
kids talk to each other and (to see) that they ran the lesson. (For
them, it's) mind blowing.

The curriculum and pedagogical changes effected in the PE Department
at Forest Edge had required Jan and Philip to reappraise and alter their
teaching methods, confront new forms of knowledge organization and
pupil grouping; but these developments had not (at least at first) challenged their fundamental belief system or ideologies about the nature and
the purpose of PE in schools. In Philip's perspective for example, it was

'the packaging that had changed, the content was not much different'. Both Jan and he had to develop and come to terms with what in their view were more sophisticated pedagogical methods, which were more capable of reaching and meeting the interests and abilities of all the children in their care than any method that they had been introduced to at college.

In essence the 'new PE' had provided these teachers with the technical prescriptions for a pedagogy of PE which their college training had largely failed to deliver:

> I mean it's much more child centred learning. Before I thought it was very much teacher based. It took me a while to get used to it . . . it had to come from the children more and I kept thinking now am I doing enough for this lesson, you know because I'm not actually giving out instruction for the whole time . . . I suppose my philosophy has changed there, (in that I now feel) I'm there to instigate the child learning, more than actually to be teaching them the whole time. (Jan)

The introduction of a health-related fitness emphasis and curriculum into the PE programme had also provided a means of realizing an aim or claim, 'that physical education is good for fitness and health', that had been present but rarely systematically expressed in their 'traditional' games orientated secondary school PE programme. As Philip commented:

> I think it (health-related fitness) is the best thing that's happened to PE since PE began. I think from the point of view of the profession it's the first time that we've really had something that can put us on the map. We're no longer games for the academics to scoff at and health related fitness had given us the chance to say 'look, its important'.
> I mean . . . a healthy body and a healthy mind has always been part of PE . . . we were just paying lip service to something that is actually important.

Jan too felt that she had been 'trained in anatomy and physiology' but fitness had never really consciously or explicitly 'come into it'. She simply hoped that children would get fit by being involved in sport and games.

The curriculum initiatives which had been effected at Forest Edge had then, involved the teachers in changing both their thinking and the curriculum and pedagogy of PE. These changes, however, reflected a radical *shift in* rather than a *rejection of* certain priorities in these teachers' philosophy of PE. They did not require any radical modification in what might be termed their foundational or fundamental ideologies. Their priorities lay now not so much with the identification and sponsorship of

sport skills amongst the physically able children but rather with culti-
vating the physical well being, the talent, enjoyment and interest in sport
of all the children in their care. The new PE had given them the means
of achieving this goal (an operational pedagogy) along with the rhetoric
(see, Sparkes, 1987) (an operational ideology) to justify the change. For
Philip, PE now had to emphasize the priority of 'sport for all'. He
remarked:

> I mean I can remember when I started here my traditional basket-
> ball lesson was a means of finding a basketball team. I'm not
> saying it was done to the exclusion of the less able but my basket-
> ball team now consists of those who want to play. (Philip)

In Jan's view the Department now shared a 'common philosophy':

> we all believe in what we are doing . . . we are not so much out
> to teach them competition and to get the children to be able to
> play well. It's each individual we have got at heart now. We are
> perhaps more worried about their fitness level really. We try
> to . . . I think we're probably more aware of those who are not
> motivated and we do try to make it so that we've got everyone
> involved and being successful at their particular level.

The curriculum initiatives which these teachers had effected had involved
substantial (radical) changes in their way of working and in what might
be termed their operational ideology and some significant shifts in the
priorities within their fundamental ideologies (Seliger, 1976). My earlier
endeavour to look for radical changes in only the latter and my failure to
adequately conceptualize the nature of ideologies (and the structure of
other forms of thought) may have led me not only to underestimate the
significance of the changes taking place for the teachers concerned but
also to inadequately document the complexity (the contradictions, the
ambivalences, the difficulties, the rational ad hoccery) of much of what
was taking place in their routine working lives.

The distinctions I make here between operational and fundamental
ideologies is drawn from Seliger (1976). Ideologies, according to Seliger,
are action orientated sets of beliefs which are organized into coherent
systems each composed of a number of elements. In Seliger's view, as
Thompson (1984) points out:

> all ideologies mix together factual description and the analysis of
> situations with moral prescriptions about what is right and good
> and technical considerations of prudence and efficiency. It is this
> peculiar mixture of factual content and moral commitment that
> gives ideology its appeal and enables it to guide political action.
> The action-guiding role of ideology is further attested to by the

element which Seliger calls 'implements' that is, rules which provide ways and means of implementing commitments and adapting them to circumscribed requirements. The final element of ideologies, described as 'rejections', calls attention to the fact that ideologies are always defined in opposition to others and thus incorporate the denial or rejection of certain principles and beliefs. (p. 78)

But perhaps the important point to stress here is that the implementation of ideologies in concerted action has an effect on the formal structure of the belief system, it leads to a 'bifurcation' of ideologies into two dimensions: 'that of fundamental principles which determine the final goals and grand vistas on which they will be realized, and which are set above the second dimension that of the principles which actually underlie policies and are invoked to justify them'. Seliger calls this second dimension 'operative ideology'. In this dimension more attention is given to norms of prudence and efficiency; whereas moral prescriptions are central in fundamental ideology, it is technical prescriptions which have priority in the operative dimension (Thompson, 1984, p. 79). Seliger's model (although it has its limitations [see Thompson, 1984]) does help us to interrogate both the complexity of ideologies and their internal dynamic. In Seliger's view the bifurcation of ideology generates a constant process of internal change. As Thompson (1984) relates

> tension and conflict arise between the principles of the operative ideology and those of the fundamental ideology, as well as between principles in the same dimension. So in order to maintain a minimum of coherence, ideologies must constantly adapt their elements and dimensions to one another, either realigning the operative principles to the original specifications of the fundamental ideology or modifying these specifications in accordance with what is actually being done or what is possible. Ideological change is also generated by conflicts between the principles of different fundamental ideologies. (p. 20)[4]

We see some evidence of this in the perspectives of the teachers at Forest Edge. It is apparent that as their curriculum initiatives developed, the concomitant shift in priorities (within the foundational ideology) and the changes effected in operational curricular and pedagogy presaged, reflexively, a reappraisal of certain attitudes within the fundamental belief system, at least amongst some of the teachers in the Department. Tension between the operational ideology and the fundamental ideology had led to some modification in the latter. Teaching boys and girls together in co-educational groups in the new PE curricula, for example, prompted Jan to review some of her gendered conceptions of the physical and intellectual capacities of the males and females in her care:

You see, like with the dance, we've done some mixed dance and I would say that affected me ... I never thought that of boys, I mean I know we do sort of, well I suppose it's more creative in as much that we've usually got a theme that suits the boys as well as the girls but I still never really thought that the boys would actually take to it in the manner that most of them did ... I never thought they could produce the movement quality that they actually do.

However, substantial and progressive changes in Philip's operational ideology and practice had tended to reinforce rather than contest some of his fundamental gendered beliefs about boys and girls.

I might get shot down in flames by the Equal Opportunities Board, but to my view girls do not have competitive instinct. If you put four boys in a room with a marble they'd invent a game. If you put four girls in a room with a marble they'd talk about it ... I think that is one of the things that teachers have to bear in mind that if you're going to extract the best from the girls it has to be done in a way, it has to have a different approach to it than you would need for the boys, because ninety-nine times out of 100 the boys are sufficiently competitive to want to achieve their maximum standard anyway, whereas you have to *extract* it from the girls.

End Comment

There is not the space here to further interrogate or explain either this teacher's point of view (which I think is sexist) or those of his colleagues. In any case my objective here is not to contest this perspective or to document the ways in which this teacher in particular endeavoured to deal with what he perceived as 'natural' differences between boys and girls, but rather it is to try and highlight the limitations in my own ethnographic research particularly in the way in which I have written about, reported and conceptualized the subjects of my studies. The processes of writing, representation and theorizing are inseparable and this brief incursion into the lives of Jan and Philip perhaps begins to convey the dynamic between them. Yet still my account does not do justice to the complexities of either the actions or thinking of these teachers. Perhaps it ought to be stressed that I have used their voices here only to try and emphasize both the multidimensionality of ideologies and the need to interrogate and explore the relationships within and between their constitutive parts. What we see in the perspectives of the teachers at Forest Edge, for example, are not just obfuscatory changes in the rhetoric that accompany the teaching of PE but rather genuine modifications in their ideologies and practices which are quite substantial and which are in the teachers' view profound and even radical. Indeed once we begin to interrogate and examine the complexity of an individual's ideologies and other thought and knowledge structures the need for caution in how we conceptualize innovation and the relationships between what teachers say and what teachers do becomes abundantly clear. It is certainly difficult to sustain the sort of dichotomy or distinction, frequently made in sociological and ethnographic texts between those thought structures which are ideologically progressive (meaning they correspond to the author's belief system), without contradiction or ambiguity, when expressed in the 'educationist context' (Keddie, 1971) and those which are reactionary, ambiguous and contradictory when expressed in classroom practice. Such a characterization of thought and of ideologies is likely to not only misrepresent teachers but also undervalue the difficult innovatory work that they do. If we are to avoid producing such accounts we do need to both rethink how we write about, represent and describe the actions of teachers, and better conceptualize the nature of teachers thinking and their subjectivity. This would involve some experimental writing; searching for different ways of describing the complexity, the multidimensionality, the organization and disorder, the uncertainty and incongruities of the social worlds that we and others inhabit. It would also mean resisting the temptation to produce texts which contain 'flat' rather than 'rounded' characters. The former according to Atkinson (1990) are unidimensional, they do tend to have a singular character trait which dominates their part in the story line or account. Such a character tends to be presented as

> highly stable and therefore predictable. Characters of this sort are often typed, that is drawn in accordance of cultural expectations, or stereotypes (whether those circulating in the sociological community or in the wider society). Round characters, on the other hand are multidimensional. They are assembled by the writer and the reader out of an accumulation of varied manifestations of the person. Characters of this complexity may be shown to change, to be inconsistent and so to surprise the reader. While rounded, multiple complex characters do not escape our conventional assumptions they may be less susceptible to typing. (p. 130)

We might then begin to both better understand the processes of educational reform and play a more active, constructive and productive part in the process.

Acknowledgments

My thanks to the participants of the St Hilda's Warwick ethnography conference, 1990, and especially to Professor Brian Davies, University College Cardiff, for their comments on this paper.

Notes

1 In July 1990 it was reported that two leading sportsmen, (Steve Ovett, former Olympic champion runner, and John Fashanu, the Wimbledon footballer, known as Fash the Bash for his aggressive play) are to join Ian Beer, the Headmaster of Harrow, on a working party to decide how sport should be taught in schools as part of the National Curriculum. Also in the team will be educationalists and people in business. (*The Times*, 12 July)

2 The reflexivity of modern social life consists in the fact that social practices are constantly examined and reformed in the light of incoming information about those very practices, thus constitutively altering their character. (Giddens, 1990, p.38)

3 Advocates of the 'Action Research' tradition of educational research at the Centre for Applied Research in Education at the University of East Anglia concentrated our attention on the first of these issues; (see Simons, 1980).

4 This is a much more telling conceptualization than Keddie's (1971) triumphalist distinction between the 'educationist and teacher contexts'.

References

ATKINSON, P. (1985) *Language, Structure and Reproduction*, London, Methuen.

ATKINSON, P. (1990) *The Ethnographic Imagination*, London, Routledge.

BERNSTEIN, B. (1986a) *A Sociology of Pedagogic Discourse*, Sociological Research Unit, Institute of Education, University of London (mimeo version).

BERNSTEIN, B. (1986b) 'On pedagogic discourse' in RICHARDSON, S. (Ed) *Handbook of Theory and Research for the Sociology of Education*, New York, Greenwood Press, pp. 200–40.

CLIFFORD, J. (1988) *The Predicament of Culture: Twentieth Century Ethnography, Literature and Art*, Harvard, MA, Harvard University Press.

EVANS, J. (1987) 'Teaching for equality: The limits of progressivism in the new PE', paper presented to the St Hilda's conference, Ethnography and Inequality, September.

EVANS, J. (Ed) (1988) *Teachers, Teaching and Control in Physical Education*, Lewes, Falmer Press.

EVANS, J. (1990) 'Defining a subject: The rise and rise of the New PE?', *British Journal of Sociology of Education*, 11, 2, pp. 155–69.

EVANS, J. and CLARK, G. (1988) 'Changing the face of physical education', in EVANS, J. (Ed) *Teachers, Teaching and Control in Physical Education*, Lewes, Falmer Press, pp. 125–45.

FINCH, J. (1985) 'Social policy and education: Problems and possibilities of using qualitative research' in BURGESS, R.G. (Ed) *Issues in Educational Research*, Lewes, Falmer Press, pp. 109–29.

GIDDENS, A. (1990) *The Consequences of Modernity*, Cambridge, Polity Press.

HAMMERSLEY, M. and ATKINSON, P. (1983) *Ethnography: Principles in Practice*, London, Tavistock.

HARGREAVES, J. (1986) *Sport, Power and Culture*, Cambridge, Polity Press.

HESS, D.J. (1989) 'Teaching ethnographic writing: A review essay', *Anthropology and Education Quarterly*, 20, pp. 163–76.

JANOWITZ, M. (1970) *Political Conflict*, Chicago, IL, Quadrangle.

KEDDIE, N. (1971) 'Classroom knowledge' in YOUNG, M.F.D. (Ed) *Knowledge and Control*, London, Collier-Macmillan, pp. 133–61.

KIRK, D. (1990) 'School knowledge and the curriculum package-as-text', *Journal of Curriculum Studies*, 22, 5, pp. 409–25.

KUTZ, E. (1990) 'Authority and voice in students' ethnographic writing', *Anthropology and Education Quarterly*, 21, 4, pp. 340–57.

LACEY, C. (1976) 'Problems of sociological fieldwork: A review of the methodology of Hightown Grammer' in SHIPMAN, M. (Ed) *The Organization and Impact of Social Research*, London, Routledge & Kegan Paul, pp. 55–76.

LEADBETTER, C. (1989) 'Power to the person' in HALL, S. and JACQUES, M. (Eds) *New Times: The Changing Face of Politics in the 1990's*, London, Lawrence and Wishart, pp. 137–49.

LUTZ, F.W. (1986) 'Ethnography: The holistic approach to understanding schooling' in HAMMERSLEY, M. (Ed) *Controversies in Classroom Research*, Milton Keynes, Open University Press, pp. 107–20.

MARCUS, G.E. and FISCHER, M.J. (1986) *Anthropology as Cultural Critique: An Experiment in the Human Sciences*, Chicago, IL, University of Chicago Press.

NELSON, J., MEGILL, A. and McCLOSKEY, D. (1987) 'Rhetoric of inquiry' in NELSON, J., MEGILL, A. and McCLOSKEY, D. (Eds) *The Rhetoric of the Human Sciences*, Madison, WI, University of Wisconsin Press, pp. 3–18.

SELIGER, M. (1976) *Ideology and Politics* London, George Allen and Unwin.

SIMONS, H. (1980) *Towards a Science of the Singular*, Norwich, Centre for Applied Research in Education, University of East Anglia.

SPARKES, A. (1987) 'Strategic rhetoric: A constraint in changing the practice of teachers', *British Journal of Sociology of Education*, 8, 1, pp. 37–54.

SPARKES, A. (1988) 'The micropolitics of innovation in the physical education curriculum in EVANS, J. (Ed) *Teachers, Teaching and Control*, Lewes, Falmer Press, pp. 157–79.

SPARKES, A. (1991) 'Toward understanding: Dialogue and polyvocality in the research community', *Journal of Teaching Physical Education*, 10, 2, pp. 103–33.

THOMPSON, J.B. (1984) *Studies in the Theory of Ideology*, Cambridge, Polity Press.

The Times (1990) 'Athlete and footballer to help decide sports course', *The Times*, 12 July, p. 15.

Chapter 10

Telling Stories from the Field?
A Discussion of an Ethnographic
Approach to Researching the
Teaching of Physical Education

Keith Lyons

People do not usually just do research. 'Results' are shared with other people. The forms this sharing takes in physical education ought to be questioned and not taken for granted. In this chapter I want to encourage you to think about research as a process *and* a product. I have found it helpful to regard research as a way of receiving and then telling stories.

Here is an example of a research story I have written.

Anush and Basketball Fever

Tuesday afternoons meant one thing in particular for 2J — forty minutes of basketball with Bob. Teacher and pupils seemed to be excited by this timetabled encounter. In 2J's other single physical education lesson in their school week, Bob focussed on skills and drills. Tuesdays were the days for cramming as many games as possible into the time available.

On this particular March afternoon, the end of the term is looming. On the last few Tuesdays, games have become more accomplished and exhibited a high degree of involvement. When I arrive, shortly after two o'clock, thirteen members of the class are already in the gym playing informal games of basketball in a mix of half-court, whole-court figurations. They have come upon a treasure trove of basketballs in the store cupboard and are making the most of their unexpected bounty.

Bob walks in a few minutes later. The boys of 2J and I look at him apprehensively. In the past, they have been 'told off' for entering the gym before his arrival. On one occasion, I had been in the gym when another group had been sent out — I had been there as an 'observer' and noted at the time the ambivalence of my position.

But today, there is no retribution.

There's no need for a whistle or command. The flurry of game activity has halted. I suppose that is what some of the prescriptive, how-to-teach texts call 'classroom presence'. Attention is focussed on Bob.

In a clear voice, he says 'Right, come in and sit down'. Once the group is collected he asks where the rest of the group is.

'They have been to swimming club and they're late back', a number of boys report.

Bob looks at the assembled group and emphasizes the kit requirements for basketball. From my vantage point there seems total compliance. (Mind you, earlier in January, I had been in a lesson when Bob pointed out to a pupil that white socks rather than no socks were required for indoor lessons.) He follows kit comments with news of this evening's basketball club which is open to second, third and fourth years, 'How many of you are coming tonight?'.

As hands go down and the whispers about the club abate, Bob draws the class's attention to a mat under one of the basketball backboards, 'Take care there, that's covering a hole in the floor'.

He organizes the class into teams and divides them into 'shirts' and 'skins', 7 v 6. In the usual way of things, the heaviest boy in the group, Anush, is in the skin team. He seems reluctant to take his shirt off which does not surprise me. A couple of weeks earlier I had helped Bob with the half-yearly fitness testing and measurement. When I came to do a skinfold test of Anush's waist, I found it difficult to give a reading (as it happened, I 'invented' one near to his previous measurement from the autumn term).

But Anush does take his shirt off and takes his place on court. The first game starts fifteen minutes into the lesson. At the tip off, Bob reminds the boys about the contact rule and recaps, quickly, the foul acknowledgment procedure.

Almost immediately, 'shirts' have a shot at the basket. 'Beautiful shot', is Bob's response. Within a short time, it is an animated game with all the boys calling for the ball when their team has possession. Some of the boys exhibit tactical sophistication whilst others seem to respond to the scale of the court and the size of the ball by passing backwards.

Bob whistles loudly and the game halts immediately. 'Stop. There's too much unproductive calling.' He dramatizes the kind of calling that has been going on. 'Let's have five minutes of silent basketball. No calling, just use your eyes and get into space to receive the ball (. . .) and help the ball carrier.'

The game is resumed. Bob starts a commentary:

'Bad luck, bad luck' as a shot hits the rim of the basket.

'Good cut, David.'

Then in a loud voice, 'I haven't seen a one-two yet.'

The game is evenly contested. Bob has stage managed the selection to make this outcome a probability. Four minutes into the game, the 'shirts' score the first basket and then a second. 'Oh (. . .) beautiful'.

One of the better players tries an ambitious pass which is intercepted and is greeted by Bob's even-handed response:

'Unlucky, Ollie (. . .) well nicked.'

The game is still a silent one, except for the teams' cheers on scoring.

There is a clumsy challenge shortly after 'skins' score the third basket. Bob stops the game with a whistle and then says, 'bad luck, Dave'. Dave puts his hand up to acknowledge his foul. Bob's teaching and Channel 4's coverage of basketball seem to be paying dividends!

The game has been going seven minutes, latecomers to the lesson have filtered discretely into the gym and have taken their place on the wallbars. Bob whistles the game to an end, 'Just hold it still. That was good play (. . .) you must still maintain urgency even though there is no noise.' He proceeds to give feedback about the game.

The eleven latecomers are divided into two teams. These two teams, 'shirts' v 'skins', take the court for the second game. Meanwhile, the original thirteen take to the wallbars as spectators. Bob starts the game and continues his commentary of play:

'Good' (. . .)

'Brilliant pass' (. . .)

'Madness at the moment' (. . .).

The game has been going for two minutes when one of the 'skins' is fouled whilst shooting. Bob whistles the foul, stops the game and explains the free throw procedure following a foul whilst shooting. There is less than complete attention from the spectators on the wallbars so Bob whistles and waits momentarily for silence.

The boy who was fouled takes his free shots but misses both of them. The game continues for another three minutes until 'skins' score a late winning basket. Bob whistles the end of the game and organizes the third game.

'Right, winners stay on and play shirts from game one.' As the 'shirts' scramble onto the court, Bob adds a latecomer to the shirts team. A hectic, four-minute game of basketball ensues. Normal commentary is resumed:

'Take a foul there' (. . .)

'Shot, Jamie, 1-0' (. . .)

As Bob announces 'Last minute', 'skins' score a second basket.

By design or good luck, his timing with exhortation is impeccable for as he says 'Thirty seconds', 'shirts' score their first basket. This is greeted by 'Oh, tremendous'.

Bob whistles to end the game. The boys leave the court to his observation 'What a great game of basketball that was'.

The last game of the lesson is organized. Anush's team are slow off the mark and remain as 'skins' for the game. There are four minutes of 'normal time' left.

The teams from game three who served up such a 'great game of basketball' are dismissed as Bob sets up game four.

'Rest of you (. . .) buzz off.' As they leave the gym for the changing rooms, those on and off court are told 'Quiet for the start'.

One of the talented players in the 'shirts' team, Matt, scores twice in a minute. Bob's response is 'Oh, magnificent'.

There is frantic activity. Bob whistles for a halt in proceedings. 'Don't all converge on the basket'. He asks the pupils to think back to previous games when they have worked on play around the basket.

The game restarts with a lot of activity but no scoring. In the last minute of the game, one of the quieter and less involved boys is hit in the face by a stray pass. The game stops briefly for a damage report. Bob checks that no harm has been done and says

'That's why we have to catch the ball.'

In the last moments of the game, in true *Boys' Own* fashion, Anush receives a pass near the basket. For the first time in the lesson, he declines to pass and . . . he scores to everyone's delight. That is the end of the game.

As the boys leave the gym, Anush asks Bob about the basketball club, 'is it still on?'

The boys from game four have three minutes to change. Bob chivvies them along.

Outside it is raining. Bob has fourth year games and will be taking Sevens practice. Almost half of 2J will be back in ninety minutes for basketball club. It must sound contrived, but Anush will be one of the first in the gym after school. This time he will keep his tee shirt firmly on.

About the Story

I wonder what you made of the story. It took me three years to write and is based on my knowledge of a teacher I have called Bob and my understanding of his class 2J. It was written to be included in my doctoral thesis (Lyons, 1989).

I visited Bob's school during the 1986 spring term and saw Bob teach 2J ten times. Thereafter I visited him regularly for a further three years to talk about teaching physical education. Our conversations were based on our shared knowledge of each other and of classes such as 2J.

Some writers regard this kind of getting to know people and settings over a period of time as 'being around'. Fortunately, we are all used to being around people and places. But it seems to me that in being around we have to be prepared to be open to what is happening to people in their social settings. I chose to write the Anush story because it encapsulated for me the wonderful relationship between Bob and 2J. In terms of the title of this chapter, I wanted it to be a 'telling story'. I saw it as a way of responding to John Van Maanen's (1988) exhortation that 'we need more, not fewer, ways to tell of culture' (p. 140).

There were four other teachers with whom I researched. Two schools were involved. Bob's school was a boys' 11–18 independent school and he was the head of physical education but not games there. The other school was a co-educational, 11–16 comprehensive school. To give you a sense of how small-scale my research was, let me share with you that, according to the Department of Education and Science (1989), in 1988 there were 16,748 qualified male physical education teachers in the maintained secondary sector. I calculate that my 'sample' constituted 0.018 per cent of the available teachers. Here is one story from this 0.018 per cent. It is about a teacher called Mark and his class 3B2.

'Exit to the Sound of Gunfire' (5 March 1986)

I walk over to the sports hall and arrive at 10.41. No one is in sight.

10.45 The sports hall is locked so that I wait outside for first boys to arrive. A cold wind is starting.

10.48 First boys arrive. Decisions to be made about options for the fourth year are the main conversation point. John Wildes shows me his completed form. Mark arrives.

10.48 JJ arrives on a bike.

11.01 Mark starts lesson. He provides a verbal exposition whilst holding on to the badminton equipment. A pupil announces that he has cut his hand on the broken glass in the sports hall door.

11.02 John Adams arrives.

11.03 Groups of four are organized on each of the three courts. Mark hands out racquets and shuttlecocks. Activity starts.

Mark polices six 'official' non-participants. John Adams goes to the small gym which links the sports hall and the changing rooms.

11.06 Mark moves from court to court explaining how to grip racquet.

Sean is a non-participant today and responds to my presence by calling me 'baldy'. (Whilst this is an accurate observation, I wonder what I have done to stimulate this response. I also wonder why it is important for him to say this.)

11.07 Mark has visited all three courts. Danny and Adrian are drawing on the blackboard. (They had not brought their kit, they tell me that they were confused about the activity for the second half of the term.)

11.12 Mark continues to move around. A command/instruction is lost in the acoustics of the hall. Mark whistles.
'In you come and sit around the court.' (It takes one minute to gather in group, they sit around the middle court.)

'What we are going to do (. . .)' (He waits for silence, the boys are restless.)

'Can you just put your racquets down in front of you?' (audible noise of racquets being put down [metal frames on hard surface]). Mark sets up demonstration in half court and asks John Wildes to demonstrate. The noise continues. Mark looks at the non-participants.

Mark explains the service rule in badminton. He then conditions a small court, 1v1 game. He and John Wildes demonstrate.

11.14   Boys are sent back to their courts. Activity restarts. Small area 1v1 games. On the middle court, Josh and Ben are moved off to accommodate two Johns. The former move to play between courts with no net.

11.15   JJ's group is still playing 2v2. Mark moves in to organize a game.

11.17   Josh and Ben have moved onto court 3 and swap places with Owain and friend.

11.18   Mark on court 1 demonstrates technique. Meanwhile two non-participants (Danny and Adrian) are playing a coin game on a mat. I try to divert three other non-participants.

11.21   Mark is on court 2. Danny and Adrian continue to attract attention of other non-participants.

At this point it strikes me that I could use friendship pairs for interviews with pupils. On talking to the non-participants, I discover that physical education (written as PE on the school option form) is included in option 2 for the next school year. Danny has made a mistake in filling in his form. He does not know that PE means physical education. He is concerned about this when he discovers his mistake.

11.26   Mark organizes court 2. Moves to court 1. Says to three non-participants 'Can I see you at the end please?' In the small gym, the players are still working quietly. Mark tries to explain serve technique to court 1.

11.30   As Mark passes by he tells me about court 2:
'They have decided that what I set up was boring so they have developed their own game. That's fine.'

11.32   Mark patrols and as he passes he says 'They are working quite well.'

11.33   Mark whistles to bring group in but this raises noise level. Mark shepherds the group to the middle court. He waits for silence. Three non-participants are told to shut up. Mark then goes through service teaching points.

11.35   Group grows quiet. Mark makes teaching points about serve and service reception. John Wildes serves. Mark shows smash response to weak serve.

11.36   Noise is growing.
        Mark: 'Paul, why don't we have our racquet down?'
        Paul: 'Because it would take too long to get up to hit.'
        Mark: 'Yes.'
        In his moment of glory, Paul turns his racquet around and uses it as a machine gun. He supplies the sound effects to go with his actions.

I made some notes about pupil response to me at this stage. I noted that the most familiar form of address was to call me 'Sir'. Robert asked me how long I was going to be with them. Daniel was worried about his option mistake 'Will I be able to change?' Whilst noting this I hear one participant say to Mark: 'Can we go in, it has gone half past.'

11.40   Mark calls group in. Paul is still machine gunning. John Wildes says 'Paul, you spastic'. John then chases Paul. Meanwhile Mark is trying to organize continuous/lives badminton on court 2. Six pupils play the game. The remainder are involved in other activity. Mark, who was playing on court 2, returns to patrolling.

Sporadic gunfire can be heard in the small gym. Meanwhile, in the sports hall, Owain and friend are at the edge of the court playing a rally game. One boy is standing on the badminton base.

11.43   Mark whistles. 'OK, finish there.'
        Three non-participants (Sean and Terry included) whistle loudly.

John Wildes asks me:

'Are you writing about all them naughty people?'

Mark collects in the racquets and shuttlecocks and supervises 3B2's departure from the sports hall. Three non-participants await his return. He tells them off about lack of kit and their behaviour. By 11.45 the sports hall is empty again.

Amongst the sounds emanating from the changing rooms can be heard occasional bursts from a lone machine gunner. Mark and I exit. In his office, we have an opportunity to talk about the lesson and teaching in general.

He refers to the energy and dynamism required to work with 3B2. We talk about his demonstrations in the lesson and I ask if he thought that one appeared to work better than the other. He thought that was the case. We chat about the lesson and Mark's day. He feels that he needs to be 'on top form' for this group. He remarks that similar content would have worked well with 3A1.

About this Second Story

When I wrote 'Exit to the Sound of Gunfire', I wanted to give the reader a sense of time and map of how the boys in 3B2 moved around within the lesson. I have resisted the temptation to provide details about Mark and 3B2 in order that you can work on the story yourself. When I came to write up the lesson in the form you have met it here, I was more convinced than ever that I should have held out for my original doctoral thesis title. I wanted to call my thesis *An Alchemy of Moments* in order to discuss the essence of teaching as I experienced and understood it — occasional moments of exhilaration within years of hard work!

In this chapter, above all, I wanted you to read about Bob and Mark. My hope is that there will be common ground between their and your experience however fleeting. I would like to think that the two stories are crafted and based upon careful but selective observation. Although the events in the stories are free-standing they are, nonetheless, part of other stories. By using direct quotations I am attempting to introduce a range of voices into *my* account. I have consciously avoided any reference to a research literature in advance of your reading of the two stories. I now want to explore why an 'ethnographic approach' to research with physical education teachers is a potentially effective way to receive and tell stories that offer parts for many voices that are rich in meaning.

An Ethnographic Approach

Walter Doyle (1979), amongst others, has pointed to the multi-dimensional, simultaneous, immediate and unpredictable quality of classrooms. During my research, I became aware of some of the particular difficulties facing me in 'open' classrooms. Stephen Cook (1985) and Andrew Pollard (1988) have discussed the characteristics of those settings where teaching and learning take place in physical education.

Throughout the research, I regarded myself as an ethnographer and was keen to be involved in three kinds of activity that characterize such a role: observation, conversation and document collection. I much prefer the description of the ethnographic researcher as 'being around' (Paul Willis, 1980) to 'participant observer'.

On some occasions, I was incorporated into lessons as umpire, referee, or as a player/spare partner in geometrically imperfect classes. On others occasions, I withdrew literally into the distance as groups disappeared to the far ends of playing fields. There were cardio-vascular demands when I was involved in introductory warm-ups with groups. Sometimes I was able to have extended conversations with captive audiences. Bored non-participant pupils provided a rich seam of talk and news. During the course of the research, one headteacher and one PE teacher had achilles tendon operations and were relatively immobile for a time — with their legs in plaster they could not even hobble away from me! 'Being around' enabled me to make a variety of notes. On some occasions I was able to make long and detailed notes. But this was not always possible. Two teachers, for example, regularly engaged me in conversation and/or involved me in their lessons and I found it difficult to make many notes. I also found it extremely difficult to make notes on some occasions either because of the weather or the nature of the lesson itself.

I was aware of a distinct change in the kind of notes I made in lessons after the half term break in fieldwork in 1986. I had used a time frame for some observations before half term but I found it increasingly helpful to make regular use of time references thereafter. I was not trying to develop the kind of systematic observation procedures favoured by those interested in time on task or academic learning time but by the end of the 1986 spring term I felt I had acquired a routine of note taking, making and developing that suited me. 'Free' time slots in the timetables at the two schools helped enormously. For one thing, I could write up some legible notes. I was able also to recall previously unrecorded comments. They were also times when I had some personal space in which to recover from the intensity of concentration I experienced in lessons. Although I did pay careful attention to my field notes their variability over time in quantity and quality surprised me. I am acutely aware, for example, that I made few notes after lunch in both schools. I want to be explicit about such shortcomings.

I made no attempt to conceal my note taking from teachers or pupils. There was no objection to this but on no occasion did any teacher ask to see my notes nor did I offer to show my notebooks to them. I would have made available to them notes of their lessons had they requested them. My main means of making public my notes (which were almost illegible to me let alone another reader) was by a kind of stimulated recall with the teacher concerned. An example of this is my discussion with Mark of his use of demonstration in the 3B2 Badminton lesson. I tried not to give the impression that my notes were some form of evaluation or a kind of teaching practice criticism.

Observations of lessons gave me a sense of what teachers did. I also talked with them about their views of teaching. With their agreement I audio-taped our conversations and eventually transcribed them verbatim in August 1988.

It was not until June 1989 that I shared with the teachers the transcript material. In some cases, the transcripts related to conversations held three years previously. I was keen to use the transcripts and so I asked the teachers to check them for accuracy(!). Some of the teachers did ask for some parts of their transcript not to be reproduced. All mentioned their surprise on seeing their thoughts in print.

During the process of my research, I gradually became aware of their enormous significance of the 'with' part of researching *with* teachers. Their openness to me, and the development of close personal relationships, imbued me with a strong sense of responsibility to and for them. In the next section, I want to indicate how relationships changed during the course of the fieldwork and how this encouraged me to think about how I would represent *our* experiences.

Intrusion, Cooperation and Intervention

Over a period of three years, I hope I moved from research on teaching to research *with* teachers. The impetus for the research came from me and I approached the two schools. This I regard as the *intrusive* phase of my research which continued, I think, throughout the intensive field work in the 1986 spring term. I was much more self-conscious of this intrusion at the comprehensive school (Bridgetown) than at the independent school (Riverside).

Let me give one example of my sense of intrusion. It comes from a talk with Mark about teaching recorded in June 1986. In a flow of conversation, I asked Mark about my presence in his lessons. He had this to say:

I found it (. . .). That term you were in, I felt (. . .) and I was struggling to keep my head above water anyway (. . .). With your presence, although I would like to have been seen to be doing some reasonable teaching, I wasn't physically or mentally able to sit down and prepare anything special. But, what it did do (. . .) it made me very conscious of the fact that I'm not doing the job as well as I ought to be. I've been aware of that for a long time but I got to the stage where they were putting all those extra demands on me, so they must expect something to fall away from the teaching.

When you were around, I became aware of the fact that I'm not doing as well as I'm capable of (. . .) that I should be doing. And yet I thought that, well, why am I not? I've been considering for a long time to say, well, I'm not actually interested in the responsibility. I'd just like to go back to Scale 1 and do the job properly. That's really what I'd like to do but from a career point of view it'd be a bad move but (. . .) at the end of the day, I'm not going to have a career worth going on with.

(*Note:* the brackets with dots (. . .) refer to a pause in what Mark had to say.)

My experience of this talk and my occasional intrusion on private 'grief' during the spring term helped to put my work in perspective. It also furthered my resolve to treat as problematic the hard edge to terms such as 'data', 'evidence' and 'interview'. In my work at Bridgetown I experienced the kind of ethical dilemmas faced by Oakley (1981) with regard to a researcher's presence at vulnerable times. I tried to deal with these dilemmas by attempting to be as helpful and supportive as possible.

I did not have the same sense of intrusion at Riverside. The head-teacher's advice not to 'cut across the fields' at our first meeting reminded me of anecdotal advice given to anthropologists to avoid the local beer. There appeared to be no perceived threat in my presence and in retrospect this seems to relate to the time available to me at Riverside to talk with and listen to the teachers there.

There were opportunities at Bridgetown to move to a more *cooperative* relationship with the teachers. I had tried to adopt a subservient role both in terms of my learning about their teaching and in acting as a 'dog's body'. Whenever possible I helped put out and collect cones and bibs, pump up, hand out and collect balls and generally just be around. I also saw participation in lessons in whatever role the teachers wanted as part of this process. I hoped that my willingness to 'substitute' for absent teachers helped to reduce pressure. However, the significance of the industrial action left me wondering whether cooperation in this sense was counter-productive. I also tried to assist the teachers to produce curriculum resources. For example, during the spring term, as I became aware of both schools' interest in a health focus, I compiled a resource pack of articles, references and contacts. At Bridgetown I also volunteered secretarial help for drafts of curriculum documents.

Whether what I took to be cooperative endeavour from my point of view was construed in the same way by the teachers is not clear. Although at various points over three years I did ask obliquely and directly about our research relationship, no teacher responded. I was left to ponder on their view of our relationships. There were occasional hints, though, as in a conversation I had with one teacher at Bridgetown about how I might help him with his interest in GCSE anatomy and physiology. When I asked if there was anything I could do to support him, he responded:

> ... teachers don't tend to use other people's material ... And you could give me material and I wouldn't use it. The reason I wouldn't use it is because I probably lack a little bit of confidence in that area. I'm not an expert in anatomy and physiology ... if you start giving me a book and I give it out to the children, I lose the controllable knowledge type of situation which I can't really afford to do ...

There were moments when I thought there was some sense of agreement about cooperation. One of the more open expressions was made by Sarah, Head of Physical Education at Bridgetown. Of my interest in work underway at the school, she said 'It's great having an outside agency. It gives a ray of hope'. Another was Mark's retrospect, in July 1987, that, 'We were apprehensive initially but it was good having you at school — we felt someone took an interest in us ... We could understand how pupils felt when we made positive remarks'. My sense of relief about these kinds of comments was tempered by my knowledge that Sarah had not had me observing her lessons and Mark had left the school some seven months earlier.

As part of my cooperative effort, I tried to maintain the professional standards of the teachers. In front of pupils I always used the title Mr to refer to the teacher concerned and at no time gave the impression that I had any authority whatsoever over decisions about who might or might not participate in lessons or what lesson content should be. At Bridgetown and Riverside, occasions arose when I was on-site before the teachers and met pupils. I also respected the confidentiality of conversations and tried not to give any evaluative comments about any teacher or school. If I was asked directly for my advice I gave it. I do not mean to suggest that my role was entirely aseptic. It is just that I was not an oracle or a paragon of virtue — just someone trying to learn about teaching with teachers.

In her work with dance teachers in secondary schools, my wife, Sue Lyons (1985) had explored the concept of interventionist research. My experience of her work at first hand encouraged me to consider my own links with teachers at Bridgetown and Riverside. Day (1984) has indicated how he adopted a research role which provided 'the necessary moral, intellectual and resource support for teachers engaged in a process of self-examination' (p. 77).

As I got to know more about the five teachers and two schools some aspects of my work took on an *interventionist* tone. An example springs immediately to mind from my links with Bridgetown. I proposed an INSET day to discuss my research and curriculum development. The idea for this emerged during informal discussions with staff and management in 1988. Early proposals for the programme centred on a report on my research as a form of feedback and discussion. In the event, the agenda agreed by the staff was to do with the National Curriculum and implications for physical education at Bridgetown.

Shortly after the INSET day, I wrote to the management, INSET co-ordinator, and physical education staff to thank them for inviting me to the day. I felt that the day had been positive and marked for me a change in relationship to Bridgetown School. Christopher Day described his research, supportive of teachers' self-examination, as:

> client-centred, where the researcher intervened in the teacher's life in order to seek questions which are perceived by the client as relevant to his needs, to investigate answers to these questions collaboratively and to place the onus of action on the client himself. (*ibid*)

I equate intervention with a process of facilitation and enablement. I do not mean to suggest that as a researcher I had any special knowledge that privileged my view of the world. My sense of humble fallibility was forged by my growing awareness of the constraints on teachers to effect change and by the gap between some educational research reports and everyday teaching in schools. The head of boys' physical education at Bridgetown, Ed, summed it up nicely in one of our conversations, 'I think that people are always critical of research if it is not done by them'.

Small-scale, local research using ethnographic methods offers, I believe, a chance to move to research *with* teachers. I am convinced that sensitive researchers can try to minimize invasion and threat. The challenge is how to re-present or textualize such research for other people.

Documentary Reality

I have tried to find ways to mediate my experience of research without denying the existence of those with whom I researched. Writing is a human process and a means of communicating experiences to others who would not otherwise know of such experiences. In education, as in other forms of activity, we are largely dependent on 'documentary reality'. Celia Lury (1981) in an admirably short Master's thesis, has argued that: 'Only a small proportion of my knowledge as a sociologist has arisen directly as a result of my own immediate experience' (p. 1).

My strategy in this chapter has been to try to privilege voices of teachers. I want to draw on their authority and their authorial voice. Ironically, my interest in doing so emerged because of my exposure to 'documentary reality' of a particular kind.

In 'Exit to the Sound of Gunfire', a third year pupil, John Wildes, came up to me and asked, 'Are you writing about all them naughty people?' Even now, some six years on, the reproduction of his question has evoked the scene in the sports hall on that day for me. I remember where I was sitting, how cold I was and what John looked like. I also remember wondering what kind of writing John thought I would be doing. It would be interesting to know if you noticed John's question in the transcript material. It is a very small example from a lot of data but it raises, in a very tangible way for me, the difficulties inherent in representing field experiences in a textual form.

With regard to the term 'text', like Tim O'Sullivan (1983) and his co-writers I use it to denote: 'a message that has a physical existence of its own, independent of its sender or receiver and thus composed of representational codes' (p. 238). These codes work at a number of levels, and a text 'is thus capable of producing a variety of meanings according to the socio-cultural experience of the reader'.

In an attempt to follow up some of the issues related to representation, I immersed myself in a range of literature that spanned literary theory, anthropology, personal construct psychology and sociology of education. The original impetus for my reading was Paul Atkinson's paper given at an Economic and Social Research Council (ESRC) conference for supervisors of higher degrees involving qualitative methodology. In it, he suggests that:

The 'writing up' of the qualitative study is not merely a major and lengthy task, it is *intrinsic* to the 'analysis', the 'theory' and the 'findings'. The success or failure of the entire project can depend on the felicity of the writing. To a considerable extent, therefore, the craft of qualitative research implies craft skill in organizing the product of that research into satisfying and plausible products. (Atkinson, 1987, p. 4)

Later in the paper he refers to 'the textual character of our productions', 'the *constructed* character of texts' and then suggests that:

It must become part of our reflexive self-awareness that we recognize the rhetorical and stylistic conventions with which we deal: not in order that textual analysis should substitute for fieldwork, but in order to bring it within our explicit methodological and epistemological understanding. Gone are the days when *writing* could be regarded as neutral. (*ibid*, p. 11)

In his concluding remarks, Paul Atkinson suggests that critical reflection be cultivated with regard to the *form* as well as the content of ethnographic writing and that:

we may need to be more open to masters and doctoral theses in which textual experimentation and exploration is a major raison d'etre; we cannot treat them as less important than any other methodological concerns. (*ibid*, p. 12)

I shared this paper with some colleagues at Dartington College of Arts and under their guidance I launched into one of my most intensive bouts of reading. In addition to literary theory texts, I was able to enjoy the work of the American poets Charles Olson and William Carlos Williams. I spent longer over Edward Dorn and Leroy Lucas's *The Shoshoneans* (1966) than many 'academic' sources and learned a great deal about an experimental educational community, Black Mountain College, from Duberman's (1974) account. Not only did the experience help me to consider more carefully some of Atkinson's arguments, it also drew me closer to the work of Eisner. The latter suggests that:

there needs to be a place for metaphor, poetic statement, the non-operational comment or insight, the descriptive assertion that one cannot measure. Why should we limit ourselves to one mode of discourse? Where is it inscribed that scientific propositions and logical analysis are the only legitimate ways to express what educators have experienced? (Eisner, 1979, p. xi)

Educational criticism as a way of rendering 'the complexity *and* ambiguity *and* richness of what happens in schools and classrooms' (*ibid*,

p. 184) now struck me as an appropriate approach to sharing fieldwork experiences with an audience. Early in 1989, I tried to write up some of my accounts in the form of educational criticism and presented an example at graduate seminars. Concurrent with this kind of work, I was also trying to make some basic headway with literary theory, to read more about the 'post-modern' debate in anthropology and follow up some leads in story-telling in personal construct psychology. The outcome has been that I have made textualization and representation a problem. If a text has the potential to operate or privilege a particular reading and a reader's interpretive practices are operators of a text then writing up fieldwork assumes a new kind of significance. In addition to the democratic rhetoric of the process of qualitative research there is also the production of the text to consider.

Literary criticism and educational criticism thus become similar activities, as Elliot Eisner has indicated, and are focussed in the form and content of the text. Iser (1974) suggests that readers of the novel are 'forced to take an active part in the composition of the novel's meaning' (p. xii). His account of this active participation is contained in his book *The Implied Reader*, and he points out that the term 'implied reader':

> incorporates both the prestructuring of the potential meaning by the text, and the reader's actualization of this potential through the reading process. It refers to the active nature of this process — which will vary historically from one age to another. (*ibid*)

Writing up fieldwork assumes a new kind of significance once the process of writing is made problematic. Anthropologists have spent a good deal of time in recent years debating this process. John Van Maanen (1988) for example, founds his monograph *Tales of the Field* on the belief that: 'the joining of fieldwork and culture in an ethnography entails far more than merely writing up the results culled from making friends, staying sane and healthy, worming one's way into back regions and taking good notes in the field' (p. 6). He challenges the persistent conviction among social scientists that: 'the problems of ethnography are merely those of access, intimacy, sharp ears and eyes, good habits of recording, and so forth', and argues that: 'a culture or a cultural practice is as much created by the writing (i.e., it is intangible and can only be put into words) as it determines the writing itself'.

In my accounts of the teaching of physical education, I am posing as problematic the documentary reality presented to the reader. My intention has been to develop an account of the writing process that will move on the debate about qualitative research in the study of physical education. Like John Van Maanen (1988), I contend that *not* to pose ethnographic writing as problematic reduces ethnography to method.

The significance of writing and the creative processes involved have been addressed by Peter Woods (1985) and Howard Becker (1986) amongst others. I take the promise of ethnography to be the multidisciplinary enrichment that it offers to accounts of everyday life. As evidenced in debates in anthropology and sociology, I believe that this enrichment will be extended by essays in literary criticism and discussions of the art of writing. The development of a reflexive approach to the process of writing in ethnography, in addition to a reflexivity to method and data, will further the debate about how to account for everyday life.

Fundamental to this debate will be the distinction between authorship and reader receptivity. John Van Maanen (1988) has suggested that ethnography must 'minimally explicitly consider':

(i) the assumed relationship between culture and behaviour (the observed);
(ii) the experiences of the fieldworker (the observer);
(iii) the representational style selected to join the observer and observed (the tale);
(iv) the role of the reader engaged in the active reconstruction of the tale (the audience). (p. xi)

He identifies three kinds of ethnographic tales: realist; confessional; and impressionistic. Each transforms unruly fieldwork experience into an authoritative written account. In exploring such narrative conventions he follows the lead of George Marcus and Dick Cushman (1982) and the subsequent work of James Clifford (1983 and 1986). According to Van Maanen (1988) a *realist* tale 'offers one reading and culls its facts carefully to support that reading. Little can be discovered in such texts that has not been put there by the fieldworker as a way of supporting a particular interpretation' (p. 53). A *confessional* tale is a highly personalized and self-absorbed mandate. It rests on a personalized author(ity) giving the fieldworker's point of view. It has a naturalness 'despite all the bothersome problems exposed in the confession' (*ibid*, p. 78). Finally, of the small number of ethnographers who write *impressionist* tales, he observes that 'their materials are words, metaphors, phrasings, imagery, and most critically, the expansive recall of fieldwork experience. These are put together and told in the first person as a tightly focussed, vibrant, exact, but necessarily imaginative rendering of fieldwork'. John Van Maanen discusses these different kind of tales in detail as vehicles to consider ethnography's role in representing culture.

Stephen Tyler (1987), another anthropologist interested in text, is critical of ethnographic text that fails to recognize itself as a 'mere monologue about a dialogue'. He contends that:

The test of true dialogue is that when it is captured in text or recording it is almost incomprehensible, a thing of irruptions and interruptions, of fits and starts, thoughts strangled halfway to expression, dead ends, wild shifts, and sudden inexplicable returns to dead and discarded topics. (p. 66)

In his book, Stephen Tyler attempts to chart a path for ethnography in a post-modern world. For him, the evocative mission of post-modern sentiment in ethnography is:

> only a preliminary move in the restoration and recuperation of the commonsense world incarnated for us not in language or representation but in speech and communication in the carnival of the mundane and the quotidian talk of everyday life. (*ibid*, p. xii)

He contends that post-modern ethnography celebrates 'a return to the plurivocal world of a speaking subject' (*ibid*, p. 172). It will be quite different in kind to that produced by ethnographers who 'have tamed the savage, not with the pen, but with the tape recorder, reducing him to a "straight man", as in the script of some obscure comic routine' (*ibid*, p. 205). In his conclusion, Stephen Tyler calls for evocative ethnography that casts off:

> scientific rhetoric which entails 'objects', 'facts', 'descriptions', 'inductions', 'generalizations', 'verification', 'experiment', 'truth' and like concepts which, except as empty invocations, have no parallels either in the experience of ethnographic field work or in the writing of ethnographies. (*ibid*, p. 207)

Text has also been made a problem in some of the contributions to the personal construct psychology literature. Peter Stringer (1985), for example, intends to stimulate reader production of text rather than reader consumption. He suggests that 'one way to liberate the reader, to give back the reader her power and responsibility, is to stop trying to produce the ultimate, inevitable ordered persuasion.' (p. 212). Removal of the author, he argues, frees us from authority. The authorless text is writable by the reader 'as she identifies the plurality of its meanings' (*ibid*, p. 213).

Miller Mair (1988) has suggested that we live through and by stories. They are habitations that: liberate the telling; value the story as a whole; are a place of battle; and are composed of many voices. He has added elsewhere (1989a) that 'our tendency, I think, has been to relegate telling . . . to secondary place in relation to the importance we give to 'getting the facts' (p. 8). Mair (1989b) has adopted a particularly interesting approach to writing in his *Between Psychology and Psychotherapy*.

Constructivist approaches to teacher education have also started to develop stories as mirrors for professional development. Maureen Pope has reminded me that, whilst on a visit to Australia in 1989, she found a paper which contained the following observation about the use of storytelling: 'the poetics of thinking yield open-ended and polysemic texts so that unified arguments are replaced by itineraries of topics'. Maureen Pope (1989) herself has attempted to draw together some of the links between personal construct psychology, teacher thinking and accounts of teaching. She suggests that:

an alternative to Kelly's root metaphor man-the-scientist, currently being explored by some personal constructivists, may be more fruitful within teacher thinking research and professional development practices which may evolve as a result. The metaphor is that of person-as-storyteller. (p. 26)

She envisions teacher thinking research making much more use of autobiographies 'since they allow more ownership and authorship of the stories told by the teachers' (*ibid*, p. 27). Patrick Diamond (1991) has added to the literature in this respect.

The availability of models of writing in anthropological, sociological, educational and constructivist research that counter conventional modes is parallelled by developments in literary theory with regard to the concept of post-modernism. I have been reluctant to discuss the concept of post-modernism in this chapter. Should you be interested in reading about some of the debates about it, you might find Bryan Turner's (1990) book helpful.

My intention has been to signal that there are important developments outside physical education that are worthy of our attention. I have found it particularly encouraging that Andrew Sparkes (1991 and chapter 11 in this volume) is beginning to raise these issues specifically in the context of physical education.

Five Teachers — Two Schools

In the two stories in this chapter, I have tried to write in, not write out real people and social settings. I have been mindful of Jeanne Favret-Saada's (1980) suggestion that 'ethnography seems to be carried forward between a native confined for all time to the position of subject in the statement, and a scholar who assigns himself the role of stating subject, though an indefinite one' (p. 28). The progressive focussing I experienced in my search for a process and form of writing was further enhanced by my reading of Fabian's (1983) *Time and the Other*. In his account of how anthropology makes its object, he notes the distancing of 'those who are observed from the time of the observer'. The task for anthropology, Fabian argues, is to remedy this by creating shared time (coevalness). Although:

ethnographers . . . have always acknowledged coevalness as a condition without which hardly anything could ever be learned about another culture . . . when it comes to producing anthropological discourse in the forms of description, analysis and theoretical conclusions, the same ethnographers will often forget or disavow their experiences of coevalness with the people they studied. Worse, they will talk their experiences away with ritualistic invocations of 'participant observation' and the 'ethnographic present'. (*ibid*, p. 33)

They do so, he suggests, by a strategic use of time 'for fear that their reports might otherwise be disqualified as poetry, fiction, or political propaganda' (*ibid*). One such strategy is to combine the ethnographic present with the third person 'non-person':

> The ethnographer does not address a *you* except, presumably, in the situation of fieldwork when he asks questions or otherwise participates in the life of his subjects. He need not explicitly address his ethnographic *account* to a *you* because, as discourse/commentary it is already sufficiently placed in a dialogic situation; ethnography addresses a reader. The dialogic other (second person, the other anthropologist, the scientific community) is marked by the present tense; *pronouns and verb forms in the third person mark an other outside the dialogue.* He (or she or it) is not spoken to but posited (predicated) as that which contrasts with the personness of the participants in the dialogue. (*ibid*, p. 85)

In such a strategy, personal experience of the field is translated into 'fact' and 'data'. Johannes Fabian contrasts the kind of distancing employed in such a strategy with a creative hermeneutic distancing from past events. It is through this latter kind of distancing that ethnographers can start to address the problems of time and otherness. Recognizing that 'hermeneutic distance is an act not a fact' (*ibid*, p. 90), leads to a distinction between *reflexion* as a subjective activity 'carried out by and revealing the ethnographer' and *reflection* 'as a sort of objective reflex (like the image in a mirror) which hides the observer by axiomatically eliminating subjectivity' (*ibid*, p. 90).

In case you are starting to think that the title of this section is referring to five teachers of anthropology and two schools of thought, I want to get us back to Alan, Ed, Mark, Bob, Tony, the teachers at Bridgetown and Riverside schools. I have made a number of statements about the significance I attached to the voices of those in our research. In the text, I have used personal and particular moments, episodes and experiences to speak about my engagement with five teachers, two schools and a cast of thousands. As such I have privileged the particular over the general. I do not want to be involved in that kind of reporting that Peter Medawar (1964) refers to as 'fraudulent' which submerges the flux of daily life. I believe that a choice is open to me in writing. I want to contribute to a collective understanding through what I hope is a distinctive approach.

Writing about five teachers and two schools can only be partial. I have taken the view that if contact with such a small number of schools and teachers over a period of three years is fallible then at the very least I would want to explore what 'significance' could be attached to large-scale, random-sampled surveys. It is not the size or scale of such undertakings that troubles me, it is the authority claimed for and by such activity.

I find the down-to-earth approach of the teachers at Bridgetown and Riverside the touchstone of my account. In trying to make them and me into us, I hope I have drawn nearer recognizing Dennis Tedlock's (1987, p. 344) point that 'multivocality is not something waiting to be originated in the discourse of a new anthropology, dialogical or 'post-modern' or otherwise, but is already present in the discourse of the natives, even when they narrate'.

Moving Practice On

Post-modernism challenges the duality of subject and object and the equating of subjectivity as opinion and objectivity as truth. As John Murphy (1988) has suggested, one of the theoretical tenets of post-modernism is that knowledge is not immaculately conceived. The time seems opportune, therefore, for sociologists of physical education to rise to the post-modern challenge. Given the state of scholarship now evident, making textualization of research reports problematic seems the logical next step. For example:

(i)   collaborative work with colleagues in other departments in higher education and schools could energize development rather than duplicate experience;
(ii) research reports could be jointly written by researcher(s) and teacher(s);
(iii) we could persuade journals and their referees to consider alternative formats for publication.

By moving practice on I believe we will get small-scale and local change. My appeal is tinged with some realism, since, as Nigel Harris (1971) points out about change in the Third World:

> One must keep a strict sense of proportion in appraising the new orthodoxies, for probably they do not go very deep, and even where they do go deeper, they are almost certainly reformulated in entirely traditional terms. Mao to an average Chinese peasant probably seems less like a champion of Marxist-Leninism, and more like an emperor-cum-prophet. (p. 201)

Whether teachers want, or ought, to move practice on is quite another matter. What I am hoping for in my work with the teachers at Bridgetown and Riverside is that all of us put a question mark over some of our assumptions. The best I can hope for is that I facilitate change, not out of a sense of personal importance but as somebody who was around at a particular time. I think I also need to be clear about the level of change possible. My 'academic' interest in political sociology has imbued me with a sense of politics as the occasional art of the possible infused with a good deal of personal desire. David Kirk (1986) and Andrew Sparkes (1987, 1988 and 1990), amongst others, have researched curriculum innovation and raise questions of the micropolitics of the school and the macropolitics of educational provision.

At Bridgetown and Riverside schools there was autonomy and control over the content of lessons which made changes in everyday teaching possible. But there seems to have been a limited range of convenience beyond that. The significance of case study material, for me, has been to indicate how the day-to-day teaching of physical education is more or less possible. Such possibilities then need to be located in wider frames of reference.

Qualitative research is becoming more acceptable in physical education. But it would not be unfair to say that qualitative sociology is not a dominant concern either for the profession as a whole or for those who control access to publication. To add a post-modern description to the work will probably reduce access even further! Once textual criticism of dominant forms of representation is undertaken some raw nerves will be touched (for a discussion of some of these issues, see Andrew Sparkes, 1991). This need not be a reason to decline textual criticism. What it does indicate however is the craft and tact essential to move debate forward. The quantitative/qualitative debate is not an either/or debate. I submit that the significance of any approach to the teaching of physical education is to be judged by what it delivers rather than what it promises.

Maureen Pope and Pam Denicolo (1984) indicate the problems facing psychologists who wish to explore intuitive theories held by pupils, students and teachers. In a discipline dominated by a quantitative research methodology, they suggest that there are no easy tabulations, no simplifying formulae into which to plug the intuitive theories data. The same problem faces qualitative researchers in physical education, as Sparkes (1989) has indicated. If we do resist the temptation to accept recognizable ordinariness then we will need to find ways of communicating 'alternative approaches' and engaging professional colleagues in debate. Perhaps we will have to agree with George Marcus and Dick Cushman (1982) that 'ethnographies will only be fairly assessed when the development of what amounts to a critical sense for the forms as well as the manifest content of ethnographic discourse becomes part of a routine of professional practice' (p. 65).

I wanted to end this chapter with another short story. Even in a book like this there are limits to space. Paul Atkinson (1990) concludes his account of the ethnographic imagination thus:

> This book will have failed if it seems to render the work of ethnography less important, or even impossible. It will have succeeded if it encourages others to find a new complexity and a new source of fascination in their own writing and the writing of others. (p. 181)

My intention has been to raise some issues that emerged during my work with a small number of teachers. I think my chapter will have failed if the content was obscure. I hope it might not fail so badly, or even succeed if you are encouraged to think about the way research is shared in physical education.

References

ATKINSON, P. (1987) 'Supervising the text', paper prepared for ESRC conference for supervisors of higher degrees involving qualitative methodology, University of Warwick, December.

ATKINSON, P. (1990) *The Ethnographic Imagination*, London, Routledge.

BECKER, H. (1986) *Writing for Social Scientists*, Chicago, IL, University of Chicago Press.

CLIFFORD, J. (1983) 'On ethnographic authority', *Representations*, 1, pp. 118–46.

CLIFFORD, J. (1986) 'Introduction: Partial truths' in CLIFFORD, J. and MARCUS, G. (Eds) *Writing Culture*, Berkeley, CA, University of California Press, pp. 1–26.

COOK, S. (1985) 'Teaching and learning in physical education: An ethnographic study', unpublished MA(Ed) dissertation, University of Southampton.

DAY, C. (1984) 'Teachers' thinking — intentions and practice: an action research perspective' in HALKES, R. and OLSON, J. (Eds), *Teacher Thinking*, Lisse, Swets and Zeitlinger, pp. 133–51.

DEPARTMENT OF EDUCATION AND SCIENCE (1989) *1988 Secondary School Staffing Survey*, London, DES.

DIAMOND, P. (1991) *Teacher Education as Transformation*, Milton Keynes, Open University Press.

DORN, E. and LUCAS, L. (1966) *The Shoshoneans*, New York, William Morrow.

DOYLE, W. (1979) 'Learning in the classroom environment: An ecological analysis', *Journal of Teacher Education*, 28, 6, pp. 51–5.

DUBERMAN, M. (1974) *Black Mountain*, London, Wildwood House.

EISNER, E. (1979) *The Educational Imagination*, New York, Macmillan.

FABIAN, J. (1983) *Time and the Other*, New York, Columbia University Press.

FAVRET-SAADA, J. (1980) *Deadly Words: Witchcraft in the Bocage*, Cambridge, Cambridge University Press.

HARRIS, N. (1971) *Beliefs in Society*, Harmondsworth, Penguin.

ISER, W. (1974) *The Implied Reader*, Baltimore, MD, Johns Hopkins University Press.

KIRK, D. (1986) 'Researching the teacher's world: A case study of teacher initiated innovation', unpublished PhD thesis, Loughborough University of Technology.

LURY, C. (1981) 'An ethnography of an ethnography: Reading Sociology', unpublished MA(Econ) thesis, University of Manchester.

LYONS, K. (1989) 'A sociological analysis of the teaching of boys' physical education in the secondary school', unpublished PhD thesis, University of Surrey.

LYONS, S. (1985) 'Dance in education: A constructivist analysis', unpublished PhD thesis, University of Surrey.

MAIR, M. (1988) 'Psychology as story-telling', *International Journal of Construct Psychology*, 1, 2, pp. 125–37.

MAIR, M. (1989a) 'Kelly, Bannister and a storytelling psychology', *International Journal of Construct Psychology*, 2, 1, pp. 1–14.

MAIR, M. (1989b) *Between Psychology and Psychotherapy*, London, Routledge.

MARCUS, G. and CUSHMAN, D. (1982) 'Ethnographies as texts', *Annual Review of Anthropology*, 11, pp. 25–69.

MEDAWAR, P. (1964) 'Is the scientific paper a fraud?' in EDGE, D. (Ed) *Experiment: A Series of Scientific Case Histories*, London, BBC Publications, pp. 35–46.

MURPHY, J. (1988) 'Making sense of postmodern sociology', *British Journal of Sociology*, XXXXIX, 4, pp. 600–14.

OAKLEY, A. (1981) 'Interviewing women: A contradiction in terms' in ROBERTS, H. (Ed) *Doing Feminist Research*, London, Routledge & Kegan Paul, pp. 30–61.

O'SULLIVAN, T. *et al* (1983) *Key Concepts in Communication*, London, Methuen.

POLLARD, A. (1988) 'Physical education, competition and control in primary education' in EVANS, J. (Ed), *Teachers, Teaching and Control in Physical Education*, Lewes, Falmer Press, pp. 109–24.

POPE, M. (1989) 'Researching teacher thinking: A personal construction', draft paper, University of Surrey, September.

POPE, M. and DENICOLA, P. (1984) 'Intuitive theories — a researcher's dilemma: Some practical methodological implications', paper presented at the British Psychological Society conference, Warwick, April.

SPARKES, A. (1987) 'Strategic rhetoric: A constraint in changing the practice of teachers', *British Journal of Sociology of Education*, 8, 1, pp. 37–54.

SPARKES, A. (1988) 'The micropolitics of innovation in the physical education curriculum' in EVANS, J. (Ed) *Teachers, Teaching, and Control in Physical Education*, Lewes, Falmer Press, pp. 157–78.

SPARKES, A. (1989) 'Paradigmatic confusions and the evasion of critical issues in naturalistic research', *Journal of Teaching in Physical Education*, 8, 2, pp. 131–51.

SPARKES, A. (1990) *Curriculum Change and Physical Education: Towards a Micro-Political Understanding*, Deakin, Deakin University Press.

SPARKES, A. (1991) 'Towards understanding, dialogue and polyvocality in the research community: Extending the boundaries of the paradigms debate', *Journal of Teaching in Physical Education*, 10, 2, pp. 103–33.

STRINGER, P. (1985) 'You decide what your title is to be and (read) write to that title' in BANNISTER, D. (Ed) *Issues and Approaches in Personal Construct Psychology*, London, Academic Press, pp. 64–77.

TEDLOCK, D. (1987) 'Questions concerning dialogical anthropology', *Journal of Anthropological Research*, 43, 3, pp. 325–44.

TURNER, B. (Ed) (1990) *Theories of Modernity and Post-Modernity*, London, Sage.

TYLER, S. (1987) *The Unspeakable*, Madison, WI, University of Wisconsin Press.

VAN MAANEN, J. (1988) *Tales of the Field*, Chicago, IL, University of Chicago Press.

WILLIS, P. (1980) 'Notes on method' in HALL, S. (Ed) *Culture, Media and Language*, London, Hutchinson, pp. 142–56.

WOODS, P. (1985) 'New songs played skilfully: Creativity and technique in writing up qualitative research' in BURGESS, R. (Ed) *Issues in Educational Research: Qualitative Methods*, Lewes, Falmer Press, pp. 86–106.

Chapter 11

Writing and the Textual Construction of Realities: Some Challenges for Alternative Paradigms Research in Physical Education

Andrew C. Sparkes

The making of ethnography is artisanal, tied to the worldly work of writing. (Clifford, 1986, p. 6)

Facts and objects in the world are inescapably textual constructions. (Woolgar, 1988, p. 73)

All scholarly or 'scientific' work must be written and read in accordance with some generic principles. There is no style-less or organization-less writing. The 'facts' of the case do not imprint themselves. Our experience of the world, both physical and cultural, is always mediated by conventions of enquiry, and that experience is equally mediated by conventions of writing. (Atkinson, 1990, p. 9)[1]

The comments by Clifford, Woolgar and Atkinson, along with the previous chapters by Evans and Lyons, signal a growing interest within alternative paradigms research about how we represent ourselves, the people we work with, and aspects of our society in the way we write. Prior to this, under the pervasive influence of positivism in the 1960s and 1970s, attention tended to be directed towards such issues as gaining access, social relationships in the field, data storage and retrieval, ethics and to a certain extent theory building, that is, the *process* of research (Agar, 1990; Atkinson, 1991; Marcus, 1980). However, as Wolcott (1990) reminds with regard to ethnography, this term refers to both a research process and a textual *product*. Alhough both are intimately related, the former ordinarily involves original fieldwork and requires the organization and editing of material for presentation while the latter refers to the presentation itself which ordinarily takes its form in prose. In relation to this Agar (1990) suggests that the product has suffered from benign neglect while Atkinson (1991) talks of a 'collective amnesia concerning literary modes of representation' (p. 165), that has partly been induced by the desire of interpretive researchers to gain academic respectability by distancing themselves from the more overtly literary aspects of their work.

Throughout the 1980s, particularly in the domains of anthropology and sociology along with others in the 'human sciences' there was evidence of more attention being given to the textual character of scholarly productions, such as books, monographs, reports, and journal papers.[2] For Agar (1990), 'The ethnographic text will never again be taken for granted' (p. 73) since textual issues like conventions of representation along with genre constraints such as the distribution of narrative and descriptive passages 'have been converted from out-of-awareness tradition into matters of conscious debate' (*ibid*). Similarly, Clifford (1986), in the introductory chapter to a book significantly entitled *Writing Culture: The Poetics and Politics of Ethnography* focusses specifically on the issue of writing — the making of texts. For him this activity is no longer a marginal, or occulted, dimension but is central to what anthropologists do both in the field and thereafter, 'The fact that it has not until recently been portrayed or seriously discussed reflects the persistence of an ideology claiming transparency of representation and immediacy of experience. Writing reduced to method: keeping good field notes, making accurate maps, "writing up" results' (p. 2).

Things have changed. What has emerged from these deliberations, according to Atkinson (1991), is a growing recognition that writing is an integral feature of the research enterprise whereby 'anthropological or sociological "findings" are inscribed in the way we write about things; they are not detached from the presentation of observations, reflections and interpretations' (p. 164). It is now recognized that there can be no such thing as a neutral report and the conventions of text and the language forms used are actively involved in the *construction* of reality. So what was once a taken-for-granted aspect of research has now been made extremely problematic. Indeed, we are left with what Marcus and Fischer (1986) call a crisis of representation in which for a range of disciplines, 'It is not just the ideas themselves that are coming under attack but the paradigmatic style in which they have been presented' (pp. 7–8). If this is the case, then there is a need for researchers of *all* paradigmatic positions to adopt a more self-conscious stance regarding the manner in which they report their findings. As Atkinson (1990) comments, 'If we comprehend how our understandings of the world are fashioned and conveyed, then we need not fear that self-understanding. Rather than detracting from our scholarly endeavours, an understanding of our textual practices can only strengthen the critical reflection of a mature discipline' (p. 176).

With the above in mind I attempt in this chapter to raise issues regarding the ways in which we write about our research. To begin this process I consider the manner in which post-structuralist thinking has undermined our view of language as something stable and dependable. Having problematized language I then move on to explore the notion that all research draws upon rhetorical strategies to persuade the audience of its worth. Following this, I focus specifically upon ethnography to indicate that there are many ways to construct our tales and suggest that those committed to alternative paradigms research need to give these serious attention in the future.

Languaging: Some Insights from Post-structuralism

As I indicated in chapter 1 of this volume, different paradigms often use the same words but give them different meanings so that different discourses produce different 'truths'. This was seen to form a major barrier to communication and critically informed discussion between researchers of differing paradigmatic views. Therefore, the questions of language, meaning and representation would seem to be a central issue in terms of initiating a dialogue and promoting greater understanding of ourselves and others as researchers. Kirk (1991), drawing on the work of Postman (1989), suggests we need to do some 'languaging' which means 'raising questions about communication, about the taken-for-granted ways in which we attempt to make sense of the world' (pp. 3–4). In relation to this the works of post-structuralist thinkers such as Jacques Derrida and Michel Foucault are important as they have focussed specifically upon the ways that we use language.[3] During the last twenty years the style of French thought that has become known as post-structuralism has had a powerful influence over many areas of intellectual life, and the recent works of Bain (1990a and 1990b), Cole (1991), Evans (1990) Gore (1990), Lyons (1989), Sparkes (1991), Tinning (1990) Whitson and Macintosh (1990) and Wright and King (1991) indicate that the domain of physical education (PE) has not gone untouched by these influences.

At the heart of post-structuralist strategies and forms of analysis lies the dismantling or deconstruction of stable conceptions of subjectivity, identity and truth (cf. Dews, 1987). According to Cherryholmes (1988):

> Deconstructive analysis suggests that texts are never what they seem. . . . This is a radical argument. Texts appear to speak with one voice. Deconstructive criticism demonstrates that texts have many voices. A text cannot be grounded on something stable and fixed beyond the sign system in which it occurs. Texts include what is not written as well as what is written, producing shifting and decentred meanings. Texts include traces of words and concepts not present, and that which is not present makes possible that which is present. (pp. 6–61)

Many criticisms can be levelled at the post-structuralist movement. For example, it has been suggested that the language it uses is elitist, exclusionary, alienating and unreadable to all but the initiated and that post-structuralist authors have actually contributed to the ongoing trend towards increasing sub-specialization and decreasing audience that they have so readily been critical of in other areas of scholarship. Furthermore, while they have been quick to critique the forms of writing produced by others and write *off* rival academic currents to their own advantage, they have been slow to apply the same critique to their own textual productions and the ways in which these are themselves a form of academic capital (reputation, promotion, tenure, publications) in the culture of professional scholarship. In relation to these, and other issues, post-structuralism has been seen by some to provide a form of analysis that is vacuous, apolitical and ahistorical, and has ideological consequences that include political inaction and despair.[4]

Having said this, I would go along with Nelson *et al* (1987a) that one does not have to accept all of what post-structuralists say in order to learn something from them. In particular, the post-structuralist turn has the potential to provide us with insights into our own engagement in the research process because it brings to the fore the relationships between language, meaning and power as they act to influence the interpretation of any text.[5] Importantly, within this framework, the person is not seen as having a unified consciousness but rather as being structured by language. This, according to Fairclough (1989), has 'profound implications for our tendency to see a speaker or writer as the *author* of her words: there is a sense, on the contrary, in which the speaker or writer is a *product* of her words' (p. 104).

Consequently, language not only functions as a means for conveying ideas to others, but it also acts as an agent that shapes what we see. For Lather (1990) language needs to be seen as both a carrier and a creator of a culture's epistemological codes, 'The ways we speak and write are held to influence our conceptual boundaries and to create areas of silence as language organizes meaning in terms of pre-established categories' (p. 71). In relation to this, Sarup (1989) stresses, 'Metaphors are not just the concern of the poet or the literary critic, not just figures of speech; they represent one of the ways in which many kinds of discourse are structured and powerfully influence how we conceive things' (p. 53). Therefore, language should not be taken as a system of meanings shared by everybody since words, expressions and propositions can change their meaning according to the positions held by those who use them (Macdonell, 1987). This means that language is not a mirror of reality since it is language that constitutes reality, and various languages will construct specific aspects of reality in their own ways. Therefore, it is an illusion to believe that meanings are fixed, centred and unchangeable.

Furthermore, for the producer of any text there are other problems to be faced since anything spoken or written is already saturated with meaning. As Eco (1984) reminds us, 'Texts generate or are capable of generating multiple (and ultimately infinite) readings and interpretations' (p. 24). This relates to the 'methodological horror' of 'indexicality' discussed by Woolgar (1988), who notes:

> The underlying reality of a representation is never fixed and always able to change with occasion of use. This means that it is not in principle possible to establish an invariant meaning for any given representation; any given sign (document) can in principle be taken as indicative of at least two alternative underlying realities (objects, meanings). It is thus always possible to nominate an alternative to any proposed meaning. (p. 32)

Since meanings are unstable and never fixed, and since the text (for example, a paper in a journal) can speak with many voices then the author often feels obliged to establish that at least one voice (that is, her or his) speaks with authority, is reasonable, is legitimate, and should be listened to. This returns us to the need to be sensitive to the ways in which language is used by researchers within any given paradigm to convince the audience of the legitimacy of their particular findings or truth, that is, of their interpretation and meanings at the expense of others that are always possible. This is an important issue because as I have indicated this legitimacy is problematic and has to be actively created by drawing upon particular forms of language use that are socially determined, that is, they call upon specific forms of discourse. All discourses are socially constructed and contain rules that guide their use and shape the discursive practices that produce a specific discourse in relation to any given paradigm in terms of textual representations (Cherryholmes, 1988; Macdonell, 1987). These rules, both tacit and explicit, govern what is said and what remains unsaid when we speak or write about research. This in turn shapes the way that researchers in different paradigms come to understand their world and influences their attempts to convince the reader of the cogency and strength of their particular viewpoint.

> When the sociologist produces a text, then he or she is inescapably drawing upon a stock of cultural codes and conventions. The text itself will be of a particular type, or for a particular purpose (essay, thesis, journal article, research report, monograph) and will in turn imply an audience (peers in a specialized field, students of the discipline, even the 'general' reader). With varying degrees of conscious control over the process, the sociologist will draw on the appropriate 'literary' conventions to construct a plausible and comprehensible text. (Atkinson, 1990, p. 11)

The points made about sociologists apply to all researchers and Edmonson (1984) reminds us that 'explanations are not only about something; they are for *someone*' (p. 1). Whoever this someone is, and whatever

epistemological or methodological claims are made for a piece of research, the text in which it is reported must be *persuasive* and in order to
accomplish this task a range of rhetorical devices are employed that need
to be understood as an essential aspect of meaning production, sense
making and truth creation in any paradigm. That is, the characteristic
conventions of writing used by authors operating within the positivistic,
interpretive, and critical paradigms act to express and legitimize differing
views of the social world, how it is to be understood, and how it should
be researched (see Sparkes, chapter 1 in this volume). Indeed, as Atkinson
(1991) reminds us, 'It is part of their paradigm-like coherence that different styles of research are embodied in different styles of reportage'
(p. 171).

For example, an analysis conducted by Atkinson and Delamont
(1990) of the ways in which teachers have been represented by British and
American ethnographic texts reveals marked differences that reflect
variations in the theoretical underpinning of interpretive research forms in
the two countries. Specifically, the British tradition emphasizes teaching
as work while the American tradition emphasizes teaching as cultural
transmission. As Atkinson and Delamont demonstrate, these national and
disciplinary preoccupations, that articulate general methodological and
epistemological differences between research traditions, intersect to define
the subject matter of particular research studies and also implicitly shape
the textual products that emerge from these differing concerns. That
is, the deep underlying differences between the traditions are expressed
rhetorically in the ways they write about teachers and schools.

Researchers and Rhetoric: You Can't have one Without the Other

During recent years there has been an upsurge of interest in rhetoric.[6] In
surveying a range of perspectives on this issue, Simons (1989) comments,
'Most centrally, perhaps, rhetoric is about persuasion . . . rhetoric is the
form that discourse takes when it goes public . . . that is, when it has been
geared towards an audience, readied for an occasion, adapted to its
ends . . . the province of rhetoric is the non-provable, the contingent, the
realm of judgement rather than certainty' (pp. 2–3). As a consequence,
Cole (1991) reminds us that '*all* researchers use writing and rhetorical
devices as part of their method and practices of persuasion' (p. 39). Likewise, Atkinson (1990) suggests that 'All scholarly or "scientific" writing
must rely on textual conventions and rhetorical methods' (p. 35), and that
it is via these devices that the authoritative text establishes its status and
its relationship with an audience. Essentially, as Nelson *et al* (1987a)
recognize:

> Scholarship uses argument, and argument uses rhetoric. The
> 'rhetoric' is not mere ornament or manipulation or trickery. It is

rhetoric in the ancient sense of persuasive discourse. In matters from mathematical proof to literary criticism, scholars write rhetorically. Only occasionally do they reflect on that fact ... even writers attacking an earlier rhetoric customarily pay no attention to their own. Modern scholars usually deny their rhetoric. Wearing masks of scientific methodology first donned in the seventeenth century, they have forgotten about the rhetorical faces underneath. Their simple repetition of official rhetoric against rhetoric serves mainly to dampen anxieties about how things really happen in the lab or library ... One way to see beneath the masks of methodology is to look at how scholars really do converse. (pp. 3–4)

To see 'beneath the mask' we can begin by considering the ways in which findings of positivistic studies are reported in 'scientific' writing. Here rhetoric is seen as something to be avoided since the objective facts are supposed to be able to 'speak for themselves'. As Firestone (1987) comments 'Scientific writing is a stripped-down, cool style that avoids ornamentation, often stating conclusions as propositions or formulae' (p. 17). He points out that the forms of data presentation are supposed to be interchangeable in that the use of tables as opposed to charts should be immaterial. Such writing also has a standardized form — the theory-methods-findings-conclusions format which itself is taken to act as constraint on rhetorical excess. Indeed, as Lofland (1974) notes, there seems to be a high level of consensus among those who draw upon models of research based on the physical sciences in that they share a highly routinized set of working procedures and schemes for reporting research. However, as Atkinson (1990) is quick to point out, this apparent uniformity is itself a textual achievement that draws upon shared stylistic features, 'The very uniformity of some scholarly genres reflects and reinforces the presumption of a single, unified scientific method applicable to an invariant world of natural or social facts' (p. 12).

The apparent absence of style is actually a rhetorical device in its own right. That is, what Gusfield (1976) has called the 'style of no-style' is the style of science. Mulkay (1991) sees this as a realist technique that allows the text to give the impression that its symbols are inert, neutral representations of the world that exist quite independently of the researcher's interests and efforts. To this we must add the image of the researcher who is presented as a neutral and disengaged analyst. Eisner (1988) draws attention to the language of identifying variables, measuring relationships between them, and describing events by using an abstracted, detached form of language with an impersonal voice that puts distance between language as written and the reality it represents. He suggests that the purpose of writing in this way is to 'objectify through depersonalization' (p. 18). Similarly, Firestone (1987) recognizes that the use of propositions is a means to empty language of emotion and thereby convince the reader of the researcher's disengagement from the analysis.

In Woolgar's (1988) terms the 'style of no-style' it is an 'externalizing device' that emphasizes the non-involvement of human agency whereby the discovered object is to be apprehended 'as neither the product nor the artful creation of scientists: scientists came upon these objects rather than creating them' (p. 75). This textual strategy plays a crucial persuasive function within a research community that believes a major threat to the validity of any conclusion is likely to come from the writer's own bias. As Woolgar argues, 'The scientist needs to be the trusted teller of the tale but, at the same time, should not be seen as intruding upon the object'. To create this impression a textual voice needs to be used that renders the actions of scientists passive and portrays entities like observations, results and information as the prime movers. For the intended audience of peers to be convinced the scientist's contribution needs to be seen as essentially coincidental with the unfolding realization about the objective state of the world. The impression is that any other scientist in the same situation would have been led to the same conclusion. Essentially, in keeping with positivistic assumptions regarding epistemology and ontology (see Sparkes, chapter 1 in this volume) this form of language has to create the impression of knower and known as separate entities. Therefore, as Eisner (1988) comments:

> We use a language that implies it is possible for the organism to grasp the environment as it *really* is. Consider how we discuss our research efforts. We talk of our *findings*, implying that we discover the world rather than construe it. We say in our discussion, 'it turns out . . .', implying that how things are is nothing for which we have any responsibility. We talk and write in a voice void of any hint that there is a personal self behind the words that we utter: 'the author', 'the subject', 'the researcher' or, miraculously we somehow multiply our individuality and write about what 'we' found. All these linguistic conventions are, paradoxically, rhetorical devices designed to persuade the reader that we, as individuals, have no signature to assign to our work. (p. 18)

Whatever else scientists may do in their laboratories or with their testing procedures, they end up writing about it. When this happens they employ a range of rhetorical strategies that express their paradigmatic assumptions and act to persuade the reader that their findings are valid and worth paying attention to.

Telling a Different Tale

Given that the basic assumptions and interests of the interpretive and critical paradigms differ from that of positivism it should come as no surprise that they often report their work differently, draw upon different discourses and utilize different rhetorical strategies to persuade the reader that their accounts are authoritative. For example, Firestone (1987) provides an illuminating example of how different forms of rhetoric operate within the texts produced by quantitative (positivist) *and* qualitative (interpretive) researchers when they address the *same* topic (in his case the influence of leadership on organizational outcomes). His analysis of the two studies in which he was involved indicates how each used different strategies to project different assumptions about the nature of organizational life and attempted to persuade the reader of the validity of each form of analysis.

In terms of attempting to persuade, the quantitative researcher deemphasized individual judgment and stressed the use of established procedures. In contrast, the qualitative researcher used the strategies of rich depiction and strategic comparison that involved the use of telling quotes from interviews, descriptions of agency staffing patterns and excerpts from agency history. These details were convincing (in the qualitative sense) because they created a gestalt that made sense to the reader and that depended upon the active effort of the reader to check these details against personal experience. In summarizing the texts of the two kinds of research, Firestone comments:

> The persuasive strategies of the two kinds of research are very different. The quantitative study must convince the reader that procedures have been followed faithfully because very little concrete description of what anyone does is provided. The qualitative study provides the reader with a depiction in enough detail to show that the author's conclusion 'makes sense'. For that reason, discussion of procedure is not emphasized. Too much attention to procedure can get in the way of the narrative line which attempts to build a concrete impression of the phenomenon studied. (*ibid*, p. 19)

This is not to imply that there is any great sense of uniformity in the way that interpretive (or critical) researchers report their work. Indeed, Lofland (1974) suggests that there seems to be a relative lack of consensus within this domain as to how findings should be reported and he points out that, 'At least in its sociological version, qualitative field research seems distinct in the degree to which its practitioners lack a public, shared and codified conception of how what they do is done, and how what they report should be formulated' (p. 101). However, this does not mean that chaos reigns in terms of reporting interpretive research and Atkinson (1990) has provided an extensive analysis of the rhetorical devices they draw upon to be persuasive.

The point to be made is that, given their basic assumptions and interests, the creation of authoritative texts for interpretive and critical

researchers is extremely problematic and a source of constant tension. As
Woods (1985) recognizes, 'The point where rich data, careful analysis and
lofty ideas meets the iron discipline of writing is one of the great problem
areas of qualitative research' (p. 104). This is particularly so in relation
to the issue of 'voice(s)' in the text. For example, Woolgar (1988) points
out that the discourse of the natural sciences tends to deny it objects a
voice, 'Although electrons, particles and so on are credited with various
attributes, they are constituted as incapable of giving opinions, developing their own theories and, in particular for our purposes, producing
their own representations. The natural science discourse thus constitutes its objects as quintessentially docile and can act upon them at will'
(p. 80). However, he adds:

> By contrast, various traditions in the social sciences wish to
> grant their objects a voice (and refer to them as 'subjects'). This
> generates difficulties for the rhetorical constitution of distance.
> In particular, in the discourse associated with interpretive
> social science, subjects/objects are granted the ability to talk back,
> have their own opinions and even to constitute their own
> representations. (*ibid*)

Furthermore, as Atkinson (1990) emphasizes, just as with texts of
biography, history or journalism, 'the ethnography claims factual status,
not by eliminating the voice of the author . . . Rather, the ethnographic
text is permeated by stylistic and rhetorical devices whereby the reader is
persuaded to enter into a shared framework of facts, and interpretations,
observations and reflections' (p. 55). As a consequence, interpretive and
critical researchers often write in the first person: the term *I* appears in the
text that announces the presence of the author. Indeed, the feelings,
actions, motivations of the *I* are often a central aspect of the way research
gets reported.

However, just incorporating the *I* into the text does not resolve
the tensions within alternative paradigms research about the ways that
people and events are represented. To illustrate some of the tensions
and problems of representation I want to consider some of the work that
has gone on in the field of ethnography where this issue has been the
focus of much attention and heated debate. In doing so I draw upon
the delineation of genre within the ethnographic tradition made by
Van Maanen (1988) in his book called *Tales of the Field: On Writing
Ethnography* where he outlines the kinds of story that ethnographers
typically recount. In presenting the narrative conventions that define a
particular type of ethnographic tale he highlights the dilemmas that
writers of this genre face when attempting to establish their tale as accurate, authentic and authoritative. Van Maanen's work also signals that
there are alternative ways to tell our tales that are worthy of consideration
in the future.

Voices in Realist Tales

Ethnographic realism, according to Marcus and Cushman (1982) 'is a mode of writing that seeks to represent the reality of the whole world or form of life' (p. 29). It has its roots in the establishment of anthropology as a discipline and the emergence of professional fieldwork as the essential prerequisite for ethnographic accounts. For Van Maanen (1988) the realist tale of culture is the most prominent, familiar and recognized form of ethnographic writing that 'pushes most firmly for the authenticity of the cultural representations conveyed by the text' (p. 45). Most certainly, this kind of tale has dominated ethnographic work within PE for both interpretive and critical researchers alike. In terms of our interest in voice, Cole (1991) provides a useful summary of its location in realist tales:

> Ethnographic realism corresponds to scientistic conventions that construct authority and objectivity through passive voice, obscuring and apparently distancing the author from the data. The writer's voice is set apart from the main text in prefaces, method sections, and footnotes as a device to indicate that a dispassionate observer 'was there, saw, and knows', asserting a contradictory 'disembodied' objective presence and 'experiential' authority. The researcher constructs and positions him/herself as a conduit through which an 'other' culture is seemingly symmetrically decoded and recoded. (p. 39).

In relation to this Van Maanen (1988) suggests that realist tales are characterized by four writing or representational conventions that make them different from traveller's tales, fiction, journalism and other forms of ethnography. For our purposes only three of these will be briefly mentioned.

Experiential Author(ity)

Van Maanen (1988) comments, 'the most striking characteristic of ethnographic realism is the almost complete absence of the author from the segments of the finished text. Only what members of the studied culture say and do and, presumably, think are visible in the text' (p. 46). He notes that, once the fieldworker has finished the job of collecting the data, he/she simply vanishes. The marked absence of the narrator as a first-person presence in the text and the dominance of a 'scientific' narrator who is manifest only as a dispassionate, camera-like observer is also commented on by Marcus and Cushman (1982). They note how in realist tales, 'the collective and authoritative third person ("the X do this") replaces the more fallible first-person ("I saw the X do this")' (p. 32). For them the resulting effect is paradoxical. Taking the 'I' (the observer) out and making the author invisible acts to enhance the narrator's authority by heightening the sense of scientific objectivity projected by the text so as to placate the audience's worries over personal subjectivities. Unfortunately, this strategy also acts to sever the relationship between what the ethnographer knows and how he/she came to know it.

The Native's Point of View

Modern realist tales go to great pains to produce the native's point of view. It is common to find extensive, closely edited quotations in the text that suggest to the reader that the views put forward are not those of the author but are the authentic and representative remarks of those people in the culture under study. However, as Van Maanen (1988) is quick to remind us, 'A good deal of typographical play, stage-setting ploys, and contextual framing goes into presenting the native's point of view. More importantly, there are epistemological stunts to be performed on the ethnographic highwire. Such fancy footwork is rarely discussed by fieldworkers constructing realist tales' (pp. 49–50). He goes on to say that what, precisely, might be called the native's point of view is highly problematic. For Marcus and Cushman (1982) this issue of how we represent the reality of others has only recently become the subject of sophisticated theoretical discussion and this debate has been influential in making anthropologists reflect on their writing practices.

Interpretive Omnipotence

This is closely linked to how the native's point of view is represented in the text, in that, however this is done, the author has the final word in realist ethnographies as to how the culture will be interpreted and how it will be presented. Van Maanen (1988) outlines several conventions of interpretive omnipotence. For example, often a cultural description is tied to a specific theoretical problem of interest to the researcher's disciplinary community. Then, field data, is put forward as facts marshalled in accordance with the light they shed on this topic of interest and the researcher's stand on the matter. The interpretation of the author is made compelling by the use of abstract definitions, axioms and theorems that work logically to provide explanation. Van Maanen notes that, 'Each element of the theory is carefully illustrated by empirical field data. The form is aseptic and impersonal, but it is convincing insofar as an audience is willing to grant power to the theory' (*ibid*, p. 51). He adds that this power is enhanced if the theoretical system is based on honoured and respectable figures and intellectual traditions. Furthermore, it allows the 'humble fieldworker to stand on the shoulders of giants (and see farther) by using well-received constructs as receptacles for field data' (*ibid*, p. 52).

Another device for establishing interpretive credibility is where the researcher rests the case on what the members say and do themselves. The data are presented conventionally as the events of everyday life. These situations, along with a generalized rendition of the native's point of view, are collapsed into explanatory constructs in such a way that the researcher's analysis overlaps with (if it does not become identical to), the terms and constructs used to describe the events. Here, as Van Maanen comments, the author's authority is embellished by utilizing the native's vernacular which suggests that the author is fully able to whistle native tunes, 'The ungrammatical and profane phrases heighten the claim that the words flow from the members, not the author. Quotes are redundant, staged, and, of course, closely edited to emphasize the fieldworker's methodological observations and analytical categories with native jargon' (*ibid*, p. 64). Likewise, Cole (1991) argues:

> The account is given increased legitimacy through representations of actual subject voices selected and excluded based on their consistency with the author's 'report'. While a sense of authenticity and objectivity permeate the narrative, the ethnographer translates the voices and visions of local subjects into his/her own. The analysis (or view from above) is bounded and legitimized by monitoring incongruent voices or anomalous moments; thus, fixing and stabilizing theory and limiting alternative interpretation by readers. (p. 40)

Therefore, while there is the presence of other voices in realist tales and while the native's voice is incorporated into the text, this does not mean that such tales are multivocal texts in which an event is given meaning first one way, then another, and then still another. Essentially, as Van Maanen (1988) recognizes, the realist tale only offers one reading and culls its facts with care to support that reading, 'It is simply a matter of closing off or nailing down an interpretation without allowing alternative views to creep into view. The narrator speaks for the group studied as a passive observer who roams imperialistically across the setting to tell, of events that happen in this way or that' (p. 53).

Realist tales, therefore, articulate voices in the text in a certain way that draws upon specific conventions of writing. According to Marcus and Cushman (1982) this realist tradition has come under increasing pressure as anthropologists have begun to ask questions regarding the possibilities of representing realistically and non-fictionally the subjectivity of another person. However, as Van Maanen (1988) points out, we should not judge realist tales too harshly as they have a long and by-and-large worthy pedigree. He suggests, 'To subject the writing to scrutiny is not to say it is false or wrong' (p. 54). Despite their limitations, they have produced, and will continue to produce, powerful, engaging, vivid and stimulating works.

Andrew C. Sparkes

Voices in Confessional Tales

Confessional tales are an increasingly popular genre and contrast with realist tales in several important ways. For example, they are characterized by highly personalized styles and self-absorbed mandates. Here, the researcher tells us what 'really' happened during the fieldwork and Atkinson (1991) comments, 'Ethnographers who have produced their realist accounts are frequently given to publishing autobiographical accounts in which the personal, the problematic, and the narrative elements are in the foreground' (p. 170). As with realist tales there are writing conventions in confessional tales of which only two will be considered here to illustrate how these tales differ from each other.

Personalized Author(ity)

According to Van Maanen (1988) the writing of confessional tales is intended to show how particular works came into being and that this requires an intimacy to be established with the reader so that a personalized authority can be developed. He points out that no longer is the 'ubiquitous, disembodied voice of the culture to be heard (for example, The police do X). In its place is a person (for example, I saw the police do X)' (p. 75). The personal character of the author-researcher is allowed expression as he/she recounts the trials and tribulations of fieldwork and provides insights into their own character flaws, personal biases and bad habits. Van Maanen suggests that the building up of this ironic self-portrait (Look, I'm just like you, full of human weaknesses) allows the reader to identify with the researcher at a more personal level.

Consequently, in confessional tales, 'the omnipotent tone of realism gives way to the modest, unassuming style of one struggling to piece together something reasonably coherent out of displays of initial disorder, doubt and difficulty' (*ibid*). The researcher often casts him/herself as someone who has come to learn the culture just as a child or newcomer would, 'Learning from living the culture is the predominant theme'(*ibid*,). Finally, the author is rarely portrayed as passive in confessional tales. Rather, he/she is a visible character who is often very street-wise, 'a trickster, or fixer, wise to the ways of the world, appreciative of human vanity, necessarily wary, and therefore inventive of getting by and winning little victories over the hassles of life in the research setting' (*ibid*, p. 76).

The Fieldworker's Point of View

Van Maanen (1988) suggests that, 'As autobiographical details mount in confessional tales, it becomes apparent that the point of view being represented is that of the fieldworker' (p. 77). Often the fieldworker's perspective is focussed on within a character-building conversion tale that illustrates how the research began with one view but was modified throughout the study by contact with the native's point of view so that it concludes at the end with a different view. This shifting view is emphasized by revelations of instances of shock and surprise, blunders, social gaffes and secrets discovered in unlikely ways and places. Frequently, the new way of seeing the world is claimed to be similar, but not identical, to the native's point of view as the impression needs to be created of someone able to shift back and forth between the insider's passionate perspective and the impassionate gaze of the analytical outsider. To lose the latter would be to infer that one has either gone native or become a cultural dope. For Van Maanen, 'Perhaps no other confessional convention is as difficult for the writer as maintaining in print this paradoxical, if not schizophrenic, attitude toward the group observed. A delightful dance of words often ensues as fieldworkers present themselves as both vessels and vehicles of knowledge' (*ibid*, p. 77).

Clearly, the confessional tale is different in many ways from realist tales. However, as Van Maanen reminds us, 'Confessionals do not usually replace realist accounts. They typically stand beside them, elaborating extensively on the formal snippets of method description that decorate realist tales' (*ibid*, p. 75). Indeed, he acknowledges that fieldwork confessions always almost end up *supporting* whatever realist writing the author may have done in the past. That is, whatever limitations are highlighted in the confessional tale it is unlikely that the author will conclude that he/she got it wrong. Furthermore, such tales are often produced separately from realist tales (usually by those who have already published realist accounts that are acceptable to a particular research community) in monographs, as journal articles, or book chapters devoted to fieldwork practices.[7] In this sense, Atkinson (1991) suggests that the confessional tale is not really an alternative genre because it 'exists in a relation of complementarity rather than contrast with realist tales' (p. 170). Futhermore, he notes the problematic relationship between the two in terms of their impact upon each other, 'To some extent, therefore, the separation of the "realist" and the "confessional" accounts leaves the former relatively uncontaminated by the contingencies reflected in the latter' (*ibid*).

Voices in Impressionist Tales

Impressionist tales *are* different. Atkinson (1991) notes how they are 'permeated with a self-conscious deployment of the more "literary" resources. The detachment of the realist genres is not sustained. The ethnography constructs a more explicitly vivid and metaphorical account' (p. 170). Van Maanen (1988) believes that there is an associative link between the writing of impressionist tales and the work of impressionist painters like Renoir and Monet who attempted 'to evoke an open, participatory sense in the viewer and as with all revisionist forms of art, to startle complacent viewers accustomed to and comfortable with older forms' (p. 101). Likewise, impressionist ethnographies attempt to startle their audience by the use of striking stories. However, rather than lumin-ous paintings their medium is that of words, metaphors, phrasing, and imagery coupled with an expansive recall of field work experience.

> Impressionist tales present the doing of fieldwork rather than simply the doer or the done ... The story itself ... is a representational means of cracking open the culture and the fieldworker's way of knowing it so that both can be jointly examined. Impressionist writing tries to keep both subject and object in constant view. The epistemological aim is then to braid the knower with the known. (*ibid*, p. 102)

As with other forms of tale a range of conventions are drawn upon.

Textual Identity

Impressionist tales use dramatic recall of events in roughly the order they occurred and include the odds and ends that are associated with the remembered events. As Van Maanen (1988) says, the idea is to draw an audience into an unfamiliar story world and allow it, a far as is possible, 'to see, hear, and feel as the fieldworker, saw, heard, and felt. Such tales seek to imaginatively place the audience in the fieldwork situation' (p. 103). The tale can stand alone or include elaborate framing devices or extensive commentary as well as analytical points made by the author. However, when such points are made they are noticed by the audience as they are clearly interruptions in the story, 'The point here is that the audi-ence knows very well what is part of the story and what is not' (*ibid*).

Ethnographers telling an impressionist tale do not try and impose one interpretation on the story. Instead, they hold back on interpretation and invite the reader to make what they will of the world presented. Therefore, the reader is asked to relive the tale with the fieldworker, 'not to interpret it or analyze it. The intention is not to tell the readers what to think of an experience but to show them the experience from the begin-ning to end and thus draw them immediately into the story to work out its problems and puzzles as they unfold' (*ibid*).

Fragmented Knowledge

Impressionist tales often read like novels which can be off-putting and certain sensibilities are jarred for those used to more realist tales. This is because the recalled events have uncertain meanings for an audience who are unsure of where it is being taken and why. Since the tale unfolds event by event, 'Matters of disciplinary or methodological concern to the audience are met, if at all, in irregular and unexpected ways ... Cultural knowledge is slipped to an audience in fragmented, disjointed ways' (Van Maanen, 1988, p. 104).

Characterization

Authors of impressionist tales, like everyone else, like to be judged charitably by their audience. They need to develop the lead character in order to tell the tale and make it attractive and individuality is expressed in terms of mixed-emotions, confusions and moral anguish etc. Also, as in confessional tales, the author is often at pains to indicate that they were not simple scribes or cultural dopes. Importantly, to make the story interesting and absorbing the supporting players in an impressionist tale need to be well developed. As Van Maanen (1988) points out, 'Characters of impressionist tales must be given names, faces, motives, and things to do if a story is to be told about them. More important, when a story is at stake, these supporting players must be given lines to speak. The fieldworker must then give individual voices to the natives displayed in an impressionist tale' (p. 105).

Dramatic Control

Since impressionist tales are about how the fieldworker came to know about a culture, their telling moves the authors back in time to events that might later have given rise to misunderstandings or confusions. In the storyworld the fieldworker's readings of these events as they occurred is important. Hence the recall is sometimes presented in the present tense in an attempt to give the tale a 'you-are-there' feel. The ending of the story must not be given away before its time tension must be maintained. In relation to this kind of writing Van Maanen (1988) emphasizes that the standards are not disciplinary but *literary* ones:

> Organizing such an illusion requires skill ... Artistic nerve is required of the teller. *Literary standards are of more interest to the impressionist than scientific ones.* A general audience unfamiliar with the studied scene can judge the tale only on the basis of its plausability or believability, not on the basis of accurateness or representativeness. In telling a tale, narrative rationality is of more concern than an argumentative kind. The audience cannot be concerned with the story's correctness, since they were not there and cannot know if it is correct. The standards are largely those of interest (does it attract?), coherence (does it hang together?), and fidelity (does it seem true?). (p. 105, my emphasis)

In summary, impressionist tales as a form of representation attempt to provoke multiple and often contrasting interpretations that illustrate how coming to understand a culture is a continuous process of interpretation that involves learning to appreciate the world in different ways. As Van Maanen comments, 'Knowing a culture, even our own, is a never ending story' (*ibid*, p. 119). Impressionist tales, therefore, are stories that are always unfinished. Their form and their dependence on the audience leads to more being discovered with each retelling as meanings are reworked again and again. Importantly, they point to the discomforting fact 'that we are unable to do much more than partially describe what it is we know or do. We know more than we can say and we will know even more after saying it' (*ibid*, p. 123). Therefore, as tales, they are a recognition and a celebration of the more literary and metaphoric aspects of ethnographic writing. Consequently, they call upon literary skills to produce evocative tales and the difficulties of this task should not be underestimated.

Future Developments in Writing: Some Hopes and Worries

The work of Van Maanen (1988), according to Atkinson (1991), makes a valuable contribution to the methodological literature but may be faulted for overstating the distinctions between the genres he identifies, in that, all three may be found within the work of a single author or even within the same monograph. However, for my purposes Van Maanen's work is useful because he illustrates clearly that there are different ways to tell ethnographic tales, that there are, indeed, different ways to tell our stories in alternative paradigms research if we wish to do so. It is unfortunate that, at present, we have so few examples of other genres in the PE literature to show us what the possibilities might look like. In this we are not alone and, along with many other disciplines, it seems likely that for the moment the style of no-style will continue as the dominant form of representation for positivistic researchers and realist tales will be the main ones produced by interpretive and critical researchers.[8] This is not surprising since, after all, these tales have served us well in the past and will continue to contribute to our understanding in the future. They are certainly not to be dismissed lightly.

Furthermore, it would be foolish to suggest that researchers of any paradigmatic persuasion within PE should rush out and produce confessional or impressionist tales. As Atkinson (1990) argues:

There is no need for sociologists all to flock towards 'alternative' literary modes. The point of the argument is *not* to suggest that suddenly, from now on, sociological ethnography should be represented through pastiche or literary forms. The discipline will not be aided by the unprincipled adoption of any particular textual practices, 'literary' or otherwise. On the other hand, we must always be aware that there are many available styles. (p. 180)

There clearly are alternatives available to realist tales that may be of great interest to those engaged in interpretive and critical research. However, there is a need to consider carefully some of the problems of telling our tales in different ways before we embark on this venture. For example, Agar (1990) acknowledges that a break with realist tales is fascinating to reflect upon but signals some dilemmas that arise in producing different stories. With regard to impressionist tales, he comments:

> In such tales one uses the scenic method to describe what actually happens. But then I start ticking off problems: How does one integrate and legitimate the expository writing to enable comprehension of the scene? How does one structure the scenes — simple chronology, thematically, topically, theoretically — and how does one mark the structure so that the reader knows what is going on? How does one organize multiple potential interpretations of a scene and support some and rule out others? How does one weave theoretical frames into discourse? These problems do not strike me as impossible, just as difficult and neglected. (*ibid*, p. 85)

These are problems associated with the creation of the final product. Further problems arise in terms of the relationship between this final product and the research process itself. On this issue Agar expresses concern over the lack of discussion that has taken place regarding the research *process* and how it would need to change to be in harmony with the final *product*. He feels that there is a danger that ethnographers, in their newly awakened enthusiasm to focus on the text as a neglected product, might engage in what Clifford (1986) calls a 'fetishizing of form' (p. 21) and thereby lose sight of the process side of what they do. When this happens there is a tendency to define process and product as separate problems when in fact they are intimately *related* to each other. Agar points out that one unintended consequence of this dislocation is that, 'theories of text can develop in isolation from the research processes whose results they supposedly represent' (*ibid*, p. 74). Having highlighted these and other issues he concludes:

> Textuality, as a consciousness-raising concept, is long overdue. But textuality, as the primary focus for what ethnography is all about, is, I think, a mistake. When process and product tug against each other, ethnographic credibility turns sour — credibility in the sense of making a good argument that displays and accounts for samples of group life. At a time when interest in ethnographic research is growing, when our sense of what it

is and how it works is improving, a move to new textual forms without more attention to the research processes that ground them would be a serious ethno-mistake. (*ibid*, p. 87)

These are timely words of warning and guard us against substituting one form of neglect (for the product) for another (the process). There is a need to be constantly aware of the intimate relationship between the two for those researchers in PE who decide to experiment with new forms of writing in the future. Such an awareness raises questions as to what a confessional or an impressionist tale might look like when written by interpretive or critical researchers and the implications that a commitment to producing these tales might have for the ways in which they conduct their research. For example, given the starting assumptions of the critical paradigm (see Sparkes, chapter 1 in this volume) what might a *critical tale* involve?

Researchers drawing their inspiration from the critical paradigm are concerned to locate individual action and perceptions in relation to the structures that shape these in the wider social context. Given that field-work studies have the potential, when used strategically, to illuminate the strands that tie the individual to these wider social, political and economic issues, then, questions arise as to how researchers should represent their work so that a critical tale is told. What forms of writing are required for a critical social research process that includes an overt political struggle against oppressive social structures? Similarly, what kinds of writing are appropriate for a research process that aspires to be emancipatory, that is, attempts to enable people to gain the knowledge and power to be in control of their own lives by changing individual and group consciousness so as to create social change? Can realist, confessional and impressionist tales be utilized, combined or transformed for this task or must they be abandoned altogether and a new genre developed?

Unfortunately, there are lots of questions but few concrete examples are available to provide any guidelines. Van Maanen (1988) mentions a few critical tales. These include the work of Willis (1977) that is defined as a realist ethnography embedded within a Marxist framework. This study, like many other critical tales with a Marxist edge, has a concern for representing social structure as seen through the eyes of disadvantaged groups in capitalist societies. For Van Maanen (1988), such tales highlight questions of power, economy, history, politics and exploitation so that, 'Unlike many other tales where the presented reality appears to be merely the unintended consequence of interacting people sharing natural problems, so that reality belongs to no one in particular, the authors of critical tales make it clear just who they think own and operates the tools of reality production' (p. 129). In relation to this Brodkey (1987), in her consideration of writing critical ethnographic narratives, argues against the use of realist forms of writing and suggests:

Critical narrators, then, are those narrators whose self-consciousness about ideology makes it necessary for them to point out that all stories, including their own, are told from a vantage point, and to call attention to the voice in which the story is being told. In critical narratives, it is from the narrative stance or conceptual vantage point of critical theory that a story of cultural hegemony is generated. (p. 71)

This seems to imply that some form of impressionist tale might be warranted since Brodkey (*ibid*) warns against the continued telling of stories that confound narrative and experience. Unfortunately, we are provided with few examples of what critical ethnographic narratives might look like. Similarly, Cole (1991) proposes a critical-feminist ethnography which depends upon a range of alternative strategies suggested by experimental ethnography and the conceptual achievements offered by feminist standpoint epistemology and minor discourse theory. Once again, the shaping of such tales is at an early stage and we will have to wait to see how they unfold in the future.

In relation to the issues raised previously both interpretive and critical researchers committed to giving *voice* to the participants in their research studies might also want to consider producing *jointly told tales*. Drawing on the work of Clifford (1983) who talks of dialogic and polyphonic authority in fieldwork representations, Van Maanen (1988) suggests the production of jointly authored texts (between fieldworker and native) in a way that opens up for readers the discursive and shared character of all cultural descriptions. Importantly, the issue of jointly told tales pushes to the fore the power relationships inherent in the research process. As Van Maanen points out, when such tales are negotiated it is usually the fieldworker who holds the editorial and publishing keys not the informant, 'Hence the negotiation is often an unbalanced one so far as the final representation is concerned: informants speak, ethnographers write' (*ibid*, p. 137). Jointly told tales challenge this power relationship. In relation to this Cole (1991) argues that critical-feminist ethnographies require symmetrical relationships between the researcher and the researched:

The problem of, and real concerns over, subject exploitation raise questions about ethnographic textual construction and shared authorial voice, characteristic of experimental work. Dialogical experiments allude to the necessity of increased interaction, co-operation, and sensitivity between researcher and local subjects in the research process. It raises questions about the rhetorical conventions used to locate and frame subjects in the texts and how their stories can most usefully be represented. Actual dialogue in the text can be useful because it demonstrates the ongoing negotiations between cultural realities; but, actual dialogue is not literal dialogue because any textual representation entails decision making: which dialogues are included and privileged, how dialogue is framed, and which dialogues are suppressed and excluded are necessary mechanisms of construction . . . In efforts not to exploit subjects, voices can be situated as central and positioned in ways that make them meaningful and productive . . . Dispersed authority challenges illusions of single textual authority by representing other authoritative voices. (pp. 44–5)

Once again, we will have to wait and see if, and when, jointly told tales emerge within PE and the implications their production will have for the research process itself. Should they surface along with, as part of, or separate from, confessional, impressionist and critical tales then they will provide a direct challenge to what so far has been defined as appropriate ways to report research in this domain (see Sparkes 1991). This challenge will be felt by those who edit journals, teachers and lecturers who provide courses on research and supervise studies, and students as they struggle to make sense of different tales and experiment with different ways to tell their stories. Quite simply, new ways of writing require new ways of reading and this will generate tensions and anxieties for both novice and experienced researchers alike[9].

One thing is for certain, the way that we write has now become problematic and we cannot ignore this central aspect of our work. Our texts can no longer be taken to be innocent or neutral. In view of this Atkinson (1991) suggests, we need to develop a reflexive self-awareness of the rhetorical and stylistic conventions we use, not with a view to substituting textual analysis for fieldwork, but rather to bring them within our explicit and methodological understanding. He emphasizes that such reflexiveness is not easy since it would require an acquaintance with recent and contemporary literary theory along with parallel work on the poetics of economics, history, law, and so on. It is also recognized that it is far easier to copy a taken-for-granted model than it is to understand other genres, to manipulate their conventions and to experiment with them. Certainly, there are different tales to be told but the writing of them is no easy matter and it would be naive to suggest otherwise. However, as Atkinson concludes:

If we recognize that the conventional formats of 'realistic' reportage are essentially as arbitrary as any other, then we can open up the possibility of alternatives. Indeed, we may come to the view that the normal canons of written scientific discourse are inappropriate for the representation of complex and multiple social realities. Of course, we do not want to encourage a spate of modernist ethnographic texts (or whatever) just in order to promote novelty. But there is surely no harm in exploring alternative modes of representation in the light of an informed understanding of literary theory. (*ibid*, p. 173)

If alternative paradigms research in PE is to fulfil its potential in the coming years then those involved should be encouraged to develop a reflexive awareness of the ways in which they write. As we become more aware of the possibilities and constraints that various forms of language impose upon us, and others, we may choose to embark upon a principled exploration of other modes of representation. These initial explorations are likely to be tentative and nervous but as our confidence grows we may become more bold in our experiments with writing. Where these experiments will lead us is impossible to predict. However, we can rest assured that there is much to be learned and enjoyed in meeting the continual challenges that the telling of tales presents us with.

Acknowledgments

I would like to thank Paul Ernest (University of Exeter), John Evans (University of Southampton) and Philip Hodkinson (Crewe and Alsager College of Higher Education) for their helpful and constructive comments on an earlier draft of this chapter. Unfortunately, time and space have not allowed me to explore all of their suggestions.

Notes

1   Atkinson (1990) tells us that the title of his book *The Ethnographic Imagination: Textual Constructions of Reality*, is borrowed from the titles of two classics in modern sociology. These are *The Sociological Imagination* (Mills, 1959) and *The Social Construction of Reality* (Berger and Luckmann, 1966). The first part of my title therefore carries on this borrowing process.

2   For an anthropological focus on the production of texts see Brodkey (1987); Clifford (1983); Clifford and Marcus (1986); Geertz (1983 and 1988); Marcus and Cushman (1982); and Marcus and Fischer (1986). For a more sociological focus see Atkinson (1990 and 1991); Atkinson and Delamont (1990); Brown (1987); Edmondson (1984); and Mulkay (1991).

3   Excellent introductions to the works of Derrida, Foucault and other post-structuralist thinkers are provided by Cherryholmes (1988); Dews (1987); Rabinow (1987); and Sarup (1989). Studies in the field of education that have been influenced by Foucault are provided by Ball (1990).

4   Tinning (1990) notes how the language of post-structuralism is obtuse, heavy, and probably elitist. Evans (1990) also comments on the elitism of the language and warns that there are substantial problems in viewing *all* social phenomena as texts along with the producers of discourse and language as the absolute captors of our minds' innermost secrets and imaginations. Sears (forthcoming) suggests that deconstructionism is apolitical, ahistorical and ethically and morally bankrupt. Furthermore, Giddens (1987) argues that post-structuralism is a dead tradition of thought that has failed to generate the revolution in philosophical understanding and social theory that was its pledge.

5 I have focussed elsewhere on the manner in which power operates both in and behind discourses so that some 'truths' are exalted above others and some voices get to speak while others are silenced in the marketplace of ideas (see Sparkes, 1991).

6 Evidence of this interest in rhetoric can be found in Atkinson (1990), Brown (1987), Nash (1989), Nelson *et al* (1987b), Simons (1989), and Leith and Myerson (1989).

7 Some examples of confessional tales in education are available in Burgess (1984, 1985).

8 That realist tales are alive and well within interpretive and critical research is evident in the contributions to several edited books for example, Evans (1986 and 1988); Kirk and Tinning (1990), and Messner and Sabo (1990). These volumes also bear witness to the powerful insights and explanations such tales can provide. Contributions to the present volume also rely for the most part on realist tales.

Much of my own work on innovation and change in PE (for recent examples see Sparkes 1990a, 1990b and 1990c), as well as my work involving life histories and the lives and careers of PE teachers (see Sparkes and Templin, chapter 4 in this volume) has been (re)presented as realist tales. The point I would like to make is that it is only in the last year or so that I have slowly become aware that I was telling any kind of tale at all, yet alone a realist tale. I was certainly not aware that there were other forms of tale available.

9 Throughout this chapter time and space have allowed me to say little about readers, reading and the interpretation of texts. However, this is an important issue and elsewhere (Sparkes, 1991) I have suggested that reading is an active process in which no one reads from a neutral or final position. Fairclough (1989) talks of the *member resources* that an individual brings to bear on the reading and interpretation of any text. These member resources are themselves socially determined and ideologically shaped by the position of the individual reader in the social structure. Therefore, as Sarup (1989) reminds us, reading should no longer be seen as the passive consumption of a product since it is actually a performance.

References

AGAR, M. (1990) 'Text and fieldwork: Exploring the excluded middle', *Journal of Contemporary Ethnography*, 19, 1, pp. 73–88.

ATKINSON, P. (1990) *The Ethnographic Imagination: Textual Constructions of Reality*, London, Routledge.

ATKINSON, P. (1991) 'Supervising the text', *International Journal of Qualitative Studies in Education*, 4, 2, pp. 161–74.

ATKINSON, P. and DELAMONT, S. (1990) 'Writing about teachers: How British and American ethnographic texts describe teachers and teaching', *Teaching and Teacher Education*, 6, 2, pp. 111–25.

BAIN, L. (1990a) 'Visions and voices', *Quest*, 42, 1, pp. 2–12.

BAIN, L. (1990b) 'Research in sport pedagogy: Past, present and future', keynote address, AIESEP World Convention, Loughborough University, June.

BALL, S. (Ed) (1990) *Foucault and Education: Disciplines and Knowledge*, London, Routledge.

BERGER, P. and LUCKMANN, T. (1966) *The Social Construction of Reality*, London, Allen Lane.

BRODKEY, L. (1987) 'Writing critical ethnographic narratives', *Anthropology and Education Quarterly*, 18, pp. 67–76.

BROWN, R. (1987) *Society as Text: Essays on Rhetoric, Reason, and Reality*, Chicago, IL, University of Chicago Press.

BURGESS, R. (Ed) (1984) *The Research Process in Educational Settings: Ten Case Studies*, Lewes, Falmer Press.

BURGESS, R. (Ed) (1985) *Field Methods in the Study of Education*, Lewes, Falmer Press.

CHERRYHOLMES, C. (1988) *Power and Criticism: Post-structural Investigations into Education*, New York, Teachers College Press.

CLIFFORD, J. (1983) 'On ethnographic authority', *Representations*, 1, 2, pp. 118–46.

CLIFFORD, J. (1986) 'Introduction: Partial truths' in CLIFFORD, J. and MARCUS, G. (Eds) *Writing Culture: The Poetics and Politics of Ethnography*, Berkeley, CA, University of California Press, pp. 1–26.

CLIFFORD, J. and MARCUS, J. (Eds) (1986) *Writing Culture: The Poetics and Politics of Ethnography*, Berkeley, CA, University of California Press.

COLE, C. (1991) 'The politics of cultural representation: Visions of fields/fields of visions', *International Review for the Sociology of Sport*, 26, 1, pp. 36–49.

DEWS, P. (1987) *Logics of Disintegration: Post-Structuralist Thought and the Claims of Critical Theory*, London, Verso.

ECO, V. (1984) *Semiotics and the Philosophy of Language*, Bloomington, IN, Indiana University Press.

EDMONDSON, R. (1984) *Rhetoric in Sociology*, London, Macmillan Press.

EISNER, E. (1988) 'The primacy of experience and the politics of method', *Educational Researcher*, 17, 5, pp. 15–20.

EVANS, J. (Ed) (1986) *Physical Education, Sport and Schooling*, Lewes, Falmer Press.

EVANS, J. (Ed) (1988) *Teachers, Teaching and Control in Physical Education*, Lewes, Falmer Press.

EVANS, J. (1990) 'Researching pedagogy and reflective teaching', keynote address, AIESEP World Convention, Loughborough, June.

FAIRCLOUGH, N. (1989) *Language and Power*, London, Longman.

FIRESTONE, W. (1987) 'Meaning in method: The rhetoric of quantitative and qualitative research', *Educational Researcher*, 16, 7, pp. 16–20.

GEERTZ, C. (1983) *Local Knowledge*, New York, Basic Books.

GEERTZ, C. (1988) *Works and Lives: The Anthropologist as Author*, Cambridge, Polity Press.

GIDDENS, A. (1987) *Social Theory and Modern Sociology*, London, Polity Press.

GORE, J. (1990) 'Pedagogy as text in physical education teacher education: Beyond the preferred reading' in KIRK, D. and TINNING, R. (Eds) *Physical Education, Curriculum and Culture: Critical Issues in the Contemporary Crisis*, Lewes, Falmer Press, pp. 101–38.

GUSFIELD, J. (1976) 'The literary rhetoric of science: Comedy and pathos in drinking', *American Sociological Review*, 41, pp. 16–34.

KIRK, D. (1991) 'Languaging and physical education teaching', paper presented at the AIESEP/NAPEHE World Congress, Atlanta, January.

KIRK, D. and TINNING, R. (Eds) (1990) *Physical Education, Curriculum and Culture: Critical Issues in the Contemporary Crisis*, Lewes, Falmer Press.

LATHER, P. (1990) 'Postmodernism and the human sciences', *The Humanistic Psychologist*, 18, 1, pp. 64–84.

LEITH, D. and MYERSON, G. (1989) *The Power of Address: Explorations in Rhetoric*, London, Routledge.

LOFLAND, J. (1974) 'Styles of reporting qualitative field research', *The American Sociologist*, 9, August, pp. 101–11.

LYONS, K. (1989) 'A sociological analysis of the teaching of boy's physical education in the secondary school', unpublished doctoral thesis, University of Surrey.

MACDONELL, D. (1987) *Theories of Discourse*, Oxford, Basil Blackwell.

MARCUS, G. (1980) 'Rhetoric and the ethnographic genre in anthropological research', *Current Anthropology*, 21, 4, pp. 507–10.

MARCUS, G. and CUSHMAN, D. (1982) 'Ethnographies as texts', *Annual Review of Anthropology*, 11, pp. 25–69.

MARCUS, G. and FISCHER, M. (Eds) (1986) *Anthropology as Cultural Critique: An Experimental Movement in the Human Sciences*, Chicago, IL, University of Chicago Press.

MESSNER, M. and SABO, D. (Eds) *Sport, Men and the Gender Order: Critical Feminist Perspectives*, Champaign, IL, Human Kinetics Press.

MILLS, C. (1959) *The Sociological Imagination*, Oxford, Oxford University Press.

MULKAY, M. (1991) *Sociology of Science: A Sociological Pilgrimage*, Milton Keynes, Open University Press.

NASH, W. (1989) *Rhetoric: The Wit of Persuasion*, Oxford, Basil Blackwell.

NELSON, J., MEGILL, A. and McCLOSKEY, D. (1987a) 'Rhetoric of inquiry' in NELSON, J., MEGILL, A. and McCLOSKEY, D. (Eds) *The Rhetoric of the Human Sciences*, Madison, WI, University of Wisconsin Press, pp. 3–18.

NELSON, J., MEGILL, A. and McCLOSKEY, D. (Eds) (1987b) *The Rhetoric of the Human Sciences*, Madison, WI, University of Wisconsin Press.

POSTMAN, N. (1989) *Conscientious Objections: Stirring up Trouble about Language, Technology and Education*, London, Heinemann.

RABINOW, P. (Ed) (1987) *The Foucault Reader*, Harmondsworth, Penguin.

SARUP, M. (1989) *An Introductory Guide to Post-Structuralism and Postmodernism*, London, Harvester Wheatsheaf.

SEARS, J. (forthcoming) 'The glass bead game of curriculum theorizing: Reconceptualism and the new orthodoxy', *Curriculum Perspectives*.

SIMONS, H. (1989) 'Introduction' in SIMMONS, H. (Ed) *Rhetoric in the Human Sciences*, London, Sage, pp. 1–9.

SIMMONS, H. (Ed) (1989) *Rhetoric in the Human Sciences*, London, Sage.

SPARKES, A. (1990a) 'Power, domination and resistance in the process of teacher-initiated innovation', *Research Papers in Education*, 5, 2, pp. 59–84.

SPARKES, A. (1990b) *Curriculum Change and Physical Education: Towards a Micropolitical Understanding*, Deakin, Deakin University Press.

SPARKES, A. (1990c) 'Winners, losers and the myth of rational change: Towards an understanding of interests and power in innovation' in KIRK, D. and TINNING, R. (Eds) *Physical Education, Curriculum and Culture: Critical Issues in the Contemporary Crisis*, Lewes, Falmer Press, pp. 193–224.

SPARKES, A. (1991) 'Towards understanding, dialogue, and polyvocality in the research community: Extending the boundaries of the paradigms debate', *Journal of Teaching in Physical Education*, 10, 2, pp. 103–33.

TINNING, R. (1990) 'Pedagogy in teacher education: Dominant discourses and the process of problem-setting', keynote address, AIESEP World Convention, Loughborough, June.

VAN MAANEN, J. (1988) *Tales of the Field: On Writing Ethnography*, Chicago, IL, University of Chicago Press.

WHITSON, D. and MACINTOSH, D. (1990) 'The scientization of physical education: Discourses of performance' *Quest*, 42, 1, pp. 40–51.

WILLIS, P. (1977) *Learning to Labour: How Working Class Kids Get Working Class Jobs*, Farnborough, Saxon House.

WOLCOTT, H. (1990) 'On making a study "more ethnographic"', *Journal of Contemporary Ethnography*, 19, 1, 44–72.

WOODS, P. (1985) 'New songs played skilfully: Creativity and technique in writing up qualitative research' in BURGESS, R. (Ed) *Issues in Educational Research: Qualitative Methods*, Lewes, Falmer Press, pp. 86–106.

WOOLGAR, S. (1988) *Science: The Very Idea*, London, Tavistock Publications.

WRIGHT, J. and KING, R. (1991) '"I say what I mean", said Alice: An analysis of gendered discourse in physical education', *Journal of Teaching in Physical Education*, 10, 2, pp. 210–25.

Notes on Contributors

Gill Clarke is a Senior Lecturer in Human Movement Studies at the West Sussex Institute of Higher Education, Chichester.

John Evans is a Senior Lecturer in Physical Education in the Department of Physical Education at the University of Southampton.

Anne Flintoff is a Senior Lecturer in Physical Education in the Faculty of Cultural and Educational Studies at Leeds Polytechnic.

David Kirk is a Senior Lecturer in the Faculty of Education and Chairperson of the Physical Education and Teaching Group at Deakin University, Geelong, Victoria, Australia.

Keith Lyons is a Lecturer in Human Movement Studies in the Faculty of Sport, Physical Education and Leisure at the Cardiff Institute of Higher Education.

Sheila Scraton is a Reader in the Faculty of Cultural and Educational Studies at Leeds Polytechnic.

Stephen J. Smith is an Assistant Professor in the Faculty of Education at Simon Fraser University, Burnaby, British Columbia, Canada.

Andrew C. Sparkes is a Lecturer in Education in the School of Education at the University of Exeter.

Thomas J. Templin is an Associate Professor of Physical Education and Director of Recreational Sports, Recreational Gymnasium, Purdue University, West Lafayette, USA.

Richard Tinning is a Senior Lecturer in the Faculty of Education at Deakin University, Geelong, Victoria, Australia.

Sherry E. Woods is currently working in Austin, Texas.

Index